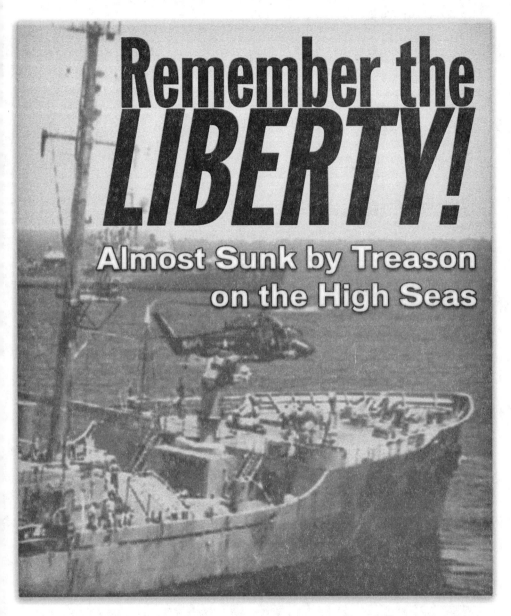

Remember the *LIBERTY!*

Almost Sunk by Treason on the High Seas

PHILLIP F. NELSON

author of *LBJ: The Mastermind of the JFK Assassination*
and *LBJ: From Mastermind to The Colossus*

with **Ernest A. Gallo**, **Ronald G. Kukal** and **Phillip F. Tourney**
survivors of the attack on the USS *LIBERTY*

Foreword by ex-CIA analyst **Ray McGovern**

Published by:
Trine Day LLC
PO Box 577
Walterville, OR 97489
1-800-556-2012
www.TrineDay.com
publisher@TrineDay.net

Library of Congress Control Number: 2017936713

Nelson, Phillip F.; with Gallo, Ernest A.; Kukal, Ronald G.; Tourney, Phillip F.
–1st ed.
p. cm.

Epud (ISBN-13) 978-1-63424-109-0
Mobi (ISBN-13) 978-1-63424-110-6
Print (ISBN-13) 978-1-63424-108-3
1. Liberty (Ship). 2. Israel-Arab War, 1967 -- Naval operations. 3. Israel-Arab
War, 1967 -- Aerial operations, Israeli. 4. Israel-Arab War, 1967 -- Personal narra-
tives, American. 5. Espionage, American -- Middle East -- History -- 20th century. 6. Johnson, Lyndon B. I. Nelson, Phillip F. II. Title

FIRST EDITION
10 9 8 7 6 5 4

Printed in the USA
Distribution to the Trade by:
Independent Publishers Group (IPG)
814 North Franklin Street
Chicago, Illinois 60610
312.337.0747
www.ipgbook.com

Foreword

Treachery at Sea

What Is So Rare As A Day In June?

How the sap creeps up and the blossoms swell;
We may shut our eyes but we cannot help knowing ...
The murder of sailors who that day fell.
The saps' cover-up is no longer going
... TO HIDE U.S. GOVERNMENT COWARDICE

Apologies to James Russell Lowell for the sobering addendum. The poet had no way of knowing how rare a day June 8, 1967 would be. Indeed, even today, scandalously few Americans have heard of the deliberate Israeli attack on the USS Liberty that day, because the cowardly U.S. political, military, and media establishment have managed to hide what happened. No one "important" wanted to challenge Israel's lame "oops-mistake" excuse. Intercepted Israeli communications show beyond doubt it was no "mistake."

Chief Petty Officer J.Q. "Tony" Hart, who monitored conversations between then-Defense Secretary Robert McNamara and Sixth Fleet Carrier Division Commander Rear Admiral Lawrence Geis, reported McNamara's instructive reply to Geis, who had protested the order to recall the U.S. warplanes on their way to engage those attacking the Liberty. McNamara: "President Johnson is not going to go to war or embarrass an American ally (sic) over a few sailors."

The late Adm. Thomas Moorer after interviewing the commanders of the U.S. aircraft carriers America and Saratoga confirmed that McNamara ordered the aircraft back to their carriers. Moorer called it "the most disgraceful act I witnessed in my entire military career."

Thanks to this book, those who care about such things can learn what actually happened 50 years ago:

(1) On June 8, 1967 Israel attempted to sink the US Navy intelligence collection ship USS Liberty and leave no survivors. The attack came by aircraft and torpedo boat, in full daylight in international waters during the Six-Day Israeli-Arab War;

(2) The U.S. cover-up taught the Israelis that they could *literally* get away with murder; they killed 34 U.S. sailors (and wounded more than 170 others); and

(3) As part of an unconscionable government cover-up, the Navy threatened to court martial and imprison any survivor who so much as told his wife what had actually happened. (This, incidentally, put steroids to the PTSD suffered by many of the survivors.)

The only investigation worth the name was led by Adm. Moorer, who had been Chairman of the Joint Chiefs of Staff. He led a blue ribbon, independent commission to examine what happened to the Liberty. Among the findings announced by the commission on October 22, 2003:

> …Unmarked Israeli aircraft dropped napalm canisters on the USS Liberty bridge, and fired 30mm cannon and rockets into the ship; survivors estimate 30 or more sorties were flown over the ship by a minimum of 12 attacking Israeli planes.…

> …The torpedo boat attack involved not only the firing of torpedoes, but machine-gunning of Liberty's firefighters and stretcher-bearers. … The Israeli torpedo boats later returned to machine-gun at close range three of the Liberty's life rafts that had been lowered into the water by survivors to rescue the most seriously wounded.

Shortly before he died in February 2004, Adm. Moorer strongly appealed for the truth to be brought out and pointed directly at what he saw as the main obstacle:

> *I've never seen a President … stand up to Israel. … If the American people understood what a grip these people have on our government, they would rise up in arms.*[*]

Echoing Moorer, former U.S. Ambassador Edward Peck, who served many years in the Middle East, condemned Washington's attitude toward Israel as "obsequious, unctuous subservience … at the cost of the lives and morale of our own service members and their families."

And the Six-Day War? Most Americans believe the Israelis were forced to defend against a military threat from Egypt. Not so, admitted former Israeli Prime Minister Menachem Begin 35 years ago:

> *In June 1967, we again had a choice. The Egyptian army concentrations in the Sinai approaches do not prove that [Egyptian President] Nasser was really about to attack us. We must be honest with ourselves. We decided to attack him.*[†]

Adm. Moorer kept asking why our government continues to subordinate American interests to those of Israel. It is THE question.

---

* As quoted by Richard Curtiss in "A Changing Image: American Perception of the Arab-Israeli Dispute."
† *New York Times,* August 21, 1982, quoting a speech Begin gave on August 8, 1982.

Fast forward to the catastrophe that is now Syria. U.S. policy support for illusory "moderate rebels" there – including false-flag chemical attacks blamed on Syrian President Bashar al-Assad – can only be fully understood against the mirror of U.S. acquiescence to Israeli objectives.

New York Times Jerusalem Bureau Chief in 2013, Jodi Rudoren, received an unusually candid response when she asked senior Israeli officials about Israel's preferred outcome in Syria. In a *New York Times* article on September 6, 2013, titled "Israel Backs Limited Strike Against Syria," Rudoren reported the Israeli view that the best outcome for Syria's civil war was "no outcome":

> For Jerusalem, the status quo, horrific as it may be from a humanitarian perspective, seems preferable to either a victory by Mr. Assad's government and his Iranian backers or a strengthening of rebel groups, increasingly dominated by Sunni jihadis.

> "This is a playoff situation in which you need both teams to lose, but at least you don't want one to win – we'll settle for a tie," said Alon Pinkas, a former Israeli consul general in New York. "Let them both bleed, hemorrhage to death: that's the strategic thinking here. As long as this lingers, there's no real threat from Syria."

Obama may have read or been briefed on Rudoren's *New York Times* article. In any event, last year he told journalist Jeffrey Goldberg how proud he is at having resisted strong pressure from virtually all his advisors to fire cruise missiles on Syria in September 2013. Instead, Obama chose to take advantage of Russian President Vladimir Putin's offer to get the Syrians to surrender their chemical weapons for destruction, verified by the UN, aboard a U.S. ship configured for such destruction. In contrast, President Trump chose to go with his "mad-dog" advisors. It is not yet clear whether he was successfully mousetrapped, or whether he saw the April 4 chemical incident in Syria as an opportunity to "retaliate," and get a bump in popularity.

There are wider ramifications of rank dishonesty and cover-up, at which Establishment Washington excels. Have we not seen this movie before? Think Iraq. Once again, the "intelligence" is being "fixed."

Back to the Liberty, Adm. Moorer is right in saying that, if Americans were told the truth about what happened on June 8, 1967, they might be more discriminating in seeing through Israel's rhetoric and objectives. Moorer insisted that we owe no less to the brave men of the USS Liberty, but also to every man and woman who is asked to wear the uniform of the United States. And he is right about that too.

This book makes a huge contribution toward those worthy ends.

Ray McGovern
April 24, 2017

Preface

A Message from The Inferno

by Edgar F. Tatro

Call the following slice of testimony what you will … an epiphany… a resolution … a confession … a warning. It does not matter to my lost soul, my lost spirit. The almighty apparitions known to you as configurations reminiscent of an armed head, a bloody infant, and a crowned child bearing a tiny tree in addition to their macabre underlings, that trio of haggard, bearded mistresses of fickle destiny, those wretched, immortal pranksters which have sealed my miserable and eternal existence, have granted me the opportunity, through a spiritual medium, to unburden my conscience, as it were, regarding past deeds of direst cruelty. Some have suspected my witting complicity, but it is apparently time to confirm those allegations for the human historical record. Perhaps those condescending mortals, who rule now, as I did then, will benefit from my errors and flaws and sins … although I doubt it.

It was I who was in attendance for all of the decisions, the debaucheries … the murders. It was I who participated in the slaying of my kinsman, my king, and my guest. It was I who mirrored the path of the floating dagger. It was I who thrust the blades of the innocent chamberlains into Duncan's unprotected bosom sending him, a most pleasant, albeit naïve, sovereign into another realm of surrealism.

It was I who secured the deepest gash across Banquo's astonished throat. It was I who administered most of the twenty mortal lacerations to his gory cranium and face while those incompetent peasants frittered away their lone chance to prevent Fleance's future reign in Scotland.

Yes, it was I who was also responsible for the immediate and inglorious demise of Macduff's issues, his noble wife and all the loyal servants of Fife. I even insured the death of those conniving spies, paid through my auspices, but residing within his castle at my behest, to prevent the release of unnecessary accounts for a future time.

I am the guilty one, drenched in blood, caked with the remnants of decayed flesh from innocent and unsuspecting victims … cousins … friends … patriots … women … babies. I am the evil perpetrator, inundated with the stench of death on my hands and royal robes, soiled for all the ages by foolhardy temptation. I am the quintessence of betrayal, the "crowning" metaphor for man's ultimate hypocrisies.

I have been dubbed through history as a mystery man, a hired killer, and a master cutthroat of peerless distinction ... a record marred only by Fleance's narrow escape. I am known to all as Banquo's THIRD MURDERER, but let it be revealed to the heavens and the Inferno and all other regions of existence that I was The Thane of Glamis ... I was the Thane of Cawdor ... I was the Usurper of Scotland ... I was the Fool of the Universe, that arrogant, headless patch who sacrificed his good name as a gallant warrior ... who betrayed his reputation as a loyal subject to the Rightful King ... who slaughtered all those who loved and admired him ... who listened to the Fates which toyed with his own self-deceiving flaws of greed ... who could not fathom the paradoxes and oxymorons laid before him ... who envisioned The Weird Sisters as riddle makers without a concerted purpose to their diabolical premonitions and plots ... who foolishly misinterpreted "Figurative" truths as "Literal" hyperbole ... who blinded himself to the concept of a moving grove and a corpse's shell as a fertile mother ... who obliterated his Nobility, his Integrity, his Pride and his Legacy for one brief, temporary moment of mindless celebration and power ... a contemptuous fragment of fallacious futility.

I WAS THE THIRD MURDERER ... I WAS MACBETH!!!!

CONTENTS

About the Authors

PHILLIP F. NELSON

Phil Nelson grew up in Indiana and studied business and economics at the University of Wisconsin (Whitewater campus), then served in the Peace Corps in Brazil in 1969-70. He was 18 years old when JFK was assassinated and had already become aware of Lyndon Johnson's criminal associations – specifically with the Texas wheeler-dealer Billie Sol Estes and Bobby Baker, who had worked with Johnson in the senate for several years – which were then being reported in national publications. After leaving his 30-year insurance management career he owned and operated his own business before selling it and retiring in 2003. Throughout his career, he had read many books related to the JFK assassination that left little doubt that it was still an "unsolved murder" that needed resolution. Upon his retirement, he began researching it intensely, recording notes from over hundreds of books and articles as well as original documents from various sources. He published his first book, *LBJ: The Mastermind of the JFK Assassination* in 2010, followed by *LBJ: From Mastermind to The Colossus* in 2014.

Mr. Nelson wrote the following note as an addendum to the above, for readers of this book:

> The previous works of other authors represent the distillation of a massive amount of research, and it forms the foundation upon which we have approached the subject of the *Liberty* attack, just as my earlier books were developed. Dozens of books on this subject have been reviewed, most of which are listed in the Bibliography if citations were made to their content. The previous books on this incident have proven beyond a shadow of a doubt that it was no "accident," therefore it was intentional, and it was clearly well planned and almost perfectly executed, except for one missing element: The ship did not sink as planned, thereby failing to fulfill that plan; this book will examine the attack in detail and offer an explanation of why the mission failed and the consequences of that failure. As before, we have approached this subject using similar methodologies as in my previous works, always guided by the Sherlock Holmes aphorism, *"When you have excluded the impossible, whatever remains, however improbable, must be the truth."*

To determine the best candidate for being the culprit for a particular crime, in this case the still-enigmatic, unresolved attack on the USS *Liberty* fifty years ago, we must start with determining – among all the possible candidates – the single most likely instigator, the "driving force" of the event: Every such action can be traced to a single person who had the most to gain and the least to lose and therefore can be presumed to be the one having the most compelling *motive*. Then one must consider which candidate was best positioned, with the most effective *means* to carry out the mission, and the resources available to create the best *opportunity*. But especially in the most brazen cases of audacious, brutally violent treacheries, that "driving force" would stand alone as one who uniquely had the kind of narcissistic, psychotic, sociopathic/mendacious persona capable of *rationalizing the action as acceptable and necessary*. Only such a person could have given it direction, momentum and resolve, together with the powerful *authority* to carry it out, as the means to an ultimate end.

Within my earlier books, certain themes were examined in considerable detail and they have been summarized within this book, including the numerous descriptions of Lyndon Johnson's life-long struggles with mental conditions based on what other authors have personally attested to, and what experts in the field of mental health have meticulously documented. Other authors, many of whom worked closely with Lyndon Johnson for years, even decades, have described numerous situations which prove conclusively that, as president, Johnson had repeated bouts of psychotic episodes, during which he became so enraged as to completely lose any semblance of self-control and rationality. A select few of those episodes have been referenced within this book as a means to put this facet of President Johnson into complete context, for it is essential that readers understand the implications of this point. None of this is "speculative," as it is all drawn from the documentation previously vetted, which in every case is cited to the original source.

The actions of President Johnson examined within this book come exclusively from people who witnessed them first-hand, or in some cases, communicated to others "second-hand," but always through highly credible military, diplomatic or other professional men or women of impeccable veracity. Exceptions to that paradigm are very few and, where names have been omitted, the reasons for that have been stated and the need for it should become obvious. Opinions expressed have been duly noted and where the line between factual statements and speculative assertions is crossed, that point is also stated. The suggestion that President Johnson's mental incapacities ultimately grew into a maniacal resolve to continue his term in the White House at all costs is of course one such point of reasoned and logical conclusion, yet it is arguably the only realistic basis for what caused the presidential treasons that will be closely examined. That his amalgamation of psychic disorders led to his forming such a grandiose plan, to accomplish another landslide election – which of course did not succeed because the *Liberty* did not sink – is admittedly a difficult point to prove with scientific certainty. Yet that premise, based upon a mountain of empirical evidence and the anecdotal "testimony" of the people who observed all of it, uniquely forms the presumptive proof of the veracity of this story. Indeed, it was the failed attempt to sink the *Liberty* that was one of the key reasons for Johnson's failure to even attempt to win that election, when he decided, less than ten months afterwards, to withdraw as a candidate.

The failure of the plan to sink the *Liberty* arguably saved the world from a nuclear confrontation between the United States and the Union of Soviet Socialist Republics (U.S.S.R.). It was the heroic actions by the survivors of the Israeli attack on the *Liberty* that should lay to rest the continuing acrimony of those whose blind allegiance to Israel causes them to curse the survivors with knee-jerk accusations of anti-Semitism: If it were not for the determination of the *Liberty* crew to keep that ship afloat, the world might have not survived that confrontation – one in which A-4 nuclear bombers bound for Cairo had already been launched, before being recalled because the *Liberty* had not already sunk as planned. It should also become obvious that, had that confrontation become conflagration, Tel Aviv and Jerusalem would have likely become "ground zero," thus the men of the USS *Liberty* deserve the gratitude of all people who were spared that calamity. The time for recognizing these heroes of the USS *Liberty* – their success in saving the ship, their contribution to saving the world from such a conflagration and their continuing, seemingly futile, efforts to bring this story to the attention of American citizens – has finally arrived.

RONALD G. KUKAL

Ron Kukal grew up in a small town in Nebraska as an only child whose mother had suffered with a bad case of rheumatoid arthritis, which impacted her ability to perform ordinary mothering functions. His schooling also suffered and by the time he graduated from high school he was ready to enlist in the U.S. Navy. He learned more discipline from the training he received to prepare for his service. That training was instrumental in providing him the skills and strength he needed in the aftermath of the attack on his ship that nearly took his life and that of his fellow sailors. It was that training, along with his belief of Divine Intervention, that enabled him to perform his duties so well after he was designated – due to his being the senior enlisted man on the crew – as the head of the "recovery and identification" team responsible for collecting and preserving the remains of the men killed in the attack. Some of the worst problems he experienced came later, as the after-effects of dealing with the lingering PTSD symptoms that resulted from that attack. The combined effects caused Mr. Kukal much personal torment and that resulted in the alienation of some of his children and his second wife. He is still recovering from decades of suffering he endured as a result of the experiences on board the USS *Liberty* in 1967.

Mr. Kukal wrote the following paragraph as a personal note to all readers of this book:

> As one of the survivors of the attack on the USS Liberty, I was the Petty Officer in Charge of the body recovery, and identification. My part of this book is dedicated to my wife, Connie, my four children, and my two step children. They are Jared, Ron Jr., Melissa, Jason, Mike and Lynda. I was not born to write, at least in my own mind, but little did I know there were plans made, maybe even before my birth, that I would. My writings are laced with scripture because so many verses run parallel to what has happened before and after June 8, 1967, at least in my own life. I will talk a lot in this book about Divine Intervention, even to the point of boring some of you to death. I still make no apologies because the truth is most simply the truth. Truth is a friend of infinite wisdom, something you never have to memorize because it is there. You saw it, you experienced it, and maybe, just maybe, just like Saul of Taurses on the Road to Damascus, you were struck by it, like lightening. That has been my experience, and I have found myself saying there are just no words to describe what I have seen, and I say that because it is true. The horrible events all of us experienced were, without a doubt, life changing. I know now why I fought so hard in an effort to find any other duty station, besides the *Liberty*.

ERNEST A. GALLO

Ernie Gallo grew up in Philadelphia, in the "Little Italy" community and went to parochial school at St. Mary's of the Eternal Church, where the American ethos was taught by the nuns, priests and scout leaders. This developed within him a firm and patriotic belief in basic American values and a love for the country and its history that was deeply shaken by the experiences described in this book. On the *Liberty* Mr. Gallo worked as a Second Class Communications Technician Maintenance Division Petty Officer, responsible for maintaining electronic equipment including cryptographic hardware associated with the mission of the Communication Technicians.. One of the most troubling experiences he has described involved being unfairly accused of "anti-Semitism" for criticizing the Israeli attack on the USS *Liberty*, despite the fact that it was an actual, undeniable, historical event. Mr. Gallo wrote a very informative and compelling book (*Liberty Injustices*) in 2013 which described the attack and its aftermath, as well as the continuing related events that defined his life throughout the last five decades as he sought to find answers to the perplexing questions about the real causes of that unprovoked yet still-mysterious event. Mr. Gallo is also the president of the Liberty Veterans Association.

Mr. Gallo wrote the following as a personal message to all readers of this book:

> I am the very proud President of the USS *Liberty* Veterans Association. The mission of our association is to make America aware of the truth of Israel's deliberate and determined attempt to sink the USS *Liberty* as well as the related events of our American officials. For those of you who believe Israel can do no wrong, take a deep breath and challenge yourself to continue reading this book as you will be presented with hard facts. And if you do not believe the contents, do your own research for the sake of the future of the United States as it is currently being guided. Because our government and media have forsaken truth for blind support for Israel, the result is that folks like author Phillip Nelson and the USS *Liberty* crew are labeled anti-Semitic and Jew haters, despite that being untrue. The crew has been living with this label for close to 50 years because we refuse to lie about the events you are about to discover. That is farthest from the truth, however, and the result is bigotry – sad, very sad as the USS *Liberty* is the most decorated Navy ship in history for a single engagement.
>
> On June 8, 1967, the Israeli Defense Forces (IDF) had a choice to make since they apparently did not want us to continue our mission. Capturing the *Liberty* was not one of their selected choices as they possessed far greater fire power than the *Liberty* and could have easily accomplished that. Yet, with no warning, the Israelis – without firing across our bow, without advising the USS *Liberty* to leave the area, and, without requesting our surrender – brutally attacked our ship. The *Liberty* was a virtually unarmed vessel and not a military physical threat. Ironically, at no time did the torpedo boats request the *Liberty* surrender as did the North Koreans involving the USS *Pueblo* in 1968. For our close ally and friend, the IDF, this was very safe target practice. The USS *Liberty* was a wonderful chance to hone their shooting and killing skills. As indicated, the Israelis had many alternatives to choose. Because they used torpedoes, is there any doubt in your mind they wanted us to sink with all hands lost? If LBJ was concerned about the so called accident, why did he not request Israel to bring the crippled ship to Israeli port to render immediate medical aid and also to prevent the ship from sinking if the internal bulkheads gave way. On the contrary, as you will read, he wanted the ship to go to the bottom,

with all hands lost. Without the involved government's providing us with an honest explanation, we can only come to a conclusion based on available facts. For a case of a so called accidental event, many documents are still very highly classified and unavailable. Finding the smoking gun is made that much more difficult, however, the Israeli apologists in the current government know that. Despite that, as you will read within this book, there are enough published documents that have become available that one can come to a logical determination for what really happened in the Eastern Mediterranean on June 8, 1967. That has now been accomplished, as described within this book.

PHILLIP F. TOURNEY

Born and raised in Colorado, on his seventeenth birthday Mr. Tourney tried to enlist in the Navy but initially failed the physical. But he was tenacious in his desire to serve, just as his two older brothers had, and he made a second attempt two months later. This time he passed the physical as well as the written examination and joined the Navy on February 6, 1964. His first assignment was on the USS *Manua Kea*, which was used to transport ammunition to Vietnam and, on the return trip to California, bring back the bodies of American soldiers who had been killed there, fighting as proxy soldiers in that civil war. From there, he was transferred back to another ship based out of Norfolk, Virginia: the USS *Liberty*. After working the first cruise in the engine room he transferred to the ship-fitter's shop and then into damage control duty (fireman), which was his assignment when the attack came on June 8, 1967. Mr. Tourney became one of the most active of the survivors in bringing public attention to the fate of the *Liberty*, including conducting many conferences and becoming the host of the radio show "Your Voice Counts" and the author of *What I Saw That Day* about the attack on the *Liberty*.

Mr. Tourney wrote the following as a personal message to all readers of this book:

> When I joined the U.S. Navy, I took an oath to protect the people of the United States from all enemies, foreign and domestic. The fact that I have received two honorable discharges from the armed services of the United States does not mean I have discharged myself from these duties to my beloved America, and that is why you are reading these words today.
>
> The day we were attacked, I was fighting just to stay alive, from one minute to the next. Therefore, I was not afforded the luxury of looking at my Timex every five minutes in order to form a perfect chronological transcript in my mind as to what happened. My main concern was not keeping perfect tabs about what was happening at

what time but rather, wondering, "Where's my next breath going to come from?"

Where does one begin, writing a story as bewildering as any that has ever been written – either fiction or non-fiction – and this one is no novel, which can be made up out of nowhere. In many ways, this story is of the "you can't make this up" variety, even though it is all true and there is nothing here that has been made up or even embellished; that would only make it truly "unbelievable." No sane person could begin to write this story even as a novel and expect it to be believable. Unfortunately, that may be the reason so many people refuse to believe it, as we will see within the pages to follow. It is an event that I have been cursed with as a disease, of "knowing" it for nearly fifty years now, and there is nothing I can do about the frustration, with each passing day and each minute, as my condition becomes ever more terminal.

And I'm not talking about the scars from the physical wounds I sustained during the attack, because those heal with time. The real wounds, to the psyche and soul, never seem to heal. They say that time heals all wounds, but that has not been my experience. Instead, time has caused these wounds to worsen and deepen; the nightmares become ever more vivid and more frequent, the anxiety never completely leaves me. Today, the pictures of death and butchery are clearer and more real than they were the day it happened. As I get closer to my grave, where I will take my story with me – but before I draw my last breath – I want this disease, this unquiet of the mind, out of my system, so that I may die in peace with myself.

I want to dedicate this book to my wife Lisa, my five children, Frankie, August, Deidre ,Bryce and Shane, as well as the 34 men named later, who did not come back with us to the United States after the attack on our ship June 8, 1967.

A Paradoxical Award from President Johnson and Admiral John McCain, II

Phillip Tourney was awarded the Bronze Star for his heroic actions during and immediately after the attack on the USS Liberty, as he literally risked his own life to save the lives of several other men who had been wounded, or trapped beneath the closed hatches in the flooding compartments where the torpedo hit. It is noteworthy that this citation makes no reference to the fact that the attacking forces were by a supposed ally, much less that it was Israeli forces who conducted it. But that is not the only paradox associated with the awarding of this medal:

THE PRESIDENT OF THE UNITED STATES TAKES PLEASURE IN PRESENTING THE BRONZE STAR MEDAL TO PETTY OFFICER THIRD CLASS PHILLIP FRANCIS TOURNEY UNITED STATES NAVY FOR SERVICE AS SET FORTH IN THE FOLLOWING CITATION: "FOR

HEROIC ACHIEVEMENT IN CONNECTION WITH THE UNPROVOKED AND UNEXPECTED ARMED ATTACK ON USS LIBERTY (AGTR 5) IN THE EASTERN MEDITERRANEAN ON 8 JUNE 1967. DURING THE EARLY AFTERNOON HOURS, USS *LIBERTY*, WHILE ENGAGED IN PEACEFUL OPERATIONS IN INTERNATIONAL WATERS, WAS ATTACKED WITHOUT WARNING BY JET FIGHTER AIRCRAFT AND THREE MOTOR TORPEDO BOATS. THE LIBERTY WAS SUBJECTED TO INTENSE INCENDIARY, MACHINE GUN, AND ROCKET FIRE AND WAS PLACED IN EXTREME JEOPARDY BY A TORPEDO HIT BELOW THE WATERLINE ON THE STARBOARD SIDE IN THE VICINITY OF THE RESEARCH COMPARTMENT. SEVERE STRUCTURAL DAMAGE AND EXTENSIVE PERSONNEL CASUALTIES WERE INCURRED. PETTY OFFICER TOURNEY, SERVING AS ASSISTANT ON SCENE LEADER IN THE FORWARD REPAIR PARTY, FIRST ASSISTED IN ORGANIZING THE EVACUATION OF WOUNDED PERSONNEL FROM THE EXPOSED WEATHER DECKS. WITH COMPLETE DISREGARD FOR HIS OWN PERSONAL SAFETY HE CONTINUED TO FEARLESSLY EXPOSE HIMSELF TO INTENSE ROCKET AND MACHINE GUN FIRE TO MOVE A FIRE FIGHTING TEAM TO THE BRIDGE. HE THEN RETURNED TO THE FORWARD WEATHER DECKS TO INSURE THAT NO MORE WOUNDED WERE STILL EXPOSED BEFORE GOING BELOW TO MAINTAIN DAMAGE CONTROL CONDITIONS OF OF COMPARTMENTS BELOW THE WATERLINE. HE REMAINED BELOW DECKS DURING THE TORPEDO ATTACK AND IMMEDIATELY AFTERWARD ASSISTED AND DIRECTED EMERGENCY REPAIRS TO MINIMIZE FURTHER FLOODING AND DAMAGE. HIS AGGRESSIVENESS AND COOLNESS UNDER FIRE WAS EXCEPTIONAL INSPIRATIONAL LEADERSHIP IN AND HOUR OF AWESOME PERIL. PETTY OFFICER TOURNEY'S INITIATIVE AND COURAGEOUS ACTIONS WERE IN KEEPING WITH THE HIGHEST TRADITIONS OF THE UNITED STATES NAVAL SERVICE."

PETTY OFFICER TOURNEY IS AUTHORIZED TO WEAR THE COMBAT "V" FOR VALOR

FOR THE PRESIDENT JOHN S. McCAIN, JR. ADMIRAL, UNITED STATES NAVY COMMANDER IN CHIEF, UNITED STATES NAVAL FORCES, EUROPE

Dedications

Those who cannot remember the past are condemned to repeat it
                                                              – George Santayana

This book is dedicated to all of the men who served on board the USS *Liberty* on her fourth and last tour of duty, all of whom came forward as patriots of their country and to serve their president. The men who died when the *Liberty* was suddenly attacked, without warning, on June 8, 1967 deserve special recognition:

LCDR Philip McCutcheon Armstrong, Jr.	CTSN James Lee Lenau
LT James Cecil Pierce	CTC Raymond Eugene Linn
St Stephen Spencer Toth	CT1 James Mahlon Lupton
CT 3 William Bernard Allenbaugh	CT3 Duane Rowe Marggraf
SN Gary Ray Blanchard	CTSN David Walter Marborough
CT2 Allen Merle Blue	CT2 Anthony Peter Mendle
QM3 Francis Brown	CTSN Carl Christian Nygren
CT2 Ronnie Jordon Campbell	SGT Jack Lewis Raper
CT2 Jerry Leroy Converse	CPL Edward Emory Rehmeyer, III
CT2 Robert Burton Eisenberg	ICFN David Skolak
CT2 Jerry Lee Goss	CT1 John Caleb Smith, Jr.
CT1 Curtis Alan Graves	CTC Melvin Douglas Smith
CTSN Lawrence Paul Hayden	PC2 John Clarence Spicher
CT1 Warren Edward Hersey	GMG3 Alexander Neil Thompson, Jr.
CT3 Alan Higgins	CT3 Thomas Ray Thornton
SN Carl Lewis Hoar	CT3 Philippe Charles Tiedtke
CT2 Richard Walter Keene, Jr.	CT1 Frederick James Walton

There were many other men who made contributions "above and beyond" their call of duty, but those noted below deserve specific mention here for the reasons explained in the narrative that follows:

PETTY OFFICER TERRY HALBARDIER

One man who, miraculously, survived the attack, deserves special recognition: Terry Halbardier's heroic action was finally recognized with a Silver Star forty-two years after the attack, in 2009. The delay was the direct result of Lyndon B. Johnson's determination to cover up not only the incident itself, due to his own cowardly actions, but also Israel's direct responsibility for the 34 Americans killed and the 174 wounded. Of the hundreds of medals awarded as a result of the attack on the *Liberty*, this was the very first one that even mentioned the fact that it was Israel which attacked the ship. The commendation reads:

> The President of the United States of America takes pleasure in presenting the Silver Star to Electronics Technician Third Class James Terry Halbardier, United States Navy, for conspicuous gallantry and intrepidity in action while serving on board the U.S.S. LIBERTY (AGTR-5), on 8 June 1967. The U.S.S. LIBERTY was attacked by Israeli aircraft and motor torpedo boats in the Eastern Mediterranean Sea on the fourth day of the SIX DAY WAR. Petty Officer Halbardier, without hesitation and with complete disregard for his own personal safety, fearlessly and repeatedly exposed himself to overwhelming rocket and machinegun fire to repair a damaged antenna in an open deck area during heavy aerial attacks. Aware that all of the ship's transmitting antennas had been destroyed and that communication with higher authority depended upon antenna repair, Petty Officer Halbardier risked his life to run connecting coaxial cable across open decks from the antenna to the main transmitter room. His efforts allowed the ship to establish communications with distant elements of the SIXTH Fleet and call for assistance. Despite being wounded, Petty Officer Halbardier ignored his injuries until the antenna had been repaired and the call for help had been received and acknowledged. His courageous actions were critical in alerting distant Navy commanders to the ship's need for assistance and were instrumental in saving the ship and hundreds of lives. Petty Officer Halbardier's outstanding display of decisive leadership, unrelenting perseverance, and loyal devotion to duty reflected great credit upon him and were in keeping with the highest traditions of the United States Naval Service.

The fact that, of the thousands of congressmen and senators who have served in the 42 years before Halbardier finally received his Silver Star on May 27, 2009, finally one persisted and managed to right that wrong should itself be celebrated. At least it was not a posthumous award, since Halbardier lived another five years after his actions were recognized. As a contemporaneous article by former CIA analyst Ray McGovern noted:[1]

In the award ceremony at the Visalia (California) office of Rep. Devin Nunes, the Republican congressman pinned the Silver Star next to the Purple Heart that Halbardier found in his home mailbox three years ago [i.e., only delayed by 39 years]. Nunes said, "The government has kept this quiet I think for too long, and I felt as my constituent he [Halbardier] needed to get recognized for the services he made to his country."

Nunes got that right. Despite the many indignities the Liberty crew has been subjected to, the mood in Visalia was pronouncedly a joyous one of Better (42 years) Late Than Never. And, it did take some time for the moment to sink in: Wow, a gutsy congressman not afraid to let the truth hang out on this delicate issue.

CAPTAIN JOSEPH TULLY, JR.
(CAPTAIN OF THE AIRCRAFT CARRIER USS SARATOGA)

A tribute by Ronald Kukal

I shall never forget Captain Tully at a reunion in Washington DC. He came up to me, and to several others, and apologized because he couldn't save us from the onslaught of the IDF. He told me he tried, and then had to recall the planes. My understanding of Captain Tully's story was that President Johnson knew all about the attack, even before it happened, and that was what had caused Captain Tully great personal grief. He had the look of a man beaten down; his clothes were wrinkled, He reminded me of several depictions I have seen of Christ after He had been beaten and was about to be crucified. Despondent in every way one could imagine, here he was, a well-decorated captain now coming to the enlisted men such as myself with an apology, one that he repeated, to each of us, as if he couldn't stop trying to get it across. I remember all of this like it was yesterday. I never blamed him personally, but he took that blame and placed it squarely upon his own shoulders.

A "Second" to Ron Kukal's tribute to Captain Tully, by Phil Tourney

As Ron stated above, at one of our reunions I also talked to this great man that had been broken by the fact that his rescue aircraft were recalled, not once, but twice. He was in tears when he came to our reunion, asking for our forgiveness; this great man was a hardened combat pilot hero, but now he was shaken to his core. He felt the Liberty crew would hate him, but we all loved that man and told him so. It was too late. The damage had already taken him over, and it was a sad sight to see and hear. I will never forget him struggling to speak because of his throat cancer that would later take his life. If anyone should be thanked and recognized, it is this icon of a man who merely wanted to do what was "right" and he was stopped by a particularly unscrupulous but powerful politician.

CAPTAIN MERLIN STARING
(SENIOR NAVY JUDGE ADVOCATE GENERAL CORPS OFFICER)

A tribute by Ernie Gallo

In Chapter 5, we will examine Captain Staring's actions in much more detail, so this will be merely a shortened reference to his heroic actions in categorically stating that the official findings of the 1967 Navy Court of Inquiry lacked credibility: specifically, that there was no evidence or testimony to support the finding that the attack on the *Liberty* was a case of "mistaken identity." This caused Admiral John S. McCain II (CINCUSNAVEUR) to recall the document from Staring's review, as Staring himself later described: "Never before had a record sent to me for review been recalled by my superior command without my having an opportunity to make a recommendation to him concerning his action on the record. In recent years I understand that some people have felt there was pressure exerted from some higher authority upon all the players in this matter, on the Court of Inquiry, perhaps on Admiral McCain, to get the Court of Inquiry completed and back there [i.e. to Washington]."[2] Thirty-eight years later, Rear Admiral Staring (Ret.) prepared another document, a "War Crimes Report," and submitted it to the Secretary of the Army, in his capacity as Executive Agent for the Secretary of Defense on June 8, 2005, the anniversary of the Israeli attack on the USS *Liberty*. No response to that report has been received as of this writing. I believe that Admiral Staring's report is an incredibly erudite, accurate and critical document and has enormous credibility for anyone wishing to learn the truth of this particular unsolved war crime. It is incomprehensible that the Navy's JAG service code of ethics was so compromised and degraded by this sordid incident as to put a permanent stain into the fabric of this storied institution. It can only be explained by the fact that is was done to protect the country from the truth of what occurred, and that truth involved "high crimes and treasons" at the highest level.

ADMIRAL THOMAS H. MOORER
(CHIEF OF NAVAL OPERATIONS FROM 1967–70 AND
CHAIRMAN OF THE JOINT CHIEFS OF STAFF THROUGH 1974)

A tribute by the authors

Admiral Thomas H. Moorer was the highest-level Navy officer to come forward and state unequivocally his belief that the attack on the USS *Liberty* was a deliberate attempt by Israel to sink the ship. He also believed that President Johnson ordered the cover-up to maintain ties with Israel. Furthermore, Admiral Moorer stated that "Israel attempted to prevent the *Liberty's* radio operators from sending a call for help by jamming American emergency radio channels [and that] Israeli torpedo boats machine-gunned life-boats at close range that had been lowered to rescue the most-seri-ously wounded." Moorer asked whether "our government put Isra-el's interests ahead of our own? If so, Why? Does our government continue to subordinate American interests to Israeli interests?" He further stated that the survivors were then ". . . betrayed and left to die by our own government. US military rescue aircraft were recalled – not once, but twice – through direct intervention by the Johnson administration. Secretary of Defense Robert McNamara's cancellation of the Navy's attempt to rescue the Liberty, which I confirmed from the commanders of the aircraft carriers *America* and *Saratoga*, was the most disgraceful act I witnessed in my en-tire military career." His full statement can be found in Chapter 5. These statements were made in 2004, while Robert McNamara was still alive and continuing to make contradictory, self-serving and deceitful statements, including outright denials of his own un-deniable, "disgraceful," record of facilitating the treasonous actions of the president who he faithfully obeyed. Three years later, still unremorseful about the *"Liberty* incident" McNamara died, taking those lies and deceit to his grave.

On another occasion, it took Admiral Moorer's personal in-tervention with the Naval Academy to reverse a decision by the directors of that academy to not honor the names of two of its grad-uates, as it has traditionally done, for those who have been killed in action. On a memorial honor wall in Bancroft Hall, where the names of its graduates killed in action are placed, two men who were killed during the Israeli attack on the USS *Liberty* – Lt. Com-mander Philip Armstrong and Lt. Stephen Toth – had been denied that privilege because their deaths had been ruled "accidental," in accordance with what Washington bureaucrats deemed to be the politically correct position. Thanks to Admiral Moorer, that injus-tice was corrected. For all of his efforts to correct the many injus-tices suffered by the survivors, as well as those who did not survive the attack on their ship, Admiral Thomas H. Moorer is recognized for his important actions.

Endnotes

1   McGovern, Ray, "A USS Liberty Hero's Passing," *Consortium News*, August 17, 2014

2   See Hounam, p. 55

Acknowledgements

The authors are indebted to all previous authors of books on the attack of the USS *Liberty*, especially those which have been cited throughout this book, of which some were referenced multiple times. The pioneering work of James Ennes in 1979 was one of the most important since it was the book that finally removed the veil of secrecy that had been placed over this story twelve years earlier. By the time his book was released, the story had long-since passed from the focal point of the main-stream news media Dozens of books have since been written, and most of them attempted to determine the real truths of the attack on the *Liberty*, but they had to counter the mythologies that were fabricated by the government's efforts to replace truths with "official" lies. The main remnant of the "Fourth Estate" that still functions, sporadically, springs from the internet and even that has been infested with moles planted there by the Dulles descendents.

Numerous others, as noted within the pages to follow, have been very helpful in different ways through their efforts to bring attention to this little-known page of American history, one that has been purposefully kept in the most secret government vaults, for reasons that will become clear by the end of the book. To say that many people want to keep it that way – and use the ugliest forms of ad-hominem attacks against the survivors and others who merely attempt to correct an historical "error" – is probably one of the biggest understatements of the last half-century.

A word of gratitude is also extended to all of the men and women who have tirelessly given of themselves to "spread the truth" about the tragedy that befell the USS *Liberty*. There are several organizations dedicated to this purpose, and they have all made important contributions toward exposing the facts of what occurred.

Several of these organizations, libraries and other entities, including especially the *Liberty* Veterans Association (http://www.usslibertyveterans.org/), have been referenced throughout the book and are noted in the Bibliography. They are all important resources for readers who seek further information about the current status of the *Liberty* veterans, and their continuing efforts to expose truths. For those who wish to support them financially as a way to contribute to this important cause, there are instructions noted on the website for how that can be done. Please also feel free to contact them if you have any questions on other ways to assist them in achieving their goals.

Finally, as we go to press, three of the most prolific writers on a plethora of subjects relating to U.S. domestic and foreign policies--having previously written on the subject of the Liberty attack--came forward to participate in "peer reviews" of the manuscript. We are indebted to David Martin (writing under the moniker "DCDave"), Greg Maybury (blogging at his website "PoxAmerikana) and Ray McGovern (an ex-CIA analyst whose non-profit organization is known as "Tell the Word") are all dedicated to the pursuit of truths and the exposure of myths. Their combined experience and knowledge base has substantively added to the public's overall understanding of this calamitous piece of history that has been kept so well hidden for fifty years.

Long-time researcher of numerous unresolved mysteries and false flag operations, Ed Tatro, also graciously volunteered his eloquent vignette "A Message from The Inferno" to the cause, which helps set the stage for the Shakespearean tragedy into which the Liberty sailed, as we have alluded to in the Epilogue.

Prologue

The truth is that like many liberal American Jews – and most American Jews are still liberal – I basically avoid thinking about where Israel is going. It seems obvious from here that the narrow minded policies of the current government are basically a gradual, long-run form of national suicide – and that's bad for Jews everywhere, not to mention the world. But I have other battles to fight, and to say anything to that effect is to bring yourself under intense attack from organized groups that try to make any criticism of Israeli policies tantamount to anti-Semitism.

– Paul Krugman, Opinion Page, *New York Times*, April 24, 2012

Regretably, any discussion of Israel, for some people, automatically produces a knee-jerk reaction in a way that does not apply to any other nation on earth: For example, criticism of Japan does not suggest one is "anti-Buddist" or "anti- Shintoism," any more than criticizing Italy is tantamount to being "anti-Catholic" or making a comment about India's policies is being "anti-Hindu, Islam" or anything else, but for whatever reason, the appellation of "anti-Semite" is inevitably triggered whenever anyone points out something that conflicts with politically-correct dogma regarding Israel. Similar demographics about the percentage of the referenced religions in those other countries are comparable to the fact that approximately 25% of Israel's population is of faiths other than Jewish. Moreover, it must also be recognized that not all Jews are Zionist, nor are most Zionists Jewish. Furthermore, in the U.S., there are probably as many, or even more, "Christian Zionists" and others whose personal beliefs might be called "Secular Zionists," than there are Jewish Zionists. So the paradigm that seems to exist is flawed on multiple levels.

Regardless of these distinctions, the more important difference is that most Zionists used lawful and peaceful diplomacy to achieve their objective, and that led to the creation of the state of Israel through negotiations in the United Nations in 1948 as a result of the Nazi Holocaust.

Yet simultaneously there existed, throughout the twentieth century, more zealously militant supporters of the Zionist cause, whose use of deadly provocations led them to be labeled "terrorists." Naturally, an individual Zionist could be positioned anywhere on the political gamut. The historical pertinence of this elementary exercise will become clearer in the following pages but it is important for the reader to understand that there were a number of ardently committed Zionists – people representing points on both ends, and different positions within that spectrum – who became chessmen in a gigantic game being played by Lyndon Johnson as he advanced himself up the political ladder.

Much of the confusion caused by the controversies that are addressed in this book are a direct result of the mistaken presumptions made by those who wish to dismiss the entire matter of the Israeli attack on the USS *Liberty* on such faulty grounds, in many cases by attempting to deny the attack even occurred. There is no doubt, it's as predictable as the sun rising in the East, that unsubstantiated criticism will be made of this book based upon this tired canard. All we can say, as the authors, is that there is not a trace of anti-Semitism either in our hearts or within the pages of this book. That said, while the authors categorically deny any shred of "anti-Semitism," it cannot be denied that being "anti-zealously-Zionist-terrorist" is quite another thing. Only that very qualified terminology gets close to the proper characterization of all of those who are merely attempting to understand the part of real history into which the USS *Liberty* began its fateful cruise into the Mediterranean on June 2, 1967.

The nation of Israel has made its share of mistakes; but that can be said of all nations, certainly including the United States. When deadly mistakes are made, if we as citizens cannot learn of them because of protocols put in place by the government to protect its true national security secrets, are misused – to protect, instead, "High Crimes, Misdemeanors, and Treasons" intentionally committed by its highest officials – then the mistakes made by the leaders of previous generations will be swept up into the dustbin of history.

Part I: Background

Dwight D. Eisenhower

Chapter 1

The Winds of War

Every man, woman and child lives under a nuclear sword of Damocles, hanging by the slenderest of threads, capable of being cut at any moment by accident, or miscalculation, or by madness.

– President John F. Kennedy at the United Nations, September 25, 1961

Democrats Urge President:
Fight Israel Sanctions, Johnson Leads Action

– Headline: *New York Times*, February 20, 1957

In that front-page article in the *New York Times*, President Dwight Eisenhower is pictured, scowling, as he returned from his interrupted golfing vacation at the Augusta National Golf Club, home of the Masters Golf Tournament. The article told how David Ben-Gurion had refused to withdraw Israel's troops from the Gaza Strip and the Gulf of Aqaba, defying a UN resolution that had Eisenhower's support. Ike had hoped to use the threat of economic sanctions against Israel to force it to relinquish control over the lands it had recently occupied. If it weren't for the fact that the majority leader of the Senate, Lyndon B. Johnson, had effectively subverted the president's foreign policy, Eisenhower may have returned to Washington, with a smile instead of a scowl. His anger was focused not only on what Ben-Gurion had already done, but also at the actions taken by the bullying Texan, then known as the "Master of the Senate." A re-examination of that incident is important to put the events that played out a decade later into proper historic context.

The infamous 1954 Israeli false-flag operation in Egypt known as the "Lavon Affair"[1] helped to set the stage for the "Suez Crisis." The rumblings of the crisis began in early 1955, when the Eisenhower administration began pressuring Israel to show some commitment to peace in the Middle East. Israel had been conducting deadly raids in the Gaza Strip, which they claimed were in retaliation for attacks made against their military from Gaza – a pattern that continues today.

On February 28, 1955, Egyptian President Gamal Nasser gave a speech on what he termed "Israeli atrocities," within which he warned of further reprisals if Israel continued the raids. Later that year, Egypt stepped closer to the Soviet Union's orbit and away from the Western powers when President Nasser negotiated a treaty with Czechoslovakia for $200 million worth of (Soviet) arms, including tanks, fighter planes, artillery, and submarines. The border clashes grew more violent and Nasser also felt that Israeli lobbyists and financial backers in America had been behind the loss of US aid for the Aswan Dam.

Nasser had previously been assured by the Eisenhower administration that financial assistance of $1.3 billion (1956 dollars) would be forthcoming, however Israeli lobbyists had pressured the Senate Appropriations Committee into blocking funding for the dam. Nasser's response was to nationalize the Suez Canal as a means to raise funds to build the Aswan Dam.[2] A result of Nasser seizing the Suez Canal was that Israel began planning to attack Egypt, colluding with France and Britain.[3]

It appears that Senate Majority Leader Lyndon Johnson was then enlisted to exercise his political muscle to prevent the UN from imposing sanctions on Israel, despite the fact that Eisenhower had already endorsed the sanctions after deciding that Israel had violated international law in plotting the attack. Eisenhower was determined to force Israel to back down from its aggression by temporarily cutting off American aid. Johnson wrote a letter to Secretary of State John Foster Dulles objecting to the proposed sanctions against Israel and then had the temerity to send a copy of it to the *New York Times*, with a request that the letter be published. Johnson was hoping to embarrass and humiliate President Eisenhower into bowing to Johnson's will; instead, the public letter only angered Eisenhower more and strengthened his resolve.

After a hurried return to Washington, Eisenhower went on radio and television to speak directly to the nation, saying, indirectly but emphatically to Senator Johnson: "America has either one voice or none, and that voice is the voice of the President – whether everybody agrees with him or not," and that the U.N. had "no choice but to exert pressure upon Israel." Ultimately, it was Johnson who lost face in the episode, as Israel, France and Great Britain all had to back down. It was not only a humiliation to all of them, but a victory for President Nasser, which was something that, undoubtedly for LBJ, "stuck in his craw." even more than his own embarrassment.

Some historians cite the Suez Crisis as being "… the end of Great Britain's role as one of the world's major powers."[4]

Israel continued using its military superiority over the neighboring Arab states in the late 1950s and early 1960s. Rumors of a nuclear reactor in the Negev Desert at a site called Dimona grew, and the city of Beersheba seemingly became a French outpost, housing nuclear scientists and engineers and their families.[5] Israel's military assets were also used in more pedestrian ways as well, such as the completion of a major new aqueduct that was built during this period and put into service in 1964 to carry the waters of Lake Tiberias to the Negev; by the summer of that year sustained pumping of water began. The Arab states had threatened to use force to prevent that, but they backed down since they did not have the military strength to enforce the ultimatum. Yet when Syria began its own water-diversion project in March, 1965, Israel immediately attacked it with artillery and tanks.[6]

These incidents from the mid-1950s to mid-1960s should be considered as early markers for a pattern that would be repeated by Israel throughout not just the lead-up to, and during, the Six-Day War and the attack on the USS *Liberty*, but for the next five decades as well. Likewise, Johnson's actions in February, 1957 established patterns that would be repeated time and again during the ensuing decade, which must be considered in the context of the remaining chapters: His unqualified support for Israel as well as his dislike of Egyptian President Nasser.

Johnson's actions were a direct defiance of the executive power of the president.

LYNDON JOHNSON'S POLITICAL PERILS: CIRCA 1964 – 1967

To understand how Lyndon Johnson's earliest presidential actions would cause him to react so severely to events that occurred in 1967 – 1968, we must begin where his presidency started to unravel. His downfall was related to his first major presidential decision, made on November 24, 1963: Exactly two days after becoming president, to reverse JFK's Vietnam policies, and make Vietnam a part of what he thought would be an important cornerstone of his presidency.

Johnson wanted desperately to be a "wartime president" just like Franklin D. Roosevelt, Abraham Lincoln, and of course George Washington. He had long sided against President Kennedy – never publicly, of course – with like minded men in the Pentagon, the CIA and among JFK's own aides in the White House. There were Cold War mainstays like Walt Rostow, McGeorge Bundy and, in the State Department, Secretary Dean Rusk, all of whom had pressured Kennedy, against his own instincts, to increase military support for South Vietnamese President Ngô Đình Diệm. Though Kennedy had listened to them for the first two years of his administration, obliging them by steadily increasing the number and scope of duty of the non-combat military "advisors," by his third year, he had begun reassessing those policies with the intention of removing all military support by the end of 1965.

Before President Kennedy was buried, Lyndon Johnson made key decisions to reverse JFK's policies on Vietnam, even while boasting that he "shall continue" to guide the ship of state as JFK would have.

The esteemed Berkeley professor, Dr. Peter Dale Scott, established the dynamics of this charade conclusively, in 1972, upon studying the

Pentagon Papers: "With respect to events in November 1963, the bias and deception of the original Pentagon documents are considerably reinforced in the Pentagon studies commissioned by Robert McNamara. Nowhere is this deception more apparent than in the careful editing and censorship of the Report on the Honolulu Conference on November 20, 1963 and National Security Action Memorandum [NSAM] 273, which was approved four days later. Study after study is carefully edited so as to create a false illusion of continuity between the last two days of President Kennedy's presidency and the first two days of President Johnson's."[7] That "illusion of continuity" became apparent in many of the statements from the new president, as he continued to evoke Kennedy's name, in the immediate aftermath of his predecessor's assassination.

Professor Scott then noted that the editing allowed for "selective censorship" or "downright misrepresentation" of the document, to allow, depending upon one's purpose, to focus on "optimism" which led to plans for withdrawal of American forces, or to "deterioration" and "gravity" which could be cited to support escalation of the war. It even provided a method to posit that "President Johnson needed to reaffirm or modify the policy lines pursued by his predecessor" and, curiously, that he chose to "reaffirm the Kennedy policies." Scott then used strong words to convey the duplicitousness of the author of the study, or "some superior" when he stated that the most important part of NSAM 273 (which had been omitted from the documents initially presented) "authorized planning for specific covert operations, graduated in intensity, against the DRV, i.e. North Vietnam." Moreover, said Professor Scott, the consequence of NSAM 273's sixth paragraph (the one which had not been leaked to the press) was "to *annul*" Kennedy's "NSAM 263 withdrawal decision announced four days earlier at Honolulu, and also the Accelerated Withdrawal Program …"(italics in original).[8]

Finally, Professor Scott concluded: "The source of this change is not hard to pinpoint. Of the eight people known to have participated in the November 24 reversal of the November 20 withdrawal decisions, five took part in both meetings. Of the three new officials present, the chief was Lyndon Johnson, in his second full day and first business meeting as President of the United States. The importance of this second meeting, like that of the document it approved, is indicated by its deviousness." Scott continued, "This deception, I suspect, involved far more than the symbolic but highly sensitive issue of the 1,000-man withdrawal. One study, after calling NSAM 273 a "generally sanguine" "don't-rock-the-boat document," concedes that it contained "an unusual Presidential exhortation: 'The President expects that all senior officers of the government will move energetically to insure full unity of support for establishing U.S. policy in South Vietnam.'"[9]

The conclusions of Dr. Peter Dale Scott can be summarized as portraying Lyndon B. Johnson, in his second day at the helm, as already making a dramatic, 180-degree change from President Kennedy's decision to begin the withdrawal of troops within weeks (starting with 1,000 in the last six weeks of the year, 1963) and to complete that process for the remaining 15,000 over the next two years, by the end of 1965, so that *no* troops would remain beyond 12/31/1965.

Johnson's new program would actually reverse JFK's plans, leading to the dramatic escalation, and finally "Americanization" of the war. Of course, none of this was known at the time, else his chances of winning the 1964 presidential election could be jeopardized.

Johnson would, within weeks, order McGeorge Bundy to begin preparing a plan ("34-A") for gradually escalating a series of provocations to North Vietnam. It was an attempt to intimidate the North Vietnamese into retaliating against U.S. Navy vessels, and to do so in the late summer of that year, just months before the November elections.

It was through "deviousness and deception" as cited by Professor Scott that a fundamental shift in policy would be kept hidden from the public. Two days after becoming president and concurrently with his approval of NSAM 273, on Sunday, November 24th, he began making the statement "We shall continue" JFK's policies in his memory, whether the point referenced was related to foreign or domestic policy. People who lived through that tumultuous period remember the constant refrain from Johnson in 1964-65, because he repeated it with almost every piece of legislation, exhorting Congress to pass bills: "in John Kennedy's honor."

Johnson's purpose – in addition to his being a wartime president, which he thought would embellish his eventual "legacy" – was to benefit his friends and himself financially, through investments in various corporations involved in the defense industry. He even admitted that, according to a statement from his CIA briefer, as cited by author Dr. William F. Pepper: As Colonel John Downie admitted, in his last session with Johnson in 1966, after he had repeatedly, "… urged him to get out of Vietnam, a frustrated LBJ pounded the table and exclaimed, 'I cannot get out of Vietnam, John, my friends are making too much money.'"[10]

It was during this same time frame that Johnson repeatedly explained to the American people how well things were going, though he admitted that they would have to carry "perhaps for a long time the burden of a confusing and costly war in Vietnam."[11]

One of the most incisive authors of Vietnam history (*Dereliction of Duty: Lyndon Johnson, Robert McNamara, The Joint Chiefs of Staff, and the Lies that Led to Vietnam*), Army Major H.R. McMaster, summarized how the mistakes that led to the "Americanization" of the war occurred:[12]

Contrary to Robert McNamara's claims of ignorance and overconfidence during the period 1963-1965, the record proves that he and others were men who not only should have known better, but who did know better.... It was during the period from November 1963 to July 1965 that Lyndon Johnson made the critical decisions that took the United States into war almost without realizing it. The decisions, and the way in which he made them, had a profound effect on the conduct of the war and its outcome.... Lyndon Johnson was a profoundly insecure man who feared dissent and craved reassurance. In 1964 and 1965, Johnson's principal goals were to win the presidency in his own right and to pass his Great Society legislation through Congress. The Secretary of Defense, Robert McNamara, was particularly adept at sensing the president's needs and giving him the advice he wanted.

By late 1966, President Johnson was in deep political trouble with his own constituents. He had spent most of the political capital that had come with winning his historic landslide victory in the 1964 presidential election. During 1964-65, he had figuratively "moved mountains" to push progressive legislation through congress. These were bills that he had previously impeded for his entire congressional career, and further vehemently opposed in the three years he spent as vice president, always telling President Kennedy that "the time wasn't right, you must wait until the time is right, we don't have the votes."

After he became president, of course, the time was right, and he was now relentless in pushing Congress to move all of it. The pressure to accomplish his "Great Society" program, and the public's reactions to the three summers of race riots, had been so great that in the 1966 elections, Democrats lost so many congressional seats that they nearly lost their majority status in both houses. The congressional changes resulted in a virtual end to the domestic programs he had envisioned to cement his "legacy."

While the majority of Americans agreed that the civil rights and voting rights legislation were long overdue, some had begun doubting parts of the progressive agenda. Worried that these actions would lead to fundamental societal changes, many pundits warned, for example, of their concerns related to bills that would extend welfare programs so greatly that they could become disincentives for gainful employment, and structured such that they might lead to family breakdowns. The "backlash" that ensued, along with the simultaneous increases in violent inner-city riots during the summers of Johnson's presidency, also caused many to question the speed at which these bills were being pushed through Congress.

But more than any of that, most Americans had begun questioning the need to invest huge numbers of young men for a war on the other side of the world – that they did not understand. A place seemingly devoid of any significant American interests. Within two years President Johnson had become distrusted, and even despised and hated by millions of people. It was the Vietnam "quagmire" that cost him tremendous loss of public support, and he knew by 1966 that, unless something was done to counter that loss, his chances in 1968 would be slim.

Moreover, as many suspected at the time and as it later became clear to the world, the events that supposedly precipitated America's entry into a wider conflict were merely a contrived pretext, a so-called "false flag": A maneuver to place the blame for an alleged attack on U.S. Navy ships – an attack that never occurred – on the government of North Vietnam.

The operation had been planned for months by the new president Johnson through his White House staff. Despite the fact that the Gulf of Tonkin "attack" never actually occurred, the purported intensity of the phantom offensive – an event that the crew of the ships involved had been conditioned to expect, aided by weather anomalies that caused radar images which helped to heighten the crew's tensions – provided sufficient drama for the frantic crew to begin shooting wildly at imaginary boats.

None of the Navy planes sent to assist the two destroyers found any sign of real boats. Indeed, one of the pilots, Commander James Stockdale, reported: "No boats, no boat wakes, no ricochets off boats – nothing but black sea and American firepower." As reported in a book titled *Dark Signals: A Navy Radio Operator in Tonkin Gulf and South China Sea, 1964-1965* by author Si Dunn, the Navy fighter jets sent out from aircraft carriers could not spot any attacking boats so they "shot up the water around the phantom radar targets" until they ran short on fuel and returned to their carriers. Among the "Flash" (highest priority) messages that were sent to the Pentagon in the aftermath of the phantom attack was this one:[13]

REVIEW OF ACTION MAKES MANY RECORDED CONTACTS AND TORPEDOES FIRED APPEAR DOUBTFUL. FREAK WEATHER EFFECTS AND OVEREAGER SONARMEN MAY HAVE ACCOUNTED FOR MANY REPORTS. SUGGEST COMPLETE EVALUATION BEFORE ANY FURTHER ACTION.

But the facts on the ground – or in the sea – were irrelevant to Lyndon Johnson at this point. He had been planning the provocations for months, and he had already gotten his aide McGeorge Bundy to prepare the wording for the Tonkin Gulf Resolution weeks before this event. Johnson immediately dispatched his frenzied aides to Capitol Hill to get the resolution voted on, before the "crisis" had passed.

The bill was carried unanimously in the House and with only two dissenting senators, it was quickly adopted without substantive debate.

Senators such as Gaylord Nelson of Wisconsin felt the resolution gave too much authority to Johnson to conduct the war without definitive limits. These concerns were rebuffed by the chairman of the Senate Foreign Relations Committee, J. William Fulbright, who – two years later – finally came to the same conclusion that Senator Nelson had previously tried to warn him about. In fact, Fulbright wrote a best-selling book in 1966 entitled *Arrogance of Power* that was implicitly aimed at Johnson's arrogant conduct of the presidency.

Finally, the *timing* of the phantom "attack" must not go unnoticed: August 4, 1964 was precisely three months before the 1964 presidential elections. LBJ's reputation as a master planner of complex events – one which would guarantee him a peak of patriotic passion amongst voters – was never more obvious, at least in retrospect. The careful choreography of this meticulous manipulation is crystal clear to anyone who examines it. Indeed, the planning started soon after Johnson ascended to the Oval Office. Marine Corps Lieutenant Colonel William R. Corson wrote about it in his aptly titled 1968 book *The Betrayal*:[14]

> "The plans to bomb North Vietnam were drawn up in the spring and summer of 1964 [i.e. even before the so-called "Gulf of Tonkin" attacks], and President Johnson told Charles Roberts of *Newsweek* that he had made his decision to order the systematic bombing of North Vietnam in October, 1964 – prior to the election. Why did LBJ procrastinate for four months – after his election – to do what his advisors deemed necessary? The answer to this question is indicative of the "necessary measures" the Johnson Administration has used to flimflam the American public about Vietnam. A suitable pretext had to be found to justify the bombing and troop escalation. The pretext was that there had been an "invasion" of South Vietnam by North Vietnamese forces. Secretary Rusk asserted before the Senate Foreign Relations Committee in April 1965 there had been an armed invasion of South Vietnam by the North Vietnamese 325th Division, which, he said, had moved across the border "as a division" between November 1964 and January 1965 ... he was counting on the image of "a division" to conjure up in the minds of the American public a picture of invading hordes of little yellow men directed by Moscow and Peking [now Bejing] attacking the freedom-loving people of South Vietnam. It was a neat trick. In March 1965 LBJ landed the Marines and began the systematic bombing of North Vietnam and the situation was well in hand."

Colonel Corson's book was written as a clarion-call to the American public, to alert them to what he felt was a major deception being foisted upon the nation, whose citizens had still been in shock in the aftermath of the assassination of their president. The public had generally been supportive of the new president the first two years of his presidency but had largely, albeit gradually, begun to understand the reason that the term "credibility gap" had recently been coined for the express purpose of describing the intrinsic lack of veracity of the new president's words. It was on March 23, 1966 that "credibility gap" was first used by David Wise in the New York *Herald Tribune* to describe the inherent statistical discrepancies of U.S. government reports on the Vietnam war. William Corson further explained that all the devious subterfuge was necessary to fool the American public, which, if they had really known what was going on, would have repudiated all of it.[15]

Even before Corson's book was published, by at least 1967, most cognitively aware people had concluded that they had been "conned" – manipulated into supporting the new president's war. That view was shared by many other leaders in both parties: It included Republican presidential candidate George Romney, whose admittance of having been "brainwashed" about Vietnam policy cost him his party's nomination. On March 25, 1966 U.S. Ambassador to the United Nations Arthur Goldberg received an honorary degree from University of California, Berkeley and attempted to defend the Johnson administration's Vietnam policies. The crowd of about 15,000 were almost entirely of the opposite view and many carried anti-war posters, some of which referenced the recipient of the honorary degree as "Arthur Goldberg, Doctor of War."

Later, when some of them gathered at a peace conference a vote was held on the Administration's handling of the war. About 7,000 voted for disapproval while less than 100 affirmed Johnson's policies. Beginning the same day, demonstrations began across the country called "Second International Days of Protest," where thousands protested the war in all of the major U.S. cities as well as others around the world.

By that point, the president must have already realized that his landslide election just two years previous would never be repeated. Indeed, in the 1966 congressional elections, the Republicans gained three seats in the Senate and forty-seven in the house due largely to a backlash against Johnson personally.

Many in the Senate had also, belatedly, come to understand the calamity that they had helped create. And many other high-profile people – from Robert Kennedy and Muhammad Ali to Martin Luther King Jr. – had switched their positions and made strong statements questioning the continuation of Johnson's Vietnam policies. Moreover, King continually drew comparisons to the "guns or butter" analogy that had been written by Richard Goodwin into the 1966 State of the Union message, to "... reconcile the war with continued progress toward the Great Society." That phrase, often used to portray the choices facing America, was implicit in many of King's speeches, such as on one occasion when he said: "We believe the highest patriotism demands the ending of the war and the opening of a bloodless war to final victory over racism and poverty."[16] Johnson was furious at him by this point, regardless of their previous pretensions of having "worked together," and at anyone else who publicly dared to speak against his policies. Johnson usually either questioned their patriotism or simply asserted that they were "communists."

LYNDON JOHNSON PLANS A NEW WAR – ONE WITH GUARANTEED POPULARITY:

HOW HE THOUGHT WAR IN THE MID-EAST WOULD SOLVE HIS SOUTH-EAST ASIA WOES

In 1967, Johnson still expected to run again in 1968 for the office he had always believed was his destiny. Johnson's paranoia had caused him to think that the protestors were being guided by foreign communists and ordered the CIA – contrary to its charter (something that never seemed to interfere with its projects) – to begin surveillance of the anti-war leadership. This program was named Operation Chaos, which, despite desperate attempts to do so, failed to produce any such evidence.[17]

Johnson then turned to the FBI, which jumped at the chance to infiltrate peace organizations to disrupt their operations.[18] The zealotry with which they tackled that objective led them to adopt certain Gestapo-type tactics which were later used by courts to throw out cases that should have been successfully prosecuted and finally led to freeing some of the most violent protestors that they had set out to arrest.

A number of aides and associates of President Johnson in 1967 have stated that, of all the people who had once been among his strongest supporters but then had turned against him, it was his Jewish constituents that upset him the most. Indeed, the protestors in Lafayette Park across the street from the White House (of which many were young Jewish men and women), whose endless chants of "Hey, Hey, LBJ, how many kids did you kill today" probably drove that reaction. He was also conscious of how Jews had been among his strongest supporters just three years previous; now they had become among his strongest opponents – all because they did not agree with his Vietnam policies. His aide Harry McPherson, interviewed by T. H. Baker for an oral history for the LBJ Library, explained how Johnson had even assigned him a role as a "conduit" to the Jewish community, charged with the task of repairing the damage and reinforcing his connection to that group: "The President could never understand why there were so many Jews who were anti-Viet Nam, and he would say – you know, to him this was a small country fighting aggression."[19] That view was confirmed by author J. J. Goldberg, in his book *Jewish Power:*

Inside the American Jewish Establishment; Goldberg stated that Johnson was upset about the prominence of Jews among the anti-war protestors and thought they were being somehow hypocritical to expect the United States to support Israel but not South Vietnam.[20]

The inevitable result of Lyndon Johnson's precarious political position in 1966-67, beginning just two years after his historic landslide election, was a resounding resolve to do whatever was necessary to get it corrected. Only the boldest, most dramatic, action – something so monumental that it could not be ignored or denied – to capture the attention of that political demographic would do, and nothing could stand in the way of accomplishing that objective. In 1967, Johnson was intensely desperate not to lose his presidency the following year, and the risk of another war, even a potentially lethal nuclear war with the Soviet Union –would not stand in the way. He probably even believed that it might even be the guaranteed ticket for him to stay in office – perhaps thinking to himself: "How could the voters abandon a president in the middle of an international conflagration?"

PRESIDENT JOHNSON – THE FIRST JEWISH PRESIDENT?

While not critical to the storyline (yet significant to understanding the deep feelings for Jewish people that Lyndon Johnson had) Johnson's natural affinity for Jews might have been due to his own heritage. Johnson's most acclaimed biographer, Robert Caro, noted that "A Johnson family friend, Cynthia Crider, observed that Lyndon's mother, Rebekah Baines (Johnson), often boasted of her Baines ancestry, but rarely mentioned the maternal side, the Huffmans. In fact, Crider recalled that Lyndon's father, Sam Johnson, used to tease his wife occasionally about her German heritage. When she would get stubborn, Sam would say, "That's your German blood again. German blood! Look at your brother's name. Huffman! Probably was Hoffmann once – in Berlin." Rebekah would respond, "Sam, you know it's Holland Dutch."[21] Moreover, Johnson's long time assistant Harry McPherson said in his third oral history interview for the LBJ Library:

> And I think he felt instinctively what I've always felt, that some place in Lyndon Johnson's blood there are a great many Jewish corpuscles. I think he is part Jewish, seriously. Not merely because of his affection for a great many Jews, but because of the way he behaves. He really reminds me of a six-foot-three-inch Texas, slightly corny, version of a rabbi or a diamond-merchant on 44th Street.[22]

In an online article "The First Jewish President?" available on various websites, further credence is given to Lyndon Johnson's Jewish ancestry.

The article states that: "According to Jewish law, if a person's mother is Jewish, then that person is automatically Jewish, regardless of the father's ethnicity or religion. The facts indicate that both of Lyndon Johnson's great-grandparents, on the maternal side, were Jewish."[23] The grandparents of Lyndon's mother, Rebecca Baines were named John S. Huffman and Mary Elizabeth Perrin, both common Jewish names, as was the name of John Huffman's mother, Suzanne Ament.[24] Moreover, the article indicates that the Huffmans migrated from Germany to Frederick, Maryland, during the 1750s before they moved on to Kentucky and ultimately Texas in the 1800s. It relates a family story about Lyndon's father "Little Sam" and his grandfather "Big Sam" who sought clemency for Leo Frank, the "Jewish victim of a blood libel in Atlanta" in 1915 and had to guard against retribution from the Ku Klux Klan by defending their farm with shotguns. Further, the article cites historian James M. Smallwood, who stated that Congressman Johnson used legal and sometimes illegal methods to smuggle "hundreds of Jews into Texas, using Galveston as the entry port. Enough money could buy false passports and fake visas in Cuba, Mexico and other Latin American countries. Johnson smuggled boatloads and planeloads of Jews into Texas. He hid them in the Texas National Youth Administration. Johnson saved at least four or five hundred Jews, possibly more."[25]

A pertinent point about Johnson's willingness to help Jews escape Europe in 1937 and his later help in the formation of Israel in 1947–48 and its substantial expansion in 1967 during the Six-Day War (to be examined shortly) is that the first person to influence Johnson to do something to help Jews fleeing Adolph Hitler was his mistress, Alice Glass (she conducted the affair behind the back of her husband, Charles Marsh, one of Johnson's primary financial benefactors and owner of several Texas newspapers). In 1937, Charles and Alice had attended the Salzburg music festival and heard one of Hitler's speeches. They were among the first Americans to realize Hitler's threat and, according to Robert Caro's research, immediately upon their return, they began assisting Jews financially and in other ways to escape Hitler's grasp, even opening their Virginia country estate to refugees. One of them was a young musical conductor, Erich Leinsdorf.[26] When Leinsdorf realized that he had received no reply for an extension of his visa, after several months, Marsh drove him to Washington where they met with Lyndon Johnson, who not only arranged to have the visa extended but developed an elaborate plan to send him to Cuba so that he could return as a regular immigrant, but one having a new status, as a "permanent resident."[27] Whether Johnson did this out of an act of kindness for a particularly worthy immigrant – Johnson had someone on his staff write a letter stating that the United States had a "Holy mission to provide a peaceful haven for musical geniuses nervously exhausted from persecution and racial bias,"[28] – or merely to impress his lover at the time, we will never know for sure.

NOVEMBER 22, 1963:
A "SEA CHANGE" IN U.S. – ISRAELI RELATIONS BEGINS

Among Johnson's closest advisers during the 1950s and 1960s were several strong pro-Israel advocates, including Benjamin Cohen (who thirty years earlier was the liaison between Supreme Court justice Louis Brandeis and Chaim Weizmann) and Abe Fortas, the legendary Washington "insider." Fortas had known Israeli Ambassador Avraham Harman since 1959, when Harman became the new ambassador to the United States. A few months later, in March 1960, Fortas hosted a breakfast meeting at his home for Israeli Prime Minister David Ben-Gurion. Senate Majority Leader Lyndon Johnson was one of the featured guests at that meeting and undoubtedly used it to emphasize how he had endeavored to be Israel's greatest friend, clearly more so than either Eisenhower or the other Democratic nominee for president, John F. Kennedy.

One of the biggest objectives of Ben-Gurion and the other Israeli leaders during that period was their desire to obtain nuclear weapons to give them an overwhelming tactical advantage over their Arab neighbors. John F. Kennedy was adamantly opposed to this, fearing that it would create such an imbalance in weaponry that the Arab nations would be forced to align themselves with the Soviet Union in order to defend themselves, and eventually to acquire their own nuclear weapons to correct the imbalance. Kennedy consistently battled with Israeli officials over giving them access to nuclear weapons or any assistance in their development of a secret nuclear weapons production facility, which had opened in 1962 at Dimona in the Negev desert. Kennedy's resistance included denying their repeated requests for the best available fighter jets, the US-built F-4 Phantom jets.

On July 5, 1963, President Kennedy wrote to the new Israeli Prime Minister Levi Eshkol (who had just succeeded David Ben-Gurion after his resignation "for personal reasons" that some said were to be related to his role in the Lavon affair). In that letter, JFK set forth the conditions, specifically that the facility could not be used for the purpose of developing nuclear weapons, and the need for "periodic visits" (i.e., "inspections") he wanted to be understood, as noted in these excerpts:

> As I wrote Mr. Ben-Gurion, this government's commitment to and support of Israel could be seriously jeopardized if it should be thought that we were unable to obtain reliable information on a subject as vital to the peace as the question of Israel's effort in the nuclear field.

Therefore, I asked our scientists to review the alternative sched-
ules of visits we and you had proposed. If Israel's purposes are to be
clear beyond reasonable doubt, I believe that the schedule which
would best serve our common purposes would be a visit early this
summer, another visit in June 1964, and thereafter at intervals of six
months. I am sure that such a schedule should not cause you any
more difficulty than that which Mr. Ben-Gurion proposed in his May
27 letter. It would be essential, and I understand that Mr. Ben-Gurion's letter was in accord with this, that our scientists have access to all
areas of the Dimona site and to any related part of the complex, such
as fuel fabrication facilities or plutonium separation plant, and that
sufficient time to be allotted for a thorough examination.

Clearly JFK's prescience in this matter has now, unfortunately, become a reality that the world is still dealing with fifty-plus years later.
Lyndon B. Johnson was instrumental in reversing Kennedy's policy and
facilitating the development of the very program that Kennedy had strug-
gled to contain. Jewish Democrats in 1960, particularly in New York, did
not completely trust Kennedy, as author Richard Reeves noted, being
"the son of a man who had been accused of being both anti-Semitic and
pro-Nazi. Nor did John Kennedy, comfortably surrounded by Jewish staff
members, trust all Jews, particularly New Yorkers."[29] In his book *President
Kennedy, Profile of Power*, Reeves quoted Kennedy explaining an incident
that confirms this point, in a conversation with Charlie Bartlett, a reporter and friend: "'I had the damnedest meeting in New York last night. I
went to this party. It was given by a group of people who were big money
contributors and also Zionists and they said to me, 'We know that your
campaign is in terrible financial shape!'...The deal they offered me was
that they would finance the rest of this campaign if I would agree to let
them run the Middle Eastern policy of the United States for the next four
years.'"[30]

Shortly after being sworn in as president, Johnson remarked to an Israeli diplomat: "You have lost a very great friend, but you have found a
better one."[31] Isaiah L. Kenen, an Israeli lobbyist in Washington, agreed: "I
would say that everything he did as president supported that statement."
Many Israelis agreed: "A number of Israeli newspapers, the U.S. Embassy
noted, '... suggested that President Johnson might be more responsive
than his predecessor to appeals from sympathizers of Israel in the U. S.'"[32]

In fact, Lyndon Johnson immediately took a "hands-off" approach to
Israel's program to acquire nuclear weapons, which was referred to by the
White House as "the delicate topic" and "Lyndon Johnson's White House
saw no Dimona, heard no Dimona, and spoke no Dimona ..."[33]

The day after President Kennedy was laid to rest at Arlington National
Cemetery, the director of the American-Israel Public Affairs Committee,

I. L. Kenen, sent a letter (marked "Not for Publication or Circulation") extolling the new president's "front-rank pro-Israel position" in contrast to the previous Eisenhower and Kennedy administrations.[34] Moreover, U.S. financial assistance to Israel went from $40 million in JFK's last year to $71 million in LBJ's first year and $130 million the next. Even more importantly than that, the assistance under Kennedy was entirely food assistance and development loans; under Johnson, 20% was in the form of military equipment in the first year and that increased to 71% the next year.[35]

The "conventional wisdom" during the first years of the Johnson administration was that Israel did not have the capacity to make nuclear weapons at Dimona, and that the (admittedly, rather cursory) inspections being conducted by the U.S. Atomic Energy Commission (AEC) had supported that view. In fact, in 1966 Prime Minister Eshkol had entered into an agreement with the U.S. for significant purchases of artillery, communications and electronics equipment, forty-eight A-4 Skyhawk planes and two hundred fifty Sherman tanks on the basis of *his promise to terminate* the atomic bomb development program begun by his predecessor, David Ben-Gurion.[36] But all of this appears to have been "window dressing" on Israel's part, because, as explained by Stephen Green in his 1984 book *Taking Sides:*

> "… Israel already had one, or at least the 'last wire' capability to assemble one in a short time, if it was needed. It is a safe assumption that Israel had nuclear weapons and the ability to deliver them at the beginning of the Six-Day War in 1967. The ingredients were there, hence the bomb was ready. Looking at the first 20 years of Israel's history, there is simply no factual basis upon which to presume discretion or restraint in matter of military development. None. Within about 25 minutes of the time Israel could have developed an atomic weapon, Israel did develop an atomic weapon."[37]

THE PERSONNEL IN THE HIGHEST ECHELONS OF THE JOHNSON ADMINISTRATION

Throughout his career, Johnson curried favor with men and women regardless of race, religion and creed; they were selected by him on the basis of their ability to meet his needs for a given opportunity, whether it be legal and above-board or not. He had ingratiated himself especially with many wealthy and influential men whom he knew could help him in various ways as he ascended the political ladder. Some were men who professed to be of a strong Christian faith, such as Bill Moyers, who had studied to be a Baptist minister and served Johnson as a high-level aide. Moyers has never been provably linked directly to any of Johnson's criminal activities, however his status as Johnson's most visible and powerful aide inevitably leads to speculation about the reasons for his abrupt departure from the White House in the middle of Johnson's term, and how much he might have known but refuses to divulge.

Another was the evangelical Christian businessman Billie Sol Estes, a very pious man on Sunday mornings, but during the rest of the week, a man who could collaborate with other swindlers to defraud the government of millions of dollars in everything from phantom fertilizer storage tanks to illegal cotton allotments, eventually being drawn into complicity in conspiracies to murder people who "got in their way." Men named Bobby Baker, Malcolm "Mac" Wallace and Cliff Carter were among those who willingly carried out heinous criminal acts at Johnson's behest, as conclusively demonstrated in the author's previous books.

A big impact on Lyndon Johnson was a Texas legislator named Alvin Wirtz, of Sequin, Texas (until the townspeople turned against him and literally "threw him out of town").[38] Johnson told his aide Richard Goodwin that "The man who had the most influence over me, more than anyone, was Texas Senator Alvin Wirtz."[39] Yet his acknowledged mentor had once been characterized by a San Antonio attorney as "a conniver – a conniver like I never saw before or since. Sharp, cunning." Another attorney who had many dealings with Wirtz described him as someone who "… would gut you if he could, but you would probably never know he did it. I mean, *that was a man who would do anything – and he would still be smiling when he slipped in the knife.*"[40]

Johnson surrounded himself in the Oval Office with a number of strident Zionists, one of the most important of whom was his long-time friend and advisor, then-sitting Supreme Court Justice Abe Fortas, who had performed a minor miracle back in 1948 in masterminding the election fraud that propelled Johnson into the Senate. That feat eventually led to his ascension to the vice presidency, which he always knew would be his route into the White House.

Other Zionist advisors, who produced a constant stream of memoranda with such titles as "What We Have Done for Israel" and "New Things We Might Do in Israel" and "How We Have Helped Israel," included McGeorge Bundy, Arthur Goldberg, Harry McPherson, John Roche, Ben Wattenberg, Walter Rostow and his brother Eugene Rostow. These men shared the same views, of the need for aggressively pro-active initiatives to advance Israel's interests.

Grace Halsell, a speechwriter who worked in the White House in 1967, has stated that President Johnson was determined to get more public support for his Vietnam policies, and wanted to enlist as many Jews as possible, despite being aware that many of them were liberals who were strongly opposed to the war. Moreover, Johnson was told by another one of his speechwriter/advisors, Ben J. Wattenberg, that if he gave all out support to Israel, "influential Jewish Americans would stop opposing his Vietnam policies. In a memo to the president, Wattenberg, whose parents had moved to the U. S. from Palestine and who was known as a strong supporter of the Jewish state, said flatly that if the president came out with strong support for Israel, he would win American Jewish support for the war in Vietnam."[41] Wattenberg asserted that, while many American Jews were "doves" on Vietnam, they were "hawks" on Israel going to war with Arab states.

The support given by the American Jewish leaders "was welcome to the president," as reporter Donald Neff observed, when at every turn Johnson was being attacked by critics, particularly in the media, of his Vietnam policy.[42] All-out support of Israel, Wattenberg predicted, would "help turn around 'the other war' – the domestic dissatisfaction about Vietnam." Immediately after Israel won the Six-Day War, he would write Johnson that: "You stand to be cheered now by those [American Jewish leaders] who were jeering last week." He added that the Mideast crisis could be "a bonus" for Johnson in the election coming the following year.

According to the aforementioned Grace Halsell, many of Johnson's advisors in the White House were Jewish men of the "zealously Zionist" variety, all uniformly and aggressively pro-Israel, to the extent that they put Israeli interests over those of the United States; none of his White House aides or associates represented the views of Israel's Arab neighbors:[43]

> There were Walt Rostow at the White House, his brother Eugene at State, and Arthur Goldberg, ambassador to the United Nations. Other pro-Israel advisers included Abe Fortas, associate justice of the Supreme Court [who had remained a close advisor to Johnson after that appointment]; Democratic Party fundraiser Abraham Feinberg; White House counsels Leo White and Jake Jacobsen; White House writers Richard Goodwin and Ben Wattenberg; domestic affairs aide Larry Levinson; and John P. Roche, known as Johnson's intellectual-in-residence and an avid supporter of Israel.

According to Seymour Hersh, Abe Feinberg's status around the Johnson White House, due to his exceptional abilities as a fund-raiser, was nonpareil. His were always in the form of cash only, and were given over not to the Democratic Party's coffers but directly to Johnson's most trusted personal aides. Johnson's special aide for Jewish affairs, Myer Feldman, put it this way: "Abe only raised cash – where it went only he knows."[44] Asked about his fund-raising role, Feinberg acknowledged that the people he collected money from were afraid to let their contributions become public, so they preferred making sub rosa cash payments to him, knowing their names would not be revealed. He admitted that "Raising money is a very humiliating process.... People you don't respect piss all over you."[45]

Johnson's long-time aide Walter Jenkins, three weeks before the 1964 election, was arrested in a Washington YMCA bathroom on homosexual solicitation charges, a news event that Johnson tried to suppress. In addition to the obvious PR problem, another immediate problem was the $250,000 in cash that was in Jenkin's White House safe. Johnson ordered Myer Feldman and Bill Moyers to clean out his safe, which they presumed would only contain Jenkin's very secret notes. When they discovered all the cash, Feldman reported: "Bill said, 'What do we do with this?' I said, 'I don't know. You handle it.'" Moyers admitted to Seymour Hersh that, though his memory was "vague," that "I think there was a private fund. There was a lot of cash washed around in Washington in those days.... I don't know what happened to it." Then Moyers, who usually measures his words carefully, made these incongruent statements about Johnson: "He'd take money from friends and adversaries just because he thought that's the way the system worked. No decisions were made on the basis of cash, but cash did give you access. I always thought Abe Feinberg had a lot of impact on Johnson; he had a big role to play."[46] But, if "no decisions were made on the basis of cash" and "cash" was Feinberg's specialty, then how should one interpret the last sentence that Seymour Hersh attributed to Moyers, about Feinberg's "impact" and his "big role to play"?

In addition to the White House staff, Johnson – like other presidents before and after him – relied on secretive, behind-the-scenes steering committees to prepare contingency plans for whatever military and intelligence exigencies became important as the result of current events. In the Kennedy administration, that committee was known as the "Special Group" – then the Special Group Augmented, when Robert F. Kennedy took over supervision of its functions – and under Johnson a comparable group was named the "303 Committee."

Some have stated that it was named after National Security Action Memorandum (NSAM) 303 (June 2, 1964) but according to the predominant view, it was so-named because it met in the elegant corner office of the Executive Office Building, physically next door to the White House, but figuratively an extension of it; the office known as Room No. 303 was occupied by the chairman of the Joint Chiefs of Staff [JCS]. According to Richard Helms, that committee was "... simply a device for examining covert operations of any kind, and making a judgment on behalf of the president, so he wouldn't be 'nailed' with the thing if it failed."[47] Under Johnson, the function of the group was much more proactive in creating plans than merely reviewing the products of others.

In 1967, the "303 committee" was composed of the under secretary of state for political affairs (Foy D. Kohler, formerly the ambassador to the Soviet Union), the deputy secretary of defense (Cyrus Vance), the CIA director (Richard Helms), the chairman of the Joint Chiefs of Staff (General Earle Wheeler) and the President's national security adviser (Walt Rostow). This committee controlled all covert CIA operations."[48] Regardless of its name, or the president, the committee was always directly under the control of the president to whom it served, and was, therefore, as James Reston, the *New York Times* columnist observed, "above even the Joint Chiefs of Staff ... charged with approving intelligence missions all over the world."[49] Clearly, and implicitly it should be noted as well, it was also above the CIA and its director, who served on it as merely one of its members.

The Joint Chiefs of Staff, nominally under the direct control of the Secretary of Defense, was indirectly under Johnson's control as well (arguably directly, given Johnson's dominance over everyone reporting to him). A third, group, also obviously under the direct command of Lyndon Johnson, were the zealously Zionist advisors within the White House, with Walter Rostow, a presence in both groups and as close to Johnson as anyone.

Together, the men on the "303 Committee" created a plan called "Frontlet 615" that included a number of subparts, one of which was called "Operation Cyanide." It appears that they began developing these plans no later than the last quarter of 1964 or the earliest months of 1965. As we will see when we examine these plans in detail in the next chapter, elements of the larger plan were already operational in the latter part of 1965.

TROUBLING SIGNS OF PRESIDENTIAL INCAPACITY

It is pertinent now to examine the issue of the mental condition of the president in the context of the subject of this book, the fate of the USS *Liberty*. In fact, it is essential to a complete understanding of the attack, which, according to Admiral Thomas Moorer, a former chairman of the Joint Chiefs of Staff, was "the most disgraceful act I witnessed in my entire military career." The reason Johnson's mental condition is so critical to the case is that it is arguably the "proximate cause" of this deed. And, paradoxically, while many other books, videos, radio interviews, newspaper and magazine articles and internet websites have been written, filmed, recorded or otherwise published, none of them have focused on this as an important aspect of the case. Some have mentioned it in passing, but they have not explored it or focused significant attention on it.

It's as if, somehow, that issue is too delicate a matter to ponder, too ephemeral to quantify, too subjective to describe or to even attempt to prove. Or, it might mean that, if it *were* proven to be the key to unraveling the case, it potentially raises too many other even more difficult questions: Such as, "How might the nation protect itself from a similar, future president who suffers from a similar amalgamation of psychic disorders, of the sort that affected Lyndon Johnson's mind?

The president's state of mind during the entire period is arguably the single most overlooked factor that might be the most critical element – the "Occam's Razor" (defined by Wikipedia as: "Among competing hypotheses, the one with the fewest assumptions should be selected") and therefore the best explanation – that led to the attack by Israel on the *USS Liberty*. There is much more background to that hypothesis of course, but this point is elemental to that overall picture, and without it, this story is too incomprehensible for anyone to fully understand

That the mental state of Lyndon Johnson throughout this episode has never been addressed in the many books that have been written may explain why the case remains unresolved and an open sore in U.S. – Israeli relations. This point is essential to a better understanding of what happened in the Eastern Mediterranean Sea on June 8, 1967, and it starts with the fact that Johnson's most famed biographers – unbeknownst to most people, or simply dismissed as mere Johnsonian eccentricities – neglected to fully explore his many incidents of mental breakdowns, or what author Robert Caro minimized by describing them as his "black depressions."[50]

Robert Dallek did mention the inherent risks of making disastrous decisions as a result of mental collapses while serving, when he observed: "Johnson's paranoia raises questions about his judgment and capacity to make rational life and death decisions … [but] Determining psychological incapacity may be impossible.… Who then is to say when a president has passed the bounds of rational good sense? No one should make light of how much his suspicions and anger toward his domestic critics distorted his judgments in dealing with Vietnam."[51] Of course, the same point can be extended to include his actions related to the USS *Liberty* "incident." But the most compelling example of Mr. Dallek's point is literally ignored or, at most, given cursory mention in every biography of Lyndon B. Johnson.

Yet other books have been written that were dedicated to this very premise, specifically about Lyndon Johnson's mental condition while serving as president; unfortunately, they have been systematically ignored in the grand biographies, by the powerbrokers and mainstream media interviewers like Bruce Lamb and Charlie Rose. These works are referenced in the bibliography of this book: D. Jablow Hershman, *Power Beyond Reason* and *Lyndon Johnson: The Tragic Self: A Psychohistorical Portrait,* by Hyman L. Muslin, MD, and Thomas H. Jobe, MD.

The conclusion of these experts in the psychiatric/psychological fields, Doctors Muslin, and Jobe, was that, "Johnson's decisions as the identified leader, and hence his leadership, were not merely flawed, they were not decisions befitting a leader of a democratic nation."[52] They stated, in layman's terms, that Johnson was an irrational man who was not in complete control of his psychological/psychiatric "issues" and that caused him to act more like a dictator than the leader of a modern democracy.

The reason that this piece of the *Liberty* puzzle has never been explored is undoubtedly due to the fact that, while he was still alive, his condition was never exposed, much less acknowledged, by anyone; it was just one of the numerous "cover-ups" that followed him throughout his entire career. The cover-up of the *Liberty* attack was merely the latest of that series. Although all of the books noted above, and below, were written after Johnson died in 1973, there were men working with Johnson in the White House who knew of his condition, but remained closemouthed about it, lamenting: "Who would believe us."

Specific documented examples of these psychotic presidential moments include those revealed by Johnson's former speechwriter Richard Goodwin, who described examples of these scenes in his 1988 book *Remembering America;* Washington lobbyist Robert Winter-Berger, writing a very detailed account of Johnson's frantic meltdown in Speaker John McCormack's office in March 1964 – so upset that he cried uncontrollably – in his 1972 book;[53] and another harrowing tale by Marine Corps Lieutenant General Charles G. Cooper, describing in his memoirs an extremely disturbing account of President Johnson's screaming, profanity-laden meltdown in front of his entire Joint Chiefs of Staff at a meeting in November, 1965:[54]

> Noting that it was he who was carrying the weight of the free world on his shoulders, he called them filthy names – shitheads, dumb shits, pompous assholes – and used "the F-word" as an adjective more freely than a Marine in boot camp would use it. It was unnerving, degrading.

These dramatic, troubling instances of Lyndon Johnson's maniacal psychotic episodes were never publicized at the time, and were hidden by those who witnessed them for their own protection, and mostly appeared only later, as books were finally published. Other stories from JFK's aide Arthur Schlesinger Jr. were withheld for over forty years, finally being published the very year that Schlesinger died, in 2007 in his last book, *Journals*. It is no wonder that the reportage so much later has never been distilled into its proper position in the legacy of Lyndon Johnson, especially since these stories are systematically ignored in certain of the "grand biographies" that have replaced factual, objective volumes such as Schlesinger's *Journals:* [55]

[Bill Moyers had told him in March, 1968] "LBJ is now well sealed off from reality," and stated that the atmosphere in the White House is "impenetrable." Moreover, the entry states that Moyers had characterized Johnson's mental state as being "paranoid" and that "four more years of Johnson would be ruinous for the country."

Another entry Schlesinger made in his diary just a week before Johnson left the White House indicated that he had talked to Bill Moyers and Richard "Dick" Goodwin about the problem faced by anyone ever trying to write a book about Johnson, because "no one would believe it." He also wrote that Moyers had said that Johnson was "a sick man" and that both Moyers and Goodwin read up on mental illness, as Goodwin personally tackled the paranoia issue and Moyers studied up on manic-depressive cycles.[56] Furthermore, Goodwin wrote in his memoirs that in July, 1965, as he sat waiting for Moyers in his office, "... when Bill walked in, his face pale, visibly shaken [Moyers then said] 'I just came from a conversation with the president. He told me he was going to fire everybody that didn't agree with him, that Hubert (Humphrey) could not be trusted and we weren't to tell him anything ..."[57]

When Goodwin, in 1965, finally tired of fighting his own convictions while working in support for a president who was willing to jettison his ambitious domestic program in order to continue escalating the "Americanization" of the Vietnam War, he acknowledged that he left because "Lyndon Johnson had become a very dangerous man."[58] Moreover, when he later explained his decision to resign his White House position to his colleague Bill Moyers, the response he received from Moyers was: "My personal integrity, what is left of it, is also on the line ... I agree with you."[59] Between these books – Schlesinger's and Goodwin's – there is a plethora of many other disturbing incidents that had occurred during Johnson's presidency, yet went unreported in real time. These powerful insights were kept from the public for three to four decades because of their lamentations that, "Indeed, what could be done – what could anyone do – about a man who was always able to impose an immensely powerful and persuasive simulacrum of control to mask his growing irrationalities?"[60] Obviously, and unfortunately for what the absence of that information has done to damage America as we know and understand it now, the world will never know the answer to that abstract and rhetorical question.

LBJ PROCLAIMS HIMSELF TO BE "KING OF THE WORLD"

One instance of how his delusions surfaced occurred in 1965, while flying high on Air Force One, when he proclaimed to several reporters on board that he had become the most powerful man in the world, as he announced to them that he was basically now the "King of the World."

It was as if he had finally succeeded in attaining his childhood dream, after working forty-five years to do so, when he had sworn his resolve to achieve that pinnacle back in 1920, as he played "King of the Mountain" at the age of twelve with some friends. Though that part is speculative, we can state factually that he did say to them, according to those same friends, who were interviewed by his biographer Robert Caro: "Someday, I'm going to be president of the United States."[61]

On board Air Force One, Johnson had invited four reporters from the press pool to share cocktails with him in his quarters. They were flying high above his domain, which was now the entire world. He was in an ebullient mood, and this phase of his mania was strengthened with each drink from his glass of Cutty Sark scotch.

As he sat in his huge, elevated, custom-designed leather chair with the reporters arrayed around him in their smaller seats, he decided to remind this select group of reporters about how fortune had smiled on them that day, to be in the presence of the single most important person in the world. Suddenly, Johnson declared, "Look around the world: Khrushchev's gone. Macmillan's gone. Adenauer's gone. Segni's gone. Nehru's gone. Who's left – de Gaulle?" AP reporter Frank Cormier said that Johnson sneered as he uttered the French president's name, "Then, leaning back in his massive 'throne chair,' as the crew dubbed it, LBJ thumped his chest in Tarzan fashion and bellowed, 'I am the King!'"[62]

After landing, Johnson's press secretary, George Christian, admonished the reporters on board not to reveal that particular revelation, however, he failed to explain that to the pilot of the airplane, Ralph Albertazzie, who had witnessed it also and later decided to put it in his memoirs.[63] The world will never know how many similar, perhaps even more troubling, incidents of that nature went unreported.

THE STILL-MYSTERIOUS FATE OF THE USS LIBERTY

In the annals of US military history, there are no doubt many unsolved and perplexing mysteries, but few could compare to the fate of the US Navy spy ship that was mercilessly attacked by one of its closest allies, intentionally and without warning. One of the reasons it is still a mystery is because it is also the only peacetime attack on a US naval vessel that, to this day, has never officially been investigated by the Congress of the United States.

The USS *Liberty* was a 455-foot, 10,150-ton electronic intercept spy ship, originally a standard-design Victory Ship – a more evolved version of the World War II Liberty Ships – which were built as supply ships, not intended for direct fighting. The *Liberty* had been converted to an Auxiliary Technical Research Ship (AGTR), known colloquially as a "spy ship," first deployed in 1965; its top speed was only 18 knots.

The unique profile of the *Liberty*, together with the dozens of antennae and other electronic communications gear – including a unique steerable dish that could bounce signals off the moon and back to the United States – on the top decks, made it one of the most distinctive ships in the world, as anyone having access to the universal mariner's guide, *Jane's Fighting Ships*, would have known, had they looked it up.

The *Liberty's* length was twice that of the Egyptian ship *El Quseir* that the Israeli navy – allegedly, mistakenly – confused it with, and the *Liberty's* displacement was more than four times larger than the old and rusty 2,180-ton Egyptian ship that had very few antennae, nothing like the profile of the *Liberty* – which bristled with antennae of every description. They filled every open deck. Rather than speeding along at over 30 knots (as portrayed in the dubious, arguably absurd, explanation offered by Israel), at the time of the attack the *Liberty* was actually sailing along at five knots in international waters, seventeen to thirty miles off the coast of Egypt. Anyone who had ever been on a boat of any size more than a day should have known how preposterous such an assertion was, by just looking at it, and to believe that highly trained men in the Israeli navy could make that mistake is patently ridiculous.

Yet the *Liberty's* fate, one of the most enigmatic, unresolved military mysteries of all time, is, paradoxically at its core, quite clear-cut and undisputed. The basic facts generally accepted by all are: On the fourth day of the Six-Day War between Israel and its Arab neighbors (Egypt, Syria and Jordan), June 8, 1967, the Israeli Defense Forces (IDF) brutally attacked the U.S. spy ship, the *USS Liberty*. Israel did that with fighter jets shooting gunfire and missiles, and dropping packets of napalm, followed immediately by torpedo/gunboats that, combined, left the *Liberty's* entire upper deck on fire – fueled by the napalm and gasoline. There were 841 cannon holes in its hull, antennae mounts, gunwales, bridge, cabins and all other equipment, as well as a 22x40 foot torpedo hole in its starboard side, mostly below the water line, which ordinarily would have sunk the ship within minutes. When the attack was over, thirty-four men were dead and one hundred seventy-four were injured to varying degrees, some near death.

Endnotes

1. The 1954 "Lavon Affair," was named after the Israeli Minister of Defense, Pinhas Lavon, who was forced to resign as a result of the controversy. According to Wikipedia, it was "part of the false flag operation, [in which] a group of Egyptian Jews were recruited by Israeli military intelligence to plant bombs inside Egyptian, American, and British-owned civilian targets, cinemas, libraries and American educational centers. The bombs were timed to detonate several hours after closing time." The mission was discovered by Egyptian intelligence agents when nine Israeli agents were captured while

they prepared to blow up the embassy and were subsequently brought to trial by Egypt, which then executed two of them.

2. See Rense.com: *"LBJ's 'Passionate Attachment' to Israel"* http://rense.com/general44/lbj.htm

3. See Department of State website: https://history.state.gov/milestones/1953-1960/suez.

4. Sylvia Ellis, *Historical Dictionary of Anglo-American Relations*. Lanham, MD: Scarecrow Press. (2009). p. 212.

5. Hersh, *The Samson Option*, pp. 63-65.

6. Green, Stephen, p. 191 (Ref. "Confidential" Department of State telegram 325 from U.S. Consulate, Jerusalem, to Secretary of State, dated May 14, 1965, NSF Country File--Israel, Volume 4 Cables 2/65 to 11/65, Lyndon Baines Johnson Library.

7. Notes from original research of Peter Dale Scott - "The Pentagon Papers and NSAM 273" (Hood College, Weisberg Collection) See: http://jfk.hood.edu/Collection/Weisberg%20Subject%20Index%20Files/T%20Disk/Tiger%20to%20Ride%20Viet%20Nam%20Withdrawal/Item%2001.pdf

8. Ibid.

9. Ibid.

10. See William F. Pepper, *The Plot to Kill King*. New York: Skyhorse Publishing, 2016, p. xxx.iv

11. See, *New York Herald Tribune*, European Edition, July 13, 1966 (also reprinted here: http://iht-retrospective.blogs.nytimes.com/2016/07/12/1966-johnson-foresees-long-war/?_r=1)

12. See PBS "Frontline" interview by Rick Young, the producer of the Frontline documentary *Give War a Chance* at the web site: http://www.pbs.org/wgbh/pages/frontline/shows/military/etc/lessons.html

13. Dunn, pp. 69-70

14. Corson, pp. 63-64

15. Ibid. p. 64

16. Burns, Stewart. *To The Mountaintop*. New York, NY: HarperCollins Publishers, Inc, 2004

17. Schulman, p. 146

18. Ibid.

19. Transcript, Harry McPherson Oral History Interview III, 1/16/69, by T. H. Baker, Internet Copy, LBJ Library. pp. 24–30

20. Goldberg, J. J., p. 207

21. Caro, *The Path*, p. 61

22. Transcript, Harry McPherson oral history Interview III, 1/16/69, by T. H. Baker, Internet Copy, LBJ Library, pp. 24–25.

23. See Holocaust website:: http://holocaust-ww2.blogspot.com/search?q=first+us+jewish+president This thesis includes the following: "A key resource for uncovering LBJ's pro-Jewish activity is the unpublished 1989 doctoral thesis by University of Texas student Louis Gomolak, "Prologue: LBJ's Foreign Affairs Background, 1908–1948." Johnson's activities were confirmed by other historians in interviews with his wife, family members and political associates.

24. Ibid.

25. Ibid.

26. Caro, *The Path*..., pp. 480–481

27. Ibid., pp. 481–482

28. Ibid.

29. Reeves, *President Kennedy*, p. 143.

30. Ibid.

31. Miller, Merle, *Lyndon*, p. 477

32. Green, *Taking Sides,* pp. 184-86

33. Ibid. pp. 165-66

34. Ibid. p. 186

35. Ibid.

36. Ibid. pp. 175-176; 187

37. Ibid. p. 176

38. Nelson, *Colossus,* p. 178

39. Goodwin, Richard, p. 259

40. Caro, *The Path,* p. 376

41. Halsell, Grace, "How LBJ's Vietnam War Paralyzed His Mideast Policymakers," *Washington Report on Middle East Affairs,* June 1993, Page 20. http://www.wrmea.org/1993-june/how-lbj-s-vietnam-war-paralyzed-his-mideast-policymakers.html

42. Ibid.

43. Halsell, Grace, Op. Cit.

44. Hersh, *The Samson Option,* p. 192

45. Ibid. pp. 192-193

46. Ibid. pp. 193-194

47. See internet video "BBC Documentary 'Dead in the Water' (at approx. 46:45) on various websites, including: http://www.bing.com/videos/search?q=bbc+documentary+dead+in+the+water&view=detail&mid=35163F5529ADE621098D35163F5529ADE621098D&FORM=VIRE1

48. Evans, Rowland and Novak, Robert. "The CIA's Secret Subsidy to Israel" *Washington Post,* Feb. 24, 1977

49. Reston, James, *New York Times,* May 7, 1969 http://jfk.hood.edu/Collection/White%20%20Files/Security-CIA/CIA%200228.pdf

50. See, for example, Caro, *Master of the Senate,* pp. 626-630; 634-636; 832

51. Dallek, *Flawed Giant,* pp. 627-28

52. Muslin and Jobe, p. 206

53. Winter-Berger, Robert N., pp. 64-66. (See Summaries of his story in: (1) Nelson, *LBJ: The Mastermind of the JFK Assassination* [Skyhorse ed. 2011-2013 pp. 571-574; Xlibris ed. pp. 593-596] (2)Nelson, *LBJ: From Mastermind to The Colossus,* pp. 347-349)

54. Cooper, pp. 3–5 (See summaries in [1] *LBJ: The Mastermind of the JFK Assassination,* p. 610; [2] *LBJ: From Mastermind to the Colossus* p. 348)

55. Schlesinger Jr., Arthur M. Journals: 1952–2000 p. 280.

56. Schlesinger, Journals, p. 306

57. Goodwin, Richard, p. 402

58. Ibid. p. 416

59. Ibid., p. 419

60. Ibid. p. 403

61. Caro, *The Path to Power,* p. 100

62. Albertazzie, p. 247

63. Ibid.

Chapter 2

Operation Cyanide/
Positioning the USS *Liberty*

*"When war comes ... some, at least, of the unpleasant facts which had been-
kept in the dark are likely to become patent to all, and the more men have
been made to live in a fool's paradise, the more they will be horrified and
discouraged by the reality.*

– Bertrand Russell, *Power,* 1921

THE PLANNING AND LEAD-UP TO THE 1967 "SIX-DAY WAR"
WITHIN THE JOHNSON WHITE HOUSE

Survivor James M. Ennes Jr., apparently after writing his ground-
breaking 1979 book, *Assault On The Liberty: The True Story Of The
Israeli Attack On An American Intelligence Ship,* discovered a docu-
ment (evidently misfiled) in the "*Liberty*" file at the LBJ Library in Austin,
Texas.[1] It indicated that a "303 Committee" had discussed secret plans
for sending the USS *Liberty,* and an accompanying submarine, into the
Mediterranean Sea, into an area that would then become a war zone.
That document, which Mr. Ennes showed on the BBC video *Dead in the
Water,*[2] (see cropped photo in endnote) was a copy of the minutes of a
committee meeting of 10 April, 1967. On this copy someone had written
"Submarine within U.A.R. [Egypt] waters" on it, and the document was
inadvertently placed into the *Liberty* file by someone unknown. It was a
serendipitous discovery by Mr. Ennes that was never meant to be seen by
anyone not "cleared" for such explosive material.[3]

The document indicates that the committee had been briefed, two
months *before* the attack, by Brig. Gen., USAF Ralph D. Steakley on the
then-current status of a larger plan, "Frontlet 615."

General Steakley died on Sunday, June 14, 2009. According to his
obituary in *Florida Today*: "... he was involved in the Cuban Missile Crisis,
the *Pueblo* Incident, and the attack on the *Liberty*."[4] No other files from the
"303 Committee" have been released, the fact that this record was left in
the file was clearly the result of either human error or divine intervention.

Wikipedia admittedly is not a completely reliable source for information, so one must exercise great caution in using it;[5] but at times it can be

useful for the careful researcher. To make that very point, here are two examples of errors that appear in the approximately 15,000 word article devoted to the USS *Liberty* "incident."

One mistake states that President Johnson "had received word from the Joint Chiefs of Staff that *Liberty* had been torpedoed by an unknown vessel at 9:50 am eastern time." In fact, he had received the "Flash" message about 90 minutes before then, but the White House logs had been changed to hide that fact. Author Peter Hounam noted the timing discrepancies and how the White House records were "glaringly" inconsistent with the records that the *Saratoga's* captain, Joe Tully, had maintained, copies of which he kept, that indicated twelve fighter jets and/or bombers had immediately been launched before Admiral Lawrence Geis, the commander of the Sixth Fleet, radioed Tully and ordered him to have all the aircraft returned, about 8:20 a.m.[EDT], minutes after the attack. Geis told Tully that he could re-launch the fighter jets in ninety minutes, at 9:50 a.m. (Interestingly, this is one minute after the edited White House logs stated that President Johnson was informed of the incident). This also reflects the fact that the first sortie of fighter jets dispatched from the USS *America* had been recalled at about 8:20 a.m., personally by Robert McNamara, who was with Lyndon Johnson in the Situation Room. It also explains the reason for the second discrepancy, below.

This other error relates to the fact that there were two recalls of fighter jet sorties, the second of which did not include nuclear-armed A-4s, but the Wikipedia article states that: "Convinced that the attack was real, President of the United States Lyndon B. Johnson launched allegedly nuclear-armed aircraft targeted against Cairo from a U.S. aircraft carrier in the Mediterranean. The aircraft were recalled only just in time, when it was clear the *Liberty* had not sunk and that Israel had carried out the attack." What that citation incorrectly states is that Johnson "launched" any aircraft; he did not, he only recalled them, twice; it also fails to make clear that this was the second time the aircraft were recalled, not the first, and that there were no nuclear-armed jets involved, because that was specifically what Admiral Geis had presumed was the reason the first sorties, launched shortly after the attack began, were recalled. The second time they were recalled, Johnson personally got on the telephone to demand that Geis recall them, saying, "I want that Goddamn ship going to the bottom. No help. Recall the wings" according to Admiral Geis. This rather major misstatement of facts illustrates the inherent risk of relying on Wikipedia.

The clearly misfiled "303" document ties the president's own hands, vicariously through his personally appointed committee of planners, to the fact that White House plans were well under way two months before the "spontaneous war" occurred in the Mediterranean Sea. This is the footnote where this critical point is noted, then summarily ignored:

> "Several *Liberty* crew members testified that they had briefly seen a periscope during the attack. In 1988, the Lyndon Johnson Library declassified and released a document from the USS *Liberty* archive with the "Top Secret – Eyes Only" security caveat (Document #12C sanitized and released 21DEC88 under review case 86–199). This "Memorandum for the Record" dated 10 April 1967 reported a briefing of the "303 Committee" by General Ralph D. Steakley. According to the memo, General Steakley "briefed the committee on a sensitive DOD project known as FRONTLET 615," which is identified in a handwritten note on the original memorandum as "submarine within U.A.R. waters." *Further Freedom of Information Act requests returned no existence of a project called "FRONTLET 615."* In February 1997, a senior member of the crew of the submarine USS *Amberjack* told James Ennes that he had watched the attack through the periscope and took pictures. According to the official ship's history from the Department of Defense, *Amberjack's* mission between 23 April and 24 July was reconnaissance within U.A.R. When contacted, four crewmen stated that they were so close to USS *Liberty* when it came under attack that some of the crew believed *Amberjack* itself was under depth charge attack. August Hubal, Captain of the *Amberjack*, insists that the vessel was 100 mi (160 km) from the *Liberty* and when told the crew believed they were closer replied "They must be mistaken". On 2 July 2003, as a result of a lawsuit using the Freedom of Information Act by Joel Leyden on behalf of the Israel News Agency requesting any evidence that the U.S. submarine *Amberjack* had gathered by means of its periscope, the National Security Agency stated that there had been "no radio intercepts made by the U.S. submarine *Amberjack*". James Ennes believes that if the submarine photography exists, it should show that the ship's flag was clearly visible to the attacking fighters and torpedo boats."[6] (Emphasis added)

The copy of that memorandum found by Mr. Ennes within the *Liberty* files (ironically in the LBJ Library) appeared to be not only misplaced but then subsequently unnoticed by whomever had approved the open files. This serendipitous "bombshell" reveals not only essential parts of Operation Cyanide, but proof of meticulous pre-planning for the USS *Liberty's* role in an overall strategy that encompassed a sophisticated plan to strengthen and expand the borders of Israel. That Wikipedia perfunctorily notes the document but ignores its intrinsic significance, and brushes it aside along with accepting fabricated White House records, speaks volumes about the lack of integrity at Wikipedia, and also how effectively rewritten "history" can replace actual provable historical records.

Furthermore, that single document clearly shows that the Joint Chiefs of Staff (JCS), was engaged in executing a plan developed by that "303 Committee" (for which no other records are available) and, as Mr. Ennes pointed out in the BBC documentary *Dead in the Water*: "Especially the fact this in the *Liberty* file suggested that it had to do with the submarine that was near us, and with Cyanide and all the other things."[7] Clearly, there was a plan to use at least one submarine as part of the operation, and it had been ordered to follow the *Liberty* into the Eastern Mediterranean.

Another point made on the same BBC documentary, according to Greg Reight (unidentified officer rank of U.S. Air Force), the Air Force allowed Israel to use four reconnaissance U.S. aircraft, repainted to appear to be Israeli, to assist and monitor the surprise attacks on the U.A.R. air bases on the first day of the war. In these sorties three hundred Egyptian aircraft were destroyed within the first 170 minutes.[8] In response to the video interview referenced, a former Israeli military intelligence officer denied the charges, but Mr. Reight rebutted that assertion, explaining that Israel had no such aircraft to be able to produce the photographic documentation that was made public and published in several news magazines shortly thereafter.

Although the *Liberty* was nominally under the control of Admiral John S. McCain, Jr., Commander-in-Chief, U.S. Atlantic Fleet (father of the Arizona senator, John McCain) while in the Atlantic Ocean, and switched to the Commander U.S. Sixth Fleet (Vice-Admiral William Martin) when it entered the Mediterranean Sea, according to Ennes: " … regardless of who was *Liberty*'s designated commander during that period, her movements were really being directed by the Joint Chiefs of Staff in the Pentagon, and any intermediate commander … served only as a conduit for JCS orders."[9] That this was a highly unusual procedure was reflected in his roommate's (Jim O'Connor), comment upon reading a message while the ship was docked in Abidjan, the capital of the Ivory Coast. When Ennes asked O'Connor about it, his response was, "It was a message from the Joint Chiefs of Staff. Whoever heard of JCS taking direct control of a ship? We're to get underway as soon as possible and make our best speed for Rota, Spain."[10]

The broader plan, called "Frontlet 615," named for the planned start date of the war (6/15/1967), called for Israeli provocations towards Egypt (then known as the United Arab Republic [U.A.R.]), Syria and Jordan, to induce border clashes that would then provoke an escalation of fighting, leading inevitably to a "flash-point." The first major error in executing the plan was in the miscalculation of the level of provocations needed to set off the flash-point.

Even before the creation of the nation of Israel, out of an ancient territory that had previously been called Palestine, there had been continuing and increasing numbers of naturally-occurring clashes between Jews and Arabs. The situation in early 1967 could be called a "tinderbox" without hyperbole.

Conflicts had already increased in frequency and violence when Israel – which had long endeavored to expand its agricultural sector – had begun using a greater share of the Jordan River's water. Ariel Sharon, who later served as Israel's eleventh prime minister, stated that the build-up to the 1967 War started in 1964-65, when Syrian engineers began diverting part of the Jordan's water flow away from Israel. He stated, "People generally regard 5 June 1967 as the day the Six-Day War began. That is the official date. But, in reality, it started two-and-a-half years earlier, on the day Israel decided to act against the diversion of the Jordan." [11]

Syria had begun to divert water at its source in the Golan Heights before it reached the river, which, according to Wikipedia, "would have reduced the installed capacity of Israel's carrier [aqueduct system] by about 35%, and Israel's overall water supply by about 11%." Israel began sporadic bombing raids on the diversion sites in November 1964 and August, 1965 and again bombed Syrian military installations in April and May of 1967.

On one of those raids, April 7, 1967, a Syrian-Israeli clash between tanks led to counter attacks by both Syrian and Israeli aircraft. Six Syrian planes were shot down on that day alone. This incident caused further retaliatory actions by both sides, and Egypt started moving troops into the Sinai Peninsula, increasing tensions between Israel and all the neighboring Arab countries. [12]

Throughout the early 1960s, as the Israeli military advantage against its Arab neighbors increased, together with suspected, but not-yet-proven, attempts by Israel to develop a nuclear weapon, the Israeli's provocations became ever more aggressive. As noted by scholar Roland Popp, in *Stumbling Decidedly Into the Six-Day War*, "With the massive raid on Samu' in November 1966, Israel destroyed 'the unwritten agreement which had neutralized the Jordan-Israel border,' in the words of King Husayn. Military activism by Israel also began to change the relationship with the U.A.R. In December 1966, reports began to reach Washington that "Israeli planes penetrate U.A.R. air space as far as Suez daily and on occasion even to Cairo." [13]

Against this backdrop, additional provocations were deliberately designed to ensure that the clashes would steadily increase and lead to the planned flash-point, as confirmed by the man who served as Israel's Defense Minister during the Six-Day War, Moshe Dayan. A letter from him acknowledging this strategy was released after his death in 1997 by his daughter Yael Dayan, a Knesset member. According to Dayan, at least eighty percent of the clashes were the result of Israeli provocations, mostly the result of sending their armored tractors to plow ground along the

Syrian border in the demilitarized zone. If that didn't cause them to begin shooting at the tractors, they would tell the soldier (disguised as a farmer) driving the tractor to go farther toward or over the border, until finally "the Syrians would get annoyed and shoot. And then we would use artillery and later the air force also, and that's how it was."[14]

Further affirmation that the Israeli provocations were planned months ahead came from yet another high-level Israeli official, Ezer Weizman, chief of the operations staff under Israeli prime minister Yitzak Rabin: "the attack on Egypt, Jordan and Syria was so that Israel 'could exist according to the scale, spirit and quality she now embodies.'"[15]

The Israeli provocations worked more effectively than anticipated. Fed up with the ever rising levels of violence, on May 22, 1967, U.A.R. President Abdel Gamal Nasser blockaded the Straits of Tiran, a waterway that was vital to the Israeli port of Eilat and the gateway to the Gulf of Aqaba on the Red Sea. This set off a chain-reaction that quickly triggered others, including the conscription of the *Liberty* into service the following day.

Even Israeli Chief of Staff Yitzhak Rabin (who would become, in 1968, Ambassador to the United States and in 1974 Israel's Prime Minister) once stated that "I do not believe that Nasser wanted war. The two divisions he sent into Sinai on 14 May would not have been enough to unleash an offensive against Israel. He knew it and we knew it." His reference to "two divisions" meant fewer than 40,000 men had been deployed in the Sinai, out of a total of 264,000 in the Egyptian military, which is the same number that Israel could have massed. At the time, Nasser had already committed too many troops in Yemen in a long, drawn-out conflict that had become known as "Nasser's Vietnam."[16]

Many others who were intimately involved as diplomats or officials on both sides of the 1967 Arab-Israeli War agree with Rabin, including the Palestinian Ambassador Afif Safieh:[17]

> Every possible study I've seen says that the Egyptian army was in defensive deployment and not in an offensive posture. I believe on the day of the confrontation, 5 June 1967, Nasser ... was sending Zakaria Mohi Edein to Washington that same morning to discuss de-escalating the crisis. That was the moment that was chosen for the blitzkrieg of six hours that devastated the region. The war was a pre-emptive strike against this diplomatic endeavor intended to avoid war.
>
> I still remember [Israeli] General [Mattityahu] Peled – who was a sophisticated general yet a peace camper – used to say, "Anybody who believes that Israel was at risk in 1967 is committing an offense and an insult to the Israeli army." So the outcome of that war was known in advance. To give you one example ... an Egyptian airplane fighter could make two sorties a day while Israeli air-

plane fighters had the capability – because of the number of the pilots, the engineers, the maintenance – to do six sorties every day. So, for example, if each of them had 500 airplanes, the Israelis, in fact, could deploy 3,000 airplanes a day while the Egyptians would deploy 1,000.

Years later, in 1982, the Israeli prime minister Menachem Begin again admitted the same point:[18]

> In June 1967, we had a choice. The Egyptian army concentrations in the Sinai approaches do not prove that [Egyptian President] Nasser was really about to attack us. We must be honest with ourselves. We decided to attack him.

All of the provocations that Israel had made to her neighbors – and admitted to by a succession of Israeli leaders as documented here – were part of the planning that had been initiated months, even years, before the war began. The provocations were designed for the purpose of instigating a war. This "war" was originally conceived within the Johnson administration in collaboration with Israeli leadership; the Six-Day War was, and still is, in many quarters, portrayed as a "spontaneous" war, but this is a myth.

By early June, the start date of the war could not be held back for much longer and it was about to explode early. This would have disastrous implications. The skirmishes had become even more frequent and violent than planned. This rising level of tensions led to further spontaneous, unplanned counter attacks which resulted in the war commencing early – on June 5, 1967. That nearly destroyed the original intentions of the plan since the *Liberty* had been ordered, evidently, several days earlier – yet still not enough – than the pre-approved schedule, to proceed on May 23, 1967, to Rota, Spain. Having arrived there on May 31st, it was then ordered into the eastern Mediterranean two days later, on June 2nd.

That scheduling snafu, the war beginning ten days early, combined with other unanticipated events – ultimately including the *Liberty's* refusal to sink – caused the entire operation to flounder. Yet the eventual results for the other key objectives – for Israel's interests, in strengthening itself relative to its immediate Arab neighbors and expanding its borders – were considered an astounding success. Israel proudly proclaimed victory with the captured territory, most of which it still holds.

Tracing Backwards: When Did The Planning Preparations Start for "Frontlet 615" and "Operation Cyanide"?

Clearly, the planning for such an elaborate and complex plan, with multiple goals for both Israel and the United States, would require considerable time to develop. Considering the fact that all of the related files have long since either disappeared, or are so highly classified that they will likely never be released, the best method for determining when the planning might have started is to examine all of the evidence accumulated to date. Thanks to the efforts of earlier researchers and authors, much of the research has already been done, and we can reference their work and "connect some reasonable dots."

British journalist Peter Hounam's investigation into the attack on the USS *Liberty* began in 2000 for a broadcast on British television. That film, a BBC documentary, *Dead in the Water,* is still one of the best videos ever produced on this subject. It is available on YouTube and other Internet sites.

Hounam concluded that the attack was the result of a secret plan concocted by the United States in collaboration with certain Israeli leaders to provide a justification for the United States to enter the war against Egypt. Hounam subsequently wrote a book titled *Operation Cyanide,* published in England. This seminal work explores the larger context of the pre-planning for the war and contains numerous examples of how the preliminary steps toward executing the plan began at least one year before the attack took place. Hounam's thorough research included many personal interviews with men who had been directly involved in the planning and execution of the overall plans for "Frontlet 615" and its critical component, "Operation Cyanide."

Joe Sorrels was one such man. He had worked in "freelance special operations" for U.S. intelligence agencies. He stated that he was deployed on a mission in "mid-1966" to work on "… a joint plan by elements of military intelligence in Israel and the United States to engineer a war with Egypt and depose its leader Gamal Abdul Nasser who, the U.S. believed, was a dangerous puppet of Moscow.… In August 1966 he was secretly sent as an adviser to the Israeli Army [and it soon] became evident [that] he was part of an extensive, covert, foreign military presence."[19] Sorrels stated that he went to Israel with others of various specialties from his base at Fort Benning, Georgia. He claimed that they were all aware that their mission was to train and tutor young Israeli officers in a "number of situations [and] venues … laying groundwork" for a war for which they were not given the date, but he knew it would be soon, because "they were in a state of total mobilisation [sic - British spelling] … it was obviously inevitable. They were organising [sic - ditto] themselves."[20] This and many other specific examples from Hounam's book and video clearly indicate the lengthy and meticulous preparations for the *spontaneous* Six-Day War.

It would be reasonable to conclude from the above that the planning for Frontlet 615 could have begun at least six months, maybe even a year, before Mr. Sorrels was recruited in mid-1966. This would imply that planning for Frontlet 615 and Operation Cyanide would have actually commenced no later than the middle-to-late part of 1965, and possibly as early as late 1964 (right after the presidential elections that year).

THE MONTH BEFORE THE ATTACK ON THE USS LIBERTY

Israeli Foreign Minister Abba Eban requested a high-level meeting with Johnson and his advisors in the third week of May, 1967. In preparation for that, LBJ's National Security Council scheduled a meeting, which included Johnson's close friend and long-time advisor, the Supreme Court Justice Abe Fortas. The NSC discussed the options that Dean Rusk presented, who had not been "in the loop" on the secret "war" plans. The assessment came down to either "unleashing Israel" or what Rusk referred to as the "multilateral fleet," which meant an attempt to organize key countries (e.g. Britain, France and Canada) to stand with Israel. Johnson used a phrase that would be repeatedly used afterwards, "Israel will not be alone unless it decides to go alone."

According to Dr. William B. Quandt, author of "The Johnson Administration and the 1967 War," in *The Jerusalem Fund*:[21]

> Johnson does tell him [Eban] in no uncertain terms that Israel should not rush to war. He says they need more time for diplomacy. He put forward the idea of the multilateral fleet. He says that it will take some time, but that it's the best solution. He shares the intelligence judgment that the Egyptians do not seem to be preparing for a strike, and he asks for time to deal with the crisis. Eban asks a lot of questions, and as he leaves the Oval Office, Johnson turns to his aides and says, "I've failed, no go."

Supreme Court Justice Abe Fortas, attending the meeting as a special guest of his friend the president, told Johnson, and the group, "You can't tell the Israelis that they will be alone if they act on their own. It's simply impossible. The kind of relationship we have with the Israelis is such that we cannot in good conscience make that statement. We have to either solve the problem for them or we have to support them as they solve it on their own."[22]

At this point Fortas – for three decades Johnson's primary adviser for everything involving his most difficult legal dilemmas – took on a new role, as a "back channel" for communications between the Israeli embassy and Lyndon Johnson.[23] When it came to Israel, Fortas was never neutral: "When they get back from Egypt," a law clerk in his Supreme Court chambers overheard Justice Fortas say, "I'm going to decorate my office with Arab foreskins."[24]

Fortas was in touch routinely with the Israeli ambassador in the weeks leading up to the war and attended another critical White House strategy meeting on the Middle East on Friday, May 26 – just three days after the Joint Chiefs of Staff and Secretary McNamara initiated the order to move the *Liberty* to its new destination, the Mediterranean. At that point, it was three weeks before the scheduled start of the war, on 15 June. The situation on the ground was becoming out of control.

The discussion at this May 26th meeting may have alarmed some in attendance who were aware of the secret plans (Frontlet 615 and its subpart Operation Cyanide). It was way too early to be triggering the conflict therefore Johnson's warning was not as Dr. Quandt presumed it to be: Johnson's warning for Israel to "not rush to war" merely meant that the start of the war needed to be delayed sufficiently to get all of the pieces in place, specifically the USS *Liberty*.

Enough artifacts have survived to conclude that the plan was unfolding much too rapidly, and then suddenly, the launch date for the Six-Day War was moved up by ten days, from June 15 to June 5, 1967.[25] This move would cause the war to be over much faster than originally planned.

The key "task" on the critical path of this project, and the apparent trigger for this succession of events, was clearly related to Johnson's ordering the Israelis to have their Air Force and Navy attack and sink his own ship as a way to justify a US attack on Egypt – and any other Arab nation that might want to join their side.[26] The original plan, based upon a June 15 launch date for the war, presumed that the *Liberty* would have been in place, and the attack would take place on the first day of the war, not the fourth, when it was already practically over.

PRES. JOHNSON ATTEMPTS TO ENLIST CANADIAN HELP; THEN COMMISERATES WITH ISRAELI DIPLOMAT ABOUT THE FAILED OUTCOME

In late May 1967, President Johnson went to Ottawa to meet with Canadian Prime Minister Lester Pearson. Johnson was hoping to enlist Canada's support for the secret plan developed through his "303 Committee." It was this plan that his "zealously Zionist" White House aides and advisors like Walt Rostow, Abe Fortas, Abraham Feinberg, Leo White, Jake Jacobsen, Ben Wattenberg, Larry Levinson and John P. Roche may have all had a hand in instigating.

Exhibit "A" for the proof of this assertion is the document detailing the minutes of the April 10 meeting of the 303 Committee. Johnson had had only one previous meeting with Pearson, which was the result of the Canadian's indiscreet comments about what he thought of the president's Vietnam policies. Johnson had immediately called him and asked him to come to Camp David to talk about that incident. When Pearson arrived, he was practically assaulted by President Johnson, who grabbed him by the lapels and shouted,

"Don't you come into my living room and piss on my rug." Pearson admitted that the meeting was acrimonious, but, eager to repair the damage his words had caused, stated that the meeting eventually ended cordially.[27] That earlier incident may have been the reason that Johnson's visit with Pearson was unsuccessful in enlisting Canada's help for his plans to join Israel in a war that had not yet started. A war that was still the subject of unfinished secret plans.

On May 26, 1967, shortly after Johnson returned from Canada, Israeli Deputy Chief of Mission Ephraim "Eppie" Evron, was visiting the White House to schedule a meeting with the president for the Israeli foreign minister, Abba Eban. When Johnson learned that Evron was there, he called him into the Oval Office. According to what Evron described and was reported in *The Six-Day War – A Retrospective*, edited by Richard B. Parker, the Israeli official was shocked at what then followed:[28]

> [President Johnson] had just returned from a meeting with Lester Pearson, who was one of the key designers, planners, of the 1957 arrangement [Pearson had played a leading role in helping to end the Suez Crisis of that year]. He wasn't complimentary ("I use diplomatic language"), in his description of the Canadian position, of Mr. Pearson personally, of the way he had been treated there.... *Obviously there was no clear Canadian support for whatever the President wanted.* [Bracketed phrases in original; emphasis added. Evron seems to be telling us that Johnson was very upset with Pearson, and used very foul language in his description of the visit].

This suggests that the conversation Johnson had with Prime Minister Pearson was related to the scheme that the president had assigned to his "303 Committee" months earlier. The long-planned operation was about to be executed by the highest-level officials in the JCS, CIA and NSA, and it was not unusual for Johnson to personally take control of key operations.

One widely-referenced example of this trait was how he attempted to micromanage the details of the bombing raids in North Vietnam; another was how he took over all detailed planning related to the Dallas motorcade event for JFK on November 22, 1963.

The scene in the Oval Office described by Mr. Evron was more than a little "bizarre" considering that the president of the United States, having noticed an Israeli embassy representative in the outer office performing a clerical scheduling task, invited him into his office in order to discuss with him "in great detail" a failed meeting with the Canadian prime minister.

But we must also consider that Mr. Evron, according to journalist Anthony Pearson (no relation to Lester Pearson), may have been only serving as the Deputy Israeli Ambassador to Washington as a "cover" for his real job: a high-level official of the Israeli Mossad.[29] Furthermore, Pearson stated that Evron "... had previously been one of the main conspirators in a plot [the Lavon Affair] to sabotage the growth of American detente with Egypt in December 1954. This was an operation planned by Mossad to blow up the American Embassy in Cairo and blame the attack on Egyptian nationalists." The scandal triggered by this incident caused Evron to disappear for thirteen years, until he showed up suddenly in Washington in May, 1967 just in time for the lead-up to the Six-Day War.

Anthony Pearson also stated that Evron "... was involved in a lot of activity with the State Department [Eugene Rostow] and the White House [Walt Rostow, among others] and seemed to have greater significance at the Israeli Embassy than his chief, Avraham Harman, in the overall Israeli power structure ... for Israeli intelligence made him a vital link in a complex plan to overthrow Nasser."[30] Moreover, having linked Evron directly to "Angleton at the CIA and Eugene Rostow at the State Department" Pearson stated that Evron's contacts, back in Israel, were to the group that had created the original plan, including "Intelligence Chief Meir Amit, Aharon Yariv (head of army intelligence), Shimon Peres (deputy minister of defense) Ezer Weizman (head of army operations), Air Force Chief Mordecai Hod, and Moshe Dayan, who soon would be minister of defense."[31]

Eppie Evron's role in the final planning and execution stages of "Frontlet 615" and Operation Cyanide – connected at both ends to the original key planners – might be why President Johnson chose him to commiserate with regarding his failed efforts to enlist Canadian "cover" for these operations, could not be more clear. That he had also played a key role in the 1954 "Lavon affair" – yet another false flag attack against their "ally" the United States – puts all of the brazen planning into greater perspective.

WHY DID PRESIDENT JOHNSON GO TO OTTAWA?

The meeting Johnson had in Ottawa with Canadian Prime Minister Lester Pearson, must be examined further because of something that had happened just a few days earlier: On May 23, 1967, Lyndon Johnson, acting through the Joint Chiefs of Staff, in concert with Robert McNamara, had ordered the Navy spy ship USS *Liberty* off its routine patrol on the West Coast of Africa and into what they knew would soon be a war zone off the coast of the Sinai Peninsula. At that point, they knew that things were starting to get "out of control," thus the decision was made to order the *Liberty* into place on a "rush" basis instead of a more routine process as had been previously planned.

It was just two days before then, on May 21, when Yitzhak Rabin, the Israeli chief of staff, visited David Ben-Gurion, to brief him on the current military situation. This visit did not turn out well. Rabin had said something upsetting to Ben-Gurion. The key to what may have upset Ben-Gurion was in a paragraph of Hounam's book, *Operation Cyanide*:[32]

> Rabin felt he was being pushed and pulled by dividing loyalties and no doubt hoped Ben-Gurion would provide him with some solace. He was utterly wrong. His recollection of what happened is dramatic: "The old Man received me warmly, but instead of fortifying my spirits he gave me a dressing-down. 'We have been forced into a very grave situation,' he warned ... Ben-Gurion kept hammering away. 'You made a mistake,' he said, referring to our mobilization of the reserves.... 'You have led the state into a grave situation. We must not go to war. We are isolated ...'"

Ben-Gurion was obviously furious with Rabin for agreeing to Johnson's audacious, dangerous plan that had the potential to become the "critical mass" leading to a World War III, with Jerusalem and Tel Aviv in the middle of it: Both targeted by the missiles of the Soviet Union, from their bases in multiple Arab countries that surrounded Israel. Ben-Gurion may have foreseen "mushroom clouds" destroying the country of which he was considered the "godfather."

Yitzhak Rabin experienced a brief nervous breakdown, ironically also on May 23, 1967, just two weeks before the attack and two days after his "dressing-down" by David Ben-Gurion. He was exhausted. He had been involved with the military build-up, all while attending numerous political and strategic military meetings. After seeking support from the revered David Ben-Gurion, and getting a harsh reaction instead, Rabin became upset, and it became so debilitating that he essentially "sat out" the war. According to his subordinate, Ezer Weizman, Rabin looked "broken and depressed," after that stinging rebuke by Ben-Gurion, and fell into a depression that caused him to take several days off.

It is noteworthy that his breakdown was of the "depressed" kind, not one of excited outrage. Weizman, who was responsible for managing and coordinating operations, visited Rabin in his apartment, the evening of May 23, 1967, at Rabin's request, after Rabin had asked him to take over his post as chief of staff due to an "error" he had committed that had left Israel vulnerable to attack by the Soviet Union – just as Israel was preparing for a fight with its neighboring nations. Weizman stated that the error involved the Israeli air force, which "will decide the war" and that he had made a "series of mistakes," the sum total of which, he believed, had compromised their ability to accomplish their mission. Weizman said that Rabin's voice was faint and weak, that he was clearly depressed and operating "below par," but that Weizman refused to allow him to resign; instead, he said that Rabin agreed to take a few days off to recover from the stress of the moment.[33]

That "series of errors" may have included having Israeli fighter jets exposed to a mission that, if discovered, would have disastrous results for the future of Israel. One facet of that might have involved, or led to the decision to minimize the risk through, the repainting of jets to eliminate the Star of David from their tail section as a means to keep their identities secret – to give them "plausible deniability."

The fact that Rabin's nervous breakdown occurred on May 23, 1967, precisely the same day that Lyndon Johnson, through the Joint Chiefs of Staff and Robert McNamara, ordered the USS *Liberty* off of its routine patrol on the West Coast of Africa, and to proceed at full speed to Rota, Spain, and later on to the Eastern Mediterranean Sea, suggests a cause-effect relationship between the two events. Perhaps Rabin's psyche had become upset by Ben-Gurion's furious response two days earlier to the military plan that was already underway. A plan that he now realized was highly audacious and potentially extremely dangerous to Israel, one that he had been forced to accede to despite his own reservations.

Using basic deductive reasoning processes, it can be posited that there may have been a connection between these events: That Lyndon Johnson, using the most polished facets of his formidable "Johnson Treatment," ordered Yitzhak Rabin to do something so outrageous that when Ben-Gurion heard of it he reacted very strongly – uncharacteristically so – which so upset Rabin that, within two days, he suffered a nervous breakdown.

All of this occurred just as the lead-up to the Six-Day War was fully underway. This overall context of the events leading up to the attack on the USS *Liberty* puts the situation into a clear perspective: That attack was merely one aspect of a much wider plot intended to establish expanded borders for Israel, strengthen its military and intelligence capabilities, secure a stronger relationship with the United States, and diminish the military power of its immediate neighbors.

When Johnson went to Ottawa, to attempt to enlist the support of Canadian Prime Minister Pearson, he was unsuccessful. Pearson's attitude towards Johnson may also have been the result of conversations he may have had with British leaders. One such man was the British Secretary of State for Defence, Denis Healey, who had such a strong dislike of Lyndon Johnson that, when he wrote his memoirs he decided to include that point in his book, and used unusually strong language to do so:[34]

> *Lyndon Johnson was a monster.* [He was] one of the few politicians with whom I found it uncomfortable to be in the same room. Johnson exuded a brutal lust for power which I found most disagreeable.... I could never forgive him for the way he destroyed Hubert Humphrey's personality while Hubert was Vice-President, thus costing the United States the best President it never had. [Emphasis added.]

When most people write their memoirs, it is generally done in a positive and uplifting manner, but the number of books which contain such negativity toward Lyndon Johnson is remarkable. There are ones by Healey, Richard Goodwin, General Charles Cooper, Lobbyist Robert Winter-Berger, Air Force One pilot Ralph Albertazzie, and those by White House officials Clark Clifford and Nicholas Katzenbach. Another is the memoirs of the late CBS News reporter Morley Safer and his recollection of how President Johnson and Bill Moyers tried to get him fired for his honest reporting of a 1965 torching of the village of Cam Ne in Vietnam by U.S. Marines. The fact that so many of these reports eventually found their way into books, but never made the news, is one of the reasons that Johnson's true legacy is still so well-hidden.

Operations Frontlet 615 and Cyanide were very secret plans, and had to be known only to a few men at the top of each country's leadership circles. In the case of the United States, it appears that only a few select men within the "303 Committee" and the Joint Chiefs of Staff had prior knowledge. It appears clear that, for example, Dean Rusk was not "in the loop," based upon his outrage, not only the attack on the *Liberty* but the consequent expansion of Israel's borders, and the fact that he was never as close to Johnson as some have portrayed. Richard Helms, the head of the CIA, in his own memoir, attempted to deny that he had been involved: "I had no role in the board of inquiry that followed, or the board's finding that there could be no doubt that the Israelis knew exactly what they were doing in attacking the *Liberty*. I have yet to understand why it was felt necessary to attack this ship or who ordered the attack." However, it must be recognized that Helms was a very skillful prevaricator and his possible foreknowledge cannot be discounted, especially as one examines that artfully-created statement: His only outright denial was in reference to the subsequent investigation of the attack, and to say that "I have yet to understand why ..." is a classic non sequitur. McNamara's obvious guilt – based on his orders to recall the rescue fighter jets, twice – is only affirmed by his complete refusal to discuss anything about the *Liberty*, knowing that the truth would have only incriminated himself, as well as Johnson.

Other than Johnson, those who can arguably be imputed to be "definites" regarding their foreknowledge of plans are Robert McNamara, Walt Rostow, possibly his brother at the State Department Eugene Rostow, undoubtedly Abe Fortas and probably some of Johnson's other close "outside advisors" such as Abraham "Abe" Feinberg. Abe had been appointed by Johnson to be the chief fund raiser for the Democratic Party, and was a liaison between Israel and Johnson. Feinberg appeared to be a guiding hand in the planning and execution of the Six-Day War. It should also be stated that foreknowledge of the larger plan "Frontlet 615" (of which the entire committee would have known about) does not imply the same degree of foreknowledge about "Operation Cyanide," which was undoubtedly known by only a few key people.

CHRONOLOGY OF EVENTS, FIRST WEEK OF JUNE

Despite the growing tensions that might cause unanticipated logistical problems with this long-scheduled Middle East war, and instead of attending the usual presidential ceremony at the Tomb of the Unknown Soldier on Memorial Day (Tuesday, May 30, 1967), Johnson left for his Texas ranch on Saturday, May 27. The president must have felt confident about the smooth execution of the upcoming "war" plans however; after all, he had delegated the handling of any problems to his able staff and now he wanted to relax back at the ranch with some of his most intimate friends. According to the aforementioned Dr. William B. Quandt, "He took none of his foreign policy advisors with him. Instead, he was surrounded by his family and friends, including Democratic party money man [who had also become his new Texas neighbor] Arthur Krim, and his wife Mathilde, with whom Johnson seemed to have, what we might now politely call, a very close personal relationship."[35]

According to author Stephen D. Isaacs in *Jews and American Politics*, Johnson routinely consulted Feinberg on Middle East policy and Arthur Krim also played a proactive role. Krim was a prominent New York attorney as well as president of United Artists Corporation of Hollywood, and served as chairman of the Democratic Party national finance committee. Johnson was especially close to Krim's wife Mathilde, who had served as an agent for Irgun, the Jewish "freedom fighter" turned terrorist group led by Menachem Begin.[36]

On Thursday, June 1, 1967, Lyndon Johnson finally returned to Washington with Mathilde Krim. Two days later, they were off to New York for a dinner-dance on June 3rd. When they arrived at the Americana Hotel, they were met by over 1,400 anti-war protestors, some of whom were carrying posters that portrayed Johnson dressed like Adolph Hitler, saluting like a Nazi soldier shouting "Heil Hitler!" beneath slogans that read "Wanted for Murder!"[37] A new record for American casualties had just been set the previous week, with 313 soldiers killed in action and nearly ten times that in total casualties. It could have been worse, since news reports indicated that the police had expected up to 5,000 demonstrators.[38] But at the last minute, Jewish organizations had been pressured to get their members to refrain from protesting.[39]

That evening, at a major fund-raiser for the Democrats as well as Israel, Abe Feinberg interrupted the president's evening with Mathilde to say that he: "had some important news from Israel. 'Mr. President, it can't be held any longer,' he said. 'It's going to be within the next 24 hours.' The President continued with the fun, and took no action on this important piece of intelligence."[40] Feinberg's point that "it can't be held any longer" referred to the fact that the planned provocations had been much more effective than anticipated; the situation had become dangerously out of control and was now close to spontaneously exploding. Mathilde Krim wrote out a statement supportive of Israel which Johnson read to Secretary of State Dean Rusk, but decided against reading it on television to the American people, as she had asked him to do.[41]

The original plan had called for the war to begin in about two weeks on June 15, so the *Liberty* was still in port in Rota, Spain, having arrived there after a harrowing trip up the African coast at full speed on May 31, which was Johnson's last day at his Texas ranch before returning to DC.

The *Liberty* was in the process of picking up supplies, as well as four linguists, including a civilian, Allen M. Blue, who worked for the National Security Agency and had been rushed to Spain straight from Washington, DC with practically no notice, leaving his wife with their new-born baby, and no details whatsoever of where he was going or what kind of mission he would be engaged in – that was the last she would ever see of him.

THE USS LIBERTY, ARMED WITH FOUR GUNS, GOES TO WAR

On May 23, 1967, the spy ship USS *Liberty* had been docked in Abidjan, the capital, at that time, of Côte d'Ivoire (the Ivory Coast) on the west coast of Africa. Many of its sailors were on routine leave in the city, most of the crew staying at the Ivorian Hotel. Although many sailors, marines, soldiers and airmen then serving in the Atlantic or Europe at that time knew that a Middle East war seemed more and more likely. The highly unusual decision, by the Joint Chiefs of Staff, to move the *Liberty* first

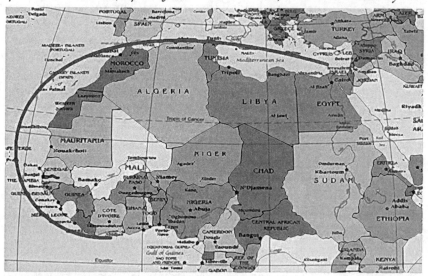

Moving the USS Liberty: 23 May - 7 June, 1967

to Rota, Spain and then to the Mediterranean Sea off the coast of Egypt caught the *Liberty* crewmen off-guard, coming as it did after only two days in port (half its scheduled resting and maintenance period).

Shore patrolmen from the *Liberty* searched the city to find the crew members and ordered them to report back to the ship immediately. The unusual haste, and the stern, urgent demeanor of the shore patrolmen, implicitly warned the crew members – who had become used to uneventful, routine missions – that a dangerous mission now loomed. The tensions had already peaked even before the order was received, since a rumor had spread among the crew that the famed columnist/prognosticator Jeanne Dixon had predicted in *The National Enquirer* that the USS *Liberty* would shortly be sunk.

Survivor Jim Ennes subsequently contacted her about that, and she denied ever making "any prediction about USS *Liberty*."[42] However, some of the survivors have stated that they remember it not as having named the *Liberty*, but rather as a more generic reference to a U.S. Naval vessel.

On June 2, 1967, the *Liberty* departed Rota, Spain and began its trip of 2,300 miles across the Mediterranean Sea. The tensions among the crew members were growing, as they knew that war in the Middle East was imminent, and they were growing more anxious about the situation daily.

On June 5th – the *Liberty* clipped across the sea at its maximum speed of 17-18 knots facing strong headwinds. Just as it was passing south of Sicily, Israel began its attack on the Egyptian air force bases.

Before arriving at its destination two days later (in response to his request for a destroyer to accompany the *Liberty* into the war zone), Commander William McGonagle received a denial from Admiral William Martin, the Commander of the U.S. Sixth Fleet. The admiral had promised McGonagle that if any kind of threat or attack arose, he would have air support from fighter jets within ten minutes, effectively the best kind of support he could hope for. Yet, as we shall see, when that kind of support was desperately needed, it did not materialize.

The reason for the lack of suport was due to direct intervention from the White House, which over-rode the Navy chain of command, and blocked the air rescues, not once but twice; help from ships in the area would also be inexcusably delayed, and all of it would then be blamed on a series of unfortunate, and very rare "communication errors." Additional incredible stories, all having in common only the most ludicrous elements of obvious prevarications – such as the one put out for American consumption that these same highly skilled, crackerjack Israeli military men would confuse an aging, rusty Egyptian horse transport ship named *El Quseir*, with arguably one of the most uniquely American warships in the fleet – would be ginned up and retold vigorously for fifty years.

While James Ennes, in his book *Assault on the Liberty*, made repeated references to the possibility that a U.S. submarine was present, labeled on the navigational charts as "Contact X," he did not attempt to identify it. His last reference to it came from literally "in the heat of the battle," as Lieutenant Commander Philip Armstrong tried to jettison two burning gasoline barrels, when a rocket hit his legs: "Meanwhile, the heretofore mysterious Contact X came to life with the first exploding rocket. Quickly poking a periscope above the surface of the water, American submariners watched wave after wave of jet airplanes attacking *Liberty*."[43] Noting that the men on that submarine were prevented from extending any help to them while making a "movie film" of the entire event, Ennes did not speculate on what submarine that might have been.

More than one book has suggested that it was the nuclear-powered USS *Andrew Jackson*, however Ennes was dubious of that because of the source – though he only referenced a "particularly inventive 'reporter' [who] described frantic messages between McGonagle and the nuclear submarine USS *Andrew Jackson*, passed during the heat of battle by your author, James Ennes ..." all of which he denied[44] – seemed to be a 1978 book titled *Conspiracy of Silence: The Attack on the USS Liberty*, by Anthony Pearson, which Ennes felt was contaminated by a number of sloppy errors and other misstatements of purported "facts."[45]

In the book's defense, however, it should be stipulated that, when Pearson's book, or his previous 1976 articles in *Penthouse* magazine on the *Liberty* attack were written, there was precious little reference material available on the subject. His magazine articles and book, which were contaminated with the disinformation planted by Johnson's decree – should therefore be recognized as "pioneering" and iconoclastic efforts despite those legitimate criticisms. There is significant true information in Pearson's book that should not be discounted and since the publication of Ennes' book, in 1979, the prominent role that the *Andrew Jackson* and other submarines played has been referenced in numerous other books, including Hounam's.

Survivor Dave ("Ed") Lewis had also been told by one of his officers about secret orders that were never to be opened, "he said there were sealed orders in my safe for Project Cyanide that involves communication via submarine in case of war ... that's all I know about it, the orders were never opened, the attack took place, there wasn't time ... I don't know what they said."[46]

One possibility many of the survivors still believe is "unthinkable," is that the purpose of having a submarine "shadow" an intelligence-gathering "Sigint" vessel (spy ship) was because they were given standing orders to "put those ships to the bottom" if they ever got in trouble. According to Ron Kukal, at a survivor's reunion in Nebraska City, Lloyd Bucher, the captain of *Liberty's* sister ship, the USS *Pueblo*,[47] made this comment to Richard Schmucker, a *Liberty* supporter. When Captain Bucher was asked why the submarine that was tracking his ship, the *Pueblo*, did not put it "to the bottom" when it was attacked a few months later, in 1968, by North Korea, he said that the sub was "out of position" and because the *Pueblo* was in shallow water, according to Schmucker.[48] It is a "possibility" that we cannot validate further, and will therefore leave it at that: "It is what it is."

Evidence of White House Clairvoyance – or Culpability

According to longtime presidential adviser Clark Clifford's 1991 memoir, *Counsel to the President*, a "communication breakdown" caused a two-hour delay in notifying Johnson of arguably the single-most important calamity, out of the many, in the Johnson administration.[49] This statement further adds to the confusion, since Clifford also stated that the White House called him "at home around 6 a.m. and asked me, without further explanation, to come to the White House immediately."[50] Since the attack had not yet occurred, and wouldn't for about two hours later at about 8:00 a.m. Washington time, an obvious question arises about why Clifford would have been called two hours before it happened.

This was not the only "timing irregularity" swirling around. Author Hounam also revealed another related story about a retired US Air Force pilot named Jim Nanjo, who stated that he and other pilots were awakened on June 8th, "between 2 and 4 a.m." California time (5:00 a.m. to 7:00 a.m. in Washington). They were stationed at Beale Air Force Base, north of Sacramento, when sirens and klaxons began sounding the alarm for all of them to go to their battle stations and remain on alert for further orders; as he jumped out of bed, it was "absolutely pitch dark in my room." He quickly dressed and ran out to his assigned aircraft, one of the half dozen B-52 bombers being readied, along with an even larger number of KC-135 tanker planes that were standing on the tarmac; they were given two and a half minutes to prepare to fly. Nanjo confirmed that the bombers were carrying thermonuclear weapons, the Mark 28 (RL) version, which was designed with special fusing and parachute systems to allow them to be dropped by a low-flying bomber. Nanjo made it very clear that this alarm, the first of its kind since the day JFK was assassinated, was not just another practice, it: "was one of the most hair-raising moments of his career."[51]

The most stunning, and revealing, point Nanjo made was his certainty that in the early morning of June 8, 1967, the alarms were sounded between 2:00 a.m. and 4:00 a.m., at least *one hour before the attack* on the *Liberty*, which did not occur until 5:00 a.m. in the Pacific time zone. The bombers would have been destined for either Cairo or Moscow if the *Liberty* had sunk, and yet they were sitting on the tarmac ready to launch at least one hour, possibly more, before the supposedly "surprise" attack had begun. It should also be noted that the mid-point of the range that Nanjo referenced, 3:00 a.m. on the Pacific coast, was exactly the same time that Clark Clifford said he had inexplicably been called to the White house, at 6:00 a.m. in Washington.

This evidence alone should be considered as presumptively conclusive that someone in either the White House, the Executive Office Building or the Pentagon – or perhaps in all three of those locations – was already up and hard at work preparing for a surprise attack, nearly 6,000 miles away in the eastern Mediterranean Sea. And on that point, the fact that the Sixth Fleet had stationed itself on the eastern end of the Mediterranean Sea, conducting a drill which included a number of aircraft already equipped with nuclear weapons, was still another unlikely coincidence.

In the meantime, the *Liberty* suddenly, and strangely, began to experience a series of missed messages to move away from the coast by a minimum of 100 miles to get it out of harm's way. Frank Raven, who supervised the NSA operations from Fort Meade, Maryland, had objected to the operation all along, and now others on his staff as well as the Joint Chiefs of Staff had become concerned about *Liberty's* vulnerability to attack.

A JCS duty officer placed an overseas telephone call at 2:00 a.m. ship's time, to the office of John S. McCain, Jr., at his headquarters in London, requesting that the ship be moved away from the coast. McCain had apparently trained his staff to be sticklers for detail, and demanded to be given a formal message, saying, "We can't revise a ship's operating orders without a confirming message." Therefore, his deputy chief of staff, Lt. Edward Galavotti, took no action to have the ship moved, and he waited four hours for a JCS message that would authorize the change. A copy of that message was sent to multiple parties,

The USS *Liberty* Before the Attack

including one that was addressed to the *Liberty*, however it was never received by the ship.

Two messages that had been intended for the ship were misrouted to the Philippines Naval Communication Station; from there they were rerouted to the Pentagon for further relay to Morocco for delivery to the *Liberty*, but the Pentagon purportedly routed it to the wrong place again. This time to the NSA communication center at Fort Meade where another error occurred when it was misfiled, and never transmitted to the *Liberty*. The JCS made it a requirement that all parties acknowledge receipt of the message, but then failed to monitor the acknowledgements to be certain they were received. Still another message was sent as "Top Secret" and to assure it was sent quickly it was given "immediate" precedence, but it too was never received, because the *Liberty* was not equipped with the kind of message delivery system that the JCS used to send it. "The fail-safe system failed" as James Ennes noted.[52] The sudden serial failure of the "secure" Pentagon communication systems might not have been merely the result of multiple coincidences and is a subject which will be examined further shortly.

Dick Carlson   Lowell T. Bingham   Ron Kukal   Jeff Carpenter
On Board the USS *Liberty*

Endnotes

1. "Apparently" is the qualifier used here since that would explain why he did not include this story in his book (in which he only referenced the possibility of an accompanying submarine, through

an "X" that had been repeatedly plotted by someone on board in a marine chart they used, purportedly marking a submarine that had been following along the same course)

2. See YouTube: "Documentary on the USS Liberty: Dead in the Water," (@ 47:00 +)

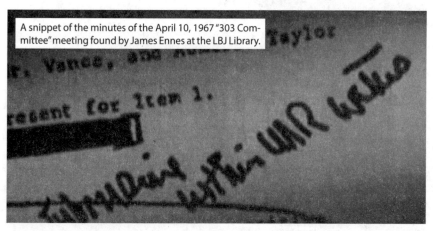

A snippet of the minutes of the April 10, 1967 "303 Committee" meeting found by James Ennes at the LBJ Library.

3. Ibid.

4. See: Ralph D. Steakley obituary: http://www.legacy.com/obituaries/floridatoday/obituary.aspx?pid=128667385#sthash.wfuC3zDw.dpuf

5. Although Wikipedia administrators claim that they allow corrections to their content, numerous people (including this author) have found that such "corrections" must meet standard "politically correct" guidelines.

6. See: https://en.wikipedia.org/wiki/USS_Liberty_incident

7. Op. Cit. (Dead in the Water video, @ 47:00 +)

8. Ibid. (@ 51:00 +)

9. Ennes, p. 34

10. Ibid., p. 9

11. See Darwish, Adel, "Analysis: Middle East Water Wars," BBC News, May 30, 2003, http://news.bbc.co.uk/2/hi/middle_east/2949768.stm

12. "United States Cryptologic History," p. 9.

13. Popp, Roland "Stumbling Decidedly into the Six-Day War" MIDDLE EAST JOURNAL, VOLUME 60, NO. 2, SPRING 2006 See: https://www.researchgate.net/publication/236885756_Stumbling_Decidedly_into_the_Six_Day_War

14. Shlaim, Avi. pp. 236–237, Also found in Wikipedia: http://en.wikipedia.org/wiki/Moshe_dayan#cite_note-66

15. Hounam, *Operation Cyanide*, p. 83

16. Ibid, p. 81

17. See: 40 Years after the 1967 War: The Impact of a Prolonged Occupation. Edited transcript of remarks titled The 1967 Occupation: A Palestinian Perspective, Afif Safieh The Palestine Center Washington, D.C. 5 June 2007 (http://www.thejerusalemfund.org/ht/a/GetDocumentAction/i/2918)

18. McGovern, Ray. "So Who's Afraid of the Israel Lobby?" *Consortium News*, October 5, 2007 (http://www.consortiumnews.com/2007/100507a.html)

19. Hounam, pp. 196-197

20. Ibid.

21. See: 40 Years after the 1967 War: The Impact of a Prolonged Occupation. Edited transcript of remarks titled *The Johnson Administration and the 1967 War*, Dr. William Quandt, The Palestine Center Washington, D.C. 5 June 2007 (http://www.thejerusalemfund.org/ht/a/GetDocumentAction/i/2918)

22. Ibid.

23. Kalman, pp. 301–302

24. Ibid.

25. Hounam *Operation Cyanide*, p. 270.

26. Ibid., pp. 28, 38, 240

27. Haley, p. 235

28. Hounam, *Operation Cyanide*, p. 266 (Ref. *The Six-Day War: A Retrospective*, edited by Richard B. Parker, University Press of Florida, 1996).

29. Pearson, Anthony, "The Attack on the U.S.S. Liberty: Mayday! Mayday!" *Penthouse* magazine, May 1976.

30. Ibid.

31. Ibid.

32. Hounam, *Operation Cyanide*, pp. 72–73

33. Ibid.

34. Hounam, *Operation Cyanide*, p. 131 (ref. *The Time of My Life*, by Denis Healy, Penguin Books, 1989).

35. Op. Cit. Dr. William Quandt *The Johnson Administration and the 1967 War*

36. Ibid.

37. Witkin, Richard, "Johnson, in City, Vows to Maintain Peace in Mideast," *New York Times*, June 4, 1967, p. 1

38. Witkin, Richard, "Protests to Greet Visit of President," *New York Times*, June 3, 1967, p. 12

39. Scott, James, p. 28

40. Hounam, *Operation Cyanide*, p. 135

41. Op. Cit. (40 Years after …)

42. Ennes, p. 14 (n)

43. Ennes, p. 64

44. Ennes, p. 218

45. The errors included some relatively minor points, including the date that the Liberty arrived in the Eastern Mediterranean, off the Gaza Strip, and, of more importance, the time zone conversions he used. But there were other points that left questions regarding the provenance of certain assertions, such as his comment that "The Captain had inquired of Major (sic) Allen Blue [who had no military title and was a civilian employee of the NSA] if there was the slightest possibility that Liberty's coded transmissions had been intercepted and decoded … Major Blue had replied that this was not merely unlikely but impossible" (p. 37). Furthermore, Pearson referred to a conference between Blue, McGonagle, James Ennis, and Philip Armstrong ,which ended at 12:15 p.m. ship's time and the general quarters drill that took place between 1:10 p.m. and 1:48 p.m. How he came across any records of these events and remarks purportedly made by Blue, and other similarly precise statements, when both Philip Armstrong and Allen Blue were among the 34 men immediately killed, and McGonagle was known for his silent stoicism, is inexplicable. The chances that McGonagle would have discussed any of this with Mr. Pearson can therefore be best described as "possible but improbable." The absence of footnotes, endnotes or any other such basis for a veritable explanation of it discredits some of his assertions, although he does refer vaguely to certain sources of much of his information, including a mysterious "Major Steven McKenna" of a

Special Air Services (SAS) regiment of the British military (pp. 3, 20-21, 64-65), and "members of the US Navy, many of them survivors of the Liberty's crew, senior officers in the Pentagon, friends and interested parties in the Central Intelligence Agency, other writers and commentators on Middle East affairs, and some important former members of the administration of President Lyndon B. Johnson" (p. 4). The fact that he was able to chronicle so much of the story, in great detail and well before any other books, articles or films/video were published, indicates he did have access to others who had to have "been there" or at least had access to certain "insiders." Unfortunately, he died shortly after his book was published, reportedly of a brain tumor that was said to have caused him to become quite paranoid about alleged tormentors, including agents of the Mossad. Certain authors, such as James Ennes, have stated that his information is very unreliable, yet others, such as the late Richard Thompson, who was instrumental in the creation of the video "Dead in the Water," considered the body of his work as being very credible. While we have been careful in referencing his works, as noted above, these caveats should be considered when weighing all citations to his book. The overall veracity of his account is considered by the authors as "cautiously credible."

46. See YouTube: "Documentary on the USS Liberty: Dead in the Water," (@ 47:30+)

47. The USS Pueblo, only seven months after the Liberty disaster, was attacked, hijacked in international waters, and then permanently held by North Korea; the crew was then imprisoned, tortured, nearly starved, and not released for eleven months. The ship is still being held by North Korea, as a war trophy on display for visitors to that dreary nation. one explanation for this incident might have been because the North Korean leader, Kim Il Sung, being of a mind not dissimilar to Johnson's, simply wanted to witness the fecklessness of the US government under President Johnson firsthand; Kim Il Sung was not the only head of state from around the world who must have pondered the real story about the USS Liberty incident, and how the most powerful albeit cowardly man in the world mishandled it and then dithered wildly as he tried to conduct the obvious cover-up of his own treason. Johnson may have even given Kim Il Sung the confidence he needed to carry on his own audacious agenda, seeing the affirmation before him: psychotics do run much of the world. The difference between the two incidents, both of which involved similar US spy ships, was that the Pueblo was attacked not by an ally, but an enemy. Instead of covering that one up, Johnson made sure that it was heavily reported, as he encouraged public outrage, even though he did nothing to protect the ship except order the drafting of fifteen thousand more reservists, and "the United States experienced a brief flush of patriotic fervor."(Shesol, p. 412). Commander Lloyd Bucher, the skipper of the Pueblo, acknowledged to the aforementioned author James Scott that the lack of a serious investigation of the Liberty was partly to blame for the Pueblo incident, that if the lessons that should have been learned, and analyzed – and the necessary procedural changes implemented – the Pueblo might have been better able to deal with the situation. Author Scott concluded by making note of the similar patterns brought out by these two attacks: "The similarities are a terrible confusion in command and control, a lack of response to desperate calls for assistance during the attack, and a cover-up for incompetency at the top."(Scott, James, p. 286).

48. Ron Kukal email to author Feb. 5, 2016

49. Clifford, p. 445

50. Ibid.

51. Hounam, *Operation Cyanide* p. 29

52. Ennes, pp. 46-48

Part II: The Survivors Speak – Chronicle of Events

John F. Kennedy

Chapter 3

The Attack on the *Liberty*

The very word "secrecy" is repugnant in a free and open society; and we are as a people inherently and historically opposed to secret societies, to secret oaths, and to secret proceedings.

– John F. Kennedy

A SUMMARY OF PRESIDENTIAL REACTIONS DURING THE EXECUTION OF THE PLANS

By the time the war began on June 5th, the people trying to manage and execute the top-secret, high-risk Operation Cyanide must have been apoplectic: Having the *Liberty* in place before war broke out would have been, in Secretary McNamara's "whiz-kids" project-management jargon, the "key task on the critical path" of the pre-established plan, and it would be absolutely essential for a successful launch. Indeed, the entire plan had been crafted around a launch date of June 15 – so important to the mission that it was reflected in its code name: "Frontlet 615". Getting that piece wrong would jeopardize the entire complex and sophisticated plan for the "spontaneous" Six-Day War, and that is exactly what happened.

On June 5th Israel launched the war ten days earlier than scheduled, first on Egypt and quickly extending it to Jordan and Syria. It had to have been Johnson's obsession with seeing Operation Cyanide go forward (despite that setback) that led to the calamitous events that then followed. For public consumption, Johnson had cautioned Israel against an attack, saying, "As your friend, I repeat even more strongly what I said yesterday to Mr. Eban. It is essential that Israel *just must* not take any pre-emptive military action and thereby make itself responsible for the initiation of hostilities," having personally added the words in italics to the cable to Prime Minister Eshkol.[1] Was his caution only related to a timing problem in starting the attack ten days early?

A day later, on June 6th, Johnson's top "national security" aide, Walt Rostow recommended that the Israelis not be forced to withdraw from the territories they had seized: "If the Israelis go fast enough and the Soviets get worried enough, a simple cease-fire might be the best answer. This would mean that we could use the de facto situation on the ground to try to negotiate not a return to armistice lines but a definitive peace in the Middle East."[2]

The next day, June 7th, after Jordan had joined the battle and Israel reacted by quickly capturing the Old City of Jerusalem, Ben Wattenberg and Larry Levinson wrote a memo to Johnson warning him that the U.N. might attempt "to sell Israel down the river." They again urged Johnson to support Israel's claim to the territories seized militarily. This was after David Brody, Director of the Anti-Defamation League of the B'nai B'rith stated his concern that the administration not force Israel to "lose the peace" after it had won the war and urging the president to stress the "peace, justice and equity theme" rather than "territorial integrity."[3] They said that such an action might even cause the American Jews protesting against him across the street in Lafayette Square to stop.

Either Johnson's known resentment for getting policy advice from relatively minor White House staffers such as Wattenberg and Levinson, or, as Joseph Califano wrote in his memoirs, Johnson was disappointed in some of his Jewish friends and staff helpfulness in drumming up more political support for him, which caused Johnson, spotting Levinson leaving Califano's office, to shout at him in a hallway as Johnson stormed towards him jabbing his fist into the air: "You Zionist dupe! You and Wattenberg are Zionist dupes in the White House! Why can't you see I'm doing all I can for Israel! That's what you should be telling people when they ask for a message from the president for their rally." Levinson later told Califano that after that dress-down by the president that he felt "shaken to the marrow of my bones."[4]

At that point the *Liberty* was on its final day of sailing into its position off the Sinai coast, having just been denied a destroyer escort that Commander McGonagle had requested.

THE "SURPRISE ATTACK" BEGINS:
THE FOURTH DAY OF THE "SPONTANEOUS WAR"

On the warm, sunny-bright day of June 8, 1967, starting at about 6:00 A.M., at least twelve, possibly thirteen Israeli aircraft of different types began surveilling the *Liberty*, some of which were only 1,000 feet or less in altitude, apparently to photograph and "map" her for later targeting purposes. The precision of the later attack could only have been accomplished through such preplanning, specifically identifying the priority targets, starting with the gun mounts to render the ship defenseless, followed by all of the forty-five different radio antennae and related transmitting equipment.

Beginning just before 2:00 P.M., three unmarked French-built Mirage III-C swept-wing fighter jets, without warning, settled into a triangular formation, aimed straight at the *Liberty* and proceeded to bore down on the ship in a fast low-level attack that began with rockets targeted at the four gun mounts and heat-seeking missiles aimed at the communications gear, with their warmed transmitters.

Senior Chief Stan White said, "It was as though they knew their exact locations ... Torn and mutilated bodies were everywhere," "Horrible sight!" [5] The Mirages shot up the ship, bow to stern, with armor-piercing rockets, missiles and a bomb that exploded near the whaleboat behind the bridge.

The crew of the *Liberty* did manage to jury-rig a new antenna and fix a broken transmitter sufficiently to begin broadcasting a call for help within ten minutes of the attack. One of the transmitters and its antenna was temporarily out of commission when the attack occurred, which prevented that transmitter from being destroyed since the heat-seeking missiles were attracted only to the transmitters that were then functional. [6]

During the attacks, Terry Halbardier risked his life to go out on the open decks as they were being strafed to string new cable from the only undamaged antenna to the main transmitter room; he was severely wounded in the process, but survived. Communications technicians James Halman and Joseph Ward quickly repaired the transmitters and patched them together to get a distress call off to the Sixth Fleet, despite intense jamming by the Israelis. "Any station, this is Rockstar," Halman signaled, using the *Liberty's* voice call sign: "We are under attack by unidentified jet aircraft and require immediate assistance." [7]

The efforts to get the message out took repeated attempts because the Israelis continued jamming not only the frequencies that had been in use by the ship and its sister ships and aircraft, but even the international distress frequency used for Mayday messages. This fact alone demonstrates advance knowledge of the planners in knowing exactly which radio frequencies to put out of commission. [8] Admiral Thomas Moorer, speaking in the video *The Loss of Liberty*, put it best: "The question is, if the Israelis thought that the frequencies they jammed were broadcast by the Egyptian ship, 'why did they jam the American frequencies.' There is no question about the fact that the jamming of the frequencies was deliberate, and was undoubtedly ordered by higher authority." [9]

Israeli apologists have never acknowledged that they did jam those frequencies, and this was one of the points that was deleted in the official Navy investigation, along with a number of other statements made by the survivors that would have been too difficult for Israel to defend. Another of those inconvenient truths was the fact that the aircraft were unmarked and still another was that the motor torpedo boats shot up two of the life-rafts that had been deployed and then took a third aboard one of the boats, apparently as a souvenir; thus, having all of these issues deleted from the subsequent Navy investigation. As survivor and co-author Ernie Gallo has stated, "It was obstruction of justice at the highest level."[10]

As soon as the Mirage jets left the scene, they were replaced by slower Super Mystere fighters, probably because they could rake the ship even more effectively. This was yet another indication of the meticulous planning that had been invested in a sophisticated attack. Another observation from Admiral Moorer is very pertinent to this point: "I have spent a large part of my life, flying over oceans and identifying ships, and this ship was perhaps the easiest ship to identify that was listed in the United States Navy: Equipped with antennae from bow to stern, pointing in every direction. It reminds one of a large, vigorous lobster, and it had a look that made it extremely easy to recognize. And so I would never, never, buy the idea that the pilots thought that this was some other ship."[11]

Chief Intelligence Officer David Lewis – miraculously saved by Robert J. "Buck" Schnell, who opened a closed hatch to save him – affirmed the precision of the well-planned attack: "The helicopters were sent to finish us off … The aircraft were sent to make us incommunicado, so that we couldn't send an S.O.S. out, the torpedo boats were sent to sink us, and the helicopters were sent to pick off survivors, so there would be no chance. It was a perfectly executed military operation… I wasn't supposed to be here; none of were supposed to be here."[12]

The strafing, with cannon-fire, rockets and gelled gasoline – famously known in Vietnam as "napalm" – continued, as though there was a concern that return fire might ensue from the ship, though the only four guns on board had been eliminated in the first strafing by the Mirage fighters. "Deafening explosions tore through the ship, and the bridge disappeared in an orange-and-black ball."[13] By this time, the Liberty was a "sitting duck", and with no other ships nearby since they had all cleared the area, having responded to the Pentagon's call for all ships to leave and remain no closer than one hundred (100) miles from the shoreline. The only ship which had not received that message was, paradoxically, the most capably equipped ship of the entire fleet to receive any form of electronic message.

After each attack, the planes would turn and circle back, making additional runs focused on the bridge, and on all other remaining communications gear and navigation equipment, including the radar, the gyro compass, the boiler deep inside the ship, even the rudder. These attacks continued for nearly twenty more minutes. The fathometer was the only instrument left that still worked, which was fortunate since there were shoals nearby. The linkages to the rudder were destroyed so the only way the ship could be controlled was to have men manually working it in the bilge, communicating with the bridge through sound-powered telephones.

In the first few minutes, five men topside had been killed and others were severely wounded, some which would shortly become fatal, including the executive officer Philip Armstrong. Commander McGonagle had received a serious shrapnel wound in his right leg, which soaked his trousers with blood as he rushed to different positions on the bridge, directing firefighting as he also attempted to take photographs of the attacking aircraft. Ensign David Lucas applied a tourniquet to the captain's leg, which allowed him to continue conning the ship.

Immediately after the Mystere aircraft attack, as if choreographed from afar, the crew were now frantically fighting the multiple fires when, at 14:24, three motor torpedo boats were sighted approaching the ship off the starboard quarter. At McGonagle's command, Signalman Russell Davis repaired the broken hoist mechanism and raised the large 7' X 13' holiday ensign to replace the original flag, which had been destroyed in the strafing attack by the Mirage jets. Minutes later, one of the motor torpedo boats flashed a message to the *Liberty*, but it could not be read due to the heavy smoke from the fires on the lower decks.

The French-built torpedo boats bore down on the disabled and defenseless ship near their top speed of 42 knots, until they were between 800 to 1,000 feet away. Then they continued to rake her decks with 20-mm. and 40-mm. automatic guns, killing four more American sailors. At 14:31, the captain ordered: "Stand by for torpedo attack, starboard side!" The first torpedo missed the stern by 75 yards and it was followed by three other misses. But at 14:35, the fifth torpedo hit the ship immediately forward of the machinery spaces, crashing outside the *Liberty's* special communications compartments. One of the numerous miracles to occur that day was that it hit an "I-beam" part of the super-structure, causing it to explode mostly outside the ship, which prevented it from destroying the bulkheads that contained the boilers. Had they been penetrated, the cold sea water hitting the hot boilers would have caused an explosion so large that the ship would have sunk within minutes, clearly what the attackers had counted on.

This sustained assault lasted nearly two hours and, including the period during which the boats and helicopters remained in threatening positions but no longer actively strafing the ship, the total was two and one-half hours, until 16:32, when the Captain himself stated "TORPEDO BOATS SEEM TO BE ISRAELI" as they retreated.[14] At this point, the only conclusion possible was that the attack had been well planned, clearly intentional, with an original objective of not merely attacking the ship, but to put it at the bottom of the sea, leaving no survivors. Had it been merely to stop its mission of data collection, that was accomplished within the first five minutes.

Therefore, the military objective had to go well beyond merely putting the ship out of commission: The only reason for all the heavy artillery was to sink the ship. Ernie Gallo stated that, as two assaault helicopters hovered overhead, he observed armed marines preparing to rappel down to the ship, however for unknown reasons the attack was called off just after the prepare-to-rappel order and all hostilities ceased.

Had those Israeli marines boarded the defenseless ship, it could only have been with the intent to rig it with powerful explosives to ensure that it sank. A possible reason for the cancellation of the final assault was the sudden presence of Russian ships nearby, making it impossible to finish the job under the cloak of secrecy without giving away who the attackers were, thus allowing the world to know the truth of the matter. The *Liberty* was finally saved only because the clock had run out. By then, the fact that the attackers were Israeli became too obvious to deny; only then did Israel stop the attack and claim that the whole thing was a terrible mistake. It was all due to their confusion over the identity of one of the most unique looking ships in the world. They claimed that this highly sophisticated, brutal attack was only to sink a smaller, worn-out hulk of a ship that was never a threat to anyone.

Photo # USN 1123509   USS Liberty maintains steerageway about 14 hours after attack, June 1967

The Crippled Liberty Steams Across the Mediterranean After the Attack
Note How the Napalm-Induced Fire Had Been Targeted to the Center (Bridge) Area

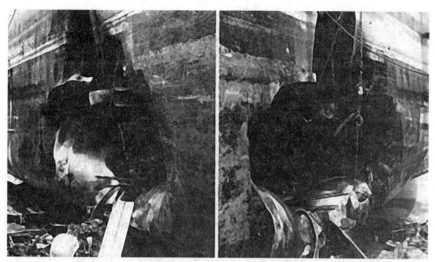

In Drydock at Malta: The Torpedo Hole (39 Feet Across at Bottom)

ON BOARD THE USS *LIBERTY*: SURVIVORS RECALL THE ATTACK:

Ron Kukal

C ome back with me if you will to June 8, 1967, come aboard the
USS *Liberty* just before, during and after the attack. Come down
with me to the dark, watery compartment where I was during the attack. Experience the power of God if you will, and learn. Believe me I
did.

This hell-raising kid who was born in Rushville, Nebraska and never
let any grass grow under his feet, learned plenty down there in a short
time, and I feel that it is not only my duty to tell you, but a command,
from our creator himself. I am approaching the age of 77, and my mind
is still pretty clear, hearing is not so good (according to my wife), but in
essence still a viable body, ready to do what needs to be done. It occurs
to me that some of us are allowed to live a bit longer because of a job you
are destined to do, and many think that is the case with me. I thank God
for whatever I can do to keep this great nation from going into the abyss,
because without change in direction, that is exactly where we are going.

The day of June 8th started out in a routine that really didn't cause
me any alarm at all, even though the men who slept in my compartment were buzzing about it very early that morning. Being the Super-
visor of one of the sections in the Research Department, I tended to
brush off the excitement, even though a prediction from Jeane Dixon,
a sort of prognosticator of that era, was in the back of my mind. She
had warned, as I remember, of a ship that would get in trouble in the
Mid-East, and in her warning she said little about the name of the ship.
She only seemed to know that it would happen. As a young Navy First

Class I poo-pooed her thoughts in a big way, and even on that very eventful day, I shoved what she had said to the back of my mind. What did she know, I said to myself, and was very satisfied with my own answer: "Nothing".

I was off to breakfast after a quick shower and shave. Breakfast was always an experience for me, and I learned to like chili beef on toast in a big way, especially the way our cooks made it. I know bragging about Navy chow doesn't happen often, but really it was always good. Breakfast was done, and I traversed my way to the research spaces, looking forward to doing what needed to be done to make my boss LCDR Ed Lewis happy.

We were scheduled for a General Quarters Drill right after noon chow, and so at 1300 I was at my GQ station, bright eyed and bushy tailed, waiting for the next orders from the 1MC (Ships Intercom) to go on with the drill. Long story short is that the drill went great and "Old Shep," our captain, was really very satisfied in the way it went. Old Shep was the affectionate name we had for Captain McGonagle. He was a stately older fellow, and was a stickler for making sure the ship was ready at all times for anything that might unexpectedly occur. Boy, was he right on that one. The GQ drill took an hour and then I headed back down to my work spaces, two decks down below the main deck. I might mention here that my work desk was about thirty to forty feet from the torpedo explosion when it happened. Keep that in mind for future reference.

I had just sat down when a sound that I had never heard before came rattling across the main deck up above me. I couldn't figure it out despite using everything in my still vivid imagination to try and call it something that would put me at peace about it all. There was nothing, absolutely nothing that could sway my mind into an inner peace that I sought. It happened again, maybe ten minutes or so from the first one, then again, and again. It could not be ignored, and little did I know right then, that my shipmates were dying – maybe twenty feet right above me. I sat there, time seemed to move forward, and backward, and then forward again. Maybe I was in a state of suspended animation, who knows?

Then I was suddenly awakened by the sound over the 1MC, and this time I became instantly awake. The voice said to prepare for torpedo attack. "What", I said to myself, "No way this could be happening, this is how other people die, not me." My mind would not accept what was going on, and I ran away in my imagination to another place and time, wherever that was. I waited and I watched the other men who were maybe ten feet from me or a little more. They were milling around, listening to their radios, trying to figure out what was going on, and then from out of nowhere it seemed like a voice came to me, and it was emphatic, "Get down, and get down now"! I didn't move fast enough and seconds before the torpedo hit, I was pushed to the deck. When it hit, only about 30-40 feet from my position, I don't remember the sound, but what I do remember is the feeling in the darkness, of objects flying through the air, and then we had an instant swimming pool, and I do mean instant. There were a couple of bulkheads between where I was and where the torpedo hit, and they were blown away like paper from the huge TNT explosion that tore up the bowels of the *Liberty*. Funny, I thought, how my whole compartment was instantly filled with water, after the distinct feeling of objects flying through the air. The men around me died, I would think, instantly. Not only would I think this, but I would hope that it was so, for their sakes. Little did I know at the time that, after the attack, I would be back down there as the enlisted man in charge of the body recovery and identification.

Some readers might ask right here, "who pushed me to the deck." You know, I never gave it a thought until years later, and it came out of nowhere again. Who told me to get down, who pushed me to the deck? There was no one around me, and so dear reader, I leave that one up to you. I like the expression: "I report, you decide." It fits quite well for me, and hope it does for you too. You see I know why I was pushed to the deck, why I am still alive, and there is no doubt in my mind. I am doing that very deed right now, writing my story for every American to see. There were other miracles that occurred that day that I didn't know about at the time, and one I heard about just a year or so ago. I often wondered why only the starboard side of the *Liberty* had the large hole, as it was my thought that a torpedo would go right through a ship, blowing up in the middle somewhere, tearing the ship apart. What I found out was simply that the torpedo had hit an "I" Beam and exploded prematurely.

So in my mind another miracle had occurred. One of the first was how I had survived the torpedo hit but then I was immediately immersed in seawater within one of the forward compartments as it flooded, and I came very close to drowning because the hatch to the deck above was dogged down (fastened from above) however, another sailor opened it from above just in time for me to escape. That was the third miracle I saw that day, although I hesitate to number them, only because I know there were other miracles happening everywhere throughout the ship, and I only observed or heard of a few.

I would never let it enter my mind nowadays, that we had survived this tragedy without help to do so. Too much devastation, left alone, with no help from the Sixth Fleet. I don't blame the Sixth Fleet at all, since I know there were men wanting to help us, but it wasn't going to happen if LBJ had anything to do with it, and I think he did. He had the help we needed in the planes that were coming to our rescue, and he had them turned around, because he had already decided to abandon us. Again, we were meant to go to the bottom with all hands on board, but even the best laid plans go awry, when Divine Intervention sets in.

Phillip F. Tourney

My first cruise aboard the *Liberty* was as a machinist's mate in the engine room. My job then was monitoring the gauges to ensure that all of the temperatures and pressures related to the ship's engines were operating normally. After a year in the engine room, I transferred to the ship-fitter's shop because I liked the type of "hands-on" work it involved, repairing broken equipment and learning other skills like welding. I worked under Lt. George Golden, the Chief Engineering Officer of the ship, who was affectionately referred to as the "Smoky Mountain Jew" because of his name, although he was known to be a Southern Baptist.

As we sailed into a war zone in the evening of June 7, 1967 we had all noticed that ships of all sorts were headed in the opposite direction. Despite this bad omen, our jittery, antsy mood had changed to one of excited invincibility, because our American flag was proudly waving high and we knew it could not possibly be unnoticed, therefore no one in their right minds would possibly attack our ship, even by "accident." That evening, our rushed 6,000 mile trip came to an end and we began slowly plying the waters off the Gaza Strip knowing that Israel had, for all intents and purposes, already won the war and Egypt, Jordan and Syria had already agreed to negotiate a peace plan at the United Nations. We finally began to relax a bit, now that the long and stressful trip was over and it looked like we had missed the worst of the war.

My job on the morning of June 8th was "Sounding and Security." I would make the rounds to ensure that everything on my check-list was in good condition and the ship was water-tight and "ship-shape" as I reported hourly to the bridge. I did not see the first over-flights by Israeli aircraft, but the other guys told me about them. We assumed that they were our "friends" and knowing that they were merely confirming that we were an American ship caused our moods to further lighten. After lunch, a General Quarters drill was conducted and right after that, I had to accompany another engineer to the starboard gun-mount on the forecastle (pronounced "foaxle") to fix the phone located there that was not working. David Skolak was the other sailor I went with and after I explained to him what needed to be done, his response was "No problem, Tourney. I'll get her working." This was about five minutes before the attack, at 2:00 p.m. As we stood there, we discussed the fact that this would be the worst possible place to be in the event of an attack on the ship, because the "gun-tub" and the guy manning it would be taken out as the first priority. I said goodbye to Skolak and the gunner and made my way down the ladder to the main deck and my workstation in the ship-fitter's shop. As I opened the hatch to go inside, I heard an order over the PA to test the motor whale boat. Just moments later, I heard a huge explosion right next to the hatch I had just closed. My immediate thought was that the test had gone wrong and the motor whale boat had blown up.

Not realizing that a rocket had just exploded directly outside the hatch, I grabbed the handle and opened it once more to go out and investigate the trouble. I had just barely put one foot outside when I felt myself grabbed by the shirt collar and violently jerked back inside. I turned and saw it was First-Class Petty Officer [Richard] Dale Neese, who ordered me to "Get Back! We're under attack!" The General Quarters alarm was then sounded and I made my way to my duty station, which was one deck above the mess decks. After going down the ladder, I slipped and fell and found myself under trampling feet of sailors as they made their way to their stations. I rolled over to my right side to get out of their way, got on my feet and joined the stampede to get to my station as well. I got into battle-dress and got my gear ready. Chief Thompson was the on-scene leader. As soon as I arrived, he said he'd been hit and was leaving to get medical care. Since I was assistant on-scene leader, this meant I was in charge. "It's all yours now, Tourney," he said as he made his way down the passage. I responded back, "Hey, thanks a lot, chief!" although I was not at all thrilled with this ad-hoc promotion.

I started my new duties by determining whether all damage control personnel were accounted for, but found out that several were missing, which was not surprising, considering the circumstances. The torrent of explosions I was hearing above and all around me had something to do with that, and the holes began appearing everywhere around us from the rocket and cannon fire was further evidence of the intensity of the attack, which I assumed must be the "enemies" of America, presumably the Arab countries that Israel was fighting against, since Israel was supposedly our "friend." In the middle of this onslaught, I caught a piece of shrapnel four inches long, in my right arm just above the elbow. I pulled it out, threw it on the deck and moved everyone in my department to the main deck. Once there, I went to the same gun-tub that I had visited earlier but saw only a pile of human remains – blood, hunks of human flesh, body parts and fragments of bone. Rick Aimetti was with me there, and we knew there was no life to be saved so we moved on; throughout this time machine-gun bullets and rocket fire were raining down on us as we crouched down behind various structures, leaping from one position to another.

Dead bodies were littered everywhere, but there were also wounded bodies that we knew had to be found and saved if possible. Between volleys of bullets and rockets, we darted out from safe cover, grabbed the wounded men one at a time, dragged them across the deck and assisted them down the hatch. Others from down below took them from there, and moved them to the mess halls where they could be treated. It took us at least fifteen minutes to clear the decks of those who were still alive and could be saved, about twenty-five men altogether. One of the worst cases I saw was Tom Reilly, a Boatswain's Mate, who was on his back and bleeding from multiple wounds and was covered with grey paint, which might have saved his life since it had become a giant bandage.

After all of the wounded had been recovered, I went to the log room, the location of Damage Control Central. I saw Ensign John D. Scott there, my superior officer, who was burning documents – standard procedure in the U.S. military. After briefing him and discussing the situation a few minutes, he ordered me to return to the deck to further assess the damages and put out any fires that were still burning. On the way back, I saw the many wounded men, bloody and moaning, begging me for help, but, as I had no medical training there was not much I could do to help relieve their pain. I got to the bridge and saw that Commander McGonagle was badly wounded in the leg but still in command. Rocket and cannon holes were everywhere and burning napalm was dripping through the holes into the bridge compartment. The CO_2 canisters were not effective in fighting that kind of fire and I requested a fire team with water hoses, but that didn't work either since the fire hoses had been shot up just like everything else. I told the Captain that I would return with some better equipment to fight the fires and he calmly replied, "Do what you can, sailor." He was always very professional and stoic, even under these incredibly violent, surreal circumstances.

On my way off the bridge, I looked at my good friend Francis Brown, a Third-Class Quartermaster, who was steering the ship. He was one of my best friends on the ship, and we hung out in better times, playing cards, drinking a few beers and joking together. We just locked eyes and communicated silently, that we might not make it through this one. I went off to find more CO_2 canisters and ran back towards the bridge, falling in the process, which caused a CO_2 canister to fly out of my hands and crash down on the deck with a bang that caused everyone, including Commander McGonagle, to look in my direction. As soon as I got up, I saw what had caused me to slip and fall: it was blood on the deck that hadn't been there moments before, when I left the bridge. It was my friend Francis Brown's blood, who had caught a machine gun bullet or a piece of shrapnel in the back of the head and his blood was everywhere. His eyes were closed but his face was swelled up like a balloon. It was something that no human being should ever have to see and especially when it is your good friend. My first thought was "Those Arab bastards, they just blew my friend to pieces." How could it have been anyone else: The Russians wouldn't have done it, certainly not our "beloved ally" Israel? Since the airplanes were not marked, it was not clear who had done this, but logic dictated that it must have been an Arab-run nation. I would soon find out about that mistake.

In a little while, after going below deck and seeing more scenes that looked like the inside of a slaughterhouse, with a cacophony of wailing and desperation in the background, the wounded men kept begging me to help them and it was frustrating for me not be able to do that, because I had to move them from the passageways and into the mess hall so they could get the medical attention they needed. Finally the jet attack was over and I went back to the top deck, and then saw torpedo boats coming at us at a high rate of speed. I saw who it was that wanted to destroy and sink our ship: The Star of David flags flying above these boats was quite a surprise and at first, I (again, mistakenly) assumed for a moment that they were there to come to our rescue. The delusion

Inspecting the Canon and Rocket Damage

lasted only a minute, because I then saw the splash of several torpedoes that they dropped into the water as they headed toward us.

Betrayal by a friend is always a very painful, heartbreaking experience, but this was more than one can adequately describe. We had been sent into that war zone for the purpose of helping them win their war and their payback for our loyalty, and the risks that we had taken to come to their assistance, was to intentionally attack us – clearly to purposely murder all of us – was *this*? I can't speak for the rest of the crew, because I can't read their minds, but for me, the knowledge that this had been done by a friend filled me with seething rage. I was determined to do whatever was necessary and at whatever cost to save the ship in whatever way I could. For whatever reason, knowing we had been betrayed by a friend made me stronger. But as angry as I was at the time, it was nothing compared to the anger I felt later, when I learned the terrible truth that we were betrayed not only by Israel, but by the highest levels of our own government.

The first four torpedoes were launched almost simultaneously. Had they all hit us, the *Liberty* would have sunk immediately and the rest of world history would have been written quite differently. Those four had, miraculously, all missed. Then the fifth one was fired and it was immediately obvious that it could not be out-maneuvered. The countdown began, we were warned to prepare for a torpedo hit and we hunkered down in "torpedo attack mode." This meant bending your knees and elbows, putting your hands against the bulkhead and relaxing your neck. And all of that is made nearly impossible as thoughts of your imminent death take over your mind.

When the explosion came it was literally deafening. I had been directly above the point where it hit, only about eight feet away, and the explosive percussion blew out my eardrums, an injury that never completely heals. We were all instantly airborne because the ship itself was picked up out of the water, then it came back down and bounced back up and down a few more times, nearly capsizing in the process. The new moaning and groaning was not coming from the wounded men, but now the wounded ship, as the rush of seawater flooding into the ship was reconfiguring some of the compartments down below. Since the ship itself did not blow up that meant that the torpedo did not hit the engine room because that cold sea water hitting the boilers would have caused the ship to be cut in half and both halves would have gone to the bottom within minutes.

Ensign Scott instructed me to determine where the torpedo had hit, so with Rick Aimetti at my side, we went to the Communication Spaces, where the spooks worked. I banged on the steel door with my fire axe, since I did not have the code to open it, and a voice told me that I was not authorized to enter the spaces. Rick and I told whoever it was on the other side to go to hell, saying that we were authorized to go wherever we had to go to keep the ship afloat. I told the person on the other side that if they did not open the door I would beat the door off of its hinges with my axe. Suddenly, the door opened. I went to the scuttle hatch and turned it, then opened it very slowly and I heard air escaping in our direction, which meant that the compartment was not filled already, but it was filling. Just as I opened it, I heard frantic banging on the other side, so I turned the wheel as fast as I could and Sgt. Bruce Lockwood, USMC, came scrambling out while pulling another sailor to safety as well. Aimetti and I grabbed the two and yanked them out of the hole. Ensign Scott came up carrying a battle lantern and ordered me to give him my belt. I did as he asked and he used it to lower the lantern into the water to check for any more signs of life. After a few moments, we looked at each other and he asked what I thought. "Sir," I said, "I think we had better seal her up."

Now the torpedo boats, having used all their torpedoes against us, began firing at us with machine guns, shooting anything that moved, including firefighters and stretcher-bearers. One of the guys I was pulling to safety got hit right above the knee with a .50 caliber slug, causing an explosion of blood and bone. I took off my shirt and tied the sleeves around the top of his leg as tight as I could get it to stop the bleeding. We got him down to the mess decks and untied the tourniquet for just a few seconds so that they wouldn't be forced to amputate his leg later, then we retied it before leaving the area.

Aimetti and I went back up to the main deck and saw that the gunners on the torpedo boats were now shooting at the ship on the waterline, aiming in the direction of the boilers and from merely thirty-five yards away. Clearly, they were trying now to blow up the ship by hitting the boilers and causing that huge explosion that their last torpedo failed to accomplish. Throughout the course of the torpedo boat attack, they circled the ship like vultures, as close as 100 feet. To suggest that they might have missed the huge lettering on both sides of the bow, in 10 foot high letters, as well as the "USS *Liberty*" lettering on the stern, would require anyone, especially a U.S. military judge or even one from Israel, to suspend any semblance of cognitive thinking ability.

All of the sounds of these machine guns and the sheer hell taking place might have been the reason that there was some controversy of whether Commander McGonagle ordered "All crew prepare to abandon ship." But I heard that order, probably because he felt that there was no possibility at that point that we could save the ship.

He was probably not yet aware that nearly all of the life boats were either destroyed by rockets, gunfire or napalm. There were only three left, and I personally put one of them into the water as I watched all three inflate, only to see them immediately shot up. Two sank but one of them was taken aboard one of the boats as a trophy. That capped the series of horrors I witnessed that day, and told me as clearly as anything else that the IDF was sent out there for the express purpose – not just to cripple the ship and take it "out of commission" so that it could not eavesdrop on their communications – but to sink our ship, and the act of destroying our lifeboats was an unmistakable sign that they wanted no survivors left to tell anyone what had happened.

Shortly after the boats left the scene, from far off in the distance but closing in fast, came the unmistakable "whomp, whomp, whomp" sound of a very large, troop-carrying helicopter approaching the ship on the starboard side. Now the 1MC system blared, "ALL SHIP'S PERSONNEL PREPARE TO REPEL BOARDERS." So now, after all the other precision military arsenals of our close ally were brought to bear on our ship, and failed to sink her, we were about to be boarded by Israeli marines armed with sub-machine guns against us, after the only machine guns on the ship had been destroyed in the first wave of attacks. Even if we could get to them in time, the only other guns on the ship were small fire arms, pistols, and a couple of shotguns that we might use to set up a last line of defense. Aimetti and I tried to open the locker with our fire axes, since the master at arms was not to be found, who was the only one with a key. Even after beating that lock nearly to pieces, we could not break it.

The commandos on board the helicopter above appeared to be ready to rappel onto the ship, ready for close-quarter combat with a bunch of defenseless, bedraggled sailors worn out from two hours of sustained attacks. It would have been a "turkey shoot," but we were not about to go without a fight for our lives. Had they proceeded, they could have murdered the entire crew and then they could proceed to use whatever explosives they had on board the helicopter to guarantee the ship's destruction.

As the helicopter hovered overhead, no more than 75 feet away, I locked eyes with one of my would-be assassins who was sitting on the floor of the helicopter. His legs were hanging out, and he had one foot on the skid below as he waited for the order to rappel down to the ship's deck and finish us off. As I stood on the deck of my bloody and battered ship, I thought about everything that had happened over the course of that afternoon, and about my good friends, Francis Brown and David Skolak, and all the other men, whose remains were strewn all over the ship. The only tool I had left was my middle finger, and I used it to let him know what I thought of him and the rest of his team. He simply gave me a sneering kind of "smile" and returned the gesture. Then, suddenly, instead of a team of commandos streaming down ropes to murder us all, the helicopter revved up its engine and hauled ass out of there like a vampire being exposed to sunlight. The sight of them scurrying off sent a wave of euphoria through the crew.

Ernest A. Gallo

The USS *Liberty* was a converted WW II Victory hull cargo vessel that had been been restored and retrofitted in the early 1960s to become one of the most advanced intelligence ships of that period. It had very large, ten feet high, US Navy markings (GTR 5) that any other ship or aircraft could see from far away, and of course could be identified quickly using the reference manual *Jane's Fighting Ships*. If there were any doubt about its identity, a quick look at its stern would clear it up: "USS *Liberty*" was emblazoned across it, also in very large letters. As well, a five-by-eight-foot American flag typically flew high on her center yardarm. The ship was under the control of the NSA, and the Naval Security Group personnel were referred to as Communications Technicians (CTs). All of the men selected for this service were subjected to close scrutiny and given secrecy clearances; they were all admonished to never discuss their activities with anyone else, including the rest of the ship's crew. Their skills included electronic and cryptographic communications and repair, signal intercept specialists (some with the old standard Morse code skills), linguists, communicators and yeomen. There were approximately 150 security group (CTs) on board, monitoring radio, radar and telemetry intercepts. Our section was located amid-ship (the center), below the main deck and in an enclosed area which was off-limits to other crew members. The area was sealed except for a single door having a cipher number keyboard to control entry to eligible personnel. There was an emergency escape hatch as well. The fact that the area was sealed off from the rest of the ship was one factor that saved the ship when the torpedo hit it, directly into our section.

The way we were suddenly ordered to proceed from our scheduled four-day "R&R" and maintenance stop in Abidjan, Ivory Coast after having just arrived there one day before, and being ordered to proceed at best possible speed to Rota, Spain was highly unusual, and alarming to all the crew. We picked up three NSA civilians and three marines, who were all linguists: Russian, Arab and Egyptian. On June 2nd we left Rota and entered the Mediterranean, observing the fact that several Russian destroyers began shadowing us, adding to our sense of imminent danger.

We were aware that Commander McGonagle had requested a destroyer escort for our protection, but that was denied, and we were left with the minimal protection of four .50 caliber machine guns against the Soviet armada, and whatever Egypt's navy might throw at us. On June 5th, as we sailed across the sea south of Italy, we heard about the start of the Israel-Arab war and how Israel had completely wiped out the air forces of Egypt, Jordan and Syria on the first day, then conquered Gaza and the left bank belonging to Jordan as well as the Sinai Peninsula. Finally, after over two weeks of sustained rushing to get there, we arrived at our assigned destination off the Sinai Peninsula on the evening of June 7th.

We found out later that the NSA commanders were also very concerned about our safety and had instructed the Joint Chiefs of Staff (JCS) to move us to a minimum of 100 miles off shore, but somehow the order got misrouted and was sent to the Philippines, of all places. And it turned out this wasn't the only such order that had been mishandled, there were at least four that did not get to us, ordering us out of the area, where we were slowly cruising off the Sinai coast, anywhere from 13 to 20 miles away from the war zone.

On the morning of June 8th, as we tended to our regular duties, we noticed several flights of low-flying Israeli aircraft over a seven hour period. I personally witnessed some of these and on one occasion a number of us waved to the Israeli pilot who was so close to us that we could see his face. He waved back in a friendly manner which was comforting to us, knowing that Israel, our ally, had dominated the war for its first three days, and all the signs were that the worst was over. All of the pilots doing this surveillance on our ship would have noticed that, in addition to the ship's markings, "Old Glory" was proudly flying and sailors were scattered around the ship on beach chairs, blanket or towels soaking up the sun's rays. This was not a fighting ship and certainly no threat to either side, except perhaps in the most intangible, ephemeral way that attended our mission, and what they all knew we were up to, which was our own method of "surveillance." For them to be giving us such close scrutiny was itself mysterious; little did we know it was for their superior's use in planning how to set up the attack for which they were then making their last minute adjustments.

The reason that those overflights were obviously done to help plan the attack is because the attack by the Israeli Defense Force (IDF) was very well planned and precisely executed in three well coordinated phases: two sets of Israeli Air Force aircraft, followed immediately by three Navy torpedo boats and then two helicopters filled with marines armed with automatic rifles who were prepared to rappel down to the ship, obviously for the purpose of finishing the job that the first waves of attackers had started. The attack was suddenly halted either because a Russian destroyer had reportedly begun monitoring the scene or because Israel mistakenly thought that American fighter jets were finally coming to the scene, when in fact, the president himself cancelled that rescue attempt, for the second time that morning. (Since all the pertinent records that might answer that question remain sealed, we cannot know which of these explanations is correct).

Suddenly I heard the first sounds of the attack by the Israeli fighter jets strafing the ship with 30mm cannon fire and rockets. The announcement came over the public address system (called "1MC"): "This is no drill – man your general quarters." The sounds from above told me that all hell had broken loose and for a few moments I felt lucky to have lots of metal between me and the action, but then I realized that some of the rockets and missiles were exploding upon impact and coming right through those metal barriers. The initial attack killed the four sailors manning the machine guns, blowing their body parts over the decks. The subsequent attacks killed three of our shipmates and mortally wounded our executive officer, Lt. Commander Philip Armstrong. Shortly after that, other jets arrived and dropped napalm bombs (gelled gasoline) onto the deck, which ignited a fifty-five gallon gasoline drum and engulfed the ship in huge flames. The pilots even shot at the firefighters, and the men who had scrambled onto the decks with stretchers as they attempted to retrieve the wounded men.

The pilots had obviously been given very specific objectives as to what to target. They were uncannily accurate in placing rockets through the ship's port holes – one of which killed the helmsman. On one pass, Seaman Larry Weaver was spotted by an Israeli pilot trying to hide behind a stanchion (a large round metal device about two feet around used to dock the ship). Apparently, the Israeli pilot who was focused on Larry returned to take him out, shooting a rocket at him and severely wounding him by opening his lower midriff. He had to push his own intestines back into his lower Abdomen and crawl into the ship for cover. Larry needed thirty-four operations over the years to repair his injuries, and found out that someone had tried to fudge his records to hide the fact that he had even served on the *Liberty*. To correct that record, and qualify for the disability that he had been denied, he was forced to retain an investigator at his own expense to prove that he was in fact on board the ship when it was attacked.

The air attack lasted twenty-five minutes, although it seemed to go on forever. There was still a fire that created a lot of smoke but the Captain saw that the flag had been shot down and ordered the Signalmen to run up the extra large flag previously reserved for holidays hoping that it would be seen, if any more attackers came, which indeed followed immediately thereafter; the new attackers came on the scene shortly after the fighter jets left, this time in motor torpedo boats but they didn't seem to have noticed that huge flag. We noticed theirs, though: the Israeli Star of David. They began strafing the ship with cannon fire and then launched four torpedoes at us, one at a time, but those four all missed the ship. A fifth torpedo was then fired at us on the starboard (right) side. I thought, "this is it, I am going to die now." I sat down and pushed myself up against equipment racks and prayed like I have never prayed before, whispering an "Act of Contrition." Right after that, I heard the loudest explosion that I had ever heard. I will never forget its sound, or the horror of how the ship rose out of the water, seemingly about to capsize as the port side pitched over into the water, before righting itself but listing about 10 degrees to port.

Commander McGonagle inspired the crew to be professional and resolute and we all tried to do that because that is what it would take if we were to survive. The helicopters, filled with armed paratroopers prepared to rappel down to the ship, still remained a threat and I asked Lieutenant Bennett if we could get weapons from the small weapons locker to prepare to defend ourselves but he refused, saying that we would wait for the Captain's orders. Then the strafing stopped so I went out to the deck to see what was going on, seeing that an Israeli helicopter with troops was still hovering overhead. Moments later, it departed; we believed that they had intercepted a message warning that the second sortie of fighter jets was on its way to protect us, despite the fact that immediately after they were dispatched, the president had recalled them. Other rumors were that a nearby Russian destroyer had come into the area and was then too close and the operation was terminated to avoid them observing the final act of sinking us. Of course, it may have been that both of these reasons applied, but we, and the rest of humanity, will probably never know for sure just what caused us not to sink under a final deadly assault that might have set off a much larger conflagration between the two world "superpowers."

OTHER VOICES

Survivor Joe Lentini stated to author Peter Hounam:[16]

> "I felt something blow on my leg; I looked down and the upper thigh on my left pant leg had a six-inch tear in it – and so did my upper thigh. That saved my life. A guy was coming toward me with a bandage. And that's the last thing I remember until I came to. [When] I woke up, it was pitch black and I was in water. I tried to stand up and put my weight on my left leg and it wouldn't support me, obviously I fell back down; I didn't know at the time I had six broken ribs, a collapsed lung, a fractured skull, both tympanic membranes in my ears were blown out, shrapnel all over me in my body ... it never occurred to me that I didn't have a leg and it never occurred to me that I was about to die."

It was only then that he realized that everyone else he had been working with at that moment had died, and as he pondered it, he became conscious of the fact that he had been the lucky one. After the eighteen-hour wait for help to arrive, he was finally evacuated to the Portsmouth Naval Hospital in Virginia, where he met a submarine sailor who told him: "We were there, [on] our submarine. We saw the whole thing. We took pictures. Then we sent an officer back to the Pentagon to deliver them."

Lentini was astonished, so much so that he failed to ask the man's name or his vessel, and he never saw him again.[17] That sailor had been on a submarine, one of three, possibly more, that, according to him and others, had been positioned in the area, although this much larger presence in the area of the war zone has never been acknowledged by anyone at the Pentagon. In fact, the USS *Requin*, one of the submarines, according to author Peter Hounam, was allegedly involved in filming the attack and to have allegedly delivered that film to the USS *Davis*.[18] Other submarines allegedly in the area include the USS *Amberjack* and the USS *Andrew Jackson*.

The Sixth Fleet, not coincidentally positioned off the coast of Crete, consisted of a huge US Navy flotilla that included two aircraft carriers, the USS *America* and the USS *Saratoga*, and many support ships as well as submarines. A CIA report stated that the "Sixth Fleet Commander had notified Washington at 8:30 a.m. [EDT] that the *Liberty* had been hit by a torpedo. A National Security Agency report said the aircraft carrier USS *Saratoga* relayed a message to its London naval headquarters that "Rockstar" (*Liberty*'s call-sign) was requesting immediate assistance, and it added: 'I AM UNDER ATTACK MY POSIT 31 23N 33 25E. I HAVE BEEN HIT.' London headquarters recorded that Saratoga relayed a signal from the *Liberty* at 8:40 a.m. saying 'UNIDENTIFIED GUN BOATS APPROACHING ... NOW.'"

At 8:45 [EDT] another message reported the torpedo hit, asking for immediate assistance.[19] After several SOS attempts the radiomen took comfort in the belief that their plight would now be known throughout the Sixth Fleet. They assumed that the Pentagon and White House would quickly react and cause help to be dispatched to them soon.[20] And there was an immediate response, though it was not apparent to the sailors on the *Liberty*: The first carrier-based bombers and fighter jets of the Sixth Fleet were launched from less than 500 miles away, soon after the SOS signals had been received. In addition to a squadron of fighter jets, two A-4 bomber aircraft were launched from the USS *America*, which carried nuclear weapons and were bound for Cairo, according to Mike Ratigan, who served on board that carrier as a center-deck catapult operator responsible for maintaining the catapult in working order. He remembered the call to general quarters (battle stations) in the early afternoon of June 8, 1967, later learning that this was due to the attack on the *Liberty*.

The A-4 bombers were each fitted with two bombs having a gold-colored tip, a type that he had never seen before. "I'd never seen that particular type of ordnance, and as we had gone into Condition November (notice of imminent nuclear war) subsequent to being in general quarters, it was definitely not a drill. Marine guards were escorting the A-4, and that was a very unusual experience. I'd never seen anything like that in the four years that I was in the Navy as a Cat operator."[21] When all the Navy aircraft were recalled by McNamara, almost immediately after they took off, the fighter jets returned but the A-4s did not reappear for another four or five days. The reason for that was explained by one of the pilots of the A-4s, who admitted that he had been carrying nuclear bombs and had been ordered to target Cairo. After being recalled, they had to be diverted to a land-based airstrip because the nuclear bombs made the aircraft too heavy and dangerous to land back on the aircraft carrier.[22]

THE ADMIRAL WHO ORDERED SQUADRONS OF FIGHTER JETS TO THE RESCUE – ONLY TO BE RECALLED

Chief Petty Officer J.Q. "Tony" Hart worked in a U.S. Navy relay station in Morocco, processing communications between Washington and the 6th Fleet; he stated that he had listened to a conversation between Defense Secretary Robert McNamara, in Washington and Rear Admiral Lawrence Geis, commander of the USS *America's* carrier battle group. In that call, Hart said that McNamara ordered Admiral Geis to recall the squadron. Geis was stunned by that order, so he explained that he had a duty to send the squadron of fighter jets to defend the *Liberty* from the attackers. Hart said that McNamara responded that "*President Johnson is not going to go to war or embarrass an American ally over a few sailors.*"[23] The first call was made at 8:25 a.m. Washington time (2:25 p.m at *Liberty*'s location off the Sinai) just after the fighter jets left, and just before the torpedo boats arrived to take their place. Had those U.S. aircraft been allowed to continue their mission, they would have undoubtedly been able to defend the ship and attack the attackers; in doing so, they would have also saved the ship from the worst damage: the torpedo that killed twenty-four men in the communication room.

McNamara's comment was stunning in a myriad of ways, not the least of which was the audacity and brutality of a White House decision that knowingly allowed a U.S. Navy ship to be savagely attacked while making no effort to either prevent the attack or even attempt to rescue the 294 men on board. But nearly as unbelievable as that, was the surprise – to the admiral – that the Secretary of Defense already knew that the attackers were known to be "allies," rather than presumed enemies. Since they had not yet been identified, even by the men on the *Liberty,* how did Secretary McNamara already know that? This alone should be sufficient to show that McNamara, ergo, Lyndon Johnson, knew all about what had happened even before it occurred. And that also explains why B-52s loaded with nuclear bombs were already on alert in California, and Clark Clifford had already been called to the White House approximately two hours before the "secret attack" was even started. If the USS *Liberty* had sunk, as Johnson wanted, Israel and the world, would have blamed Egypt.

The second time McNamara recalled the fighter jets – over an hour later, after the jets were reconfigured to remove any notion that they carried nuclear bombs – he told Admiral Geis that President Johnson had ordered the aircraft to be returned, saying "He would not have his allies embarrassed, he didn't care who was killed or what was done to the ship."[24] According to other sources, President Johnson, known for his ruthlessness and vile profanity, told Geis, *"I want that goddamn ship going to the bottom. No help–recall the wings."* Tony Hart, the Navy communications technician stationed at the U.S. Navy Base in Morocco in June 1967, reported that McNamara added, "We are not going to war over a bunch of dead sailors."[25] That same Robert McNamara, in 2003, denied all of it, saying "I'm absolutely certain that's false.... I don't know what the hell happened, and I haven't taken the time to find out"[26] (Implicitly stating that the matter is of no significance to him, and that it shouldn't be to anyone else either. Just before he died at age 91, in 2007, McNamara was still denying his obvious involvement, telling the *Chicago Tribune* that he had "absolutely no recollection of what I did that day," except that "I have a memory that I didn't know at the time what was going on."[27]

Survivor George Golden, the *Liberty's* chief engineer, provided the most revealing of Hounam's interviews; according to him, "'They didn't want any survivors,' he said. 'I was told when we got into Malta – and I'm not going to mention any names – that their orders were to sink that ship and kill everyone on it. I have nothing to prove it, [but] I have a lot of messages – secret messages; even in Washington they tried to get some of these from me. I won't say where some of this came from. The crew all feel that McNamara and Johnson were looking for an excuse to jump in and help Israel." Golden also stated that the alleged messages to warn the *Liberty* to stay 100 miles away from the danger zone were "*deliberately blocked*" and not simply "misrouted" as the cover-up story alleged.[28] [Emphasis added]. This point – rarely raised by researchers amazed by the stunning coincidence of a sudden breakdown of the sophisticated communications systems unique to that ship, that caused messages intended to warn the *Liberty* to leave its position, to be lost – should be taken as a sign that perhaps the assertion is true; it certainly conforms with many other indications that the *Liberty* was purposefully put into harm's way and deliberately left there during and after the attack.

It also conforms with a story reported in the 1978 book, *Conspiracy of Silence: The Attack on the USS Liberty*, written by author Anthony Pearson, as previously noted does contain certain errors in basic facts, such as the date the ship arrived at its post off of the Sinai coast. That does not mean everything in it is in error. Indeed, there were certain assertions made in the book that were strongly denied, for decades, by critics of that book, which were ultimately vindicated; one of which was Pearson's claim that the Soviet Union had stationed two Echo-class missile submarines off the coast of Israel during the Six-Day War which they planned to use if Israel escalated the war through missile attacks against Baghdad, Cairo or Damascus (pp. 161-162).

It was later determined that there actually were Russian submarines nearby ready to nuke Israel under certain conditions, according to Richard Thompson, who helped produce the BBC documentary *Dead in the Water*. Thompson learned from Russian naval historian and author Nikolai Cherkoschin – who interviewed the captain of a nuclear submarine that was there – who said of the missiles: "These missiles were armed with nuclear warheads and could be used to attack the shore in the worst case scenario. If in an extreme situation, under high command, it was possible to attack Haifa, the largest Israeli seaport." Another assertion made by Pearson was that secret congressional hearings were conducted in the immediate aftermath which revealed that "two of the pilots involved in the attack had been Americans – ex-Navy fliers." Furthermore, he stated that Israel had routinely recruited American ex-pilots who "emigrated" to Israel and that he had personally met two captured "Israeli" pilots from the Yom Kippur War (1973) who were actually Americans.[29]

Regarding the highly credible George Golden's assertion that the messages to the Liberty were intentionally blocked, according to Pearson, "It had quickly become clear to the observers on [the] *Liberty* that the strength of the Israeli offensive lay in a superb intelligence capability … Somewhere between Cairo and Amman in a field relay station hastily constructed in Sinai, [Arabian] messages were being blocked by the Israelis, reconstructed and passed on so swiftly and effectively that there was no apparent break … In the language of electronic intelligence this type of interference is called 'cooking.'"[30] This "factoid" is not conclusive in and of itself and might have not been the cause of all the lost or misdirected messages. However, given all the other mysteries and unresolved anomalies connected to this story, neither should it be lost between the cracks. Yet the fact that the attack itself, as well as the larger plan for employing U.S. military assets to work covertly for Israel in its conduct of the war, had been planned for months before the war commenced, makes it just as likely that the lost messages were always a part of that plan, regardless of the methods used to keep them from being received by the *Liberty*.

When asked whether the orders not to help the *Liberty* came from the president, George Golden responded, "Yes" and then said that he knew two of the officers who came to Malta to investigate the incident and one of them said to him, "George, they really did it to you, old boy.… You were a damned guinea pig."[31] Finally, Golden told Hounam that he had talked to Captain William McGonagle at length before McGonagle died, and Golden intimated to Hounam that McGonagle had been warned to expect a mild "strafing attack" as part of a set up. McGonagle went on to say that "'Those SOBs [sons of bitches] really did us in, George.' I said, 'What are you talking about?' and then he told me that [it was] the President and McNamara – that he had straight information, through Fort Meade [NSA], that *when they sent us up from over in Africa, we were there to have this happen.*"[32] [Emphasis added.]

This is a startling, yet sobering, comment: *"when they sent us up from over in Africa, we were there to have this happen."* George Golden was a man well respected by all his fellow shipmates for his plain-spoken, non flamboyant manner, whose reputation was as solid as the Rock of Gibraltar that they had passed as they sailed on their way to their "fate."

The only solace in the failure to sink the USS *Liberty*, if anything comforting can possibly be said about that sordid tragedy is that a series of miracles and the toughness of the survivors on board kept it from sinking. And it is they who have continued their heroic efforts for five decades, and kept the issue alive so that the rest of us may learn from the past.

A working hypothesis begins with the premise that President Lyndon B. Johnson initiated the overall plan for Frontlet 615 (what would become known as the Six-Day War), as a confrontation between Israel and its Arab neighbors, chiefly the U.A.R., [Egypt]. As we noted previously, the evidence already collected by other authors indicates that the earliest parts of the plan had already commenced by 1965, with some military operations already in progress, including the mission that Joe Sorrels became involved with doing "freelance special operations" on a joint plan between Israel and the United States involving elements of military intelligence to engineer a war with Egypt and depose its leader Gamal Abdul Nasser. By August 1966, he was already working in that capacity as "part of an extensive, covert, foreign military presence."[33] The mission was to train and tutor Israeli officers for a planned war that was-imminent.

In order to reach a broader understanding of what really happened to the USS *Liberty*, the hypothesis would have been to provoke a war between Israel and Egypt, and set it up so that the blame would be put on Egypt, while portraying Israel as the "innocent" party. That would enable Israel to keep the "spoils of war" – the expanded borders and enhanced military strength for them, while simultaneously weakening their Arab neighbors.

There was a precedent for a "false flag" operation taking place when it did: The similarity was the long-planned provocations in 1964 that led to the Gulf of Tonkin (phantom) "attacks" precisely three months before the November presidential elections that year. That operation guaranteed Johnson's landslide re-election in 1964; the resulting war had since backfired on him and he knew that he could use an even larger, more ominous event to guarantee him re-election in 1968. When the *Liberty* refused to sink, so did his chances for being re-elected.

The hypothesis includes a smaller, even more audacious sub-part of the plan, called Operation Cyanide, that involved sacrificing the USS *Liberty* as the means for Johnson to insert the U.S. military machine on the side of Israel, to "defend" her against the marauding Arabs who would be portrayed as having sunk a great, highly valued naval vessel and killed a crew of nearly three hundred in the process.

The nation, according to this purported plan, would have immediately understood the reason for his quick and decisive retaliation. It would be done under the battle cry of "Remember the *Liberty*!" and finally the war protestors would see and understand how their great leader had been correct about his efforts to halt the growth of communism. A thankful nation would rally around him and give him another victorious landslide election, maybe even by larger margins than his previous one.

LESSONS NEVER LEARNED

In 1964, millions of copies of a book, *"A Texan Looks at Lyndon"* by James Evetts Haley, on some of Lyndon Johnson's earliest crimes were distributed (in Texas, it was second only to the Bible in sales that year). The voting public – anxious to avoid an unnecessary war that Johnson had pretended to also want to avoid, and in memory of John F. Kennedy – decided that he had performed well in his first year, so decided to elect him to his own term, by a landslide. And again, in 1968, a book was published in Germany by Joachim Joesten titled *The Dark Side of Lyndon B. Johnson,* which went even further than Haley's book, stating: "I openly accused Johnson of complicity in the assassination."[34]

Nearly all previous books on the USS *Liberty* attack have given Lyndon Johnson the benefit of the doubt regarding his possible complicity in pre-arranging the logistics of making it happen. Some have noted his disgusting actions *after-the-fact* and have left it at that, as though the acts were done merely in a reflexive, unplanned and spontaneous haste to protect Israel. Anthony Pearson's 1978 book, which preceded the Ennes book, described a situation in Washington, where Congressmen Craig Hosmer, a Republican from California and Thomas Abernethy, a Mississippi Democrat, among others, complained about the the president's unwillingness to take meaningful action and to determine what had happened: "Washington was 'as quiet as the tomb' about the whole event. Where was American pride? Where was her indignation at the affront to her dignity?"[35] He went further, saying that those congressmen, as well as the Joint Chiefs and others who had been indignant about the attack, "… had never been privy to the secret war plans of the CIA and the highest advisers of Lyndon Johnson. If they had been, they might have been appalled; but at least they would have understood the reluctance of the Government (sic) to approach the problem. Its plan was simple: it had to cool everything, to cover up."[36]

Besides the Pearson book, which was the first book written on the subject as well as the first to at least suggest a similar plot, another early one was Stephen Green's 1984 book *Taking Sides: America's Secret Relations with a Militant Israel,* which posited the idea that it was from within the White House that the planning and the succession of preparations for war emanated, and that there were many indications that the ensuing operations "were being orchestrated" from the White House[37] (an interesting footnote to that sentence stated that the staff which coordinated it " … wished to specifically exclude the State Department from the group of "orchestrators."). Then the author asked, rhetorically: "Was all of this merely naive and simplistic, or was it something else – part of a 'scenario' in which the Israelis were 'unleashed' … The answer to that question depends, of course, upon whether Rostow and the Johnson White House were merely reacting to the events of the war, or had a hand in planning them, even participated in them."

Another book which alluded to this possibility was the previously cited British author and film-maker Peter Hounam, who outlined the broader aspects of it when he wrote that the focus of his seminal book *Operation Cyanide* was "… also on the Johnson White House and the President's desperation about being re-elected. The Vietnam War was being lost and his dream of a second term was fading. In the midst of trying to revive his popularity, he nearly blundered into a nuclear war."[38]

Author Philip Giraldi, in a March 17, 2011 article in *The American Conservative*, titled "Sinking Liberty: Who will write the final chapter on Israel's 1967 confrontation with the U.S. Navy?"[39] also pointed directly to the the same premise as we present here (which, coincidentally, we humbly suggest, may ultimately be the response to the question he raised in the sub-title):

> Confirmation that the *Amberjack* was in the area and that it had made a film and photo record of the attack suggest a number of lines for further inquiry. First and foremost has to be the issue of possible prior knowledge or even connivance by the White House in what was about to take place. Was it happenstance that the submarine was in the same location as the *Liberty* or was it by design? Was there any advance notice to Washington that an attack might take place? Could the USS *Liberty* have been an intended victim of a false flag simulated Egyptian attack, leading to American involvement on behalf of Israel in the fighting? Though that line of inquiry might appear implausible, the White House ordered the return of US warplanes sent to assist the *Liberty*, suggesting that Johnson knew who the attackers were in spite of the fact that the Israelis had covered over their aircraft markings in an apparent attempt to blame the Egyptians. One might also recall the Gulf of Tonkin incident.

In a sense, we are merely taking the germ of an idea planted by these previous news articles and books, and extrapolating, as we put many other aspects of the story together under a microscope and begin "connecting the dots" from one to another, and so on, linking them linearly, until the entire sketch is done. The one major gap left by the earlier works is their failure to link Lyndon Johnson's psychological state during the period of his entire presidency, which we have examined in the context of everything else.

It was known immediately that at least 25 men were killed and over 100 men injured, but these statistics were withheld from the public. They were told the numbers were 4 dead and 53 wounded. Within a few days, it had been established that 34 men were killed and 171 injured (later revised to 174 injured). Yet President Johnson announced that only "10 men" were killed and 100 injured, and amazingly still used those figures in his memoirs, *Vantage Point,* published *four years later.* That he could still state this lie as a "fact" four years after the event is the clearest evidence one could ask for as to the effectiveness of

the cover-up he had engineered. This strange lapse, not only of the press generally, but of the publisher and the ghost-writer, Doris Kearns, who let that distortion stand, should have itself been major news. But in this case, the presidential myth was to be completely unquestioned, and by then, the news media and the public seemed to accept Johnson's prevarications as merely extensions of his presidential "eccentricities," simply a fact of life which did not rise to the level of comment, much less indicative of his "inability to tell the truth," to paraphrase JFK's famous observation about his vice president.

This was understandable in a sense, because throughout his life, he would believe whatever "facts" he wanted to believe because he honestly could not tell the difference in truth and lies. Having told so many lies, he would convince himself that whatever he believed was the "truth" and everyone else was supposed to accept that. To him, the myths were much more powerful and important than whatever "facts" one wanted to believe.

These observations are not simple hyperbole of his chroniclers; all of these assertions have been made by the most prolific of Johnson's biographers. One example came from his aide George Reedy, who once said about Johnson's veracity: "Whatever Johnson tells you at any given moment he thinks is the truth."[40] His aide Joseph Califano wrote that he "would quickly come to believe what he was saying even if it was clearly not true."[41] And on another occasion "Califano, listening to Johnson tell a story which Califano knew was not true, and which Califano knew that Johnson himself knew, or at least had known at one time, was not true, writes of 'the authentic increase in the President's conviction each time he recited it.'"[42] It was this aspect of Johnson's personality – his intrinsically jaded character – that explains why, from the immediate aftermath of the attack, he announced that only ten men were killed and 100 wounded. Those numbers never changed.

Endnotes

1. Hounam, p. 87

2. Ibid., p 136.

3. Green, p. 219

4. Califano, p. 205

5. Bamford, p. 211

6. Ibid. pp. 28, 38

7. Ibid.

8. Ibid. p. 29

9. See Youtube video "USS Liberty cover-up 'Loss of LIberty'" See: https://www.youtube.com/watch?v=ZluFfyQ7sAI (@ 27:50)

10. See: Youtube video "Ernie Gallo: The USS Liberty -- what really happened? What did not?"

(https://www.youtube.com/watch?v=rLr9fjg6cmM

11. Op.Cit. @ 30:50

12. Ibid. @ 20:15

13. See: http://historynewsnetwork.org/article/191#sthash.AQNFqXhS.dpuf

14. Ennes, (Appendix "P" - Extract From Combat Information Center Watch Officer's Log, from 1358 to 1632), pp. 281, 282

15. Hounam, p. 248 (Israel immediately admitted that this was a "mistake" in the "IDF Court of Inquiry Report"- See Pearson, p. 68)

16. Ibid., pp. 32-33

17. Ibid. p. 112

18. Ibid. p. 255

19. Ibid. p. 90

20. Ibid.

21. Ibid., p. 181

22. Ibid., p. 182–183. Also See YouTube: "Documentary on the USS *Liberty*: Dead in the Water," (@ 25.30), http://www.youtube.com/watch?feature=endscreen&Nr =1&v=va0shuZyJwU

23. Crewdson, John, *Baltimore Sun* October 2, 2007 (See http://www.baltimoresun.com/news/chi-liberty_tuesoct02-story.html#page=1)

24. Findings of the Independent Commission of Inquiry into the Israeli Attack on USS Liberty, the Recall of Military Rescue Support Aircraft while the Ship was Under Attack, and the Subsequent Cover-up by the United States Government, Capitol Hill, Washington, D.C., October 22, 2003

25. See: "USS Liberty White House-sanctioned attack, June 8, 1967" – Excerpt from the video, *Terrorstorm* by Alex Jones @3:30 (See: https://www.youtube.com/watch?v=ZnTdn1bSo-Q)

26. See BBC documentary video "Dead in the Water" (@ 28:40)

27. Op. Cit, Crewdson, *Chicago Tribune* and *Baltimore Sun*

28. Hounam, p. 240

29. Pearson, Anthony, p. 98

30. Ibid., p. 31

31. Hounam, p. 241

32. Ibid. p. 242 (Also see the BBC video "Dead in the Water" (Op. Cit.) @ 45:00)

33. Ibid. pp. 196-197

34. Joesten, p. 378

35. Pearson, p. 98

36. Ibid.

37. Green, p. 202

38. Hounam., p. 17

39. See: http://www.theamericanconservative.com/articles/the-uss-libertys-final-chapter/

40. Nelson, *LBJ: The Mastermind* …p. 32 (Ref. Lasky, Victor, *It Didn't Start with Watergate*, p. 136)

41. Caro, *The Passage*, p. 82

42. Caro, *Master of the Senate*, p. 886

One of the four gun mounts on the *Liberty*.

Shot-Up Moon-Bounce Dish

31.45 N

20   33.30 E   40   50   34.00 E   10

06:30

USS Liberty course:
app. distance by knots
c/c and c/s from deck logs

08:00

??

torpedo attack

31.30 N

14:30

Matching returns from
radar bearing log:
time, bearing, range as shown

air attack

14:00

11:30

09:00

9:05 sighting,
Deck Log: 20 nm
bearing 203

Capt's NCOI test:
14:00 - 25.5nm,
142 bearing,

31.15 N

ISRA

Bearings from El Arish

El Arish

20 nm

EGYPT (U.A.R.)

Shots directed to the ship's identification letters

GTR5

Chapter 4

The Immediate Aftermath and Recovery – On to Malta

Ok fellas, now I'm an admiral again and I want each and every one of you to understand something. We're talking about National Security here, not your personal feelings, not what you did or did not do… I could really give a shit about any of that. You listen to me once, because this is the only time you're ever going to hear it. You are NEVER to repeat what you just told me to ANYONE – not your mother, your father, your wife – ANYONE! Including your shipmates. You are not to discuss this with anyone, and especially – ESPECIALLY – not with the MEDIA, or you will end up in PRISON, or WORSE!

– Rear Admiral Isaac Kidd Jr., to USS *Liberty* survivors

AFTER THE ATTACK: THE SURVIVORS STORY

Phil Tourney

After the aircraft, torpedo boats and helicopters filled with armed paratroopers finally departed the scene, about two and a half hours after the attack began, we started the long wait for help to arrive. Knowing that our S.O.S. messages had been transmitted, we naturally assumed that the great American military fifty-ship armada known as the Sixth Fleet would soon come to our rescue. The time was about 4:30 p.m. and we were adrift for awhile until we managed to get the crippled ship underway, still not sure what to expect next or even whether the ship would sink or not. Thus began "Eighteen Hours of Hell."

To call it a long night is a big understatement. None of us slept, for two reasons: First, we were afraid of the dark. Not like little kids, but rather because we knew that criminals prefer the cover of darkness when doing their dirty work. Those responsible for the previous day's attack might return to the scene of the crime to finish what they failed to do earlier. Second, we didn't know if the ship would even stay together. Although we were not sure of the exact size of the hole in the starboard side, we knew that it was big, very big. There was also a lot of work that would be needed just to keep the ship afloat and moving away from the danger zone; and with all the men killed or wounded, only a skeleton crew remained to do this.

Those of us who did survive were glad of that of course, but we all felt an enormous amount of survivor's guilt. "Why me? Why us?" – we asked ourselves silently. "Why had we been spared while others had not?" The dead included two of my good friends: Francis Brown, who was shot in the head with a .50 caliber machine gun round, and had his brains splattered all over the bridge; David Skolak, who I had been with just minutes before the attack. He was also caught in the machine-gun fire and had been blown to pieces – too many to count. I went to the mess deck to see if I could help with the severely wounded men. As soon as I entered, the sheer mass of human suffering moved me to such emotion that my knees got weak, but I dared not to let it show as I went from broken man to broken man, asking what I could do to help him feel more comfortable.

As I was doing this, Commander Phillip Armstrong, the ship's Executive Officer, called my name. I thought that his condition was not critical because he was active and alert and seemingly in little pain. He asked me for a cigarette, so I lit one and put it in his mouth for him. He asked me many questions about the numbers of dead and wounded and the Captain's condition, while I heard the agony of men all around us.

I left him for a few minutes to try to find anything to help comfort the men and by the time I returned to check on Commander Armstrong, to my great shock and sadness, I found that he had just died. Then I went to the Ward Room, the mess hall for the officers. There I saw another one of my friends, Gary Blanchard, an enlisted seaman whose front showed no signs of a wound, but he was lying in a puddle of his own blood that seemed to get bigger second by second. He asked me to remove his socks because his feet were on fire. I did as he asked. Then he asked if he was going to make it. I could do no more than shake my head "no." I always hated myself for not lying to him, or at least ignoring the question and changing the subject. But I did hope that my response allowed him the chance to make peace with his maker before the final curtain. These four men were among the nearly three dozen killed that day, many of whom I had never gotten a chance to know.

I had met the ship's only doctor there in the Ward Room, Doctor Richard Kiepfer. He came over and began to operate on Gary, however, it quickly became clear that it was too late. As soon as he opened him up, he then had to put stitches in him to hold him together before Doc moved on to his numerous other patients, all of whom desperately needed his attention. If anyone aboard that ship deserved the Congressional Medal of Honor, it was Doc Kiepfer.

As time marched on, we went about our regular duties, now modified because of the precarious condition of the ship. We didn't want to think that the attack was a deliberate attempt to sink the ship on anyone's part, but that thought could not be erased from everyone's minds. And we were still unsure of why it had been attacked, and by whom. Israeli flags had been seen on at least one boat, and the helicopters, but the thought that our "friend and ally" would do something so treacherous was unthinkable. But nothing was "normal" anymore and that thought was the only possible explanation; the brutality, intensity and long duration of the attack and the obvious fact that they wanted to kill us all and sink the ship had become quite clear to all of us. Why else would they destroy our only means of escape, by shooting up the life boats?

There was also a growing suspicion that our government was up to something big – and "hush-hush" – which might explain why no airplanes, ships, boats, helicopters or any other conveyance with a U.S. flag, or any other flag for that matter, had come to our rescue or even inquired about our condition. To say that the feelings we were all experiencing were "surreal" is an understatement, but by dusk that was pretty much what it was.

As I began to resume my regular duty, "Sounding and Security and Damage Control," I realized that my heroic shipmates had saved the ship that day by remaining at their posts while under attack. As I would later come to understand, by saving the ship, we also possibly saved many others, perhaps tens, even hundreds, of millions of people because it prevented a possible nuclear confrontation between the two major superpowers in the world.

I started making my usual rounds, which now included both bulkheads encompassing the CT (Cryptologic Technician) spaces where the torpedo had hit. The walls, made of plate steel no more than an inch thick, if that, were sweaty from the cool ocean water on the other side. I could even hear the water sloshing around, knowing that if the bulkheads ever gave way, we would all be goners. There were cracks in the steel walls caused by the enormous pressure being exerted against them by the Mediterranean Sea. They were ballooning outward from that pressure and I feared that the cracks would get larger and larger until finally they would give way; they looked like they were alive and breathing as they heaved in and out with the movement of the ship and the pressure of the water. I got shivers standing in such close proximity to them, knowing that the only thing standing between me and my own death was a plate of steel that was ready to come crashing in to the boiler room at any second. That thin steel wall was the only thing keeping the seawater from flooding into the interior of the ship. If that happened, of course the ship would have immediately sunk from a huge explosion when the cold water hit the hot boilers.

After waiting overnight and well into the next morning, some of the men had gathered on the top deck milling about because we were still not sure the ship would not sink. At sunrise, I noticed a ship on the horizon at our stern, which I later found out was a Russian ship that had been following us throughout the night. Then I saw two other ships coming up behind the Russian ship, both of which were moving quickly; it soon became apparent that they were two U.S. Navy destroyers, the USS *Davis* and the USS *Massey,* coming to our rescue. Right after that, the Damage Control Officer John Scott approached me, saying, "The old man wants the ship cleaned up." He didn't have to explain it any further, as I knew exactly what he meant: The ship's deck looked like the floor of a slaughterhouse, with pieces of flesh, bone, hair, various organs and everything else covered the deck, held in place by dried blood. The bodies that could be identified had already been collected and stored but the rest of the remains needed to be cleaned up.

Rick Aimetti and I found some undamaged fire hoses and began hosing off the deck with a "suicide nozzle" on it that sprayed water in a very concentrated, high-pressure stream. It took both of us to handle this hose, because it was like a giant python and one man could not do it alone. It was the most gruesome, heartbreaking task either of us had ever done because every piece of flesh was the remains of one of our fellow sailors, many of whom were friends.

As Aimetti and I went about this ungodly task, tears streamed down our faces and I prayed to God for forgiveness in how we were forced to treat the remains of these men so sacrilegiously. In the gun-tubs we found a shoe with a foot still in it, which we put aside for collection. Many of the bloodstains would not come off, even with that special hose, because of previous day's intense heat – not just baking under the sun's heat, but from the rockets and napalm that had been dropped on the ship by the attacking Super Mysteres. We found out the hard way how hot our government's most brutal weapon can burn: It can get as hot as 2,000 - 2,200 degrees Fahrenheit, which explains why that blood could not be completely cleansed from the steel decks.

Despite the fact that it had taken so long to arrive, all the men on the *Liberty's* crew were excited to see the ships with American flags finally coming to our rescue. Thankfully, the water was flat, like a sheet of glass, without even a ripple in it as the USS *Davis* came alongside the *Liberty*, separated only by inches as we tied their lines to our crippled ship. A plank was put across and the men from the *Davis* began boarding, about thirty or forty in all. Over and over again, we heard them apologize for taking so long to get to us, but of course there was nothing that any of them could have done any differently, given that official orders controlled all ship movements. Some of the men inspected the damage, running their hands over the holes and shaking their heads in disgust and outrage, some cursing like sailors, though others cried like babies at the incredibly horrendous sight. But they all remained orderly, professional and somber, just as they had been trained to be.

The crewmen of the *Davis* and *Liberty* started moving the most seriously wounded men from the mess halls and passageways up to the main deck. Shortly thereafter, the aircraft carrier USS *America* maneuvered itself into the area, keeping enough distance away to allow it to launch fighter jets if necessary. Helicopters came over from the *America* and hovered over the *Liberty* since there was no open areas to land, and life stretchers were hoisted up to the helicopters with cables. One by one, the wounded of the *Liberty* were ferried over to the *America* and taken to the hospital on the carrier, followed by the same methods in removing what was left of the dead men.

The *Davis* crewmen joined with us to quickly evaluate what was needed for emergency repairs. There was no time for architects or structural engineers to do lengthy plans and blueprints; we were looking at bulging walls that were designed merely as bulkheads, not for being the exterior skin of the ship and the pressures of seawater on the other side. If they gave way, the ship would sink so fast that we would be lucky to escape from those lowest decks.

Thankfully, the *Davis* carried all the tools and shoring timbers we needed to quickly set up strong braces, using as many triangles as we could, designing it as we went; the improvised wooden structure allowed us to finally get the ship into dry dock. The huge torpedo hole in the starboard side was covered by a canvas tarp that was secured with straps wrapped around the bottom of the ship and up around the port side; the straps could not hold the tarp adequately, which resulted in some of the bodies of dead crewmembers floating out the torpedo hole. I found out later that the USS *Papago*, which followed us all the way to Malta, retrieved bodies that had floated out of the spaces.

Along with Rick Aimetti, James Smith and Duilio Demori, we had been "volunteered" to regularly check the shoring that had been built to reinforce the bulkheads. This involved crawling into the spaces below with a battle lantern, going in to the skin of the ship on the starboard side to examine each crack to see if any were getting any bigger as we went along. It was like crawling into a coffin, because if all hell broke loose and those walls gave way, that was it. There would be no way out and you were going to die right there. We had to crawl out backwards in the same way we crawled in, rechecking each crack. Each time, we felt as we crawled back that we had successfully cheated death yet again.

All the crew assumed that we would be allowed passage to the closest dry dock that could repair the nearly "totaled" ship, which would have been Crete, a little over a day's passage. When Lt. George Golden, our engineering officer, announced our destination, we were all a little stunned: "Boys, we're not headed for Crete, so get ready for just a little bit of a ride." We had already been on a "little bit of a ride" over the last day or two. What was ahead now?

We were not told where we were heading, I suppose to control our fear about whether we would even get to our destination. By the time we heard "through the grapevine" that it was Malta, where we had never been before, and we were still two days away. Only afterwards did I realize there was a method to the madness, given that it took nearly a week to make the trip, compared to the day and a half trip it would have taken to go to Crete. We were forced to take a treacherous journey across the deepest, choppiest waters in the Mediterranean, apparently because "someone" was hoping we would sink along the way.

DR. JEKYLL AND MR. HYDE (A.K.A. ADMIRAL ISAAC KIDD JR.)

Admiral Isaac Kidd Jr. had met separately with small groups of sailors, starting each meeting in a very relaxed and friendly setting. When it was our turn, it was quite obvious that he had done the same "presentation" with other groups and would do the same with still more, until every last man on board our ship had heard the same message, undoubtedly in the same way and heard the same exact words. It became clear that the first such meeting was with the ranking officers and many of us noticed a change in their demeanor, right after Admiral Kidd had arrived on the ship, beginning with Commander McGonagle. It was a very uncomfortable feeling, following what we had all been through, because these officers had now become sullen and morose, then seemingly more bitter, confused and even angry.

The attack had happened on a Thursday. On the following Monday, after we were finally underway, I was ordered to report to sick bay, and saw that several other sailors were there as well. A few minutes later, a voice called out "OFFICER ON DECK!" We stood at attention while Admiral Kidd came in and shut the door behind him. He prepared us by first taking off his stars, as he told us in a kind and fatherly voice, "You have no reason to fear me. In fact, I'm going to take off my stars now" as he tossed them onto a metal table, causing them to make a metallic "ping" sound when they landed. It was his way of coming *down* to our level and just being one of the guys.

"Gentlemen, I am trying to piece together what happened, and I can't do it without you. I know I'm a flag admiral, but right now I am here to congratulate you and to let you know that your testimony is very, very important to me and my staff. I know that since the attack you fellas have had a lot of time to reflect about what happened and this is what I want to dig out of you. I'm not an admiral anymore, I am just like you – a third-class petty officer, a seaman recruit or a Lieutenant Commander. Feel free to speak up with anything you think is important. Also, this is off the record, so I want you to speak freely."

Now we could all breath normally again, feeling that this admiral was like a kindly father, a big brother, or a favorite uncle to each of us and now the weight of the world, at least the heavy emotions that we had all carried from the absolute horror we had just experienced the last few days, was finally going to be lifted from our shoulders. He spoke to each of us, asking us questions like, "Did you see any markings on the recon aircraft in the morning before the attacks began?" and "What about the attacking aircraft, were there markings? Did you see the torpedo boats? Did you see the torpedo boats machine-gunning life rafts? Are you sure the U.S. flag was flying over the ship?"

When it was my turn, I described everything I had seen – the surveillance flights, the attacks, the fires, the wounded, the life rafts being shot up, the flag flying high on the yardarm until it was shot down, then quickly replaced, when we had a brief break in the strafing, by the much bigger flag; I told him everything I saw, as best that I could describe. And throughout my description he never interrupted me once, which gave me even more confidence that he was there on a mission, and it was to flesh out the horrid story and make sure that justice would be exacted from the attackers.

We were all feeling great that, at last, we were able to tell our stories. Admiral Kidd had listened well, taking detailed notes the whole time; it was as if he was a great and magnanimous sheriff, just like Matt Dillon on the old *Gunsmoke* TV show, and now he was prepared to strap on his double holster with his six-shooter revolvers, go find the bad guys and make them pay – big time.

Then he asked if there was anything else that anyone wanted to say. Buoyed on by the fatherly way he had treated us, I raised my hand and asked him, "Sir, why didn't we get any help?"

An immediate change transcended through the room, and I think all of us felt it. It was as though the temperature dropped, the lighting became darker, the sense of hope began receding and it was as if funeral music, or the musical score from old movies like *Dracula* or *Frankenstein* might have been heard at low volume. We saw immediately that he did not like that question, because his attitude changed immediately and his face went from pale to red almost as if he had gotten an instant sunburn. Without answering my question, he walked over to the stainless steel table onto which he had tossed his stars an hour earlier and put them back on his collars. The pins slipped easily into the same holes from which they had come a little while before that, indicating that this wasn't the first time he had practiced this routine.

As soon as his two stars were in place on each lapel – perfectly, just as they had been when he had entered the room – he spoke directly, and threateningly. Dr. Jekyll had now become Mr. Hyde, as he delivered his warning, noted in the epigraph at the beginning of this chapter: to NEVER say ANYTHING to ANYONE else, ESPECIALLY the media, or we would end up in PRISON, or WORSE! As he said the word "worse" he scowled. His face twisted and turned into a mask of hatred and rage. He presented that mask to each of us personally, one at a time. When it was my turn, I knew that I was looking into the eyes of the devil himself. We found out later that this was similar to all the other presentations he conducted throughout the ship's roster, and what we saw might have won him an Oscar, had it been done in Hollywood, instead of the high seas, and for real.

I know in my heart that he hated the fact that we were still standing in front of him, alive and breathing. That was not the plan. He started out of the room, stopping to look back at us. We were standing there in the same relaxed mode which he had encouraged us to adopt when the interrogation first started. Now he seemed to be offended that we had not come to attention as he was leaving. "ATTENTION ON DECK" I shouted, fearing that if I and my shipmates did not stiffen up right then, he might kill us all and throw us overboard right there. He opened the door himself – gently. But before leaving, he turned his entire body in our direction and stared at us for at least fifteen seconds. I thought I might piss my pants, I was so scared. Then, after finishing his glare, never once blinking his eyes, he stepped through the door and slammed it, and it slammed so hard that the steel on steel sounded like a bomb that had gone off in the room, leaving us all completely speechless. At that point, we didn't know what to think, for all we knew, he would re-enter the room at any moment and shoot anyone who had not remained at attention. Maybe he was still outside, listening through the door to determine if anyone was already disobeying his orders not to discuss anything … to anyone?

When I think about what we went through during the attack, the fear of dying at any minute, the general uncertainty of ever making it out alive: the pain of re-experiencing it never fades. But even worse than all of that was how we were treated by Admiral Kidd, after first pretending to befriend us then turning on us like a vicious, man-eating beast. It had scarred me, like an animal being branded with a red-hot branding iron; only instead of on the rump it was on my heart, mind and soul. I know I am not the only one who feels that way.

Whenever I think about what Kidd did to us, my impulse is to scratch myself all over and take a shower, but knowing that no matter how much I might wash myself, I would never be clean again. Even at the ripe young age of twenty at that time, my gut told me that I had been conscripted against my will into participating in something so ugly – an incredibly horrible treason – that was committed against my country, a betrayal that I had no control over, yet I realize it was still an unforgiveable act. It is something that can never be forgotten by those of us who were forced to participate in it. The men who I have talked to, despite Kidd's warning not to, all agree that the worst part of the experience was being made to feel like *we* were the criminals, for not obeying the orders to sink and go to the bottom as commanded by the president himself.

Ron Kukal

The attack was over somewhere in the area of two hours. We were supposed to be at the bottom, or floating in sea water, quiet, unresponsive, and quite dead. That thought has been, and always will be, very sobering to me. What it means, to me, is that every action to put us to the bottom failed, every rocket, every torpedo, all that napalm, and still we were alive and floating. You had to have been there to understand; of course my mere words will never capture the essence of what really went on. But I will attempt to describe it as best that I can, to convey the scene we were faced with and what happened after the attack.

When the attack was finally over, we were then faced with the dilemma of bulging bulkheads that could go at any minute. Thank God for the men of the *USS Davis* that showed up the following morning on June 9th to go down below and shore up the ones that needed it. In talking to Larry Broyles, a USS *Davis* crewmen, I was informed that when they went down below they had locked themselves in, just in case those bulkheads gave way while they were shoring them up. What powerful testimony these men could give about the effort put forth to keep the *Liberty* from going to the bottom. It is also a great testimony to the training that we all received in boot camp, and I thank those who trained us. I hope the training has not changed. Why fix something that is not broken?

We had no after steering and so it was up to some of us to go down below to steer the ship by hand. Turning a rudder of that size was difficult enough, but the extra added weight of the water filled compartments, and the list made that task even more difficult. When I was relieved from that duty I went topside out to the fantail and our wake looked like a slithering snake across the sea. We were ordered to sleep topside out on the deck, but I was so highly medicated I really didn't care what happened. There was never any argument about sinking, and according to some I have talked to who were in the know, it was not "were we going to sink;" but when? Still it made little difference to me, and I went down below anyway. I had some great sleep from the load of Seconal that I was taking, and it just seemed like the right thing to do.

It took us five days to cover the 1,000 mile trip to Malta, and we found out later that six of the bodies floated out of the torpedo hole as we made our way. The *USS Papago* picked these bodies up, and the *USS Massey* was there to do the same thing. I have had occasion to talk to one of the crewmen from the *Papago*, and to this day it is something they cannot forget. They had no body bags as I understand it, and what was left of a body was put in their reefer (military jargon for "refrigerator"). Being exposed to something like this had to have affected them, more than likely for the rest of their lives. That appears to be so at least with one of the crewmen of the *Papago* that I talked to.

On arrival in Malta we were headed straight to dry dock, and once we were in, it was up to the great crew at Malta to get us set up for repairs and whatever else needed to be done. What never occurred to me was the grisly duties that were about to be laid squarely on our shoulders. In my case, as senior enlisted man on the crew, I was put in charge of recovery and identification. I will admit I tried to talk my way out of this one, but I was told those were my orders, and I followed them.

That hour arrived sooner than I wanted, as we made our way down to the dark hole below. No one knew what to expect, and I was extremely apprehensive about what we would see. For forty-eight years I have said little about what I saw, because I wanted to spare the loved ones of these men that cruelty if I could. With the writing of this book, and the distance in years, I think I can at least say that the scene could compare to a wrecking yard of autos. But these were human body parts strewn everywhere, carnage that escapes description with mere words, and there were more bodies that were down below which were brought to me to try to identify. Those bodies were wedged between steam pipes, and in places that a body wouldn't fit.

If I bring tears to any of the loved ones with this description, let me console you with this. Those men never knew what hit them, they couldn't have. It had to have been instantaneous. The task was grim but I must tell you that strange things happened to me in the process. There were some that said they couldn't stand the smell, and yes it must have been indescribable, and I say this for a reason. In the days that I spent down there, I had men like Ernie Gallo come up to me, and ask how I could do this. For the most part much of it has been blocked out of my mind, and I only know that I did it. Phenomena occurred that I couldn't begin to explain, and I have spoken about the smell for a reason.

That smell cannot be described by me, because I never smelled a thing. No, nothing, absolutely nothing. Again some pretty strange things went on down there. Working in the midst of this for about three days was tiring, and of course no one gets used to what we were seeing. Twenty-five men, with some of them slipping out the torpedo hole. We could not identify all, and so as bad as it sounds we gathered up the unknown parts, put them in a body bag, and called it the six men we couldn't find. They are buried in Arlington, and may God have mercy on their souls. Again I say to the families and loved ones of these men, it is not my intention to dredge up old memories, just to make sure that true history is not forgotten.

Ernie Gallo

After sailing nearly a week to get there, living on a ship drenched in the blood of our dead and the seriously wounded shipmates who were no longer on board, we finally arrived in Malta and put the ship into a dry dock, which finally allowed the water to be removed from the flooded lower decks. One group of CTs, headed by Ron Kukal, was ordered into the classified spaces to remove the bodies. I participated in a second group, which was led by Senior Chief Stan White, to recover all classified documents and materials. This assignment was, for me personally, more horrific than the attack itself, because until now, I had not had to handle or even observe the body parts of my friends and fellow CTs "up close and personal." Remorse hit me like a ton of bricks and I will never forget the carnage of my shipmates, now dead for a week, some impaled on pipes, others caught in overhead equipment as they frantically tried to escape in the last moments of their lives. The stench of death was mixed with a heavy black oily substance mixed with the seawater and was insufferable. It was the blackest and bleakest, most morbid, depressing scene that one can possibly imagine, yet we had a job to do and we just had to put all of that aside and get it done.

It was hard to keep the work separated so neatly between the two groups, because in order to do our tasks of collecting the classified materials, in many cases we had to uncover it from body parts that had been blasted by the torpedo's shrapnel into small pieces. The black coating over everything hid some of it such that it couldn't be seen until the equipment racks and cryptographic material were picked up. We moved from one area to the next, clearing all debris as we went, which often included a finger or a toe, to get to the item that we were attempting to retrieve. This was a very emotionally painful and draining experience for all of us, and we all broke down at one time or another as we went about this awful, yet sacred, work.

The ship was patched back together, all 821 holes including the big asymmetrical torpedo hole that measured approximately twenty-five by forty feet. The ship had been destroyed sufficiently to render it a "total loss." The ship, which had been refurbished just three years earlier, was now made seaworthy again for its last trip across the Atlantic. The ship was reduced to salvage once it was back in the U.S.

While we were in dry dock, naval officers came to Malta to conduct a Naval Court of Inquiry. The crew had reason to hope that this impressive group – a Rear Admiral and four Navy Captains – would dig out the truth of what happened as they took four days of testimony. Unfortunately, that was not to be, as the entire process was a sham, and an extension of the gag order that had already been ordered by Admiral Kidd. Like everything else, it was set up to hide the actual truth, even down to the point that although Israel was the attacker, that fact was purposely left out of this supposedly official "inquiry." It quickly became clear to all that the Naval Court of Inquiry was given one week to complete its work for a reason: There was no interest in a thorough, rigorous investigation that would uncover the truth of what had happened to us. It was to be a "sham" that had all the markings of a process that someone, a person clearly very high in the command structure, created for his own mysterious purposes and designed to vindicate the attackers, to guarantee their protection from reprisal.

Finally, after the debris was collected and bagged, most CTs were transferred to Norfolk and given new assignments, where everyone was sent off in different directions so that we could not reminisce together over forbidden secrets. We were all now supposed to put these painful memories behind us and join new crews on different ships and act as if this "incident" had never occurred; those were the *orders* and that was that.

Although selected crew members were asked to present testimony, it was eventually discovered that nothing that anyone said about the machine-gunning of stretcher bearers and life rafts made it into the final report; the presence of the flag was questioned, despite the insistence of everyone who saw it flying, therefore left as an uncertainty rather than an unquestioned fact. Since some Israeli authors and other apologists still use that document as "gospel" to prop up falsified accounts, they can still find "factual" support for their specious assertions even now.

I discovered that for myself in 1995, when, as a CIA staff officer, I sent a Freedom of Information (FOIA) request for related documents and, even with my own extensive classified clearances (Top Secret / SI Crypto), I was surprised to find how much information had been redacted, based upon the security manager's determination that "I did not have a need to know." However, they did provide me with a copy of the 1967 Navy Court of Inquiry, which included Lt. Lloyd Painter's testimony, except for the most incriminating parts. In addition, the detailed statement provided to the court by the Officer of the Deck's Morning Watch report had been deleted. The White House lawyers had also removed all written testimony provided to the court by sixty-five *Liberty* crewmen.

Examining The Center of the Plot: Complete White House Capitulation

For about twenty-four hours after the attack, President Johnson, apparently only for appearances, acted as if he was upset with Israel because the attack on the U.S. ship was deliberate. This reaction was recorded in the minutes of a White House meeting of the National Security Council the following day.[1]

In the immediate aftermath of the failure of the *Liberty* to sink, Johnson tried to place the blame for the war firmly on Egypt, citing President Nasser's reaction to the series of provocations set in motion by Israel as planned and America's highest-level staff as described earlier, when Johnson announced: "If a single act of folly was more responsible for this explosion than any other, it was the arbitrary and dangerous announced decision by Egypt that the Strait of Tiran would be closed [to Israeli ships and Israeli-bound cargo]."[2] However, that pretense ended at that point and, over the next several weeks, disappeared completely.

There was an immediate effort to quash the growing backlash in Washington. On the following day Secretary of Defense Clifford, according to the NSC minutes, said: "It was inconceivable that Israel destroyed the *Liberty* by error, as is claimed."[3] U.S. Ambassador Walworth Barbour, who had spent much time during the war within the Israeli war room and shared the jubilation, both in Israel and much of America, in the wake of Israel's victory. He also shared Israel's efforts to downplay Israel's attack on the *Liberty*.

While Barbour's colleagues back in the U.S. were angered by the attack, according to Seymour Hersh, in *The Samson Option*, it was Barbour who first reported that "Israel did not intend to admit to the incident and added: 'Urge strongly that we too avoid publicity. (*Liberty's*) proximity to scene could feed Arab suspicions of U.S.-Israel collusion ... Israelis obviously shocked by error and tender sincere apologies."[4]

Barbour initiated other actions at Israel's request, one to discontinue the monitoring of Israel's nuclear facility at Dimona, and another to stop undercutting the Israeli's by discontinuing operations with British or Canadian counterparts: "Israel is going to be our main ally [now], and we can't dilute it by working with others," he informed William N. "Bill" Dale, the chief of mission in the immediate aftermath. And there was a second message, according to Dale: "Barbour said, 'Arab oil is not as important as Israel is to us. Therefore, I'm going to side with Israel in all of my reporting.' 'And maybe he was right,' added Dale. 'From that time on, it was a different Wally Barbour.'"[5]

According to author Hersh, Barbour was always in Israel's lap, from the time he was sent there by Johnson, he admitted that he was there as Johnson's personal representative, with instructions to "keep the Jews off my [LBJ's] back." He admitted to his colleagues that his instruction was "To keep them happy" and that "I go back to Washington every year to see the President and I get my orders directly from him – not from those pipsqueaks (at State)."

Barbour also instructed Bill Dale to send embassy reports by mail to avoid cables being intercepted, because "Israel has friends all over the State Department."[6] Barbour's reference to the "pipsqueaks" in the State Department is undoubtedly a reflection of Johnson's view as well, since we know that Dean Rusk was there as a "yes man" who quickly got the message that the president wanted only men who would go along with his decisions, not anyone who exhibited any independence of thought; as LBJ would say, often, "No Mavericks!"

101

The official position of the United States after the Six-Day War had originally been based upon a presumption that Israel would return the Palestinian territories won during the war. Yet it quickly became clear that, despite the initial claims that Israel had merely responded to a war begun by Egypt, in fact the war had been planned weeks, even months, in advance, so its rights to "spoils of war" were non-existent, and made no sense at all given that the territories "won" were mostly from Palestine, which was not one of the Arab countries involved in that war. The only way to be able to rationalize Israel's action to retain these territories was to portray themselves as the victims of Arabian aggression.

Likewise, the U.S. position regarding the proposed sale of fifty F-4 jets, and Israel's continued development of nuclear weaponry, had always been premised upon Israel's allowing International Atomic Energy Agency (IAEA) inspections and their acceptance of the Nuclear Non-Proliferation Treaty (NPT). At least, these were the positions held by everyone in the State Department and, even more intensely, at the Pentagon by Clark Clifford, who had replaced Robert McNamara as Secretary of Defense.

When the CIA confirmed that Israel possessed nuclear bombs it exposed a secret, and when Clark Clifford took McNamara's place at the Department of Defense he did not even know where Johnson stood on the important questions of Israel's acquisition of nuclear bombs, or their (non) commitment to sign the NPT, much less his position on the sale of the F-4s. Shortly after Clifford took over, Johnson scheduled a US-Israeli (Johnson-Eshkol) summit meeting at his ranch. Eshkol and his advisors including Effy Evron, now the Israeli ambassador, sat through a day of briefings at which State and Defense Department officials argued against selling the F-4s to Israel, so they were not happy with the proceedings at that point.[7]

President Johnson finally announced, "Let's all go piss" and off they went to Johnson's huge bathroom to have a group urination break. When Johnson saw his friend Effy looking dejected, he asked him what was wrong. Effy said, "We're not going to get our F-4s" and Johnson replied, "Oh goddam, Effy, you're going to get the F-4s, but I'm going to get something out of Eshkol. But don't tell him." This meant that Johnson's staff had told him they wanted to get Israel to at least join the "nuclear club" by allowing IAEA inspections at Dimona. But Effy, and his boss Eshkol took that to be a commitment to sell the F-4s, and told Abe Feinberg about it, and together they held him to it, using as leverage Feinberg's grip on Johnson. Then, when CIA Director Richard Helms told Johnson about the fact that Israel had already built four nuclear warheads, Johnson ordered him to bury the report, and Helms, being the loyal and unquestioning acolyte, complied without objection.[8]

In the meantime, since no one else in the administration knew about their acquisition, but strongly suspected it, Clifford and Paul Warnke, an assistant secretary of defense for international security affairs, attempted to press for "due diligence" attempts to pressure them to agree to the IAEA inspections. When Warnke began pressing the newly designated Israeli ambassador, Yitzak Rabin, on this question, he asked for a definition of what a nuclear weapon was, to which Warnke replied, "It's if you've got a delivery device in one room and the nuclear warhead in another room." To which Rabin then responded, "Do you have a nuclear weapon unless you say you do?"[9] President Johnson responded to that news by ordering the CIA to *not disclose that information to anyone else in the administration.*[10] He was highly skilled in such things as keeping secrets from people who he deemed to have no "need to know."

Unbeknownst to Clark Clifford, Johnson had yielded to Abraham Feinberg's pressure to disconnect the conditions for the sale of the then-state-of-the-art F-4 Phantom jets from Israel's acceptance of the NPT.[11] When the negotiations began to flounder because of this disagreement, Feinberg reminded Johnson of his concession. That was all it took for Johnson to fold – to capitulate entirely on what had been a major point. When Clifford called the president to seek clarification, Johnson said, *"Sell them anything they want."* Clifford, despite having always been a strong supporter of Israel, responded by saying "Mr. President, I don't want to live in a world where the Israelis have nuclear weapons." President Johnson, responding in typically abusive fashion, screamed *"Don't bother me with this anymore"* and hung up the telephone (emphasis added).[12]

Even in Johnson's State Department of 1965, Israel's request for these brand-new, "state-of-the-art" fighter jets had been denied through normal channels; but *after* the Six-Day War, and ironically after the horrific attack by Israel on the USS *Liberty*, the Johnson administration capitulated – completely, to practically everything Israel requested as evidenced by his remarks to Clifford, including even providing the pilots to train them how to fly the planes.[13] Johnson did this because in the latter part of 1967 and up to March 30, 1968, he still intended to run for re-election and he did not want anything to happen that might impact his fund raising capability for that campaign. Whatever principles he might have ever had (and there weren't many to begin with) would be suspended when it came to doing anything that might diminish his political power.

The numerous proofs of Lyndon Johnson's central role included his own words, "I want that ship going to the bottom. No help. Recall the wings." And his orders to have the Navy's Court of Inquiry report rewritten by his White House aides, to make certain that all references to the visible flag, life rafts being shot up and that had Israel blocked the specific radio frequencies used by the *Liberty*, were removed. Also, his later orders to Clark Clifford to "Give them whatever they want" (F-4 fighter jets to deliver the nuclear bombs he knew they possessed) was the icing on the cake that showed his intent. These actions, many of which took decades to unravel, are what had protected the lies and deceit, and kept the veil of secrecy in place for as long as it was.

As the *Liberty* was being attacked, the word spread quickly to the sailors on ships throughout the Sixth Fleet. Gilad Atzmon, the author of *Remembering the Liberty: 45 Years Later and Still No Answers*, on the website maintained for the *Liberty* survivors, described a former Navy pilot who affirmed this: "I was a 6th [Fleet] Navy's pilot," he said. "We were deployed to the Mediterranean Sea on that day in June 1967, we heard it all, the sailors on board of the *Liberty*, they were begging for help, it was a real agony, we were fuming, we wanted to get on the planes, we were about 10–12 minutes away, we wanted to save our brothers, but they didn't let us onto the deck."[14] Similar frustrated expressions came from men on many other ships of the Sixth Fleet after the squadron of fighter jets had returned to the carrier, immediately following the first launch.

President Johnson's reactions to the reality that the ship was not sinking as it was supposed to do, evidenced by the recall of all the navy aircraft and the subsequent, otherwise inexplicable, delays in sending other ships to the *Liberty*'s rescue, were also apparent in the numerous discrepancies regarding the official logs of the president and his cabinet officers.

Those disparities begin with the time that the White House was purportedly notified of the attacks. The official records state that Walt Rostow, Johnson's special adviser, first telephoned the president about the attack at 9:49 a.m., stating that the *Liberty* had been torpedoed, even though it made no mention of the air attack that began thirty minutes before the torpedoes were launched. However, as author Hounam stated, the Pentagon claimed that it learned of the attack at 9 a.m., which is also inconsistent with many other records, including one that indicates it was 8:24 a.m. in Washington when McNamara ordered the first recall of the rescue aircraft that had just been dispatched – just a few minutes after President Johnson had called McNamara from his bedroom.[15] This mishmash of inconsistencies betrays an obvious, albeit failed, effort to fudge official records to cover up presidential misdeeds of the highest level.

Though the White House records were brazenly revised, that part of the deception was not extended to other Pentagon and State Department records, leaving them inconsistent with other records, for example, those kept by the USS *Saratoga*'s captain, Joe Tully. That was obviously due to the cloak of secrecy that was immediately invoked, which Johnson undoubtedly assumed would remain forever. Thankfully, Tully kept copies that indicated twelve fighter jets and/or bombers had immediately been launched before Admiral Lawrence Geis, the commander of the Sixth

Fleet, radioed Tully and ordered him to have all the aircraft returned, at 8:24 a.m.[EDT], minutes after the attack (At about the same time, the *Liberty* received a message "about 12:20Z" [Zulu] or 14:20 Sinai, that "help was on the way" and then again at 13:05Z, or 15:05 Sinai – or 9:05 a.m. in Washington).[16]

Geis told Tully that he could re-launch the fighter jets at 9:50 a.m., the time which Johnson and McNamara set, evidently, figuring the ship would be sunk by then anyway. Interestingly, this is also just one minute after the edited White House logs stated that President Johnson was informed of the incident, clearly reflecting that the White House logs had already been modified when that time was set, just so that the record would show how Johnson reacted so quickly, within one minute of hearing the awful news.

Joe Tully remained furious for the rest of his life that he had been prevented from rescuing the *Liberty*; he never realized that Lyndon Johnson was behind the order recalling that mission. The White House falsified records stand as a testament to one of the most egregious actions of a president of the United States ever.[17]

NSA DEPUTY DIRECTOR: "A NICE WHITEWASH"

As this was going on in the Oval Office, just after 10:00 a.m. in Washington (4 p.m. in the eastern Mediterranean) NSA Deputy Director Louis Tordella was informed by the deputy director of the Joint Reconnaissance Center (JRC), Captain Merriwell Vineyard, that: "According to NSA documents – classified top secret ... some senior officials in Washington wanted above all to protect Israel from embarrassment." Captain Vineyard had mentioned during this conversation, wrote Tordella, "that consideration was then being given by some unnamed Washington authorities to sink[ing] the *Liberty* in order that newspaper men would be unable to photograph her and thus inflame public opinion against the Israelis. I made an impolite comment about the idea."[18] Tordella angrily scrawled, "A nice whitewash for a group of ignorant, stupid and inept [expletive deleted]" across the top of the report. He wrote a memo of the conversation for the record, and stored it away.[19]

As the *Liberty* lay smoldering, President Johnson ordered the second fleet of fighter jets to return to their carrier. James Bamford, the author of *Body of Secrets*, described that scene more fully, and even more graphically: "*President Lyndon Johnson came on with a comment that he didn't give a damn if the ship sank, he would not embarrass his allies.*" [Emphasis added.] Admiral Geis told Lieutenant Commander David Lewis, the head of the NSA group on the *Liberty*, about the comment, but asked him to keep it secret until after Geis died. It was a promise that Lewis kept.[20]

There are a number of websites devoted to keeping the mystery of the unresolved attack on the USS *Liberty* in the public eye, many of which include a detailed timeline of events.[21] What the timelines reveal is that, as US sailors were being massacred in cold blood, Robert S. McNamara, US secretary of defense, as demanded by President Lyndon B. Johnson, cancelled a rescue mission from the Sixth Fleet carrier aircraft, ordering them to abandon the mission.[22]

Some people now evaluating this long held secret – one that is only now becoming known to more and more people – might even dare call it "treason." But this single order to abandon all protection for a US Navy spy ship is, lamentably, only incidental to an overall story about greater deceits and treachery. The timeline referenced in the previous citation goes on, to include much of the continuing developments covered within this chapter. There is one entry in particular on that extended timeline that is of more than the usual interest, under the date of June 14, 1967, six days after the attack: "*Liberty* arrives in Malta. Total news blackout imposed. Rear Admiral [Isaac] Kidd, acting on orders from John McCain II, warns crew: '*You are never, repeat never, to discuss this with anyone, not even your wives. If you do, you will be court-martialed and will end your lives in prison, or worse.*' Secretary of Defense McNamara informs media that, '*Department of Defense will have no further comment.*'" [Emphasis added.]

It is sobering to ponder what could possibly be "worse" than "ending your life in prison," and why would McNamara announce that the Department of Defense would have no further comment; this was a rather unusual statement, considering the circumstances. The last entry on that timeline was from November 1998: "Captain McGonagle breaks his long silence: 'After many years I finally believe that the attack was deliberate. I don't think there has been an adequate investigation of the incident…. The flag was flying prior to the attack….' McGonagle will die four months later, on March 3, 1999."

Lloyd Painter, a survivor of the attack who later became a Secret Service agent, lamented the fact that his skipper was not completely honest about what had happened. Painter said that he "witnessed a cover-up take place of the highest magnitude" and that in exchange for McGonagle's silence, he was given his choice of duty in the Navy.

Furthermore, author Hounam also wrote that a US intelligence agent who studied the attack on the *Liberty* determined that McGonagle was briefed to expect a superficial strafing attack, that would be used as a pretext for attacking Egypt, a repeat of the same kind of maneuver that Johnson had used at the gulf of Tonkin to produce a surge of patriotic fury that enabled him to take complete authority over another war. McGonagle had not been expecting the kind of vicious attack that actually occurred.

This same source stated that the war had started ten days prematurely; in fact that was the reason the operational code name was "Frontlet 615," which was the date that hostilities were to begin. It was a name that had been adopted the previous year, in a secret political agreement between the United States and Israel, one objective of which was to destroy Nasser. The code name given for the execution of the plan to sink the *Liberty* by the military was Operation Cyanide.[23]

WHO REALLY ORDERED THE ATTACK ... AND WHY?

A previously classified CIA document stated that:

> [REDACTED] said that [Moshe] Dayan personally ordered the attack on the ship and that one of his generals adamantly opposed the action and said, 'This is pure murder.' One of the admirals who was present also disapproved the action, and it was he who ordered it stopped [two and one-half hours later] and not Dayan. [REDACTED] believe that the attack against the US vessel is also detrimental to any political ambition Dayan may have.[24]

Given the fact that so many of the files on the USS *Liberty* and Operation Cyanide have remained closed, the extreme secrecy that was immediately invoked, and the fact that the files that were opened have been heavily redacted, it may be presumed that no paper document exists that is presently available which might be called the "smoking gun."

However, there was really only one man who was in a position to give Moshe Dayan that order: President Lyndon B. Johnson uniquely qualifies as the one man with the power, the manic resolve and the sociopathic absence of guilt required to solicit the highest ranking military official of Israel and his own specially-placed men in all the right places, all of them trained to help carry out whatever instructions he might order. Failing in his effort to recruit Chief of Staff Yitzhak Rabin to carry out these special orders, he would naturally turn next to Moshe Dayan, the Israeli Defense Minister. Mr. Dayan had no apparent motive, only Lyndon B. Johnson had such motives, and they had to do with his highest priority: Ensuring his tenure in the office he had always prized, which he had always considered as his rightful destiny. As his most prolific biographer, Robert Caro has elegantly stated:

> Johnson's hunger was for power "... in its most naked form, for power not to improve the lives of others, but to manipulate and dominate them, to bend them to his will ... it was a hunger so fierce and consuming that *no consideration of morality or ethics, no cost to himself – or to anyone else – could stand before it*. (emphasis added).[25]

Some people, reading these passages for the first time, may find this part of the thesis to be somewhat "speculative," however a better term might be "elucidative ... an attempt to clarify the inexplicable."

For example, Peter Hounam came to the conclusions that "... the *Liberty* was sent to its position off the Israeli coast precisely in order to be attacked,"[26] and "'Nuking' Egypt seems an act of madness,"[27] but in the end, he could not close the circle, ending it with these observations: "Is it credible that an American President would sanction the use of nuclear weapons in these circumstances? It is the most baffling of a series of riddles ... But it does not explain why Johnson, knowing the sordid truth about the *Liberty* attack, saw advantage to himself or his country in pushing the button."[28]

The last sentence of Mr. Hounam in the above paragraph says that nothing explains how Johnson saw an advantage to himself, is the key to solving the "series of riddles" that he referenced. But the reason those riddles and mysteries remain unsolved is that no other researcher or author has ever looked at the larger "enigma" in quite this way. The reason is that Lyndon Johnson's psychotic behavior, and his combination of untreated psychological and psychiatric issues over decades have been completely ignored by every other researcher, author and video producer. And that is exactly the "key" to solving the mystery of such an audacious event. If it all seems a bit convoluted, it is because the picture must be framed around the foibles of a man with a shady past, who was himself full of contradictions and insecurities and whose tortured mind occasionally overrode all barriers to irrational behavior, and that picture describes precisely the man who was the personification of the term "enigma."

As author Hounam continued his examination of these anomalies he seemed to come to a better understanding of what might have accounted for them, inexorably concluding that President Lyndon B. Johnson's actions were more than merely puzzling. After scheduling a meeting with his military advisers for the next hour, he then called his secretary and ordered her to begin compiling information about his reelection campaign plans for the following year, beginning with a listing of all the states he had visited, by year, since he became president. He gave her twenty minutes to complete the task; it was done in fifteen minutes.[29]

George Ball wrote the tragic denouement of the Israeli attack on the *Liberty* and its aftermath in his 1992 book *The Passionate Attachment*, which recalled George Washington's admonition that the United States must avoid "a passionate attachment" to another nation that could create "the illusion of a common interest ... where no common interest exists."[30] It was Ball's claim that the unparalleled cost of America's support of Israel, and its practically unqualified commitment to help it defend itself, are precisely what Washington warned against; it was also what so concerned

James Forrestal and others about the formation of the new country of Israel, whose mysterious death just after crossing paths with Lyndon Johnson is yet another unsolved cold case.

Endnotes

1. See BBC documentary video "Dead in the Water" (@ 31:15)

2. See Morris Smith, 5 *Towns Jewish Times* March 7, 2016, "Our First Jewish President Lyndon Johnson? – an update!!" http://5tjt.com/our-first-jewish-president-lyndon-johnson-an-update/

3. Hersh, The Samson Option, p. 168, f/n(*)

4. Ibid., p. 168

5. Ibid.

6. Ibid. p. 161

7. Hersh, *The Samson Option*, pp. 186-189

8. Ibid.

9. Hersh, *The Samson Option*, p. 190

10. Neff, *Fifty Years of Israel*, p. 153

11. Hersh, *The Samson Option*, pp. 189-191

12. Ibid.

13. Green, *Taking Sides* p. 194

14. See http://www.gilad.co.uk/writings/what-phil-saw-that-day.html

15. Hounam, pp. 89-91

16. Ennes, p. 77 f/n; p. 236 Appendix C.

17. Hounam, pp. 91-92

18. Bamford, p. 223.

19. Ibid. Also see http://historynewsnetwork.org/article/191#sthash.AQNFqXhS.dpuf

20. Bamford, p. 226. Also see YouTube: Documentary on the USS Liberty: Dead in the Water," op. cit. (@ 28:20).

21. See: http://www.ifamericansknew.org/us_ints/ul-ameu.html

22. See Margolis, Eric, 'The USS *Liberty*': America's Most Shameful Secret; and http://www.lewrockwell.com/ orig/margolis12.html; also http://www.ifamericansknew.org/us_ints/ul-ameu.html;

23. Hounam, p. 270

24. See USS *Liberty* Document Center: http://www.usslibertydocumentcenter.org/doc/upload/CIA_from_Tel-Aviv_1967.pdf

25. Caro, *The Path* ... p. xix

26. Hounam, p. 261

27. Ibid., p. 262

28. Ibid. p. 271

29. Ibid., also Ennes, p. 98

30. Ball, pp. 57 - 58

Part III: The Ensuing "Investigations"

Chapter 5

The Official Investigation Begins ... and Quickly Ends

Public sentiment is everything. With public sentiment, nothing can fail; without it, nothing can succeed. Consequently, he who moulds public sentiment goes deeper than he who enacts statutes or pronounces decisions.

– Abraham Lincoln

I know from personal conversations I had with Admiral Kidd that President Lyndon Johnson and Secretary of Defense Robert McNamara ordered him to conclude that the attack was a case of "mistaken identity" despite overwhelming evidence to the contrary.

– Ward Boston, Jr., Captain, JAGC, USN (Ret.)

How LBJ's 1967 Telephone Logs Belied the "Trap" He Created for Nasser

In contrast to President Kennedy's abhorrence of secrecy, throughout his public life, Lyndon Johnson was very secretive about anything that might be harmful to his political or financial aims, and careful about anything he might say or write that could become a part of the public record. If he had to communicate something that involved unethical, immoral, illegal, or unconstitutional matters, as he would explain to his associates or aides, it should never be done in writing; telephone conversations were better, unless of course there was any chance the telephone was bugged. The best type of communication for those kinds of conversations was the personal kind, and if there was a possibility that they could be recorded by the other party – or a third party – then all communications should only be done eyeball to eyeball, or through other means, such as hand or eye motions and other body language, and arcane Texas colloquialisms like "that dog won't hunt" or "let that sleeping dog lie," to reach an "understanding." He had practiced these methods of deceit for decades, teaching others such as his long-time colluding lawyer Ed Clark to follow them as well. An attorney in Clark's Austin, Texas firm, Barr Mc-

Clellan, noted a number of them throughout his book *Blood, Money & Power* including this example: "Clark [had] insisted that his lawyers put everything in writing. By 1952, Clark knew better when the transaction was incriminating and went outside the secret, privileged files. 'No evidence, no crime,' sayeth Clark."[1]

Another example came from his partner-in-crime, Billie Sol Estes, who explained that when LBJ came to Texas to discuss with him the plans for handling the employees who had become involved in their criminal activities, Johnson's assistant Cliff Carter had accompanied them, to take notes of Johnson's decisions on each of them. Carter acknowledged Johnson's reactions to each name they discussed, including those communicated only through body movements (e.g., head, arm, hand and finger pointing, or similar motions) and eye contact and, on several occasions, "only silence." (Based on the tone and hidden meanings of their communications as described by Estes, this implicitly meant that those people's fate would either be tabled for a later, private, discussion between Johnson and Carter, or there was already an understanding in place as to the disposition of people in certain categories.) The fact that five people on those lists wound up dead (all deemed to be "suicides") over the next two years indicated which list they were on.[2] Johnson had also trained his secretaries to keep detailed notes in his diary, sometimes including the gist of telephone conversations that he recorded. Not all conversations were recorded however, since he could control which ones were with a button on the telephone set or in his desk.

Compared to the numerous calls on every other subject, however, there were *none* recorded about the planning or management – before, during or after – the 1967 Middle East war, indicating that all of them involved subjects which had to be hidden. This point was made, paradoxically, by a scholar writing in *The Jerusalem Fund*, Dr. William B. Quandt, whose essay was purported to be a defense of the position that Lyndon Johnson was *not* the cunning manipulator behind what he called an "Israeli-American trap that was being set for Egyptian President Nasser, who unwittingly fell into it."[3]

> I had hoped that by now we would have more evidence, particularly from what Johnson was saying to his most intimate advisors and friends in his almost obsessive telephone conversations during the crisis. What we do know is who Johnson talked to. Telephone logs were exquisitely well-kept by his secretaries and we know that from the earlier sixties, 1964/1965, Johnson had a habit of pushing the little button on his phone to record the conversations. [When] the LBJ Library in Texas got around to releasing the tapes from 1967 … I thought we would find a treasure trove of new materials telling us what Johnson really said to whom in the crucial weeks of May/

June 1967. *Alas, he stopped pushing the little button in 1967. There are a few tapes from 1967,* [but] *none of them have to do with the Middle East crisis.* (Emphasis added)

What Dr. Quandt ironically, and clearly inadvertently, did was to produce evidence that showed the opposite of his thesis; it indicates that he was unaware of Johnson's long history of manipulating the public record to show only what he wanted it to show, while hiding that which would expose his real agenda. In the process, Dr. Quandt has paradoxically validated a portion of our thesis, which was that President Johnson, as we have previously demonstrated, had indeed set up the specially designed trap for Nasser to react to, so that Johnson could then blame him for initiating the very war for which Johnson had set the stage. In his attempt to show Johnson's innocence, Dr. Quandt revealed that Johnson, as he had always done, favored personal contact with his quarry; these schemes would never be recorded, nor would written records be maintained if possible to avoid them. If that was not possible, they would be highly classified and put away in top-secret files. It has been only by fortuitous error that key pieces of evidence were inadvertently released over many years..

But Dr. Quandt also revealed other points that indicated a lack of perceptiveness, as when he wrote: "Johnson surrounded himself with a fairly impressive group of advisors; they were men of considerable experience, diversity of views, and Johnson actually listened to them, unlike some presidents who have not paid too much attention to people around them. And they were not all of one mind."[4] That he misread these men as having "diversity of views," does not square with what so many others have stated about the facts that Johnson only wanted "yes men" around him and that he did not want to hear "bad news" from them, as shown in the random examples summarized below:

- According to the research of the highly credentialed author John Newman, Lyndon Johnson himself told his cabinet, on his second day on the job as president, November 24, 1963, that he had *"never been happy with our operations in Vietnam"* and that there had been "serious dissension and divisions" between the cabinet members that must be cleaned up. Furthermore, he declared that there would be *"no more divisions of opinion, no more bickering and any person that did not conform to policy should be removed."*[5] [First phrase emphasis in original; second phrase emphasis added.]

- Johnson dominated the cabinet just as he had dominated every other committee he had ever chaired. A good illustration of the point was reported contemporaneously by *Life* magazine about the Democratic Senatorial Campaign Committee: "It was a committee in name only, for Johnson controlled it absolutely," This article continued, "money was given only to senators and senatorial candidates whom Johnson felt he could control; in the words of a Senate insider quoted by the magazine ... 'with no talk back. No mavericks.'"[6]

- Dean Rusk, the secretary of state, admitted that none of the cabinet members would *ever* challenge the president, afraid that doing so would automatically get them fired, when he stated in his memoirs: "At most cabinet meetings Lyndon Johnson asked Bob McNamara and me to comment on Vietnam, and then he would go around the table, asking each cabinet officer, 'Do you have any questions or comments?' Everyone sat silently."[7]

- Arthur Goldberg, who went from secretary of labor, to Supreme Court justice, to UN ambassador within the Johnson administration, stated that a colleague who served with him in Kennedy's cabinet said, "Kennedy didn't mind disagreement. It didn't bother him. But disagreement really bothers this President. He is going to do what you dislike anyway; so let's not upset him by having an argument in front of him."[8]

- George Reedy affirmed all of these assertions when he stated that the discussions were "very gentlemanly" and were "really monologues in which one man is getting reflections of what he sends out."[9]

- Richard Goodwin also noted the same point in his memoirs, when he described White House meetings, and how Johnson's presence dominated and immediately set the tone for every meeting, generally as a reminder not to contradict or question him; to do so was tantamount to calling him a liar, "And one didn't call Johnson a liar, not to his face."[10]

- Richard Goodwin also said that Johnson would begin cabinet meetings with the question: "What are you doing here? Why aren't you out there fighting against my enemies? Don't you realize that if they destroy me, they'll destroy you as well? ... Questions about Vietnam were discouraged, and, if asked, went unanswered."[11]

- Robert McNamara once said, "*I don't believe the government of a complicated state can operate effectively if those in charge of the departments of the government express disagreement with decisions of the established head of that government.*"[12] [Emphasis added.] In other words, McNamara had come to agree with Johnson that only "Yes" men could be tolerated throughout his administration.

Except for the short period of time that George Ball had remained on the White House staff after JFK's assassination, the entire group of advisors to Lyndon Johnson were all sycophantic "yes men." All were afraid of him, and would never confront him on anything of consequence because they valued their high level, prestigious government positions more than taking an interest in ensuring that the "ship of state" was prudently guided. That many of them even knew, or should have known, that the president they served had often experienced psychotic episodes meant that they were partly responsible for how, not only that ship but the one called *Liberty*, was put in jeopardy. George Ball later recalled that "McNamara treated his [Ball's] dissenting memos rather like 'poisonous snakes.' He was 'absolutely horrified' by them, considered them 'next to treason.' We met then for two Saturday afternoons to discuss this thing. As I say, the general attitude of the conferees was to treat it as something that really shouldn't have been done. Although I think that Rusk and Bundy were more tolerant of my effort to put it on paper than Bob was. He really just regarded it as next to treason, that this had been put down on paper."[13] Johnson's aversion to leaving paper trails had obviously been adopted by McNamara for the same reasons as his boss.

Unlike Presidents Truman, Eisenhower and Kennedy – who had all endeavored to maintain a comfortable distance between the US and Israel, in order to keep a neutral position from which to promote peaceful relations between Israel and its Arab neighbors – President Johnson moved quickly to drop all pretense of neutrality. Within days of his ascendency to the Oval Office, after JFK's murder, Johnson told the Israeli ambassador, "You have lost a very great friend, but you have found a better one." Afif Safieh, a Palestinian Roving Ambassador for Special Missions based in London, wrote in his essay, *The 1967 Occupation: A Palestinian Perspective,* another interesting contrast of President Johnson's attitudes:[14]

> I remember 35 years ago reading the memoirs of Golda Meir ... In one of those pages [recalling when she went to JFK's funeral] Lyndon Johnson bends over her to tell her, "With me in the White House there will be no repeat of the Eisenhower incident of 1956." Eisenhower, with just one phone call to Ben Gurion, obtained Israeli total withdrawal out of the Sinai in 24 hours. This is extremely indicative and revealing of Johnson's personal inclination and preference.

It is clear that Johnson had lost no time in using JFK's assassination to ingratiate himself with all of Israel's leaders, reassuring them that their "wish lists" would now be honored. As historian and author Donald Neff observed, "Up to Johnson's presidency, no administration had been as completely pro-Israel and anti-Arab as his."[15] Before the end of his presidency, he would out-Zion his most jealously Zionist advisors, practically giving Israel everything they asked for, even in some cases more than they had dared to dream.

But it is more than a little ironic that this would be the direct result of the intentional, vicious Israeli attack on an American warship. That Israel achieved such enormous, long-term benefits from an action that should normally have resulted in severe penalties and sanctions suggests that the real story is comprised of lethal secrets, discrete blackmail and ransom disguised as foreign aid. In the final analysis it is an explanation of why there still exist so many untold secrets, locked away in vaults in such places as Washington, DC, Arlington and Langley Virginia, and various locations in Israel. And, there were probably even more that once existed but will never be found.

President Johnson pretends (for one day) to be angered by the attack

For a very brief period, lasting about one day, Lyndon Johnson pretended to be angered by the Israeli attack on his ship. He was even the anonymous source for *Newsweek* reporter Charles Roberts, who wrote an article for the magazine which claimed that Israel had "carried out a deliberate attack because the *Liberty* had intentionally engaged in electronic espionage." That message was nearly identical to the information presented at a State Department background briefing the day following the attack.[16] The day after that, Israeli diplomats discovered that the leak had come from Johnson himself; this should not come as a surprise to people who have studied Johnson's tactics, because that kind of sleight-of-hand comment was his pro-forma method of sowing confusion when he wanted to implicate others for a deed that he himself had perpetrated.[17]

Richard Helms confirmed much of that: "The White house was at first angry, but after 24 hours President Johnson just disappeared out of the picture."[18] This is an astonishing remark coming from the ex-director of the CIA, a well-established prevaricator like Richard Helms, therefore we must closely consider this comment: Helms basically explained Johnson's behavior as angry, but only for 24 hours. Not only was this a very untypical Johnson response to such an enormously explosive situation, but it probably means that Johnson only *pretended* to be angry at first, because that would be expected. Then he just dropped it and immediately set in place all the blockades that would ensure the real story became lost in the shuffle as a planted story about an Israeli "mistake" replaced it. Planting lies to replace truths.

It is axiomatic that Lyndon Johnson would have been the first to realize that the number one priority at that point would be to order absolute secrecy to every sailor, navy officer, and civilian NSA technician on board that ship. That this particular perfidy precisely fits what actually happened is undisputed by anyone. Indeed, it also explains why the story remained a secret for as long as it did.

There was a quite rational, albeit troubling, reason for McNamara's previously noted reticence about discussing the USS *Liberty*: Doing so, he must have realized, would be tantamount to standing on the top step of the front portico of the US Supreme Court, with hundreds of reporters present, and voluntarily announcing that he, along with former President Lyndon B. Johnson, was guilty of the high crime of treason.

Peter Hounam's interview with Robert McNamara exposed his complete denial and loss of memory on one of the most critical events of his period in office. In that interview he kept repeating things like, "My recollection of the circumstances around the *Liberty* is very vague ... I have nothing to say on the *Liberty* ... I don't recall it, but everything ... well, I'm not going to go further. I'm not going to say anything on the *Liberty* ... I don't know what the hell happened and I haven't taken time to find out ... I know nothing about it. I don't want to say I didn't at the time, but today I have no knowledge of it."[19]

Later that same day, a general cover story for the *Liberty* was outlined that would be handed down from the highest military officer, the commander-in-chief, to the secretary of defense, through the Joint Chiefs of Staff to Admiral John S. McCain, Jr., Commander-in-Chief, U.S. Atlantic Fleet, who would order others in his command, including Rear Admiral Isaac Kidd and Captain Ward Boston, Jr., to begin implementing the order, adjusting it as necessary to severely limit any real investigation.

The avenue the investigation followed was engrained into the system, whereby senior officers could expect complete obedience from their subordinates, and it repeated down through the chain of command, until carried out by the men at the bottom of the chain. When such orders are proper and legal, the system works; unfortunately, it may be perverted when the man at the top is unprincipled and has no scruples. In the "investigation" of the attack on the *Liberty*, it is clear that the process was sabotaged from the start: determining the truth was never the objective. Indeed, it has been demonstrated by the Navy officers involved that the investigation was preplanned to hide the most important facts – not expose them.

The US Naval official inquiry, to be examined next, was deliberately falsified. Details acquired were either changed or dropped so that the official U.S. Navy's report would complement the Israeli version, both of which would conclude that that the attack was a tragic mistake despite the multitude of facts that disproved such a conclusion.

THE "OFFICIAL INVESTIGATIONS" INTO WHAT REALLY CAUSED THE ATTACK ... AND WHY THEY WERE INCONCLUSIVE

Unlike any other attack on a US Navy vessel, there has never been an official congressional investigation on the USS *Liberty* attack. The perfunctory initial Navy investigation lasted only eight days, which was, according to author James Scott, the son of survivor John Scott, "less time than it took to bury some of the dead. The Navy's top-secret final report proved a muddled mess with typos, misspellings, and contradictory findings."[20] It has since been acknowledged to have been an intentional cover-up, by the attorney who originally oversaw it, Captain Ward Boston. It had come from Johnson himself, through Robert McNamara, who assigned it to Admiral John McCain II, who then commanded others to create the primary cover-up document: It was to be a superficial, non-investigation to create a bogus report designed to hide the real story in an elaborate "official" account presented ceremoniously to the highest government officials. And all of it was done simultaneously with orders to clamp the lid of secrecy on everyone and everything connected to it.

Ernie Gallo stated that "While we were sailing to Malta, Admiral Isaac Kidd helicoptered out to the ship to ensure the crew did not discuss the attack with waiting newsmen. He interviewed some of the crew to obtain a preliminary idea of the event. After we arrived in Malta, he chaired the Navy Court of Inquiry which included Captain Ward Boston as his legal counsel. Selected crew members were asked to give testimony under oath. Some discovered later that their testimonies of the IDF machine-gunning stretcher bearers and life rafts were absent from the finished report.

We later learned the testimonies of the wounded on the USS *America* and USS *Little Rock* (a cruiser and Sixth Fleet Flag Ship) were considered important by the court but were over-ruled by Admiral McCain in London. They also wanted to interview Israelis, however McCain insisted the court conclude as soon as possible. Members of the crew who gave critical testimony obtained a copy of this report and they indicated that their testimony was left out if it indicated Israeli brutality."

A summary of the official report is presented below, as described in a document prepared in 2005 and submitted to the Secretary of the Army as "A Report: War Crimes Committed Against U.S. Military Personnel, June 8, 1967." This report was submitted in accordance with official guidelines for requesting war crimes investigation, yet it has never been resolved, or even responded to. Those provisions state, in part:

> a. The Armed Forces of the United States will comply with the law of war during all armed conflicts, however such conflicts are characterized, and, unless otherwise directed by competent authorities, the US Armed Forces will comply with the principles and spirit of

the law of war during all other operations. Specifically, reference A provides that it is the policy of the Department of Defense to ensure that:

(1) The law of war obligations of the US Government are observed and enforced by the US Armed Forces. (2) An effective program designed to prevent violations of the law of war is implemented by the US Armed Forces. (3) *All reportable incidents committed by or against members of (or persons serving with or accompanying) the US Armed Forces are promptly reported, thoroughly investigated and, where appropriate, remedied by corrective action.* (Emphasis added).

The full 38-page War Crimes Report, which readers are encouraged to review in detail to gain a complete understanding of the awful truth of the *Liberty* attack, is available to the public at many of the USS *Liberty* websites, including: http://www.gtr5.com/evidence/warcrimes.pdf).

The following excerpts from the 2005 War Crimes Report convey how the original flawed report of the 1967 Navy Court of Inquiry was intentionally written, not to identify the causes of the attack, but to cover them up:

"Convening initially in London, the Court proceeded immediately to the Mediterranean and conducted its inquiry both aboard USS *Liberty* as she limped under escort to Malta, and in succeeding days as she lay in dry-dock there. Concluding their inquiries there, the President of the Court, with the Navy Judge Advocate General's Corps officer who had been appointed as Counsel to the Court, and with a Navy court reporter who had been assigned from the London headquarters to assist, returned to London on June 16, 1967 (eight days after the attack), with their results.

"Within 24 hours of the attack, the United States Navy convened a formal Court of Inquiry into that attack – a standard investigative procedure reserved for such serious events or circumstances. This procedure was unusual in only one respect – the President and members appointed to the Court of Inquiry by the Commander in Chief, U.S. Naval Forces, Europe (CINCUSNAVEUR), [Admiral John McCain, Jr.,] headquartered in London, *were directed orally by the appointing authority to conduct and complete their investigative proceedings within one week – a most unusual requirement in light of the nature and magnitude of the events they were ordered to investigate* (Emphasis added). Convening initially in London, the Court proceeded immediately to the Mediterranean and conducted its inquiry both aboard USS *Liberty* as she limped under escort to Malta, and in succeeding days as she lay in dry-dock there. Concluding their inquiries there, the President of the Court [Rear Admiral Isaac C. Kidd, Jr.], with the Navy Judge Advocate

General's Corps officer who had been appointed as Counsel to the Court [Captain Ward Boston, Jr.] and with a Navy court reporter who had been assigned from the London headquarters to assist, returned to London on June 16, 1967 (eight days after the attack), with their results.

"At London, the Navy court reporter supervised the final production of a written record of the Court's proceedings and findings – a document over 600 typewritten pages in length. On the afternoon of June 17, 1967, that record of the Court's proceedings was delivered to the senior Navy Judge Advocate General's Corps officer [Captain Merlin Staring] on the CINCUSNAVEUR (Commander-in-Chief, U.S. Navy Europe [Admiral John S. McCain II]) staff for his review and recommendation to the appointing authority concerning his required endorsement and action upon the Court's proceedings and record. The CINCUSNAVEUR Staff Judge Advocate [Staring] thus charged with that review – *in full compliance and accord with standard Navy requirements and practice – turned immediately to his detailed examination and consideration of the record. He continued that process steadily into the early morning hours of June 18, 1967, then after a four-hour rest break resumed his review at 6:00 AM on June 18th. In the midforenoon of June 18th an emissary from his Commander, the appointing authority, appeared and inquired of the Staff Judge Advocate concerning the status of his review and when it might be expected to be completed. The Staff Judge Advocate advised that he had by then read only about a third of the record – that there were many clerical and typographical flaws in the record that should be remedied before it was formally forwarded to the high governmental authorities who undoubtedly awaited it – that, more importantly, the reviewer had not yet been able to find, in the parts of the record he had so far reviewed, testimony or other evidence to support some of the Court's stated conclusions – and that he could not yet estimate when he could complete his review and recommendations but was continuing to devote himself solely to that task. The emissary from the appointing authority departed with that information , then returned about 20 minutes later with the message that CINCUSNAVEUR, [Admiral McCain] the appointing authority, had directed him to come and get the Court's record from the Staff Judge Advocate and bring it back to the appointing authority. The Staff Judge Advocate [Captain Staring] accordingly surrendered the record to the emissary exactly as he had received it; he was neither then nor later asked for any of his work or opinions so far; and he had no further contact with the Court of Inquiry or its results at any time in his active Navy career.* [Emphasis added by authors].

"The records of the Navy Department reveal that the written record of proceedings of the U.S. Navy Court of Inquiry into the Israeli attack upon USS *Liberty* was formally submitted by the President of the Court of Inquiry to CINCUSNAVEUR, [McCain] the appointing authority, by a written letter dated 18 June 1967, the very day that the record had been withdrawn by the appointing authority from his Staff Judge Advocate. The written record also reveals that the appointing authority, on that same day, placed upon that record of the Court's proceedings, a five-page First Endorsement, transmitting that Record to the Judge Advocate General of the Navy in Washington as required by the Navy's investigative procedures.

"Mr. Secretary, it is respectfully submitted that, even based solely upon the facts and circumstances outlined above, the Navy Court of Inquiry into the Israeli attack on USS *Liberty* – the sole official investigation by the United States Government into that attack – was deficient and prejudiced, even at its outset, by the unreasonable haste imposed informally by the appointing authority. In addition, the processing of that Court's hasty result was further compromised by its peremptory withdrawal from its initial and prescribed legal review in the field, and its hurried transmission to the seat of the U.S. Government under cover of a purported official endorsement that could not conceivably have been based upon even a cursory complete review of even the hasty work of the Navy Court of Inquiry. Inexplicably, the Court record was classified Top Secret and withheld from public scrutiny for many years."

Another attempt to investigate the incident was completed thirteen years later when, in 1980, an eighty-three-page secret report was completed, which was only released to the public in 2011, and still heavily redacted, with many entire pages blank. Entitled, "United States Cryptologic History – Attack on a Sigint Collector,"[21] it does contain much basic information, even though it stops short of insightful explanations. For example, on page 13, it states that "The decision to deploy [the USS *Liberty*], it should be noted, came before the Six-Day War erupted." Technically, and narrowly, that is correct, but is far from the complete truth as we know it now: The decision to deploy it was merely one step toward initiating a war that had been planned for months.

Another example, on page 40 – after noting the messages sent to Moscow regarding the attack, to explain that aircraft were sent to investigate it – the report blithely states: "Thereafter instructions were issued by JCS and Commander, Sixth Fleet to withdraw the aircraft launched to defend the *Liberty*. By 18:49 hours Sixth Fleet reported all planes recalled and accounted for." Just as so many other puzzling questions were never answered, this report glosses right over the most obvious one: *No explana-*

tion whatsoever was given as to <u>why</u> the US Navy was clearly abandoning its own ship and all of the men aboard that ship. It should also be noted, for the record, that the heavily redacted report makes no mention of the strafing attacks on the lifeboats. That was likely in the excised material since it only "adds fuel to the fire" of extreme outrage that such information might otherwise ignite. Also missing are the profane quotes from the president of the United States, as were reported elsewhere by Admiral Geis and others, regarding his orders to "recall the wings." As evidenced by the number of pages that have been either entirely redacted or nearly so, there is much that the government is still hiding fifty years after the attack.

It is essential to remember the context: the war was practically over, and would have been over had Johnson not purposely delayed work on a cease-fire treaty as revealed by Nicholas Katzenbach in his 2008 memoirs. He stated that most administration officials, including Navy personnel, did not believe the Israeli explanation that it was "a case of mistaken identity." He acknowledged that Johnson accepted the apology for political reasons but that they should offer the families "generous compensation," undoubtedly with the understanding that they would be reimbursed for that by the United States anyway as part of the annual aid package they received. Moreover, he admitted that the State Department had angered many in the Jewish community through its issuance of a statement of neutrality, which was considered in retrospect as unwise. That controversy apparently caused Johnson to back off efforts to obtain a ceasefire at the United Nations, where a disagreement regarding the language about the definition of territories had materialized.[22]

Stephen Green's book, referenced previously, went further in its explanation of the delay in the peace negotiations, stating that it was necessary because "The IDF needed time ... By the evening of June 6, a cease-fire resolution had been passed. But during those first two critical days of furious bargaining on the matter, the U.S. delegation, led by Ambassador Arthur Goldberg, resisted any cease-fire resolution that would (a) brand Israel as the aggressor or (b) include a demand for a troop withdrawal to the June 4 borders. This in spite of the fact that the Johnson White House knew that Israel had carried out a massive sneak attack that had, in the case of Egypt, destroyed 300 planes on the ground in the first 170 minutes ..."[23] Green also described Johnson's duplicity in this same period, between what he did publicly and what he did secretively, practically simultaneously: Just as he had authorized emergency shipments to Israel, of armored personnel carriers, tank and Hawk missile spare parts, bomb fuses, artillery ammunition and gas masks, he had publicly declared an arms embargo for anything going to the Middle East. That message was obviously meant for the Arab countries, since it clearly didn't apply to Israel.[24]

The subject of the still-unexplained *Liberty* attack continues to arouse passions among many, not only those who actually survived the attack. Most of the books on the subject were written, consciously or not, to support one side or the other in this debate; to one degree or another, all can be said to be tendentiously weighted to an unstated agenda. If there is any doubt about the veracity of the previous statements concerning the real purpose of the Navy's original "investigation" and report of the Court of Inquiry, the reader should study the following document closely. It was written by the author of that report, before he realized the travesty of justice that was being engineered inside the White House. After remaining silent for thirty-seven years, as ordered by the President of the United States and communicated by the military chain-of-command, Captain Ward Boston, Jr. finally came forward to document the fact that the 1967 report was a pack of lies. He was enraged (as he himself noted in this document) that the book by A. Jay Cristol published in 2002, attempted to re-prove those lies and thereby help make the "official story" permanent. That the State Department then used Cristol's book to permanently close the case and seal it once and for all, with their January, 2004 "Hearing" was the catalyst that caused Boston to issue this statement just two weeks before that officious event.

Declaration of Ward Boston, Jr., Captain, JAGC, USN (Ret.)

I, Ward Boston, Jr. do declare that the following statement is true and complete:

1. For more than 30 years, I have remained silent on the topic of USS *Liberty*. I am a military man and when orders come in from the Secretary of Defense and President of the United States, I follow them.

2. However, recent attempts to rewrite history compel me to share the truth.

3. In June of 1967, while serving as a Captain in the Judge Advocate General Corps, Department of the Navy, I was assigned as senior legal counsel for the Navy's Court of Inquiry into the brutal attack on USS *Liberty*, which had occurred on June 8th.

4. The late Admiral Isaac C. Kidd, president of the Court, and I were given only one week to gather evidence for the Navy's official investigation into the attack, despite the fact that we both had estimated that a proper Court of Inquiry into an attack of this magnitude would take at least six months to conduct.

5. Admiral John S. McCain, Jr., then Commander-in-chief, Naval Forces Europe (CINCUSNAVEUR), at his headquarters in London, had charged Admiral Kidd (in a letter dated June 10, 1967) to

> "inquire into all the pertinent facts and circumstances leading to and connected with the armed attack; damage resulting therefrom; and deaths of and injuries to Naval personnel."

6. Despite the short amount of time we were given, we gathered a vast amount of evidence, including hours of heartbreaking testimony from the young survivors.

7. The evidence was clear. Both Admiral Kidd and I believed with certainty that this attack, which killed 34 American sailors and injured 172 others, was a deliberate effort to sink an American ship and murder its entire crew. Each evening, after hearing testimony all day, we often spoke our private thoughts concerning what we had seen and heard. I recall Admiral Kidd repeatedly referring to the Israeli forces responsible for the attack as "murderous bastards." It was our shared belief, based on the documentary evidence and testimony we received first hand, that the Israeli attack was planned and deliberate, and could not possibly have been an accident.

8. I am certain that the Israeli pilots that undertook the attack, as well as their superiors, who had ordered the attack, were well aware that the ship was American.

9. I saw the flag, which had visibly identified the ship as American, riddled with bullet holes, and heard testimony that made it clear that the Israelis intended there be no survivors.

10. Not only did the Israelis attack the ship with napalm, gunfire, and missiles, Israeli torpedo boats machine-gunned three lifeboats that had been launched in an attempt by the crew to save the most seriously wounded – a war crime.

11. Admiral Kidd and I both felt it necessary to travel to Israel to interview the Israelis who took part in the attack. Admiral Kidd telephoned Admiral McCain to discuss making arrangements. Admiral Kidd later told me that Admiral McCain was adamant that we were not to travel to Israel or contact the Israelis concerning this matter.

12. Regrettably, we did not receive into evidence and the Court did not consider any of the more than sixty witness declarations from men who had been hospitalized and were unable to testify in person.

13. I am outraged at the efforts of the apologists for Israel in this

country to claim that this attack was a case of "mistaken identity."

14. In particular, the recent publication of Jay Cristol's book, *The Liberty Incident*, twists the facts and misrepresents the views of those of us who investigated the attack.

15. It is Cristol's insidious attempt to whitewash the facts that has pushed me to speak out.

16. I know from personal conversations I had with Admiral Kidd that President Lyndon Johnson and Secretary of Defense Robert McNamara ordered him to conclude that the attack was a case of "mistaken identity" despite overwhelming evidence to the contrary.

17. Admiral Kidd told me, after returning from Washington, D.C. that he had been ordered to sit down with two civilians from either the White House or the Defense Department, and rewrite portions of the court's findings.

18. Admiral Kidd also told me that he had been ordered to "put the lid" on everything having to do with the attack on USS *Liberty*. We were never to speak of it and we were to caution everyone else involved that they could never speak of it again.

19. I have no reason to doubt the accuracy of that statement as I know that the Court of Inquiry transcript that has been released to the public is not the same one that I certified and sent off to Washington.

20. I know this because it was necessary, due to the exigencies of time, to hand correct and initial a substantial number of pages. I have examined the released version of the transcript and I did not see any pages that bore my hand corrections and initials. Also, the original did not have any deliberately blank pages, as the released version does. Finally, the testimony of Lt. Painter concerning the deliberate machine gunning of the life rafts by the Israeli torpedo boat crews, which I distinctly recall being given at the Court of Inquiry and included in the original transcript, is now missing and has been excised.

21. Following the conclusion of the Court of Inquiry, Admiral Kidd and I remained in contact. Though we never spoke of the attack in public, we did discuss it between ourselves, on occasion. Every time we discussed the attack, Admiral Kidd was adamant that it was a deliberate, planned attack on an American ship.

22. In 1990, I received a telephone call from Jay Cristol, who wanted to interview me concerning the functioning of the Court of Inquiry. I told him that I would not speak to him on that subject and prepared to hang up the telephone. Cristol then began ask-

ing me about my personal background and other, non-Court of Inquiry related matters. I endeavored to answer these questions and politely extricate myself from the conversation. Cristol continued to return to the subject of the Court of Inquiry, which I refused to discuss with him. Finally, I suggested that he contact Admiral Kidd and ask him about the Court of Inquiry.

23. Shortly after my conversation with Cristol, I received a telephone call from Admiral Kidd, inquiring about Cristol and what he was up to. The Admiral spoke of Cristol in disparaging terms and even opined that "Cristol must be an Israeli agent." I don't know if he meant that literally or it was his way of expressing his disgust for Cristol's highly partisan, pro-Israeli approach to questions involving USS *Liberty*.

24. At no time did I ever hear Admiral Kidd speak of Cristol other than in highly disparaging terms. I find Cristol's claims of a "close friendship" with Admiral Kidd to be utterly incredible. I also find it impossible to believe the statements he attributes to Admiral Kidd, concerning the attack on USS *Liberty*.

25. Several years later, I received a letter from Cristol that contained what he purported to be his notes of our prior conversation. These "notes" were grossly incorrect and bore no resemblance in reality to that discussion. I find it hard to believe that these "notes" were the product of a mistake, rather than an attempt to deceive. I informed Cristol that I disagreed with his recollection of our conversation and that he was wrong. Cristol made several attempts to arrange for the two of us to meet in person and talk but I always found ways to avoid doing this. I did not wish to meet with Cristol as we had nothing in common and I did not trust him.

26. Contrary to the misinformation presented by Cristol and others, it is important for the American people to know that it is clear that Israel is responsible for deliberately attacking an American ship and murdering American sailors, whose bereaved shipmates have lived with this egregious conclusion for many years.

Dated: January 8, 2004
at Coronado, California

(Signed)
Ward Boston, Jr., Captain, JAGC, USN (Ret.)
Senior Counsel to the USS *Liberty* Court of Inquiry
* * *

FULL STATEMENT OF ADMIRAL THOMAS MOORER

America's HIghest Ranking Naval Officer
Admiral Thomas Moorer (1912 - 2004)
Former Chief of Naval Operations
and
Chairman, Joint Chiefs of Staff
Rejects the Israeli Excuse
MEMORANDUM:
From: Admiral Thomas H. Moorer
Subject: Attack on the USS *Liberty* June 8, 1967
Date: June 8, 1997

I have never believed that the attack on the USS *Liberty* was a case of mistaken identity. That is ridiculous. I have flown over the Atlantic and Pacific oceans, thousands of hours, searching for ships and identifying all types of ships at sea. The *Liberty* was the ugliest, strangest looking ship in the U.S. Navy. As a communications intelligence ship, it was sprouting every kind of antenna. It looked like a lobster with all those projections moving every which way.

Israel knew perfectly well that the ship was American. After all, the *Liberty*'s American flag and markings were in full view in perfect visibility for the Israeli aircraft that overflew the ship eight times over a period of nearly eight hours prior to the attack. I am confident that Israel knew the *Liberty* could intercept radio messages from all parties and potential parties to the ongoing war, then in its fourth day, and that Israel was preparing to seize the Golan Heights from Syria despite President Johnson's known opposition to such a move. I think they realized that if we learned in advance of their plan, there would be a tremendous amount of negotiating between Tel Aviv and Washington.

And I believe Moshe Dayan concluded that he could prevent Washington from becoming aware of what Israel was up to by destroying the primary source of acquiring that information the USS *Liberty*. The result was a wanton sneak attack that left 34 American sailors dead and 171 seriously injured. What is so chilling and cold-blooded, of course, is that they could kill as many Americans as they did in confidence that Washington would cooperate in quelling any public outcry.

I have to conclude that it was Israel's intent to sink the *Liberty* and leave as few survivors as possible. Up to the point where the torpedo boats were sent in, you could speculate on that point. You have to remember that the *Liberty* was an intelligence ship, not a fighting ship, and its only defensive weapons were a pair of 50-caliber machine guns both aft and on the forecastle. There was little the men could do to fight off the air assault from Israeli jets that pounded the *Liberty* with bombs, rockets, napalm and machine gun fire for 25 minutes.

With the *Liberty* riddled with holes, fires burning, and scores of casualties, three Israeli torpedo boats closed in for the kill. The second of three torpedoes ripped through a compartment at amidships, drowning 25 of the men in that section. Then the torpedo boats closed to within 100 feet of the *Liberty* to continue the attack with cannons and machine guns, resulting in further casualties. It is telling, with respect to whether total annihilation was the intent, that the *Liberty* crew has reported that the torpedo boats' machine guns also were turned on life rafts that were deployed into the Mediterranean as well as those few on deck that had escaped damage.

As we know now, if the rescue aircraft from U.S. carriers had not been recalled, they would have arrived at the *Liberty* before the torpedo attack, reducing the death toll by 25. The torpedo boat commanders could not be certain that Sixth Fleet aircraft were not on the way and this might have led to their breaking off the attack after 40 minutes rather than remaining to send the *Liberty* and its crew of 294 to the bottom. Congress to this day has failed to hold formal hearings for the record on the *Liberty* affair. This is unprecedented and a national disgrace. I spent hours on the Hill giving testimony after the USS *Pueblo*, a sister ship to the *Liberty*, was seized by North Korea. I was asked every imaginable question, including why a carrier in the area failed to dispatch aircraft to aid the *Pueblo*. In the *Liberty* case, fighters were put in the air not once, but twice. They were ordered to stand down by Secretary of Defense McNamara and President Johnson for reasons the American public deserves to know.

The captain and crew of the *Liberty*, rather than being widely acclaimed as the heroes they most certainly are, have been silenced, ignored, honored belatedly and away from the cameras, and denied a history that accurately reflects their ordeal. I was appalled that six of the dead from the *Liberty* lay under a tombstone at Arlington Cemetery that described them as having "died in the eastern Mediterranean," as if disease rather than Israeli intent had caused their deaths. The Naval Academy failed to record the name of Lt. Stephen Toth in Memorial Hall on the grounds that he had not been killed in battle. I intervened and was able to reverse the apparent idea that dying in a cowardly, one-sided attack by a supposed ally is somehow not the same as being killed by an avowed enemy.

Commander McGonagle's story is the stuff of naval tradition. Badly wounded in the first air attack, lying on the deck and losing blood, he refused any treatment that would take him from his battle station on the bridge. He continued to direct the ship's defense, the control of flooding and fire, and by his own example inspired the survivors to heroic efforts to save the ship. He did not relinquish his post until hours later, after having directed the crippled ship's navigation to a rendezvous with a U.S. destroyer and final arrival in Malta.

I must have gone to the White House 15 times or more to watch the President personally award the Congressional Medal of Honor to Americans of special valor. So it irked the hell out of me when McGonagle's ceremony was relegated to the obscurity of the Washington Navy Yard and the medal was presented by the Secretary of the Navy. This was a back-handed slap. Everyone else received their medal at the White House. President Johnson must have been concerned about the reaction of the Israeli lobby.

The *Liberty* Veterans Association deserves the encouragement of everyone who wants the facts of the *Liberty* incident revealed and proper homage paid to the men who lost their lives, to their families, and to the survivors. I have attended many of their reunions and am always impressed with the cohesion of the *Liberty* family. They arrive in town with their whole entourage grandmas, grandpas, grandchildren. They promote the memory of the boys who were killed and I respect them for that. They are mostly from small country towns, probably a lot like Eufaula, Alabama, where I grew up, and they represent the basic core of America that has enabled us to be a superpower for so long. These are the kind of people who will make certain that our *Liberty* and freedom survive if fighting is what it takes.

[signed] Admiral Thomas Moorer

Endnotes

1. McClellan, p. 105

2. Nelson, LBJ: From Mastermind to the Colossus, pp. xxix - xxx.

3. See: *40 Years after the 1967 War: The Impact of a Prolonged Occupation*. Edited transcript of remarks titled *The Johnson Administration and the 1967 War*, Dr. William Quandt, The Palestine Center Washington, D.C. 5 June 2007 (http://www.thejerusalemfund.org/ht/a/GetDocumentAction/i/2918)

4. Ibid.

5. Newman, p. 443

6. Wheeler, Keith, "Scandal grows and grows in Washington," *Life*, November 22, 1963, p. 41

7. Rusk, p. 467.

8. Schlesinger, *The Imperial Presidency* ..., p. 185

9. Ibid., p. 186

10. Goodwin, Richard, p. 461.

11. Ibid., p. 410.

12. Herring, p. 8

13. Transcript, George Ball oral history Interview I, 7/8/71, by Paige E. Mulhollan, Internet Copy, LBJ Library, p. 10.

14. See: *40 Years after the 1967 War: The Impact of a Prolonged Occupation.* Edited transcript of remarks titled *The 1967 Occupation: A Palestinian Perspective,* Afif Safieh The Palestine Center Washington, D.C. 5 June 2007 (http://www.thejerusalemfund.org/ht/a/GetDocumentAction/i/2918)

15. Neff, *Fifty Years of Israel,* p. 219

16. Scott, p. 195

17. One of the many examples of that occurred when, in retirement, he told Walter Cronkite that he never really believed his own Warren Commission finding that Lee Harvey Oswald was the "lone assassin," and that he had always suspected an international conspiracy involving Fidel Castro, who allegedly wanted to get back at the Kennedys for their plotting to assassinate Castro. This was a multi-level deception that not only pointed the finger away from himself, but even implicated his arch-enemy Robert F. Kennedy as having been an unwitting instigator in the assassination of his brother.

18. Hounam, p. 239

19. Ibid. pp. 236-238

20. Scott, James, p. 4.

21. See unclassified report United States Cryptologic History: Attack on a Sigint Collector, http://www.nsa.gov/public_info/_files/uss_liberty/attack_sigint.pdf

22. Katzenbach, pp. 251–252

23. Green, pp. 201-202

24. Ibid.

Chapter 6

The Israeli Response: Recriminations Abound

The men of the USS Liberty represented the United States. They were attacked for two hours, causing 70 percent of American casualties, and the eventual loss of our best intelligence ship. These sailors and Marines were entitled to our best defense. We gave them no defense. The American people deserve to know the truth about this attack. We must finally shed some light on one of the blackest pages in American naval history. It is a duty we owe not only to the brave men of the USS Liberty, but to every man and woman who is asked to wear the uniform of the United States.

– Admiral Thomas Moorer, Chairman of the Joint Chiefs of Staff (Ret.)

THE MOST IMMEDIATE RESPONSE:
FROM AN ISRAELI PILOT WHO REFUSED HIS ORDERS

One of the attacking Israeli pilots, Evan Toni, told Congressman Pete McCloskey that while on air patrol on June 8, 1967, he immediately recognized the USS *Liberty*, informed headquarters of its status, and was told to ignore the American flag and attack. When he refused and returned to base, he was arrested on the spot for refusing to follow orders. Another pilot confirmed this report, stating that orders came directly from IDF – the Israeli Defense Force – to attack the *Liberty*, and when he said that he saw an American flag, they once again told him to "attack it."[1]

A similar, compatible story, separately and independently reported by the former (1967) American ambassador to Lebanon, Dwight Porter, stated that the following exchange of radio communications, between one of the Israeli pilots ordered to attack the USS *Liberty* and the war room of the Israeli Defense Forces which managed that operation, was intercepted by the NSA aircraft flying high above the Mediterranean Sea at 2 p.m. local time on June 8, 1967. It was routinely deciphered, typed up, and then, inadvertently, cabled to CIA station chiefs around the world:

> **Israeli pilot to IDF War room:** "This is an American ship. Do you still want us to attack?"
>
> **IDF War room to Israeli Pilot:** "Yes, follow orders."

Israeli pilot to IDF War room: "But, sir, it's an American ship – I can see the flag!"

IDF War room to Israeli Pilot: "Never mind; hit it!"

This communications intercept was confirmed personally by author and *Liberty* survivor James Ennes with Ambassador Porter in 1991. Then he passed the information on to columnist Rowland Evans Jr., who published it in his syndicated newspaper column "Inside Report," which immediately came under fire by major news outlets. Was this part of *Operation Mockingbird*, which had been established forty years earlier to spread CIA propaganda, by such CIA luminaries as Allen Dulles, Richard Bissell, and Cord Meyer? Ennes described that residual blowback on his website USSLiberty. org as follows:

> Rowland Evans confirmed the details with Ambassador Porter by telephone and then wrote a syndicated column that was widely distributed on November 6, 1991. Evans and his writing partner Robert Novak came under immediate and severe attacks by Abe Rosenthal of the *New York Times* on November 8 ([who called it] "a lie") and by Hirsh Goodman on November 21 ([who asserted that it was] "a piece of fiction"). Evans defended the original position in print on November 20 and again on December 19, 1991.[2]

Mr. Ennes also explained that Jay Cristol, the author of the deeply flawed book *The Liberty Incident* claimed, incredulously, that "Porter's story cannot be true because the intercepted communications have not shown up in any of the FOIA releases of embassy traffic, is unknown to people queried by Cristol, and could not possibly have been intercepted in Beirut because the distance is too great for line-of-sight UHF communications."[3] This knee-jerk response came despite the fact that Ambassador Porter had clearly stated to Cristol that the distance argument was not pertinent, because the intercept came from the direct transmission caught by the NSA, "... almost certainly those intercepted by the Air Force C-130 operating near *Liberty's* position, then sent in real time to the 6931st Security Group of the USAF Security Services stationed on Crete, where they were placed on dedicated Sigint communications by watch officer Captain Richard Block."[4]

THE INADVERTENT RELEASE OF CIA/NSA INTERCEPTS

According to Mr. Ennes, that same cable was reportedly seen by several others who have come forward over the years to confirm that it was in fact a part of the record, and is undoubtedly still a part of the numerous files that remain closed in both countries – probably forever. The inadvertent release of the intercepts, to CIA and NSA offices around the world has been confirmed by men who saw them, in one case as recently as May 13, 2016: A man identifying himself as James E. Vigiletti, attorney at law, writing a (one star) review of Cristol's book on Amazon stated: "I was a communication officer at NAS Argentia, Newfoundland [and] had the opportunity to read the (sceds), the top secret messages that came in at the time of the Liberty affair, and Cristol (not a real Federal judge but an ALG who hears Social Security case[s] who got the job by taking a test) white-washing of the affair and letting the Israelies of[f] the hook on the issue of intent (necessary for criminal responsibility) is an insult and I believe he has an ulterior motive."

Ernie Gallo has also identified some of those men who saw it, including Air Force Captain Stephen Forslundan, who came forward after retiring from the Air Force, "after twenty-six years of service, after reading *Assault on the Liberty*," the Ennes book.[5] Forslundan was an intelligence analyst for the 544th Air Reconnaissance Technical Wing at Offutt Air Force Base in Omaha and, according to an article in *Digital Journal* by Ralph Lopez dated November 14, 2014, stated that the Israeli military:[6]

> "…made specific reference to the efforts to direct the jets to the target which was identified as American numerous times by the ground controller. Upon arrival, the aircraft specifically identified the target and mentioned the American flag she was flying. There were frequent operational transmissions from the pilots to the ground base describing the strafing runs. The ground control began asking about the status of the target and whether it was sinking. They stressed that the target must be sunk and leave no trace."

Another witness to this event was James Ronald Gotcher, who saw the same intercepts as a U.S. Air Force Intelligence Analyst with the 6924th Security Squadron, in Da Nang, Vietnam.[7] Army Colonel Patrick Lang was another, who stated that he saw the intercepted material at an advanced cryptographic logistical course at Fort Holabird, Maryland a few months after the attack. When the error in sending this information to CIA posts around the world was discovered, extensive efforts were made to collect them and destroy those copies, however, the men who read them apparently did not get the memo advising them that they should not repeat that information.[8]

Through his uncanny ability to obfuscate truths and replace them with fabrications, A. Jay Cristol still maintains that, since those records cannot presently be retrieved then all of the credible people who have stated that they saw them must be ignored. Throughout this book, we have noted numerous other anomalies, misstatements and discrepancies in the disparate versions of the purported "official findings" of both the United States and Israel, as well as the books since written which have been exposed as obvious efforts to prop up the original fabricated stories. That all of these pieces of critical evidence, when combined, point to the real causes and motives, can only be attributed to random incidents of serendipity. Or, as some prefer, "Divine Intervention."

REGRETS, CONDOLENCES AND RECRIMINATIONS BEGINS

On June 10, 1967 Israel's ambassador to the United States expressed deep condolences to the "Government of the United States and its sympathy to all the bereaved families." He also stated that Israel is "prepared to make amends for the tragic loss of life and material damage."[9] The same day, the official American reply was made, missing by two hours the timing of the attack (the attack was stated to have occurred between "16:05 and 16:25 hours local time" rather than 14:00 to 16:30.) This was all part of a purposeful misstatement of material facts that was intended to distort, a point originally made by researcher/author Peter Hounam.

The letter to Israel's ambassador did state a number of reasons that their explanation was less than satisfactory and that the attacks "must be condemned as an act of military recklessness reflecting wanton disregard for human life." Moreover, it stated that "there is every reason to believe that the USS *Liberty* was identified ... by approximately one hour before the attack." It continued on, stating that the U.S. vessel "should have been scrutinized visually at close range before the torpedo attack, and that it expects, not only, for Israel to make amends for the "tragic loss of life," but that Israel should "take disciplinary measures which international law requires in the event of wrongful conduct by the military personnel."[10]

Two days after that came a response by the Israeli ambassador, which rejected much of what was stated in the U.S. reply: It stated that the assertion that the *Liberty* was identified was "unfounded;" that Israel rejected the statement that the attack be "condemned as an act of military recklessness," and that "drawing of such conclusion before a full investigation" is unwarranted. The letter then stated that the Chief-of-Staff of the Israeli Defense Forces (i.e. Moshe Dayan) would "make a full investigation of all the facts and circumstances. Furthermore, the letter stated that "... as soon as this tragic error occurred it immediately informed the Government of the United States what had taken place [and] ... assumed responsibility for this error and conveyed its apologies and deep regret for what had occurred and for the grievous loss of life."

Finally, it stated that Israel had already taken the initiative to offer to make amends for the tragic loss of life and material damage, and that "assistance was offered by the personnel of the Israel Defense Forces to the USS *Liberty*, but these personnel were informed by the USS *Liberty* that such help was not needed." The letter went on to admonish the Government of the United States about the fact that "it was not given prior information ... about the presence of a United States vessel in an area which the United Arab Republic had warned neutral vessels to avoid."[11]

Finally, on June 18, a classified document was received by the State Department from the Israeli Court of Inquiry, which was a synopsis of their findings that stated: "There was no criminal negligence and the attack was made by innocent mistake," and that there was actually a chain of three mistakes.[12] According to this official cover-up document, the list of reasons Israel used to base its opinion were:

1. The first mistake was decisive. Navy and Air Force Headquarters had received a number of wrong reports stating Al Arish [sic] was being shelled from the sea. This wrong information formed the background and main factor leading to the attack on *Liberty*. The IDF Commanding Naval Officer and assistants were convinced that shelling was being done by an unidentified ship or ships which were discovered at the time near the shore of Al Arish [sic] ... The IDF Navy is not responsible for the mistaken report of shelling and the reasons for the mistaken report are outside the scope of the inquiry at hand.

2. The second mistake which when added to the first resulted in aircraft attack on *Liberty* was a mistaken report that *Liberty* was steaming at 30 knots. This mistake had two significances: (A) When *Liberty* was identified in the morning her maximum speed was determined from *Jane's Fighting Ships* to be 18 knots. Therefore, even if the unidentified ship were thought to be *Liberty* the fact that she was reported to be making 30 knots would have denied the identification. (B) In accordance with IDF Navy Standing Orders an enemy ship in any waters which is attacking Israeli ships or shelling the Israeli shore may be attacked. If there is information of enemy ships in the area any ship or ships discovered by radar which are determined to be cruising at a speed above 20 knots may be considered an enemy. Since the speed of the unidentified ship was fixed at 28 to 30 knots, the IDF Navy was entitled to attack without further identification in view of the background of information on the shelling of Al Arish. Israeli Defense Force naval operations section had ordered the MTBs [motor torpedo boat] who reported *Liberty's* speed at 30 knots to recheck and only after confirmation of that speed was the information considered reliable and aircraft were sent to attack. The question of possible negligence in establishing the

speed at 28 to 30 knots, when in fact the *Liberty's* top speed is 18 knots, is discounted by the IDF commanding naval officer who testified 'that such estimations require expertise and in an MTB there may be great discrepancies in fixing the speed of a vessel moving in front of it, especially if the estimate was made only over a short interval of time. It is quite feasible that there may be such a mistake, even if you measure it twice or more.' As a result of the incident maybe the Standing Order should be reconsidered but no criminal negligence is found in the MTBs' fixing of *Liberty's* speed.

3. Third mistake caused execution of the second stage of attack on *Liberty* this time with torpedoes from MTBs. This was the mistaken identification of *Liberty* as the Egyptian supply ship *El Quseir*. Here I (that is, the officer conducting the inquiry, Colonel Ram Ron) must state my doubts whether the identification was not done with a certain over-eagerness as this happened when serious doubts were already beginning to arise as to the identification, as an Egyptian ship. [That this ship was implicitly considered capable of making 30 knots should have been considered even more absurd than the presumption that the *Liberty* was]. It has been established by the Commanding Officer of the MTB division that the doubts which had begun to arise in the pilots as to their accuracy of identification did not get to the Commanding Officer of the MTB division at that time but he already knew that the ship was not a destroyer but a supply or merchant ship and this should have caused extra carefulness in identification. On the other hand, I must state the extenuating circumstances and difficulties of identification under the following conditions:

   i. The ship was covered with thick smoke.

   ii. When asked to identify itself the ship did not do so and behaved suspiciously.

   iii. It appeared to the division's commander that there was a gun on the forecastle of the ship and that the ship was firing towards the MTBs. These observations were recorded in the War Diary at the time of action.

The document continued on, with similar efforts to explain the inexplicable and shift the blame back to the victims, as this (condensed) statement indicates: "... it is clear that the American ship acted with lack of care by endangering itself to a grave extent by approaching excessively close to the shore in an area which was a scene of war ... without advising the Israeli authorities of its presence ... the ship made an effort to hide its identity first by flying a small flag which was difficult to identify from a distance ... by beginning to escape when discovered by our forces and when it was aware of the fact that it had been discovered ... by failing to identify itself by its own initiative by flashing light and by refusing to do so even when asked by the MTBs. From all this I conclude that the ship *Liberty* tried to hide its presence in the area and its identity before it was discovered and even after having been attacked by the Air Force and later by the Navy and thus contributed a decisive contribution towards its identification as an enemy ship."[13]

US Naval Attaché Commander Ernest Castle wrote in his cover telegram that as Lieutenant-Colonel Efrat read some of the points being made in the document he appeared to have a look of "surprise and incredulity," and when finished he asked what the "U.S. Naval Attaché' (Castle) thought of the findings 'off the record.'" Castle pretended not to hear the question and thanked the Colonel for his time.

Author Pearson also stated that Lieutenant-Colonel Efrat, the personal aide to General Yitzak Rabin, later told Castle that "Rabin had never been so angry as when he read the current *Newsweek* magazine comment on the *Liberty* incident (*Newsweek* 19 June 1967, Periscope column said in part: 'High Washington officials believe the Israelis knew *Liberty's* capabilities and that the attack might not have been accidental. One high level theory holds that someone in the Israeli armed forces ordered that *Liberty* be sunk because it had intercepted messages which revealed Israel had started the fighting'). Commander Castle replied that he took no notice of news media reporting on the incident. He did not indicate to Lieutenant-Colonel Efrat, who was obviously fishing for such an indication, that American intelligence had identified the 'someone in the Israeli armed forces' as the Israeli Defence Minister and Supreme Commander, General Moshe Dayan."[14] Nor did he admit that the reference to "High Washington Officials" was *Newsweek's* code for none other than the highest such official, the commander-in-chief himself.

It is instructive to consider that last statement, that "Rabin had never been so angry" when he read that *Newsweek* article: That is what one might expect, if he had known that the real culprit was not himself, or even Moshe Dayan, who carried out the order, but the one person who had really been behind the attack was also the one who caused *Newsweek* to place the blame elsewhere. Only when that statement is considered in such a context does it begin to make any sense at all; and then, it makes perfect sense. And the statement made elsewhere within these pages, that Johnson had attempted to avoid "further angering Israel," adds further to this point.

THE NEGOTIATIONS COMMENCE

Within four days after the Six-Day War, France, which had previously been Israel's primary source for military as well as nuclear research and related equipment, cancelled their contract for fifty more Mirage fighter jets. And within that four day period, Israel began negotiations with the United States for fifty Phantom F-4 fighter jets, a much more advanced aircraft. That confluence of events led to delays in the Israeli damage payments, since the latter issue became the leverage for the former, at least it appeared to the survivors that way. But one year later, damages averaging about $100,000 each for the men killed on the *Liberty* were paid. Nearly two years later, just after the deal for the F-4s was settled, but before the planes were delivered, claim settlements were paid out to injured men based upon the percentage of their disabilities. A few months after that, Israel received her first consignment of F-4 Phantom fighters, along with U.S. airmen to train the Israeli pilots.[15]

Some people have concluded that these events were "connected" in a way that suggested a "quid pro quo" arrangement, involving incentives for Israel to "do what was right" through rewards for each step along the way, arguably financed through the financial and military aid package that has steadily increased over five decades to $3.1 billion per year as of 2015. And according to a November 4, 2015 news report by Reuters, Israel requested an increase, to $5.1 billion per year.[16]

THE CURRENT ISRAEL POSITION

The following summary of the Israeli position on the USS *Liberty* issue, adopted immediately by Israel in collaboration with White House staff and attorneys as prescribed by the president himself, and held firmly for fifty years and counting, has been excerpted from "The USS *Liberty* Incident: History & Overview" by Mitchell Bard, posted on the Jewish Virtual Library website.[17]

> The Israeli attack on the USS *Liberty* was a grievous error, largely attributable to the fact that it occurred in the midst of the confusion of a full-scale war in 1967. Ten official United States investigations and three official Israeli inquiries have all conclusively established the attack was a tragic mistake.
>
> On June 8, 1967, the fourth day of the Six-Day War, the Israeli high command received reports that Israeli troops in El Arish were being fired upon from the sea, presumably by an Egyptian vessel, as they had a day before [In the IDF's Court of Inquiry Report, this was noted as a "mistaken report of shelling and the reasons for the mistaken report are outside the scope of the inquiry at hand. The Navy and Air Force Headquarters took the reports at full value."][18] The United States had announced that it had no naval forces within hundreds of miles of the battle front on the floor of the United Nations a few days earlier; however, the USS *Liberty*, an American intelligence ship under the dual control of the Defense Intelligence

Agency/Central Intelligence Agency and the Sixth Fleet, was assigned to monitor the fighting. As a result of a series of United States communication failures, whereby messages directing the ship not to approach within 100 miles were not received by the *Liberty*, the ship sailed to within 14 miles off the Sinai coast. The Israelis mistakenly thought this was the ship shelling its soldiers and war planes and torpedo boats attacked, killing 34 members of the *Liberty's* crew and wounding 171. Ships from the Sixth Fleet were directed to launch four attack aircraft with fighter cover to defend the *Liberty*, but the planes were recalled after a message was received at the White House that the Israelis had admitted they had attacked the ship.

Numerous mistakes were made by both the United States and Israel. For example, the *Liberty* was first reported – incorrectly, as it turned out – to be cruising at 30 knots (it was later recalculated to be 28 knots). Under Israeli (and U.S.) naval doctrine at the time, a ship proceeding at that speed was presumed to be a warship. The sea was calm and the U.S. Navy Court of Inquiry found that the *Liberty's* flag was very likely drooped and not discernible; moreover, members of the crew, including the Captain, Commander William McGonagle, testified that the flag was knocked down after the first or second assault. [END]

This treatise puts the blame squarely on the "confusion" caused by wartime conditions and the communications failures between the U.S. military and the *Liberty*.

All of this "confusion" came after up to thirteen overflights were conducted all morning during which the ship was surveilled, and undoubtedly photographed for the benefit of the planners to target the specific defenses and vulnerabilities of the ship. To say that this "justification" is a bit surreal is a considerable understatement. However, it is essentially the same tack that has been advanced for the last five decades by Israel.

QUESTIONS POSED BY NICHOLAS DEB. KATZENBACH:

"RIDDLES WRAPPED IN MYSTERIES INSIDE AN ENIGMA"

Nicholas Katzenbach, who was moved by President Johnson from the Justice Department and appointed as an assistant secretary of state a few months before the *Liberty* attack, may have inadvertently left some of the most revealing clues as to what was really going on *behind the scenes* during the USS *Liberty* episode in his 2008 memoir, *Some of It Was Fun: Working with RFK and LBJ*. Within his book, he cited a number of points that he still pondered about, over forty years later that still made no sense to him. There is no indication that Katzenbach had any foreknowledge of the attack, in fact, there are numerous indications that he was nowhere near being "in the loop."

He stated that most administration officials, including Navy personnel, did not believe the Israeli explanation that it was "a case of mistaken identity." He acknowledged that Johnson accepted the apology for political reasons, but felt that Israel should have offered the families "generous compensation," with an understanding that they would be reimbursed. Moreover, Katzenbach admitted that the State Department had angered many in the Jewish community through its issuance of a statement of neutrality, which was considered in retrospect as unwise.[19]

That "neutrality statement" began during a State Department briefing when some of the officials became giddy over Israel's successes. As described by Grace Halsell in her previously noted article, "How LBJ's Vietnam War Paralyzed His Mideast Policymakers": "With a wide smile, Eugene Rostow said, 'Gentlemen, gentlemen, do not forget that we are neutral in word, thought and deed.'"[20] Shortly thereafter, press spokesman Robert J. McCloskey repeated those words for reporters. This statement caused much consternation among the Israeli leadership and within the White House.

According to the memoirs of Joseph Califano, the reason it was such a "political problem [that] reached white heat" was because it could be interpreted as an invocation of the Neutrality Act, which meant that Israelis would be constrained from raising money in the United States and that might prevent the United States from shipping supplies to Israel. Califano said that Abe Fortas was among those who expressed concern to him about that issue, however it was in the context of his having "deep reservations" that it applied.[21]

Abe Fortas, a sitting Supreme Court justice, was simultaneously serving as one of Johnson's primary advisers, while also serving as a liaison between Johnson and Israeli leaders, as well as attending meetings of the National Security Council, and thereby becoming directly involved in the planning of the Six-Day War. Even as he played these multiple roles he was apparently oblivious to the inherent conflict of interests. Fortas had previously been Johnson's personal lawyer for over twenty years, including having played a primary role in Johnson's theft of the 1948 senatorial election and being his chief collaborator in the months after JFK's assassination – to squelch the multiple Senate investigations into Johnson's criminal past. Throughout all of it, he was a personal witness to Johnson's long history of criminal activity, evidently becoming one of Johnson's primary enablers. Abe Fortas was facilitating Johnson's efforts to subvert constitutional, legal, moral and ethical rules of conduct, and was assisting the president to use U.S. military might to support a war of aggression by a U.S. ally on its neighbors. To ensure the war did not end before the

Liberty arrived in its position, Johnson had ordered U.N. Ambassador Arthur Goldberg to resist efforts to obtain a ceasefire at the United Nations, where a disagreement regarding the language about the definition of territories had materialized.[22]

But three other points raised by Katzenbach must also be considered in relation to tracing the events as they unfolded in the White House. Whether taken separately, or together as a whole, these confusing and contradictory statements should have raised multiple red flags:

(1) Katzenbach stated that Israel initially refused to pay anything toward compensation for the victims because it was a regrettable accident. Others made similar statements, including George Ball, who also noted that Israel's apology was "reluctant and graceless" and that the reparations for the families of the men killed and the injured survivors were "parsimonious and slow in coming."[23] Ball admitted that Johnson had tried to downplay the enormous damage to the ship and the thirty-four dead and scores of other wounded sailors through an "elaborate charade" to silence the crew, but admitted that the "sordid affair" was too damaging to ever "possibly be concealed." His poignant conclusion was that the Israelis decided that if they could get by with an attack of this enormity, they could "get away with almost anything."[24]

If Israel had been at fault for this egregious, inexplicable "error" – given the close dependency it had to the United States as its primary ally – then a logical presumption would suggest that they would have implicitly understood the need to at least act contritely, to acknowledge and apologize for the error, and offer to make a generous financial settlement with the victims of such an accident involving their most important patron, without the need to be coerced; even if it was all for "show," just to get the monkey off their back. But according to Katzenbach, George Ball and the many others that was not happening.

However, there is a counterpoint to that: If the Israeli officials felt that they had been put into an impossible position in the first place by the American president, to attack his own ship, for his own political purposes, and that they were being forced into having to accept the blame and "bite the bullet" when things went wrong and the ship didn't sink, then it follows that their reaction was not as insensitive as Katzenbach and the others have interpreted it. Perhaps they felt that they had been "had" by the American president, and they did not relish the idea of becoming the scapegoat for something they – specifically the "Godfather" of Israel, David Ben-Gurion – had even desperately tried to warn against, furiously berating Yitzhak Rabin so severely for acquiescing to it that it caused Rabin to suffer a nervous breakdown just days later. Looking at it from that prism, if indeed that was their perspective, then their resistance to paying restitution to the victims seems a bit less "unreasonable," and that leads us to a clearer understanding of what actually happened. Pending release of all the files that remain closed, on both continents, this issue will remain, as Winston Churchill once famously said about Russia: "A riddle wrapped in a mystery inside an enigma."

(2) Another point that Katzenbach made was that President Johnson, curiously, did not want to anger the Israelis any further. This assertion, considering the circumstances, is quite astounding, given that, even under the ostensible cover story, that the "incident" was merely a case of "mistaken identity," still put the onus on Israel to make matters right, at least to act contritely and with an adequate level of remorse for the awful "mistake." Could Israel have operational knowledge that could be used as blackmail?

(3). Finally, and even more confusing than any of the other points that Katzenbach stated, was Johnson's decision "to make little effort to obtain a ceasefire" for several days. What possible explanation for his wanting to delay a peaceful solution? Was it because of his re-election hopes, and that Operation Cyanide was not yet in play? That may be an explanation for why Johnson, and Goldberg at the U.N., deliberately stalled the efforts going on by the United Nations to secure an early peace.

Was this all part of a grand move in a chess game the president was playing, acting as the "King of the World," involving one of his pawns? That Katzenbach was still pondering these enigmas forty years after the fact, when he wrote his memoirs, is a poignant reflection on how so many men, who had observed Lyndon Johnson in dynamic real time, failed to completely understand him.

ISRAEL'S MILITARY COURT: DISMISSES EVERY CHARGE, AGAINST EVERY MILITARY OFFICER

The following summary illustrates how the "charges" against various Israeli officers were dealt with. The Israeli military court "charges" and the rationale it used to dismiss every single one of them in order to avoid actually making criminal charges against any of its officers. One example of this, to illustrate how it decided to hold no one culpable of even mere negligence – never mind gross negligence or extreme, willful criminal conduct – the court ruled as follows on charge number 6:

> **6. Charge:** That it was negligent to order the torpedo boat to attack the ship upon an unfounded presumption that it was an Egyptian warship, and this as a consequence of not taking reasonable steps to make proper identification.

> **Finding:** The examining judge considered it noteworthy that the identification of the target as the El-Kasir [sic] was made both by the division commander and the commander of a second torpedo boat. Upon examining photos of the two ships, he was satisfied that

a likeness existed between them, and that an error of identification was possible ...

The irrefutable fact that the ship-shape *Liberty* was nearly five times larger (in displacement), and over twice the length of the rusty old 1920s era horse transport ship, and that it was flying an American flag (originally five feet by eight feet, until that was shot down, at which point the holiday flag, seven feet by thirteen feet, was then hoisted up), that it was clearly marked in large (ten feet high), lettering on the bow, its name emblazoned on the stern, and that it "bristled with antennae" (forty-five of them in all, according to this very report) and that it was slowly proceeding in international waters, or that Israeli planes had surveilled the ship with up to thirteen overflights before the attack – the pilots even exchanging smiles and hand waves at the men on the top deck – none of that entered into the judge's deliberation of this issue. As the report concludes, regarding the Israeli court findings, "When NSA's Deputy Director read the decision of the Israeli Defence Forces Preliminary Inquiry, he summed up his personal feelings on the subject by calling it 'a nice whitewash.'"[25]

The seriously flawed book *Six Days of War*, written in 2003 by Michael B. Oren, the Israeli ambassador to the United States from 2009 until 2013, can be considered as a thirty-six year anniversary official Israel attempt to strengthen and affirm the original "whitewash." Within it, the author explicitly admits an inherent bias: Oren acknowledged that he wasn't completely objective and that he took "strong stands" regarding war and peace, but that he attempted to overcome his biases.[26] The book describes what the author portrayed as a succession of events that preceded the attack on the *Liberty* claiming that all of the overflights occurring in the eight hours before the attack were involved only in looking for Egyptian submarines. According to author Oren, shortly before the attack, an Israeli fighter jet observed it as an "unidentified ship ... sighted northeast of al-Arish," where an ammunition dump had exploded.

Oren also stated that the ship was steaming toward Egypt, at an estimated speed of thirty knots (in the seaman's standard reference book, *Jane's Fighting Ships*, the *Liberty*'s maximum speed was eighteen knots). Oren also claimed that Israeli torpedo boats gave chase at their maximum speed of thirty-six knots, but that it was not possible to catch up to the ship because of its speed.[28]

Additionally, the veracity of his account of this incident would have gained credibility if he had addressed the issues raised in James Ennes' 1979 book, which was written over one and a half decades before *Six Days of War*. Or, better yet, the assertions of James Bamford in his book *Body of Secrets*, written two years before Oren's, including allegations of war crimes that had become well known by then: "Aryeh Yitzhaki [an Israeli military historian] said, 'The whole army leadership, including [then] Defense Minister Moshe Dayan and Chief of Staff [and later Prime Minister Yitzhak] Rabin and the generals knew about these things ... senior Israeli officials tried their best to cover them up by not releasing a report he had prepared on the murders in 1968.''[29] These allegations gave rise, for some critics, to a presumption that the primary reason that Israel initiated the attack on the *Liberty* was to contain its ability to eavesdrop on the alleged massacres that were said to be going on at El Arish. The presumption was that, if Israel (i.e., someone high up in the hierarchy of the Israeli government or its military) ordered the attack, this might explain why they would want to destroy the capability of the *Liberty* to intercept or transmit reports of such activities. But there were other ways to accomplish that without sinking the ship of an ally and all the men aboard, including simply jamming the radio frequencies used by the ship, which is exactly what occurred just before and during the attack. That argument fails on another level as well: Sinking that ship would not have accomplished the goal since there were Elint aircraft flying continuous rotations overhead that also captured the same communications, yet they were not attacked.

Despite these myriad distortions, the primary newspapers of the mainstream press, the *New York Times* and the *Washington Post* gave Oren's book positive reviews, the latter calling it " ... not only the best book so far written on the Six-Day War, it is likely to remain the best." That should prove to any objective reader the subjective biases of these seemingly-objective newspapers.

George Ball, then the Undersecretary of State, wrote in his far more credible memoirs that:

> The sequel was unedifying. The [Johnson] administration tried vigorously to downplay the whole matter. Although it silenced the crew, casualties to the sailors and damage to the ship could not possibly be concealed. Thus, an elaborate charade was performed. The United States complained pro-forma to Israel, which reacted by blaming the victims. The ship, they rejoined, had not been clearly marked but looked like an Arab ship-which was definitely untrue. Nor did the Israelis even pretend that they had queried the American Embassy in Tel Aviv regarding the status of the well-marked ship.

Mr. Ball's assessment of the USS *Liberty* incident, written twenty-five years after the event, succinctly and accurately describes the continuing, "unedifying," and still-unsatisfactory, result of the epic tragedy that remains a virtually secret part of American and world history, circa 1967.

Endnotes

1. See: http://www.wingtv.net/documentaries.html

2. See USS *LIberty* Organization: http://ussliberty.org/dwightporter.htm

3. Ibid.

4. Ibid.

5. Gallo, p. 23

6. Lopez, Ralph, "Declassified Israeli cables add evidence USS Liberty no accident." *Digital Journal*, Nov. 14, 2014 See: http://www.digitaljournal.com/news/world/declassified-israeli-cables-add-evidence-usaliberty-no-accident/article/414951#ixzz496DwlSFy

7. Op. Cit. Gallo

8. Lopez, Ralph (Op. Cit.)

9. Ennes, Appendix R

10. Ibid., Appendix S

11. Ibid. Appendix T

12. Pearson, pp. 66-68

13. Ibid.

14. Ibid., p. 69

15. Ennes, p. 198

16. See: http://uk.reuters.com/article/uk-iran-nuclear-israel-usa-idUKKCN0ST2SV20151104

17. See: http://www.jewishvirtuallibrary.org/jsource/History/liberty.html

18. See Pearson, p. 66

19. Katzenbach, pp. 251–252.

20. See: Halsell, Grace "How LBJ's Vietnam War Paralyzed His Mideast Policymakers", *Washington Report on Middle East Affairs*, June 1993, Page 20 (http://www.wrmea.org/1993-june/how-lbj-s-vietnam-war-paralyzed-his-mideast-policymakers.html)

21. Califano, pp. 204-205

22. Katzenbach, Op. Cit.

23. Ball, pp. 57 - 58

24. Ibid.

25. Ibid., p. 49 (p. 41 in original document).

26. Oren, pp. 333–334

27. Ibid.

28. Ibid., p. 265.

29. Bamford, p. 203 (ref. original cite: *Newsday*, August 17, 1995).

Robert McNam

Chapter 7

A Review of "The Liberty Incident" and Other Failed Attempts to Reframe History

"The evidence was clear. Both Admiral Kidd and I believed with certainty that this attack, which killed 34 American sailors and injured 172 others, was a deliberate effort to sink an American ship and murder its entire crew. In particular ... Jay Cristol's book, The Liberty Incident, twists the facts and misrepresents the views of those of us who investigated the attack. It is Cristol's insidious attempt to whitewash the facts that has pushed me to speak out."

~ Captain Ward Boston, Captain, JAGC, USN (Ret.)

INESCAPABLE CONCLUSIONS

The strange actions by Lyndon Johnson and Robert McNamara went well beyond the mere refusal to order protection for the ship after the initial attack that killed about ten sailors and seriously injured many more. Had they allowed the fighter jets to complete their mission, the subsequent torpedo attack might well have been averted, which would have saved the lives of at least twenty-four men. It has finally become obvious from their own actions that they had ordered the ship into the area for the very purpose of having it attacked, and when it didn't sink, they abandoned it for over seventeen hours and then ordered a massive cover-up of the entire incident. Simultaneously with the scramble to hush their own military men, from the highest Pentagon officials to enlisted men throughout the Sixth Fleet, especially the survivors of their planned massacre, they collaborated with Israel in fabricating a story blaming the attack on a "series of blunders" by both the United States and Israel. Eventually, these lies were pieced together and written into two books, both of which have been verbally attacked by practically everyone familiar with the real facts of the case. The first, published in 2002, was titled *The Liberty Incident*, by A. Jay Cristol, a former bankruptcy judge.

The other one, *Six Days of War*, by the American-born former Israeli ambassador Michael B. Oren (whose given name, Michael Scott Bornstein, was changed when he immigrated to Israel, later renouncing his U.S. citizenship)[1] was described earlier. But two other items of interest regarding Oren's works must also be considered in this evaluation: His 2012 appearance at the Naval Academy in Annapolis, and an examination of an earlier appearance of Mr. Oren at a 2004 conference, which was purportedly held to bring together so-called "experts" on the subject of the tragic fate of the USS *Liberty*. It should be noted that, despite that objective, certain experts including the survivors of the vicious attack were not invited to participate; in fact, even those who did attend the event were denied opportunities to simply question those "experts."

During his term as the Israeli ambassador, Mr. Oren spoke to the midshipmen at the U.S. Naval Academy, evidently arranging with officials to order the students not to ask any embarrassing questions about what happened forty-five years earlier. This incident was reported in an article by award-winning journalist Thomas E. Ricks, titled "Was There Academic Freedom at Annapolis during the Israeli Ambassador's Visit?" in the January 23, 2012, issue of the magazine *Foriegn Policy – National Security*.

> " … students were instructed not to bring up the USS *Liberty* incident, reports one midshipman. The midshipman says the pre-visit instructions were along the lines of, 'It is not appropriate, in a setting like this, to bring up any major points of contention during conversation, current or historical. It is okay to talk about issues like Iran or the two-state solution, where our nations have a largely common view. But it's not okay to bring up grievances like the USS *Liberty*, if you are familiar with that incident."[2]

The fact that the midshipmen of this institution had to be ordered to keep their lips sealed regarding the attack on the USS *Liberty* so as not to "embarrass our ally," suggests that it may have become a permanent, standing order.

The State Department Conference

"1967 Arab-Israeli War and USS Liberty"
January 12, 2004

As a preface to a review of Mr. Oren's appearance at the State Department's conference on the USS *Liberty* in 2004, a little background is in order: Just a few hours before the attack on the *Liberty*, a spy-plane, colloquially called a "ferret," officially known as a Navy EC-121, and of a type called an "Elint" aircraft (meaning that it was designed to monitor electronic intelligence), left its base near Athens and headed out on a two-hour flight to the eastern Mediterranean to begin its regular patrol.

On board that flight was Navy Chief Petty Officer Marvin E. Nowicki, who was both a Hebrew and Russian linguist. When the EC-121 arrived on the scene, according to James Bamford's seminal 2001 book *Body of Secrets*, battles were already underway on shore, causing them to go "crazy trying to cope with the heavy [intercepting signals] activity."[3]

For nearly 35 years the NSA had kept many of the secrets related to the attack on the USS *Liberty*, however Mr. Bamford's book exposed some of them, and thus they were forced to open some files before the 2004 conference. Among the previously hidden files was the fact that a Navy EC-121 ferret was overhead at the time of the incident, eavesdropping on what was going on below. The intercepts had been among the NSA's deepest secrets.[4]

Bamford wrote that Nowicki and the other linguists had to work quickly to keep up with the traffic and that Nowicki had said that he heard one of the Hebrew linguists shout, "Hey Chief ... I've got really odd activity on UHF. *They mentioned an American flag.* I don't know what's going on." (Emphasis supplied). Immediately after that exchange Nowicki tuned in to the same frequency, and later reported, "Sure as the devil ... Israeli aircraft were completing an attack on some object. I alerted the evaluator, giving him sparse details, adding that we had no idea what was taking place."[5] (The "evaluator" was the person at the NSA who would listen, or read the transcripts that were produced.)

The comment about "an American flag" that Mr. Nowicki made was raised three times during the January 2004 conference at the State Department, first by Michael Oren (then-Israeli ambassador to the United States), who referred to it during his presentation at this conference. It was in the context that it was part of the "new evidence" which had come to light since he published his book the previous year. He stated that it had confirmed his initial findings, then he asked rhetorically, "*Why would Israel attack the ship with 'clearly marked' planes and boats, then allow the ship to survive?*"[6] (Emphasis supplied.)

To make that stunning assertion – with respect to the fighter jets, given that every officer and enlisted man on board the *Liberty* who saw the planes categorically denied that any of them were marked – is stunning. But such an assertion can be made because all of their testimony on that point had been *erased* from the original record, the 1967 "Court of Inquiry Report." This same point was also raised by other speakers that day, and they were able to do so because the censored "official" record was based upon a perfunctory "investigation" that had been designed to reach a predetermined conclusion: that the "incident" was just one huge mistake – the sum total of numerous smaller errors. Because not only were those planes not marked, but the larger point – that the ship ultimately *survived*, – had nothing to do with Israel *allowing* it, as Oren insinuated.

The fallacious report – which many of the speakers at this conference praised, since it reinforced their own sophistic and/or intentionally deceitful versions of the story – has been thoroughly discredited by everyone who has examined it objectively. Indeed, it was later disavowed by its primary author, Ward Boston, Jr., who had been ordered to write the report in the first place. This same point also explains why those survivors who attended this conference were not allowed to speak – it might "embarrass our ally."

In his presentation, Mr. Oren stated that he had reviewed Israel's taped transcripts of the attack, and found that they were consistent with the transcripts released by the NSA; though admitting that these were only "partial" transcripts, he gave no indication of how much remained unreleased, much less the possible content of the redacted information. He stated that "the Israelis thought they were attacking an Egyptian ship and ceased firing the minute they identified the ship as American."[7]

Yet ten years later, in 2014, it was reported that a new tape of Israeli military transmissions was broadcast for the first time, " ... which established that the ship was confirmed to be U.S. by 2:14 p.m. that day, local time ..." [i.e. 14 minutes after the assault began, but over an hour before it ended]. The report indicated that the existence of those tapes had been confirmed in the *Jerusalem Post* back in 2004, when Oren made his conflicted statements at the State Department conference.[8]

In that 2004 speech, Oren then referenced the Hebrew linguist Mr. Nowicki, who, he asserted, had stated that in his opinion, the "attack was accidental."[9] Unfortunately, Mr. Nowicki was not a present at this event, and Professor Charles Smith of the University of Arizona in his presentation stated that Nowicki had in fact denied the statement that James Bamford had attributed to him.

Later, during the question and answer period at the end of the conference, Mr. Bamford explained that he had received a lengthy (15-20 page) email from Nowicki, who he said had initiated the contact; he also acknowledged that Nowicki had always believed that the attack must have been a mistake, which Bamford had acknowledged within the book.[10] Yet Oren (followed by Professor Smith), had misstated the point, both of them suggesting that Bamford had misrepresented Nowicki's position, which was not true. This incident did reveal something important however: Rather than exposing erroneous statements in Bamford's book, what it did reveal was the degree to which Ambassador Oren was willing to go – by attempting to subtlety insert a misstatement of fact into the record – in his efforts to reframe actual history with the cloak of mythology. Fortunately, the astute James Bamford caught that "sleight of hand" maneuver and managed to correct the record.

Oren continued, "And yet, in spite of massive evidence and rational case for the friendly fire explanation, there are still those – and not just hate mongers and not just quacks but including senior former U.S. officials, who continue to insist that the attack was deliberate; how can we explain it?"[11] Then Oren proceeded to attempt to do just that, citing a number of other "similar" incidents such as the downing of an Iranian airplane by a U.S. warship, "that does not evoke the same kind of controversy, the same kind of conferences, certainly;" and then the involvement of the NSA "a highly secret organization that is the subject of many kinds of 'conspiracy theories' not just that of the *Liberty*." Then he stated that "... above all, and this must be said, there is the aspect of Israel--the Jewish state. And the various conspiracy theories [unintelligible] to this Jewish state feed into classical cabal-style conspiracy libels. Now purveyors of these allegations [unintelligible] often call for an official U.S. investigation of the incident, or an independent investigation of the incident, and on this point alone, I cannot disagree. Such an investigation, I am convinced, will turn up nothing new on the Israeli side, all the information is out there, everyone has given their testimony under oath; on the American side, there may be some difficult questions to ask, as to why the *Liberty* was sent into somebody else's war zone, lightly armed and totally unannounced."[12] He then reiterated that, while he invited such an investigation, he was confident that it would only validate what has already been established.

James Bamford then gave a powerful rebuttal to Professor Smith's suggestion that he had incorrectly embellished his book with "rumors" of Israeli atrocities involving mass murder of Egyptian prisoners of war. Bamford cited numerous news articles, including a lengthy piece in *Time* magazine (October 2, 1995), "Opening Grave Wounds: Evidence of Israeli Atrocities in During 1967 War with Egypt Threatens Fragile Ties," as well as articles in other publications including the *New York Times* and the *Washington Post*.[13]

Finally, Bamford effectively demolished Ambassador Oren's incorrect assertion that the reason the torpedo boats had fired on the *Liberty* was to return fire that the ship had supposedly directed at them; as Mr. Bamford adroitly explained, the machine gun nests were the first thing the Mirage fighter jets had taken out (along with the men who had been in those positions). Furthermore, he read from the transcripts of conversations of the pilots themselves that there had been no fire coming from the ship. He also noted that the supposed confusion about the ship's identity (presuming that there was any) could have been resolved by checking its profile with the universal warship registry *Jane's Fighting Ships* that every military ship should have. Finally, he referred to one of the "newly released NSA documents" that Oren previously claimed – incorrectly – had validated everything that Oren had said or written: "Helicopter informed torpedo boat, that 'GTR 5 was written on the ship and inquired if this meant anything.' The torpedo boat replied, 'Negative, it does not mean anything.'" Bamford then asked, not rhetorically, as a specific question to Oren, "How could it not mean anything? You're about to blow up a ship with five torpedoes!" At this point, without giving Oren the time to answer, assuming that he might have wished to do that, the moderator cut in to the discussion, saying, "Jim we have to cut now ... we only have a few minutes left and I would like to take at least a couple of questions from the audience."[14] Oren had been caught in his own fabrications but, just in time, the moderator saved him.

Joseph C. Lentini was the first (and, it turned out, the only) *Liberty* survivor to address the panel, and he began attempting to correct a number of misstatements that had been made during the conference but was cut short by the moderator, State Department Historian Marc Susser. But before he was cut off, Lentini was able to correct the record in one respect, regarding Jay Cristol's comment that Lentini was "a friend:" Lentini explained that he had met him previously, but that to characterize their relationship that way was erroneous, that he was merely "an acquaintance."[15] Furthermore, said Lentini, Cristol's statement that he had been a friend of the late Captain McGonagle was, in his estimation, a similar mischaracterization. Later in the program, Cristol also claimed to have been a friend of Admiral Kidd, yet another gaffe, if one accepts Captain Ward Boston's statement (in Chapter 5), whose affidavit stated that "At no time did I ever hear Admiral Kidd speak of Cristol other than in highly disparaging terms."

Judge Cristol, in response to another question, maintained that all the "facts" that he has seen form the real history of the event, whereas the story rendered by the survivors, and authors such as James Bamford, was the one full of errors. His ability to twist words and substitute myths for truth, while making empty promises of hope for an early closure, can be seen from many of his utterances, such as this one from that State Department conference: "Sadly, I think that it is unfortunate ... (unintelligible) from a historian's point of view, because we're here to find history, and if there is any new evidence out there that anyone has, send it to me and I'll incorporate it in my work, if I find proof going in a different direction, I'll gladly disclose it, but I think ... unfortunately, people who have their own agendas keep this thing alive and keep torturing the survivors, like Joe Lentini who, after these years, he wants to believe that the attack was intentional; if that gives him comfort, then bless him, let him so believe, but I suggest to you that if you're interested in the history, then look at the facts and make your own decision."[16]

A. J. CRISTOL'S TURGID BOOK: *"THE LIBERTY INCIDENT"*

In his review of that book,[17] Joe Meadors, a survivor of the attack, has explained many of the reasons Cristol's book was merely meant to extend the Johnson-McNamara-McCain 1967 cover-up. Cristol used the fraudulent results of the long-discredited report of the Navy's Court of Inquiry – which has since been rendered worthless by its primary original author, Captain Ward Boston – and used it as the basis for his book.

Review of "The Liberty Incident Revealed: The Definitive Account of the 1967 Israeli Attack on the U.S. Navy Spy Ship" by A. Jay Cristol

Prepared by Joe Meadors, *USS Liberty* Survivor

Cristol's work reads more like a poorly written legal brief than a highly-touted, impeccably-researched work of historical accuracy.

Barely 38 words into the opening flyleaf he claims there were 171 wounded during the attack. I can only assume he is not including the 34 who were killed in that number. After decades of researching the attack on our ship you would think he would have learned there were 174 Purple Hearts awarded to the survivors. A small point? Obviously to him and to those who have heaped praises upon his work. Not to those of us who survived the attack and we hope not to those in the USN community.

That same mistake is repeated by the NSA Historian in the NSA 60th Anniversary Book. Then again, the NSA historian isn't the best source authority when it comes to the USS *Liberty*. He has the USS Liberty already on station when the Six-Day War broke out when, in fact, we didn't arrive until the fourth day of the war.

That NSA historian is cited by Cristol as claiming "the attack was a tragic mistake." He doesn't know how many were wounded during the attack, he doesn't know when we arrived on station and he hasn't interviewed a single USS Liberty crewman but he does know that "the attack was a tragic mistake."

Another fact missing from Cristol's work is that among the awards won by the officers and crew of the USS *Liberty* are the Medal of Honor, two Navy Crosses, eleven Silver Stars, twenty Bronze Stars, nine Navy Commendations, 208 Purple Hearts, 294 Combat Action Ribbons, the Presidential Unit Citation and the National Security Agency Exceptional Service Civilian Award which makes the USS *Liberty* arguably the most decorated ship in US Navy history for a single event.

In his advertising, Cristol claims he interviewed every living USS *Liberty* survivor. A legitimate historian interested in telling the complete story about the attack would have. Cristol did not.

I personally invited Cristol to attend a USS *Liberty* reunion in order to address and interview the crew. He refused.

To date not a single crewman has indicated to me that he was interviewed by Cristol and some have told me that interviews Cristol claims to have conducted with them didn't happen. If he wants to create a complete history of the USS *Liberty* attack why doesn't he interview the survivors? Why does he refuse to attend a USS *Liberty* reunion? Why does he lie about interviewing all living USS *Liberty* survivors?

On page 1 he tells us that the air attack was initiated when the Mirages dropped out of the west from 10,000 feet and began their strafing run. If Cristol had bothered to interview USS *Liberty* survivors instead of just claiming he did he would have known that that is not how the attack began. They didn't initiate their attack from 10,000 feet out of the western sun. They initiated it at *low-level* out of the *east*. The author would have known this if he had only interviewed the USS *Liberty* survivors instead of just claiming that he did.

We had just secured from general quarters and were on a westerly course. Lt. Jg Lloyd Painter noticed very high speed contacts coming up our starboard side traveling so low that they were visible on our surface search radar. Thinking that this would be just another circling of our ship as had occurred so many times that morning a number of us (including me) ran up to the Signal Bridge to watch the aircraft.

They flew at very low level up our starboard side. When they got a bit ahead of our ship they turned left. Instead of continuing on their anticipated circuit, when they got almost dead ahead of us they turned and began their initial strafing attack.

On Page 2 of his book we see another example of Cristol's stunning research. There he subjects the reader to the myth of the 10 US government investigations claiming that the evidence and testimony submitted during those investigations support the conclusion that there is no evidence the attack was deliberate. Those "investigations" didn't ask for nor receive any evidence and testimony about the intent of the attackers. They could just as easily have concluded that Mary had a little lamb or the cow jumped over the moon.

None of those reports are based on an investigation of the attack on the USS *Liberty*. The report that comes closest to being an investigation of the attack is the report prepared as a result of the 4 days of testimony taken during the US Navy Court of Inquiry. One glaring omission from that report is the testimony of Lloyd Painter who testified before the court about his witnessing the torpedo boats deliberately machine gunning our life rafts in the water. Painter's testimony has been removed from the record. Not redacted. Removed. A fact nowhere to be found in Cristol's work.

Dare I mention the "missing" written statements provided to the Court by some 65 USS *Liberty* crewmen at the request of the President of the Court? Strange that there is nothing about this in Cristol's "the truth, the whole truth and nothing but the truth" account of the attack. Even

ADM John McCain who is the convening authority of the court provided a *qualified* endorsement for the record of the Court.

Why Cristol claims the evidence and testimony supports his theory of "mistaken attack" is open to conjecture – as is his decision to interview few if any of the living *USS Liberty* survivors all the while allowing the myth that he interviewed all of us to continue unchallenged by anyone except the *USS Liberty* survivors ourselves. Why Cristol claims his book is "the truth, the whole truth and nothing but the truth" when it is not is open to conjecture as well. He opines that we are just "motivated by hidden agendas" and we "wish to keep alive conspiracy theories." In fact, our agenda has never been hidden.

If Cristol had bothered to attend our reunion he would have spoken with countless *USS Liberty* survivors who would have told him that during the attack:

- We were attacked by unmarked aircraft;
- Our radios were jammed on both US Navy tactical and international maritime distress frequencies;
- Life rafts we had dropped over the side in anticipation of abandoning ship were deliberately destroyed by machine gun fire from the attacking torpedo boats;
- Attacking torpedo boats slowly circled the torpedoed and sinking ship while firing upon *USS Liberty* crewmen who ventured topside to help our wounded shipmates; and,
- Two flights of rescue aircraft that had been launched from Sixth Fleet aircraft carriers were ordered recalled while we were still under attack and calling for help.

Our efforts are focused on ensuring the attack is completely and publicly investigated by the US government. Nothing more and certainly not less. The investigation we are advocating for will have evidence and testimony given under oath with the penalty of perjury attached. Cristol operates under a far less stringent standard than we do. He has the luxury of claiming he is presenting "the truth, the whole truth and nothing but the truth" in a format that doesn't hold him accountable for anything he says.

Given he is a retired US Naval aviator and US Navy JAG officer sworn to protect the US constitution against all enemies foreign and domestic one has to wonder why Cristol has gone to such lengths to destroy his reputation and credibility in the US Navy community by writing what clearly is an apologia for the forces who attacked our ship when all he has to do is support our effort to ensure the attack is subjected to the complete and comprehensive public Congressional investigation that routinely follows an attack of this kind but that has been denied the attack on the USS *Liberty*.

Cristol's book "is a tale told by an idiot, full of sound and fury, Signifying nothing."[18]

Endnotes

1. See Wikipedia: "https://en.wikipedia.org/wiki/Michael_Oren"

2. See FP National Security, http://ricks.foreignpolicy.com/posts/2012/01/23/was_there_academic_freedom_at_annapolis_during_the_israeli_ambassador_s_visit

3. Bamford, pp. 212-213

4. See: : http://historynewsnetwork.org/article/191#sthash.AQNFqXhS.dpuf

5. Ibid., p. 213

6. State Department Hearing 1/20/2004: http://www.c-span.org/video/?179892-1/1967-arabisraeli-war-uss-liberty (starting @2:08:45)

7. Ibid. (@02:09:00)

8. Lopez, Op. Cit. "Declassified Israeli cables add evidence USS Liberty no accident." *Digital Journal*, Nov. 14, 2014

9. State Department Hearing, Op. Cit. 2004: (@02:09:35)

10. Ibid. (at 02:40:30)

11. Ibid. (@02:10:00)

12. Ibid. (@ 02:10:45)

13. Ibid. (@02:42:30)

14. Ibid. (@02:44:55)

15. Ibid. (@02:46:35)

16. Ibid. (@02:49:38)

17. The 2002 book *The Liberty Incident: The 1967 Attack on the U.S. Navy Spy Ship* was written by A. Jay Cristol, a federal bankruptcy judge and former Navy aviator. In its essence, the book is an apologia clearly biased toward acceptance of the questionable Israeli claim that the attack was a case of "mistaken identity."

18. From Shakespeare's The Tragedy of Macbeth, Act 5 Scene 5

Part IV: The Long-Term Aftermath

Fortas getting a friendly Johnson "treatment."

Chapter 8

First Betrayed – then Deserted

By the Navy League, the American Legion and My Country.
— Ernie Gallo, USS *Liberty* Survivor

Never before in the history of the US Navy has a Navy board of inquiry ignored the testimony of American eyewitnesses and taken, on faith, the word of their attackers."

— Captain Dr. Richard Kiepfer, USS *Liberty* Survivor

How Their Attempt to Reveal Truths Has Redounded on the Survivors

"My Navy League Suspension"

By Ernie Gallo

I have been suspended from all Navy League functions for threatening their "501 (c) 3" charitable status by using the Navy League to foster my USS *Liberty* agenda. This is not true, nor am I anti-Semitic.

Jim Ennes, the author of *Assault on the Liberty*, initially signed me up with the Navy League in Washington state, and it seemed like a neat idea. Then, in the Fall 2005, I was asked to give a speech about USS *Liberty* to the St. Augustine Navy League (SANL). I was warmly received, and I liked this group of people. So, I moved my affiliation from Washington to SANL. As time passed, I enjoyed the interaction with other veterans at the navy ships at Mayport, the navy air wing at Jacksonville Navy Air Station, the coast guard facility and ships at Mayport, the air wing at Cecil Field, and the Marine Logistics Command at Blount Island. As a matter of fact, I had the opportunity to go aboard the boomer, the USS *Tennessee*, and tour the boomer school at Kings Point, Georgia. I was having the time of my life and at every opportunity I was keeping the USS *Liberty* story alive. There was *never* a hidden agenda.

Furthermore, when one of our members wrote a great navy story, "Heroes of the Hook," the SANL explored passing this book to the components we supported. I suggested that I could also supply a book entitled

Assault on the Liberty and a DVD *Dead in the Water.* They were receptive to the idea. I then suggested that we could collect used books, box them up, and give them to our typical components, and also to every ship at Mayport. The SANL approved the project and I named it "The Captain William McGonagle Memorial Library," and received overwhelming support.

Since I started this project, over 5,000 books have been distributed, including the USS *Constitution* and the USS *Freedom.* When I presented my box of books to the respective command, I talked freely about Captain McGonagle, his Medal of Honor, and how he got us out of harm's way. But, I discovered that if I indicated that the attack was a brutal and deliberate attack by Israel, I received some irritated comments by a few SANL members. If I was in a good mood, I refrained from mentioning Israel and if not, I gave the historical rendition. Nevertheless, my project was very successful and I was always warmly greeted at the ship's quarterdeck. None of the commands ever complained about the USS *Liberty* story.

I wondered why SANL directors were not making any attempt to publicize what we were doing to Washington. *Sea Power* magazine often cites positive actions by either personnel or councils, and I was happy just giving back to the sailors and marines – that's all that counted.

I had received a President's award in December 2009, and one of the reasons I had received the award was that I had come to the aid of the USS *Farragut* (DDG 99), an Arlie Burke destroyer. I was the SANL liaison, and the ship had hit heavy seas. The Ward Room 46 inch LED TV came off its mounting and broke. They did not have the funds to replace it and they asked for help. I acquired $250 LVA support and raised $600 from SANL. Everyone was very happy, and my rapport with the *Farragut* was so good that when I came aboard I was piped aboard as "SANL arriving" or "*Liberty* arriving." I was even invited to an overnight sail for a Tomahawk Missile Launch Test firing, and was given the Commodore quarters. Wow! During that cruise, the CTs, now called Cryptologic Technicians, make up the Electronic Warfare Division, asked that I give them a USS *Liberty* briefing in *their* spaces. I was flying high as a member of the SANL.

At the end 2009, I was elected Vice president for Military Affairs. I continued to carry my USS *Farragut* liaison duties, and, continued the Capt. William McGonagle Memorial Library project. *Then my trouble started with our new elected 2010 SANL President.*

At our February meeting, he invited a Lt. Colonel Ranger who had been very much involved in fighting the fanatical, fundamentalist Islamics. He spoke three of their languages fighting them in Iraq, Afghanistan, and North Africa. He was very much into their mind set. When he finished, I asked a hypothetical question. I said, "I deeply respect what you do and I deeply appreciate your service to our country. As a USS *Liberty* survivor, most of us have become students of the Middle East to attempt to understand what happened to us. I have completed much research and I believe we are facing a religious war. Therefore, if we stopped supporting Israel and told them to make peace with the Palestinians, would the fanatical Islamics stop coming after us?" Before I could get my question asked, our new President jumped all over me and said, "We will have none of that." But at the same time, others at the council shouted to me to ask the question, and I did.

While I was angry, I did not say anything, as I planned to talk with the SANL President after the meeting privately. However, towards the end of the meeting he publicly trashed my Middle East politics and indicated that I was an anti-Semite. I demanded a public apology and never got it, and he saw to it that I was drummed out of the SANL. I have since learned there were others who also were tired of me "trashing the good name of Israel." Or, was I telling the truth of the *Liberty* attack and they simply did not want to hear it anymore?

From that point on, as I insisted that I was the wronged party, it all went down-hill. I was told that I threatened the "501 (c)-3" status of the Navy League. Unless I am missing something, I have never asked the Navy League to lobby congress, business, or the media to investigate the USS *Liberty*. In the beginning, I had asked the Navy League Florida directors to push for an investigation. They complied and wrote letters to Washington, and were told that the Navy League does not get involved in these situations. I understood that and put it behind me. I have asked council members individually to write to the president and their congressmen, and no problems were cited. But now all of a sudden "I threaten the Navy League's charitable status?"

Before I close, I also want to say that they have engineered this dismissal so that I cannot speak to the SANL board of directors or the council itself. Fair? No, just label him anti-Semitic and kick him out. On April 30th, 2010, I visited the Navy League Headquarters to determine if the SANL president and the All Florida president can ban me from Navy League functions. The individual I talked with began by giving me a lecture indicating that the USS *Liberty* Veterans Association (LVA) has been a thorn in their side for years. Needless to say, I knew I was not going to get any help. In fact, the individual said I should read Jay Cristol's book on the attack.

The basis for their lack of empathy comes from their belief that the attack was accidental. That is, they acquired this position from Judge Jay Cristol and his book, believing the myths which he regurgitated – rather than the truths of the actual history. They believe he is a much respected federal judge. I knew I was in trouble. I countered and indicated that his book is full of lies, half truths, and incorrect statements, and I gave them examples. I was also told that Admiral Thomas Moorer did not help by convening an investigative panel indicating that the attack was deliberate. He was very critical of Admiral Moorer, seemingly oblivious to his status as a war hero and his life accomplishments that left a magnificent legacy as one of the greatest American patriots.

With that statement, I understood why the LVA has been a problem for them. That is, the Navy League wants to believe that the attack was accidental and therefore, we should also. I pleaded with him to read James Scott's book *The Attack on the Liberty*. Nevertheless, I indicated that the SANL board of directors had no say in my termination and I did not feel that was fair. While he would not commit one way or the other, he did indicate that I should "work it out with the board". The All Florida president and the SANL president has forbidden the SANL board of directors to discuss my termination or reinstatement.

When I was interviewed on the 48th anniversary of the attack, in the service at Arlington National Cemetery, I was asked why isn't it sufficient to accept Israel's apology. I responded with this statement: "When you apologize, you apologize with the truth. Not with a lie. So it's not an apology. Not as far as I'm concerned and our government is just as bad for going along with it." Moreover, I explained, the sailors selected to serve on the *Liberty*, were limited to those having an outstanding service record, and were chosen for their honesty and moral character. "Someone is lying here," says Gallo, "and it isn't us."[1]

THE AMERICAN LEGION FIASCO

By Ernie Gallo

In 2011, my shipmate Glenn Oliphant was joined by USS *Liberty* supporter Ms. Alison Weir to operate a booth at the American Legion (AL) Convention. Everything went well until someone engaged Ms. Weir in a conversation regarding the plight of Palestinians. Ms. Weir is very informed and told the individual what she knew, indicating the negative and brutal treatment of Israelis toward Palestinians. The individual did not like her honest comments and complained to AL security. Solely based on that conversation, they then escorted Ms. Weir off and out of the AL convention and told her she was not welcomed ever. Glenn remained at the USS *Liberty* booth and continued his normal business of passing out information and answering questions from passing AL members with no problems or issues from AL security.

I attended the 2012 convention of the American Legion in Indianapolis, Indiana with another *Liberty* survivor, Glenn Oliphant. We submitted the paperwork and fee to AL headquarters to get a booth to use to pass out information about the *Liberty* incident from our decorated booth.

Another LVA supporter, Ted Arens, from Michigan, was also planning to attend, with a resolution to present to the convention that supported a congressional investigation. Ted had arrived in advance, on August 22, in order to confirm that he would be speaking there to announce the *Liberty* resolution and, attempting to find the LVA booth, was told there wasn't any. On August 23rd, Ted went to AL security, wearing his USS *Liberty* baseball cap. Seeing the ball cap, Mr. Dick Holmes immediately and provocatively said to Ted, "I am sick of you bastards and I am going to throw you out on your ass." Ted replied, "Hold on – I am a delegate from Michigan representing Legionnaires advocating my resolution; get out of my face." As Ted walked away, they had more words. Ted was angry and immediately walked over to Legion headquarters where he found Judge Advocate Phil Onderdonk. Ted introduced himself and asked Onderdonk what he knew. The next words out of his mouth were unbelievable, "The ship should never have been there – it was a spy ship." He also said, "Your resolution is going nowhere." The fix was in.

Due to an oversight, our application and fee were never sent so we asked to see whoever had the authority to remedy the problem, never thinking that it would be a problem. I had flown there from Florida while Glenn drove down from Minnesota to attend the event. Ms. Andrea Watson arrived, with two or three security guards in tow; in response to our question, she replied that no, there would be no way to do that and she could not negotiate it. She told us that they were there to escort us out of the premises. We politely pleaded with them, never raising our voices but they adamantly refused, in a very rude and abrasive fashion. Glenn, a longtime American Legion member, was distraught by their actions and, distraught, flicked his membership card at Ms. Watson, which got him into trouble as they now accused him of bad behavior and they now considered us trouble makers.

The following is the report submitted by Ted Arens:

> "I always thought that the word judge implied impartiality and a person who would look at things fairly, but that was not the case. It became very apparent that many phone calls had been made to the Michigan AL headquarters regarding the resolution before I ever got to Indianapolis. Never mind that the entire resolution was approved at the State AL convention in Kalamazoo, MI. Democracy does not exist if national headquarters does not want it. You would think that the American Legion would realize that there is no greater gift one can give than to give his/her life for their country. The executive leadership of the AL is so blinded by their own power trip that they no longer understand the sacred obligation they have in defending that gift. Onderdonk and Holmes had absolutely zero sympathy for the crew of the *Liberty*. The fact that the ship was a

sitting duck, had over 3,000 rounds of cannon fired at them, na-palm and phosphorous and then a torpedo that blew men to hell and then purposely left abandoned for eighteen hours (so it would sink) with thirty-four dead and 174 wounded and one doctor aboard – made no difference to Holmes and Onderdonk. I wonder what kind of battles they were in – if any. The USS *Liberty* is the most decorated ship in Naval history for a single engagement, or perhaps ever? Strange, several years ago I was told that the ship was not even on the Navy's Vessel Registration website. It took a half a year for me to get the *Liberty* back on the website – I had to shame the Navy into it. They have tried to cover it up for a long time."

"In discussions with many Legion members they already told me that the fix was in before I ever went to the meeting – I would not be allowed to speak. Lo and behold they were right. I went to the committee meeting on foreign affairs and when the American resolution came up I raised my hands and said I wanted to speak. They said I could not. I said that I was a delegate from Michigan as-signed to the foreign policy committee. They said my name was not on the list even though Pat Lafferty and I personally went down, talked to Joe Socci – went over to the secretary and saw her enter my name in the computer. The judge advocate had the paperwork changed."

This brings us to calendar year 2013 and the American Legion's letter telling us in advance that the USS *Liberty* Veterans Association was not welcome at the 2013 convention. The letter was dated April 10, 2013 and reads as follows:

> Dear Mr. Shafer (USS *Liberty* Veterans Association Treasurer)
>
> On April 8, 2013, the American Legion received your applica-tion and check for a booth in the exhibit hall at the upcoming American Legion Convention in Houston, Texas, August 23-27, 2013. Based upon your organization's actions in the last two years, we decline to have your organization participate.
>
> Returned herewith is your application and check
>
> Very truly yours,
> James E. Koutz
> National Commander

Alison Weir, the author of the highly acclaimed book *Against Our Better Judgment: How the U.S. was used to create Israel,* wrote a brief history of the American Legion's long history of desultory relations with the USS *Liberty* survivors, in her article "American Legion Honchos Betray *Liberty* Veter-ans," on May 16, 2014 in the on-line publication *Counterpunch*.[2]

The American Legion was the first organization to support *Liberty* survivors and call for an official investigation of the attack. However … this quickly triggered anti-*Liberty* pressure that caused Legion management to back off, and today the American Legion does not have a single live resolution regarding the USS *Liberty* – this despite the fact that three resolutions on the *Liberty* have been passed by the general membership, and that many American Legion posts around the country have attempted to introduce others. In recent years, none of these has been allowed to make it to the convention floor.

The Legion's stance is in stark contrast to that of other veterans' organizations. The Veterans of Foreign Wars (VFW), Disabled American Vets, The Retired Officers Association, and other veterans' groups have placed wreaths on the *Liberty* graves at Arlington National Cemetery; the Legion has been conspicuously absent. The VFW has at least seven resolutions on its books calling for an investigation of the attack, the most recent passed in July 2013. The Legion has none.

How The Attack on the Liberty Affected My Life for Fifty Years, and Counting

Ron Kukal

I never realized what the aftermath would do to me– for years to come. I feel so very strongly for those that have been put in similar situations, and then try to make a life for themselves. You do strange things to survive. I cannot explain all the things I might have done, only my first wife and my mother could tell you that story. My mother is gone. I lost her during the most emotional period of my life, while I was trying my best to forget the attack. To lose her was like losing a part of one's own body. She was a bulwark of support to me, as was my first wife Karol.

The aftermath of the attack is something that requires a lot of thought for me, as so many things happened. I will go into some depth, because I think it might just help other veterans. I will readily admit having had thoughts of just doing away with myself as a quick answer, but since I am sort of "chicken," I thought the best way was to drink myself to death. I also thought I might as well have some fun on the way out, and of course I never discussed this with my first wife. Karol did not deserve the hurt that my own troubles caused her to suffer, and that is one of my biggest regrets. If I had come home without the attack in my past, I think things would have gone well. I could have gone to college, as I had wanted to do, but it soon became a nightmare. How does one start trying to describe what happened? Where does one pick up his life after being exposed to this kind of destruction? I have thought long and hard about it, and in the first years I was just a "vegetable." I even began practicing with alcohol, and asked what might happen if I over imbibed. Like any task, I guess one needs to be informed how to go about it all. So the first six or seven years I hardly worked at all. I spent my time hunting and fishing, in bars, and just doing next to nothing.

There just seemed to be one travesty after another, and finding out my wife wasn't able to have children was very devastating, as I was an only child, and wanted to fill my life with kids – I was thinking four or so. My mom gave a lot up birthing me, as she had rheumatoid arthritis, and my birth came close to completely devastating her body. Even more was the wild little boy, who made his way through grade school and on to high school. I often think the only reason I graduated was simply because they wanted me out of the building.

Getting back to the traumatic aftermath subject, I did try college, and things may have gone well except for sleeping in dormortories was not for me. I think my roommates would have liked to have put me under a microscope to see what caused the the nightmares and screaming at night. Mind you the attack was bad enough, but recovering the bodies was a trip that I don't think even the dictionary has words for. I have described it as best I could, and still I hedge around it, because there are no words in the thesaurus that go beyond "chaos" or "destruction" or "monstrous carnage" etc. If one strung all those words together, and all the other ones that might apply to the scene I witnessed for nearly a full week, it could still not adequately portray the devastation that I not only witnessed, but had been assigned the grim task of the recovery of the bodies.

What it did to me after I came home only Karol can tell you, and of course the boys that slept in the dorm might have some words. You see I don't know what I did in my sleep, and at the time my VA doctors were always asking me about things that I really never understood. I know now they were very concerned about a lot of things, but they mainly wondered if I could maintain my sanity. The reader needs to know at this point, that I did a lot of praying, I really did. Prayer for me was talking to God, and just asking that his will be done. To add to that I felt that every muscle in my body was frozen, and I was afraid to say anything to my physicians. I didn't want them to think I had gone over the edge, and in an attempt to shut the worst out of my mind. I froze up – I really did.

When one is exposed to death, and the terror surrounding it, I believe your body goes into that protective mode, and when you think you are going to die, and you don't – problems begin. I have taken a lot of medication, and some of it may have been experimental, but it was the only way I could sleep, and yet I lived many years afflicted with sleep deprivation. My doctors, with the exception of one, were very sympathetic and wanted to help. When I first told my story and what happened to me, they were aghast. They actually called Washington DC to see if this attack really happened, since it had never been in the news because of the massive cover-up.

I remember one pastor who ate breakfast with me, whom I told the story to, getting up and walking out, saying that I must be hallucinating. I do hope this story might help other veterans, and I am doing my best to describe everything that actually happened. This is not fiction. Moving along, I endeavored to become a valuable part of our nation's work force, and went into the electrical trade.It took a year to become qualified, and I was very impressed with the trade, mainly because I had to use my brain, and my brawn, to make a living. It was great work, and along with making good money, I continued to satisfy my hunger for the truth about the USS *Liberty*. I worked for many years, but after awhile my back injury, and undiagnosed severe PTSD started to cause trouble. Telling the story was always hard, but to see the looks of disbelief on people was very heavy on my heart.

Coming home to tell the truth, I thought folks would listen, and then finding out they wouldn't, really took its toll. My own family was turned against me. This was devastating. My own kids could never understand what had happened to me because for many years years (13) I lived under the edict that had been burned into my brain: I could never tell anyone what had happened to the *Liberty*, under penalty of prison, "or worse."

Even after James M. Ennes Jr.'s book was published in 1980, many of us could still not talk about it. Our family relationships were already shattered. How could my children understand the trauma that I had lived. How could I earn their respect, which was lost? I don't blame them for that. How could they know? I just couldn't tell them. How could you tell anyone when most people just looked at you like you came from outer space? These feelings will tear you from limb to limb, it will break you down, and leave you standing with your heart in your hand.

It is not so bad now. When you talk to someone, one of two things happen: Complete anger, or complete disbelief. You just never know what is going to happen when you get to the end of the story. My family is still in turmoil. My daughter who hasn't spoken to me in twenty years. In looking back at this, I can't blame any of them, including my former spouse. The real blame belongs to a government.

Bringing up my family is extremely hard. The mundane attitude, from those whom I have tried to speak to, has been even more devastating. And over the years my work has always been laced with the added burden of trying to get the truth out. Was I simply supposed to sit back and let life go by, living a lie?

I have seen those lies work out quite well in many cases. The effort to keep the truth out of the public eye – not only by the 1967 Johnson administration, which invoked a massive cover-up, but all administrations since then. In my mind it is not possible to accept this, it's just not possible.

There have been many strange things that have happened in the past fifty years, and one is so prevalent that I feel I must bring it up here. I believe it was in the year 2000, I drove up the hill to my work place one snowy early morning. I had a cell phone with me, and it was new to me at the time. I would guess it was six in the morning and close to Christmas. My cell phone starting ringing and I fumbled for it, finally finding the right button. A voice on the other end was that of a man who was sobbing beside himself. I could hardly understand him, but he stayed on long enough to make sure his story was told. He said he was a former crew member of the submarine USS *Amberjack,* and they were right below us when the torpedo exploded. He could hear the dying men *in the compartment where I had been.* He said he had to tell someone about this, and that he had picked me.

He had recently read my story about the body recoveries, and decided that I was the one. He told me his name, and out of respect for this man who was scared to death about even bringing the subject up, I will just let it suffice to say that his efforts were valiant. Scared as he was, he called me, and for years I have wondered what goes on in a man's mind to cause him to do what he did. How deep does a knife have to be thrust into one's conscience before you have to let it out? By the same token I had never thought about the effects on the psyches of the men who were serving on the other ships around us. Take George Sokol, for example who was serving aboard one of the ships that finally came to our rescue. God help me, I never realized what this had done to him.. He told me that bringing the wounded on board was devastating to him. He was also ordered to never talk to his shipmates, or to his family, or to anyone about what he saw that day. The threats and warnings to never talk were abundant on every ship around us, as I understand it.

Is this the beginning of the destruction of a country? Living a lie, and keeping this horrendous happening from reaching the public eye. Would you call this solid ground to stand on? I certainly wouldn't, and consequently, those of us who felt strongly about this have done our level best to not let it drop. Still, to this day, when you mention the USS *Liberty* story, people look at you like you have gone off the deep end. If I were to do this all again, knowing what I know now, I think my decision would have been different. Family did not come first with me, in my mind I felt I was protecting every family in this country, by endeavoring to get the truth out – I still feel that way. I was not an easy person to be around, as there was no one going to get in my way of trying to save this great nation from itself. That was ingrained in me.

Under the circumstances, I believe that it is no longer possible to do what you consider to be the right thing for your country, without creating all of the havoc that it creates in your life. I sometimes doubt it. There is a phrase from a Bible Scripture that fits this quite well. "The truth will be exchanged about God for a lie". I see it every day, and I see the average person accepts it as part of their daily lives.

Surviving the attack on the *Liberty* has changed me profoundly, and completely. I no longer see things the way the average person might see them. Living this, comparing it to the things I have been taught over the years, and realizing that there is more truth than the average person may think in the Bible, has put me on a level that even I don't understand at times. I am still far from perfect, but I do know one thing for sure: this great nation cannot do as it wants, it cannot defy the laws of God, and survive. Of that I know for sure. Look around you, are things as you would like? Do we really have the freedoms we used to have? Well for some they could not answer that, but for those of us who saw what a great country we had, they will know. I can guarantee they will know.

I want to make a stand for the women who went through hell just being around and living with me. In my case it is my children who also deserve my praise. My kids have said for years that they want me to forget my past, and be their father. My kids are good kids, but I never got much of a chance to raise them.

Another item I would like to bring up, and sort of a thorn in my side, can be described thusly: After the attack the most seriously injured men were taken off the *Liberty* as soon as possible. I can say little about what they went through, simply because once they were airlifted off the ship, that was it. A second group of men had to stay to do the cleanup, plus in many cases those with undiagnosed injuries, and that would have included me. There was more to that duty than most would imagine. I would be remiss if I didn't say that I tried to get out of that duty, and the very thought of recovering my own shipmates held a horror for me that I can't even think of a word for.

I did as ordered. Recovering the bodies and identifying them was not a picnic, and I ended up being the Petty Officer in charge. Lastly in the third group were those that went through the attack, did the cleanup, and took the ship home. I can only give you second hand knowledge of what it was like taking the ship home, simply because I wasn't there. I was airlifted home by commercial jet from Madrid, after the body recovery was done. There are some who have said they have no symptoms of PTSD They can consider themselves very fortunate, because practically every man exposed to the condition of the bodies, has big time symptoms. God help us all, as I was one of them with PTSD and a physical injury that didn't get diagnosed until later.

The reader needs to understand that at the time the VA did not have PTSD in their manual of diagnosis, so no treatment was available. One time my doctor told me this information, and he wanted to know how we survived it all. There is no survival of this I told him, the only survival technique I used was to roll with the punches, and there were plenty of them. The USS *Liberty* incident left me an empty hulk. I think a lot about the PTSD when I was shoved into the court room, stripped of my home, my children taken from me, and my only crime was coming home, and trying to survive it all. I was stereotyped as a combat veteran, made to look dangerous. My life is still one of getting up every day, knowing some of my children have been alienated from me, and wondering, yes wondering if you will ever see them again. Go ahead and love your country folks, never back away from the truth, stand your ground – I say, you won't like it.

There was no one there for me, absolutely no one. Accused of everything in the book, and guilty of none of it except the anger. First of all I have VA doctors that will say I am still very much in control of my faculties, that I have passed their tests in every way. Next you could dig out my records and see that I have never been in jail, or even seen the inside of one in my life. If I were guilty of all I was charged with, I should be locked up forever. What I am guilty of is caring about this nation, loving it to the point of giving up my own family, and in that process, making sure that yours could have the protection they need. Trying to tell those in a court room that don't have a clue, is next to impossible, I suggest don't even try it. The highly intelligent will look down their nose at you. Their reaction, "You must be one of them, I stereotyped you, how could you be anything else"? Yep that would be their reaction. In defense of the VA, I would like to say that I have never had any real problems with them, really there just wasn't any. Yes, I had to cross every "t", and dot every "i", but what is wrong with that? They were just doing their job. I am very aware that there are veterans that try to duplicate the symptoms of PTSD, and try to get something for nothing, and I am sure the VA has plenty of problems with those types. Again, I just can't find any major problems with the VA, and I did work for them for 23 years.

In closing and in trying to be positive, I want to thank our mayor in Sheridan, Wyoming, Mr. Dave Kinskey who is now a State Senator, for reading the book, "*Assault on the Liberty.*" Thank you to the Official Naval Museum in Norfolk, Virginia for exhibiting my uniform God Bless this once great nation, as it certainly needs all the blessings it can get.

The "*Liberty* incident" and the massive cover-up put into effect by Lyndon B. Johnson have had a profoundly negative and lasting effect on our country. I have never seen this country like it is today, never in my whole life. Leaders that don't want to lead, dumbing down of our children and most of all, the absolute loss of patriotism what I have known for so many years have deeply damaged the United States of America. In closing I can only say one thing. God Bless this great nation, at this point I don't know of another country that needs His blessing like we do now.

The USS Liberty Memorial Library, Grafton, Wisconsin
How the Name of the Town Library Became Offensive to Some

In March of 1988, the *Liberty Veterans Association* announced in their newsletter that the city of Grafton, Wisconsin was planning a new public library that would be named the USS *Liberty* Memorial Public Library in honor of the shipmates who died on June 8, 1967. The name was suggested by a local family who wished to remain anonymous, who contributed $250,000 toward construction. Three months later, the newsletter reported that the names of the anonymous donors were Benjamin and Theodore Grob, who owned a Grafton machine tool business. The Grobs suggested the name after reading a speech made by survivor Phil Tourney. There was an immediate outcry from supporters of Israel who deemed the name was somehow an attack upon Israel and an anti-Semitic slur. Rabbi Gideon Goldenholz of a nearby synagogue was quoted as calling the project a "cynical" way to bring the *Liberty* attack to public attention, and is therefore "insulting to Jews." He said, "The U.S. acted in a way unbefitting an ally, the blame ought not to be on Israel."

James Fromstein of the Milwaukee Jewish Council appealed for reconsideration of the name. According to Fromstein, "The USS *Liberty* incident … is a sensitive subject considered offensive to...Jewish people everywhere." Hostile press interest developed in Milwaukee, a federal commitment to contribute $83,000 to the library had been "delayed" for reasons unclear and at least one large donor had been asked to withdraw his donation. Fromstein and an associate met with Grafton mayor Jim Grant at Grant's home on May 10 while three newspaper reporters and two TV cameramen waited outside. Fromstein threatened to force selection of another name and he said he would call a session of the Milwaukee Jewish Council to consider their next move. The situation got increased TV and press attention in Milwaukee.

Liberty survivors John Hrankowski and Joe Meadors were invited by the Grafton Library committee to attend a forum at the American Legion Hall on June 8, 1988. Congressman Pete McCloskey was also invited and approximately 400 people attended the event. Hrankowski and Meadors explained that the name was merely a memoriam for the men killed on the American Naval ship of that name and strongly denied that the name was anti-Semitic in any way. The people of Grafton showed wonderful support and love for the *Liberty* representatives. On July 26, 1988 the ground breaking ceremony for the library was conducted despite the presence of protestors. Despite the presence of those who thought the name "USS *Liberty*" was chosen for anti-Semitic reasons, or to embarrass Israel, most of the local people considered the name as it was intended, to honor the memory of men who were killed in the attack made on it, regardless who or what the cause of that incident might have been.

The USS *Liberty* Memorial Library, Grafton, Wisconsin

Janet Staszewski, staff writer for the *Cedarburg News Graphic Pilot*, wrote on June 15, 1989, about the library memorial service: Ida Goss, whose son Jerry Goss was killed in the attack, praised the village

John Hrankowski Presenting *Liberty* Jackets to the Grob brothers at Dedication of USS *Liberty* Memorial Library, Grafton, Wisconsin, June 10, 1989

Ron Kukal giving the invocation

for the service and for naming the library after the *Liberty*. She had traveled from Indiana to see her son's name on the stone. Lorna Stopper, whose brother Duane Marggraf is memorialized on the stone marker, was overwhelmed by the love and generosity of the people of Grafton. John Hrankowski, vice-president of the LVA, indicated the memorial service was very emotional. John said as the stone was unveiled, "the unveiling of this stone will mark a spot which preserves the memory of 34 brave men who died unnecessarily in the service of their country." Joe Meadors, of Corpus Christi, Texas, said, "It's all kind of overwhelming after 22 years." Jim Grant, village president said, "The agony of uncertainty that the survivors and family have experienced must be addressed." He further honored the survivors and those killed with this tribute to them. And it was Steve LaTorre, who spoke for the survivors in displaying how they all felt, as he stood on the top step of the library, turned to the crowd and said... "THANK YOU, GRAFTON!"

Several Milwaukee-area groups, including the Milwaukee Jewish Council, had criticized the village for the name of the library and asserted that the attack had been used to foster hatred toward Israel and the Jews. The police escorted two buses carrying *Liberty* veterans and scattered other police officers throughout the area. Survivors of the Israeli attack reported that SWAT teams were dispersed on the roofs of the library and other buildings on the street. Procedures included a search of the library and nearby buildings with bomb-sniffing dogs. Despite fears of disruption, the 40-minute ceremony went off without a hitch. Captain McGonagle proudly wore his Congressional Medal of Honor he received and lauded and paid tribute not only to those who died but to the survivors. U.S. Representative Pete McCloskey urged the government to use the Grafton memorial as the beginning of official recognition for the men of the *Liberty*.

CONTINUING DENIALS AND ACCUSATIONS: REVERSE BIGOTRY

Of the many websites dedicated to getting the story of the still-nearly-secret attack on the USS *Liberty* publicized, one having the URL "www.HonorLibertyVets.org" has recently placed billboards on highways around the country. These billboards show background pictures of the disabled ship on one side and injured men on the other, with the words, "HELP THE USS LIBERTY SURVIVORS: ATTACKED BY ISRAEL."

News articles labeling the ads as "vicious" and "anti-Israel propaganda," and which accuse the billboard companies of anti-Semitism, have been the predictable result as illustrated in the referenced articles.[3] Further, one article by reporter Pamela Geller, published in *Brietbart.com* on

Honor Liberty Vets Billboard

April 25, 2016, erroneously states that the ad "aggressively promotes the discredited theory that Israel intentionally sank (sic) the USS *Liberty* warship in 1967. In reality, the sinking (sic) of the ship has been thoroughly investigated (sic) by the U.S. government and deemed an accident." Finally, the article laments, paradoxically, the George Orwell quote, "The further a society drifts from truth the more it will hate those who speak it." That quote is certainly a true reflection of the situation, but unfortunately in the opposite context intended by the author of the referenced article.

The articles reference the Anti-Defamation League (ADL) and its attempt to defame Alison Weir, whose mission is merely to publicize what is still a clearly misunderstood (as evidenced by the multiple errors in these articles), practically still-secret historical event, one that automatically provokes knee-jerk cries of outrage amongst those who prefer to keep it a state secret. And they repeatedly charge the survivors with anti-Semitism, yet another "blame the victims" tactic.

The billboards have caught the attention of a lot of people who just wish the controversy would go away, as it is too uncomfortable for them to have to contemplate. Another example occurred on May 20, 2016, in reply to an email sent by Ron Kukal, which informed others that he had just been called a "bigot" by a Pennsylvania state representative named Stan Saylor in response to Kukal's only statement to him: "I quoted former president Calvin Coolidge to Rep. Saylor, in which he said, 'A nation that forgets it's defenders, will be forgotten itself." That is all I said to Rep. Stan Saylor, to which he replied, "You are a bigot." Phil Tourney called Saylor about it and was hung up on, and *Liberty* supporter Phil Restino, of Daytona Beach, FL, also called Saylor to explain it but didn't get through; Saylor later returned his call, but still wasn't ready to listen, as Mr. Restino described it:

PA Rep Saylor just phoned me from his cell phone … [he] went on and on about survivors and supporters of the USS *Liberty* pitting veterans against veterans and that what happened with Israel and the USS *Liberty* was not important because it happened over 40 years ago. He said that we should be concentrating on helping our veterans. He confirmed that he was one of the dozen or so PA legislators who publicly opposed the USS *Liberty* billboards put up in PA, stating that they were "bigoted," [before hanging up on Mr. Restino].

The confusion and mis-directed anger resulting in these encounters and error-filled articles about the ad are unfortunate enough, but the fact that they support the original lies caused by Johnson's iron-fisted clampdown on the truth fifty years ago illustrate anew how the politically-correct mythologies have overtaken what George Orwell was saying in the referenced quote above in the *Brietbart* article. And how the writer of that piece, Pamela Geller, has completely transformed Orwell's warning, obliviously reversing it 180 degrees and essentially treating the grand "myths" as being the "truth." The convoluted way that the author of the article has misused Orwell's works is an unfortunate reminder that some people seem to have missed the point of *1984:* It was not written as a guide, or manual on how to achieve the society it described, or for the uninformed to absurdly reverse the axioms he put forth, wittingly or unwittingly reinforcing the myths; it was intended to be a warning about how to avoid that dire and bleak existence. Unfortunately, despite Orwell's magnificent efforts, that warning seems to have fallen on deaf ears as the nation marches on, seemingly unmoved by his prescience.

It is the upside-down, "black is white and white is black" mind-numbing effect evoked by George Orwell's dystopian police state, one which its modern practitioners have nearly perfected, that must be examined in the remaining chapters as it is an essential aspect of the still-unresolved "mystery" of the USS *Liberty* legacy.

Endnotes

1. See: http://www.aljazeera.com/blogs/americas/2015/06/israel-uss-liberty-attack-150608204015123.html

2. See: http://www.counterpunch.org/2014/05/16/american-legion-honchos-betray-liberty-veterans/

3. Geller, Pamela. "Geller: Lamar Advertising Runs Libelous Anti-Israel Billboards" Breitbart.com, April 25, 2016. See: http://www.breitbart.com/middle-east/2016/04/25/lamar-advertising-runs-libelous-anti-israel-billboards-refuses-afdi-pro-freedom-billboards/. And: http://blog.adl.org/international/alison-weirs-new-billboard-campaign-promotes-uss-liberty-conspiracies

Captain McGonagle on the bridge 16 hours after the attack.

Chapter 9

Beyond the Seas: The Flushing of Secrets From The USS *Liberty*

Captain William McGonagle: *"Those SOBs [sons of bitches] really did us in, George."*

Lieutenant George Golden: *"What are you talking about?"*

Captain William McGonagle: *"It was the President and McNamara, when they sent us up from over in Africa, we were there to have this happen."*

– Lieutenant George Golden, USS *Liberty* Survivor

THE "EXPLOSIVE" FIFTH TORPEDO

There is a reason that the next subject appears here, and was not a part of the narrative in Chapter 3, where the subject was focused on the details of the attack on the *Liberty*. That reason will become ever more clear as we proceed through it, however even before beginning, the pertinence of something touched upon in Chapter 1 will now become more obvious as well.

Before we examine the "alternate story" regarding the fifth torpedo that actually hit the *Liberty*, recall from Chapter 1 the words of Marine Corps Lieutenant General Charles G. Cooper, as he described in his memoirs an extremely disturbing account of President Johnson's screaming, profanity-laden meltdown in front of his entire Joint Chiefs of Staff at a meeting in November, 1965. They are so important that they have been repeated here, to add emphasis to this highly critical, essential point. As soon as the JCS chairman, Earle Wheeler, had finished his presentation, as Johnson stood facing away from them momentarily, then, suddenly whirling around, he began his vicious assault, screaming and cursing each of them in turn. Lieutenant General Cooper summarized his recollections of that frightening day:

Noting that it was he who was carrying the weight of the free world on his shoulders, he called them filthy names – shitheads, dumb shits, pompous assholes – and used "the F-word" as an adjective more freely than a Marine in boot camp would use it. It was unnerving, degrading.[1]

Author Cooper's stunning description of presidential behavior to his visitors that day, as he quoted more of Johnson's statements – for example, those "…idiots gave him stupid advice, [adding that] he had the whole damn world to worry about" – bespeaks more than the mere words in these excerpts say. This was obviously another of many Johnsonian meltdowns, an incident that suggests the president was suffering multiple incidents of psychotic rage, just like those that Richard Goodwin described, much too gently, in his book, or the very vivid, dramatic account of lobbyist Robert Winter-Berger in his book, as he told of Johnson's meltdown in Speaker McCormack's office in March 1964 (both of which are summarized in *LBJ: From Mastermind to the Colossus,* but the books cited – and noted in the Bibliography – are also available in many libraries, or at internet sites for new and/or used books).

Cooper's account showed Lyndon Johnson more vividly than the summaries found in the few other books that have alluded to this facet of presidential frailty – exploding in front of his highest-level-ranking military leaders as a result of his own failures of leadership in the direction of his war, one that many in the Pentagon didn't want, knowing its futility and fearing that it would lead down an impossible path to certain defeat – and it speaks volumes about how the whole "Vietnam Quagmire" came about. During this meeting, the chairman of the JCS, General Wheeler, had attempted to empathize with the president's situation and the tremendous pressure Johnson was under, but the president was not moved; Johnson asked the other participants if they agreed with General Wheeler and each of them explained the rationale for their concerns. During the discussion he had returned to a calmer demeanor, but before they were dismissed. Johnson returned to his attack mode, screaming and cursing, throwing the "F-bomb" at each of them, telling them he was "disgusted" with all of them. They had tried to make a serious presentation about the options available to him, assuming that he wanted to hear alternatives that might "win the peace" with war, but he demeaned and belittled them. All in all, it was probably the worst experience that each of them had ever endured. In fact, on the drive back to the Pentagon, Admiral Wesley McDonald even said as much, declaring that it "was the worst experience that I could ever imagine."[2]

The reason for this trip "into the weeds" of Lyndon Johnson's episodic rages will now be put into better context, as we return to an unspeakably atrocious possible consequence, that occurred in the afternoon of June 8, 1967 (still before lunchtime back in Washington, D.C.).

THE OTHER, "UNTHINKABLE," POSSIBILITY …

In the first edition of this book, we did not name the survivor, or the U.S. submarine involved, regarding his statement about that "fifth torpedo." The reason for that was because the assertion had only been made on an internet radio program (audio only) and it was felt that it had not been sufficiently vetted. Since then, on the 50th anniversary of the attack, that sailor, Richard Larry Weaver, produced a widely distributed video, including the referenced websites, stating that President Johnson personally ordered the captain of the submarine USS Amberjack to fire a torpedo at the Liberty. He said this was done after the Israeli motor-torpedo boats had fired four torpedoes, all of which missed. That torpedo hit the ship but failed to sink it, as explained previously. Weaver is considered by his peers to be an honorable and reputable man, and that imbues his statement with credibility. His comments are summarized as follows:

> According to the man [Mr. Weaver] who made the assertion, an investigator he had hired saw top secret documents which revealed that the four torpedoes fired, nearly simultaneously, from the Israeli torpedo boats all inexplicably missed the *Liberty*. President and Commander-in-Chief Lyndon B. Johnson – apparently in a fit of blind rage and exacerbation upon hearing that news, together with the news that the Israeli motor-torpedo boats had no more torpedoes left – then ordered the captain of one of his submarines to fire a torpedo at his own ship. It was that torpedo which purportedly hit the USS *Liberty*, nearly sinking it, but for the fact that a series of "miracles" occurred which prevented that from happening, as previously noted.[3]

Though there is no direct corroboration for this account, Mr. Weaver has stated that he has spoken with two men who were on board that submarine, both of whom acknowledged to him that it happened. For reasons that should be obvious, because this information would unfairly lead to so many other men, both alive and deceased, who might have participated – indubitably, only very reluctantly, with trepidation and fear, as they were forced to make an instantaneous "life and death" decision whether to obey, or not, a presidential order – they have understandably chosen to remain anonymous. So this aspect must also be considered as part of the "unsubstantiated rumors file" which we are merely conveying "for what it's worth." To suggest otherwise would only devalue the import of everything else reported herein, which has been carefully assembled and presented to ensure that it is as close to the truth as it is possible to be. Again, it cannot be stressed enough, this story is not being reported as "fact."

Unfortunately, however, it must also be said that another point which ultimately does give the rumored story "legs" is that it is consonant with so many of the other documented assertions made about the erratic behavior of President Johnson, including stories that were recounted throughout the previous chapters related to this sordid episode of U.S. Naval history. Included among them are the statements from credible men, George Golden and Dave Lewis, who were told by other highly credible men (Admiral Geis and Captain McGonagle) the stories that implicated President Johnson directly in treasonous actions. The story that Admiral Geis told to Mr. Lewis was one of the key pieces of the puzzle, as noted earlier; the fact that it was not revealed until two decades had passed, on the occasion of the twentieth anniversary reunion of the *Liberty* Veterans, caused the real story of what happened to nearly be lost, and would have, had Mr. Lewis not outlived Admiral Geis. That piece of invaluable evidence was one of the many elements of this incredible presidential scandal to finally become exposed. Even more important to resolving it was the story that Captain McGonagle told to George Golden.

It took the veterans twenty years to learn that truth, and even longer for it to become known to the rest of the American public, which had continued to think that Lyndon Johnson was merely a victim of unfortunate circumstances, rather than a president who had acted in a cowardly, treasonous way. But over two to three decades, as one piece at a time of the myriad of secrets came out, the matter was no longer of interest to the "main stream media," which was still highly controlled by three broadcast networks, and a handful of "nationally based" newspapers, none of which was interested despite its blockbuster, earth shattering nature. What was once a potential political scandal of immense proportions that should have received immediate attention, was now just a cold postscript that was swept into the dustbin of history.

Our task now is to bring that story out of the dustbin, put it under a microscope, and give it the attention that it deserves. Pieces of the puzzle have taken five decades to become known to the public, and in the meantime, many people have been hard at work attempting to keep the darkest secrets of the Johnson presidency under wraps, as others have worked to build the myths to create the illusion of a great president.

But the troubling evidence presented so far, when combined together, shows that months of extensive planning preceded the allegedly "spontaneous" Six-Day War, and that even the earlier provocations by Israel to her Arab neighboring countries were all part of that plan. And that the plan had its genesis in the White House, specifically in the mind of Lyndon B. Johnson. Furthermore, it can also be posited here that a major part of that planning, called Operation Cyanide, was specifically designed by him as a "false flag" attack on the USS Liberty, for the purpose of intentionally sinking it and taking every one of the 294 men with it to the bottom of the Mediterranean Sea. The story only becomes understandable when it is viewed in the context of the other stories – for example, Johnson's treatment of the same Joint Chiefs of Staff just two years earlier – which explains why so many others who had the misfortune of seeing first-hand how the president experienced episodes of psychotic behavior were so frightened of him. One of the most compelling reports came from another, later, chairman of the Joint Chiefs of Staff, none other than the very honorable Admiral Thomas Moorer, who observed that the president's handling of the *Liberty* attack was "... the most disgraceful act I witnessed in my entire military career."

WHO DECIDED TO HOLD THE OCCUPIED TERRITORIES. HINT: IT WAS NOT THE "USUAL SUSPECTS"

Israel, despite this so-called "incident," had won the war that it provoked – according to no less a figure than Moshe Dayan, whose affirmation of that can be found elsewhere within this book – with an all-out attack on the U.A.R.'s [Egypt] air force installations before they could prepare for their defense. At the previously noted January 2004 conference hosted by the State Department, David Satterfield, Deputy Assistant Secretary of State for Near Eastern Affairs acknowledged it, saying that the Six-Day War, "... defined the shape, literally, of the continuing Middle East conflict and physically changed the face of the region."

By the end of the Six-Day War the maps of the Middle East had to be redrawn because of the old refrain, "to the victor goes the spoils." The territories gained from what had been Palestine were suddenly now Israel's. The fact that even fifty years later, the "losers" (Palestinians, who had not even been involved in the fight) still regard those territories as only being "occupied" by Israel, shows clearly that the matter still remains "unresolved." Yet the general population of Israel, and of the majority of Americans, dismiss that point of view.

A recent poll revealed that the majority of Americans believe, incorrectly, that it is the Palestinians who now "occupy" Israeli territory, rather than the other way around. This troubling opinion is uniquely American, and is not even shared by other North Americans – neither Canadians nor Mexicans – or anywhere else in the world.[4] Moreover, as the author of the referenced article, Grant Smith, described the current situation:

> UN Resolution 242 called for withdrawal of Israeli armed forces from territories Israel occupied in order to establish peace in the region. Instead, Israel annexed East Jerusalem in 1980 and the Golan Heights in 1981. Neither move has been recognized by the international community. Israel's annexation of Jerusalem was declared "null and void" by UN Security Council Resolution 478, while UN resolution 497 de-

clared the same over Israel's annexation of the Golan. Israel withdrew military forces from Gaza in September 2005, but retained control over Gaza's frequency spectrum, tax revenue, airspace and coastline. Israel continues to be designated as an occupying power by the UN.[5]

In a MSNBC news story on October 15, 2015, the above graphic appeared in a discussion between anchor Kate Snow and reporter Martin Fletcher, to show the steady growth of Israel as well as the loss of Palestinian land.[6] There is also a video at the referenced website which captures that discussion. As the report on the backlash that ensued notes:

> "Supporters of Palestinian human rights on social media praised what they saw as a rare example of honesty about the occupation from TV news. But some media critics, and especially the Israeli media, criticized the segment, calling the graphic inaccurate. *The Jerusalem Post* referred to the image, which closely resembled a similar graphic widely circulated among activists, as "a map commonly used by Palestinian propaganda groups…"

The two major "complaints" were said to be that the map indicated that " …in 1946, present-day Israel was under Palestinian rule, leaving out the fact that it was under British Mandatory rule until May 14, 1948, when the British Mandate came to an end" and, the graphic reference to the "UN plan" was incorrect because that plan was never agreed to by the Arab neighbors. So four days later, MSNBC apologized for using the map because it was "not factually accurate." Correspondent Fletcher also explained that there was never a "recognized country called 'Palestine' in 1947, [though] twice as many Arabs as Jews lived in the region [so named] at that time."[7] The Institute for Middle East Understanding supported the map's accuracy, though acknowledging that Britain did not recognize Palestine as a "country," the map "accurately depicts the land that has been forcibly taken from Palestinians since 1946, two years before Israel was established" in preparation for expelling nearly a million Palestinians in the process of establishing the Jewish state.[8] All of the "factual inaccuracies" stem from the fact that the name "Palestine" had existed for about two millennia, well before other countries came into existence, but it was never formally constituted as an independent nation. Some might call this oversight in creating the graphic a "technicality" rather than a grievous factual "error."

The paradox of Israel having expropriated lands from Palestine as a result of the 1967 war – one which Palestinians had nothing to do with, least of all in starting it – and then adamantly refusing to relinquish that territory, is the root cause of the confusion of so many regarding that "occupation." That conundrum now manifests itself in further convoluted discourse, and begets automatic charges of "anti-Semitism" should one attempt to even mention it. A recent example of this appeared in *The Daily Beast*, in reference to the point of the Palestinian's demand for the right to return to their pre-1967 homes. The rationale for not allowing that – where the "occupied vs. disputed" status of this territory was glossed over, and taken as a "given" that it was indisputably Israeli territory – was stated as "A Palestinian right of return would mean forcing a nation of 8 million to accept as many as 4 to 5 million immigrants, many of whom are hostile to its statehood ..."[9] The fact that the issue involved the rights of indigenous people to "return" to their 1967 homes was reframed, to define them as "immigrants," speaks volumes about the nature of this "debate." Regardless of whether one likes or dislikes the subject of this article, Ann Coulter, one thing cannot be disputed: That this issue of the "occupied or disputed" nature of that territory can be so glibly dismissed, as to suggest that the matter is settled, in anyone's mind.

Before the 1967 war, and in its early stages, Israel had steadfastly denied that there had been any intention of holding on to the captured lands. But when it was over, on June 10, 1967, Israel was in control of more than double the amount of land that it had controlled the week before, as well as the indigenous Palestinian population living there. This fact has been a key element in the Arab-Israeli conflict and in efforts to end it ever since.[10] At the 2004 State Department conference previously referenced, Mr. Satterfield explained how UN resolutions 242 (November 1967) and later, 338, which called for Israel's withdrawal from those territories, have been the basis for every peace proposal since, including the "Roadmap" for a two-state solution. However, he admitted, "hope has evaporated" more than once in all of the negotiations since 1967.

Yet, according to reliable sources, neither Moshe Dayan nor David Ben-Gurion were entirely comfortable with the notion of retaining all of the occupied territories. Following the war, Ben-Gurion, even though out of power, was in favor of returning all the captured territories apart from East Jerusalem, the Golan Heights and Mount Hebron as part of a peace agreement.[11] And Moshe Dayan had doubts as well, which led him to become an advocate of unilateral disengagement from all the territories occupied in 1967. This turnaround came after a disagreement with Menachem Begin led to his resignation from the government before then founding the Telem party, which advocated ceding back the occupied territories.[12] Their view was that the return of those lands was an opportunity to trade the land back, in exchange for an assurance of achieving a sustainable peace.[13]

If some of the foremost leaders of Israel had not advocated the expropriation of these lands, then one may reasonably ask: Who then, led them in that direction, and what incentives were put before them to change their minds and retain the "spoils of war," for a war that the evidence previously presented shows was started by Israel after months of planning and aggressive provocations? In his autobiography, Dean Rusk agreed that the Israelis had denied such an intent as the war broke out, even though things changed as they conquered more territories. When he reminded Abba Eban, the Israeli Foreign minister, that they had previously stated that they "had no territorial ambitions," the response he got was, "We've changed our minds."[14]

When Abba Eban declared that they had changed their minds and decided to hold on to the new territories gained during the war – the old City of East Jerusalem, the Sinai and the Gaza Strip, the Jordanian territory west of the Jordan river known as the West Bank, the Golan Heights on the Israeli-Syrian border, and Sheba's Farms – it meant not only a tremendous geographic growth but the acquisition of the Arabs living in the areas formerly part of Palestine. The premise of that decision was based on an assumption that the "Palestinian problem" that came with it could be contained eventually. In the weeks and months following the Six-Day War, the UN Security Council deliberated the possible ways to force Israel to withdraw from the territories captured during the Six-Day War. U.N. Ambassador Arthur Goldberg (who Johnson had appointed as the successor to Adlai Stevenson in 1965) supported a modified resolution 242, which required that Israel withdraw "from [the] territories" taken in the war. Goldberg successfully removed the word "the" before "territories," and with that subtle, hardly noticeable change in wording, thereby allowed Israel to redefine what land would be returned. It also provided the pretext for them to delay further actions to begin such withdrawals until the Arab nations accepted the terms of the UN resolution. The ambiguous terminology that Goldberg (ergo, Johnson, who indubitably dictated his moves) left for future generations to interpret, could be construed in many ways – only the Sinai Peninsula has been returned as of this writing – but the remaining territories are considered as "occupied Palestinian Territory" by Israel's neighbors and the Palestinians living within its new borders.[15] The dilemma, as described above, is part of the unsung legacy of Lyndon Johnson.

The source of how Israel's border expansion really came about could not be more clear; it was planned and directed by Lyndon Johnson himself. This point was even acknowledged and described in a February 14, 2016 article titled "Our First Jewish President Lyndon Johnson?–an Update!!" in the on-line Israeli newspaper "5 *Towns Jewish Times*":

> The crafting of UN Resolution 242 in November 1967 was done under Johnson's scrutiny. The call for "secure and recognized boundaries" was critical. The American and British drafters of the resolution opposed Israel returning all the territories captured in the war. In September 1968, Johnson explained, "We are not the ones to say where other nations should draw lines between them that will assure each the greatest security. It is clear, however, that a return to the situation of 4 June 1967 will not bring peace. There must be secure and there must be recognized borders. Some such lines must be agreed to by the neighbors involved." [Arthur] Goldberg later noted, "Resolution 242 in no way refers to Jerusalem, and this omission was deliberate." This historic diplomacy was conducted under Johnson's stewardship, as Goldberg related in oral history to the Johnson Library. "I must say for Johnson," Goldberg stated. "He gave me great personal support."[16]

The fact that this was accomplished nearly seamlessly in the immediate aftermath of a war that had been meticulously planned, then aggressively provoked by Israel in collaboration with Johnson's White House staff, should become clear to all by this juncture. This critical point, which was described in detail in the first two chapters, becomes the basis for what followed.

HOW A "WIN-WIN" GOAL BECAME A "WIN-LOSE" FACT: DOOMING LBJ'S PRESIDENCY

There is considerable irony that the original objective – to weaken its enemies while strengthening Israel through expansion of those borders – was achieved even despite the fact that the plan was severely impacted by the early start of the war, which should have caused the planned sinking of the *Liberty* to be cancelled. Because the attack was delayed until the fourth day of the war, at a point where the Arab countries were conducting peace negotiations, the planned sacrifice – the "false flag" operation called Operation Cyanide – had now become almost impossible to cover up, even if the ship had sunk. The desperate, completely irrational decision to proceed with the attack, despite the fact that victory was already at hand, came close to exposing the false premise of the supposedly "spontaneous" war.

The fact that the *Liberty* and its crew refused to sink only compounded the problem, but that was mitigated by the enormously effective cover-up that ensued: the veils of secrecy imposed on everyone having anything to do with it – especially the *Liberty* survivors – complete with threats of prison, "or worse," and the lock-up of all true records, which were then replaced with abbreviated or completely fabricated false accounts, allowed everything else to fall into place, not the least of which was the expropriation of most of the rest of Palestine. Unfortunately, the cost to the United States was very high, especially in terms of the intangible loss of valued integrity, respect and honor to its friends and allies. Even to Israel itself, which Undersecretary of State George Ball concluded, poignantly, resulted in the Israeli's coming to believe that, if they could get by with an attack of this enormity, then they could "get away with almost anything." It may explain why Israel gets the most foreign aid dispensed by the U.S., but still wants more. Their 2016 request is up to $5 billion per year from $3 billion in recent years.[17]

The loss of honor – to America's friends and allies, but more importantly, to its own citizens, especially to the men on the *Liberty* who were abandoned, then as now – was brought about by the abrogation of normal military protocols designed for legitimate national security purposes, but compromised and degraded in this case because they were used for deceptive and treasonous purposes for the personal political objectives of the president. His goals had nothing to do with "national security," and were only related to strengthening his chances to be re-elected in order to extend his tenure in the White House. Johnson knew that being a "wartime" president only worked if the war being fought was a popular one. That he used the highest national security secrecy and classification protocols – developed over decades, even centuries, for the protection of the constitutional authority of the country itself – for the most crudely despicable personal purposes, was bad enough; but to then brutally force honest and patriotic men to use the same cunning and deceitful methods was arguably another of his many treasons.

Lyndon Johnson's presidency had been shredded into tatters by the end of 1967, when even his staunchest supporters had deserted him, the latest being his faithful sycophant Robert McNamara. Much of it was due to the public anger over the futile "war" in Vietnam and Johnson's growing "credibility gap." In February, a new play opened on Broadway called "MacBird!" that openly compared the president to the murderous Shakespearean character Macbeth; by the middle of March, 1968, his national approval rating had sunk to 36 percent and support for his handling of Vietnam sank to 26 percent, which was roughly the number of people who would support anything a president might do. In a closed-door meeting of Senate Democrats, Missouri senator Stuart Symington said that "Lyndon Johnson could not be elected dogcatcher."[18]

By September, 1967, *Newsweek* magazine (which had until then been among his strongest supporters) reported that:

> "He is the first President in U.S. history to be beset simultaneously with a major war abroad and a major rebellion at home – neither of them going well or holding forth any promise of the kind of sudden and dramatic improvement that alone could reverse the rising tide of anger, frustration and bitterness that is cresting around the White House. He is also a President whose own personality has become an issue in itself – an issue, indeed, that seems increasingly to be producing almost as much criticism and contention as the war in Vietnam and the tumult in the ghettos."[19]

In November, Robert McNamara and Lyndon Johnson became estranged over their "irreconcilable differences" and McNamara left his position under such strange circumstances that it is still not clear whether he resigned or was fired.

Some people on Johnson's staff stated that he had begun to talk about not re-running for the presidency in late 1967, and his top aide Marvin Watson said he had privately told him that in January, 1968. It was at this point that the Vietcong initiated the Tet Offensive, a surprise attack launched simultaneously throughout South Vietnam, setting off bombs and attacking even the "invulnerable" American embassy in Saigon. It was a huge operation that shook even the most strident supporters in the U.S. Finally, the majority of Americans began to realize that they had been lied to by their president and all of his high level surrogates about the "light at the end of the tunnel" and the enemy body counts, all of it. That was also the impetus that caused Robert Kennedy to re-evaluate his position against running for president that year, and he finally had begun to think about running. On March 12, Minnesota Senator Eugene McCarthy won 40% of the votes in the New Hampshire primary and that caused Kennedy to make his announcement three days later that he would challenge Johnson. The next primary was scheduled for April 3 in Wisconsin, where the entire state had been covered by the energized band of "McCarthy kids" and Johnson rightly feared the results from that contest.

For Johnson to finally decide to sacrifice his presidential powers, giving up his life-long dreams on March 31, 1968 when he officially announced that he would not run for the presidency, meant that he had undergone a powerful transformation. For him to voluntarily give up the presidency that he had lusted for his entire life could only mean that he had to surrender it in order to accomplish even "greater" objectives, ones that would help assure that his tenure as president would be enshrined forever in a legacy befitting one of the "greatest presidents of all time." Only a position in the same tier as George Washington, Abraham Lincoln and Franklin D. Roosevelt in the pantheon of U.S. presidents would be adequate for him. But to accomplish that, he would have to ensure that no one then alive and in a powerful position to succeed him any time in the future – anyone who might wish to destroy the myth of his "greatness" – would ever be allowed to follow him into the White House.

Four days after Johnson's announcement, Marin Luther King, Jr., was murdered in Memphis. It was, perhaps, not merely coincidental that the man he had feared the most might ever become president – Robert F. Kennedy – would then be assassinated just two months later. A friend of RFK's, Paul Schrade, who was with Kennedy when he was shot – and who was himself shot by Sirhan B. Sirhan – never believed that Kennedy was shot by the accused assassin. Schrade believes that Sirhan was "set up" in a very sophisticated conspiracy to eliminate Robert Kennedy. On the occasion of a February, 2016 parole hearing Schrade stated that while he thought Sirhan had shot himself, but "…a second unidentified shooter killed Kennedy."[20] A short excerpt from an AP article published in the *Washington Post* stated:

> The AP noted that "Schrade's voice cracked with emotion during an hour of testimony on his efforts to untangle mysteries about the events of June 5, 1968." The 91-year-old Schrade, a Kennedy family friend, was working as the labor chairman of the senator's presidential campaign in 1968. He was walking behind Kennedy when the Democratic candidate was shot four times. In part because Kennedy was struck from behind, Schrade has long advanced the argument that Sirhan fired shots that night – but not the ones that killed Kennedy. The fatal bullets, Schrade argued, were fired from a different shooter's gun.

Other books have pointed convincingly to a high-level government controlled operation that led to the murders of both Martin Luther King, Jr., and Robert F. Kennedy. While that topic is beyond the scope of this book, perhaps eventually the many anomalies left regarding these murders and their similarly clouded, highly-suspect cover-ups may also be put under closer scrutiny, and closed with the long-awaited finality that they so greatly deserve.

THE DEVELOPMENT OF A WORKING HYPOTHESIS ON WHAT REALLY HAPPENED TO THE USS LIBERTY

Based upon the information that has incrementally surfaced over the last five decades, it is now possible to develop a hypothesis about the still lingering mystery of what went wrong, and why the *Liberty* was attacked. Consider the "someone" who *Liberty* sailor Phillip Tourney ominously posited was behind the entire episode, a person who apparently still wanted the ship sunk even after help had finally arrived, eighteen hours later, to evacuate the wounded.

The fact that help would not arrive for almost eighteen hours, when fighter jets were within fifteen minutes of its location, is proof enough. When Israel called off its attack due to the appearance of a Russian ship on the scene, making it impossible to sink the *Liberty* undetected, that same "someone," in a final act of desperation, evidently decided first that no help would be dispatched until the following day and that the ship would then have to fight its way to Malta and, with any luck, would not make it. Only someone capable of enormous acts of self-delusion would even think that he could replace truths with lies, and that the lies would become the truth, could possibly been behind this tragic story. Only a person whose hold on sanity – and the last traces of rationality were intermittent and tenuous at best and completely lost at worst – could come to believe that an outrageous act of treason such as this could be politically beneficial to himself and therefore worth the risk of failure, or worse, public exposure.

There was only one person who met those criteria, and he was not in the Israeli military or government. The "someone" referenced by the sailor/survivor/author Phillip Tourney could have only been the president of the United States, Lyndon B. Johnson.

The benchmark being set for this case is simply that the perpetrator must have been someone known to have episodes of becoming "psychotic" – in this case, no other possible cause makes sense, because no one in their "right mind" could have done something so heinous. Just as there is also no known evidence to support an assertion that some lesser, maverick military officer made such a stunning and intrinsically outrageous order on his own.

All of the signs previously noted point to Lyndon Johnson as the instigator and the others as merely the planners and facilitators. This statement is based partly upon the descriptions furnished by some of Johnson's closest aides of what can be called his "documented psychosis" during this period of time. The scenario described here uniquely fills in all the "missing links." Naturally, these assertions are subject to the scrutiny of others and, pending further investigation and the complete release of all files still being withheld.

The ultimate test of its veracity – and any rebuttals to it – must address specifically the known mental condition of Lyndon B. Johnson during this period.[21] As to the issue of Israel's culpability – arguably, even being the victim of an enormous dosage of Johnsonian manipulation, according to this thesis – it becomes the only realistic alternative to the widely held presumption that the war was already won and therefore there was nothing about the attack that could be considered as having been in the interest of Israel or any of its leaders to initiate that attack. If it had ever been the case, by June 8th, it clearly was not. By then, with the war essentially over, it could only have been at the insistence of a deluded president who still thought it could win him another landslide re-election the following year.

For all of these reasons, it can be stated beyond a shadow of a doubt, that the attack on the USS *Liberty* was not a case of "mistaken identity." What rational Israeli official, knowing that victory was already in hand, would have initiated orders to knowingly and mercilessly attack and sink an American Navy ship, their closest ally, with the specific intent to murder every one of its officers and enlisted men? The only realistic answer is "none" of them. The only logical explanation for this sordid chapter in American history is that the person responsible for it was an irrational, embittered, sociopathic, narcissistic, paranoid, and psychotic individual in the middle of a major manic-depressive meltdown. The only man who was known to have suffered from this amalgamation of psychic disorders was the man who had placed himself at the pinnacle of power within the military apparatus of the most powerful nation in the world and subsequently deemed himself, before a handful of reporters on Air Force One, the "King of the World." The best, and only realistically possible candidate for the question "Who ordered the attack on the *Liberty?*" was President Lyndon B. Johnson himself.

Johnson's sole focus throughout his career – indeed, his entire lifetime – was the "politics" of everything that happened, or even more importantly, had been planned to occur. In this case, in the middle of the crisis, according to his domestic affairs aide at the time, Joseph Califano, Johnson ordered press secretary George Christian and Secretary of State Rusk to back away from the previous statement of neutrality. Moreover, Califano stated that Johnson had told him to call Arthur Krim, Lew Wasserman, and Edwin Weisl, and to reassure them that he would stand by Israel and that their help was needed to make this known to the Jewish community in order to get them "off his back."[22]

Califano also made some revealing comments about events in the White House during this period relating to Johnson's reaction to advice he had received from two Jewish staff members, Larry Levinson and Ben Wattenberg, who had suggested that he address a meeting of American Jews in Lafayette Park about his intent to support Israel. The idea was that this would "neutralize" the State Department's neutrality statement, and reap political benefits through negating some of the Vietnam protests.[23] An indication of Johnson's psychological state of mind at that point (the memo referenced was dated June 7, 1967, and it is unclear whether Johnson read it that day or the next, which was the day the *Liberty* was attacked) is revealed in what Califano then reported: Johnson told him how disappointed he was in how some of his Jewish friends and staff had not been very helpful in drumming up more support for him. Just after this exchange, Johnson spotted Levinson leaving Califano's office and, as he jabbed his fist into the air, he yelled down a hall at him, saying, "'You Zionist dupe! You and Wattenberg are Zionist dupes in the White House! Why can't you see I'm doing all I can for Israel. That's what you should be telling people when they ask for a message from the President for their rally.'" Levinson told Califano afterward that he felt "'*shaken to the marrow of my bones.*'"[24] [Emphasis added.]

Johnson's state of mind on June 8 was highly agitated by other events that had taken place on the day before that. Congress had remained split over many issues, including the on-going racial divide, the stalled Great Society initiatives, and of course the growing quagmire called Vietnam. On June 7, the house had voted against the Johnson administration's bid to increase the debt limit, which was a major setback that stalled the federal government at many levels because, within three weeks, its ability to borrow money would come to a halt. On the same day, Johnson demanded to see a list of all the Democrats who had not voted for his bill and found that the representative of the affluent New York district of Westchester County, Richard Ottinger, had voted against it as a jab against the war because it was taking priority over domestic spending. Johnson, of course, was furious and swung back at him, threatening to build a public housing project in the middle of Ottinger's high-rent Westchester District.[25]

These other highly charged issues would have indubitably caused Johnson to become even more agitated, perhaps contributing to the events of the following day, June 8, 1967 and his apparent insistence on carrying out the planned Operation Cyanide. Three days earlier, Walter Rostow, Johnson's special assistant for National Security Affairs, had sent the president a memo deriding Egypt's failed defense in the battle on the first day, as Israeli fighter jets destroyed the Egyptian air force on the ground at their air bases, as a "turkey shoot.'"[26]

On the next day, Rostow had sent another memo to Johnson, recommending that Israel be allowed to keep the captured territories. This was a recommendation for a "sea change" in US policy since the previous clash in 1956, when Eisenhower had forced Israel, threatening economic sanctions, to return the captured territories in that skirmish. Rostow's memo became the basis for de facto US policy: Lyndon Johnson immediately acquiesced to Israel's new position, no doubt anxious to show them his resolve to continue supporting their agenda in exchange for them doing the same for him. It was no wonder, then, that Ephraim "Eppie" Evron so loved Lyndon Johnson that he actually volunteered to remain in the

United States and campaign for him in 1968. Presidential counsel Harry McPherson pleaded with Johnson to authorize "Eppie" to "spill the beans," sending him a long memorandum; Johnson marked it up with "No, no, no!" in the margins, but Eppie still went around to Miami, New York, and Los Angeles, meeting with large groups of Jews, telling them how great a man LBJ was.[27]

Peter Hounam interviewed a veteran CIA agent, John Haddon, who for ten years worked for James Angleton. Haddon confirmed that Angleton did not have the power to make such a policy decision, that such an action could *only have been authorized by the president*: "It was what the President of the United States thought that had the only meaning.... There was the White house and the Pentagon all set to give the Israelis a green light" [to invade Egypt on the fourth day and go all the way to Cairo][28] Hounam's conclusion was that the presence of the Sixth Fleet generally and the USS *Liberty* in particular, was all part of a prearranged deployment to support Israel in its planned war with its Arab neighbors: "It implied a degree of foreknowledge at a time when few people were expecting a war."[29] This astonishing assertion, an "implied degree of foreknowledge," applies equally to the JCS decision to move the USS *Liberty* into the area over two weeks before the war began.

Had the *Liberty* sunk, and taken every man aboard to the bottom of the Mediterranean, Lyndon Johnson could have immediately entered the war in the Middle East (which is precisely why he had aircraft loaded with nuclear bombs that were ready for take-off hours before the ship was attacked), and forced a confrontation with the Soviet Union that could have provoked a major war, possibly a nuclear war between the two superpowers. Indeed, as previously noted, two A-4 bombers loaded with nuclear bombs bound for Cairo had already been launched with the first sortie of fighter jets sent to rescue the *Liberty*, before they were all recalled when it became known that the ship had not sunk as expected. He may have been counting on Soviet Premier Alexei Kosygin to back down, but it is difficult to put oneself into the deluded mind of a man who had declared himself "King of the World."

Johnson probably expected this confrontation to have given him the collateral benefit of distracting the students who were protesting the Vietnam War. Johnson still expected to run again for the presidency the following year, and he would have tried anything to dampen those protests by an act of deception even greater than he had already accomplished three years earlier with the contrived "attack" by North Vietnam, which he then used to secure carte blanche authority from Congress to insert the US military machine into their civil war.

Admiral Geis, a very loyal Navy man whose conscience impelled him to share his words with Lt. Commander Lewis, did so because he wanted that piece of explosive information to be put into the public record so that history would have a chance to be corrected. Rear Admiral C. A. Hill Jr., added additional context to that event, when he wrote the following about Admiral Geis:

> No better example of that man's courage may be found than his attempt to save the lives of the officers and crew of the *USS LIBERTY* when that ship was under aggressive attack by a foreign power. That was the year before (June 8th of 1967) with his flag on the *USS AMERICA* when he responded to *LIBERTY's* desperate call for aide by authorizing *AMERICA's* Captain, Don Engen, to launch fighter aircraft that could have, *by their mere presence,* ended any mistaken identity claim by the attackers without further bloodshed! (Emphasis in original).

> When Secretary of Defense McNamara, by telephone, directed him to recall those aircraft he refused to comply unless ordered to do so verbally by President Johnson. When the President came on the line he ordered Admiral Larry Geis to recall our aircraft despite the full knowledge that American sailors were being killed in an unprovoked attack. Then he had no choice except to follow the orders of the Commander-in-Chief.[30]

McNamara died forty years after the event, consistently denying anything of the kind, but further stating that he did not remember anything about the *Liberty* attack. This, while promoting his books and video about how he eventually came to realize that he had been an enabler to Lyndon Johnson in promulgating a war, one that he couldn't deny, which he claimed was all because of the confusion related to the "Fog of War." Mr. McNamara had been beguiled by all of the publicity afforded him as JFK's secretary of defense and the numerous times his eminence appeared on the cover of *Newsweek, Time* and assorted other magazines in the 1960s, generally referenced (erroneously) as one of the "best and brightest" men in Washington.

McNamara had always believed that he had to perform his duties as a classic "Yes Man." In this perverted version of being a "team player" there was no allowance for one to speak his or her mind when it came to judgments of policy, not to mention morality or even legalities. He once said, "I don't believe the government of a complicated state can operate effectively if those in charge of the departments of the government express disagreement with decisions of the established head of that government."[31] In other words, he had come to agree with Johnson that, *whatever the president ordered him to do* – regardless of the niceties of due process, the fealty to constitutional governance, the mundane observance of moral principles or ethical standards, even the impediments related to basic legalities – *he would follow those orders without question.* He must have slept through the morass of the Nuremberg trials, where even low level soldiers were held to a higher standard than that.

But there were others in the chain of command who could have also changed the course of history. Had Admiral John S. McCain II not been so accommodating as a facilitator of presidential treasons, the others on down the chain of command would have not been able to carry out the outrageous orders. It wasn't until Captain Merlin Staring stated his objections to the miscarriage of justice, as previously noted, that anyone raised their voice against the presidential orders. Rear Admiral Staring's letter "U.S.S. *Liberty* Alliance" dated September 30, 2006 is printed as Appendix B and his letter of September 21, 2005 (also under the "Liberty Alliance" letterhead) to Ron Kukal is printed as Appendix C. Captain Ward Boston, Jr. similarly stepped forward years after the incident, powerfully redeeming himself for his capitulation in carrying out the orders he had been given in 1967 (as cited in Chapter 5).

The deceit about the real mission of the *Liberty* and its attack by an ally remains a sore point in the relationship between the United States and Israel to this day. The reason it still persists is the inevitable consequence of the cover-up immediately invoked by Johnson, which caused the truth to be hidden for so long, specifically the fact that all officers and enlisted men who survived the attack were sworn to secrecy. Years later, when some of the sailors did begin talking about it, AND others became involved, some reacting very aggressively.

It is easy to see how this issue has exacerbated the divisions within our own nation regarding Israel, and the tenuous relationship it created between the two; this incident has become a part of the continuing and growing, ageless chasm that has long divided the world as the distrust it created has still not receded. Regardless of how one looks at it, the Six-Day War was only one battle of a very long string of battles, a centuries-old clash of civilizations.

The bottom line of the results, which can readily be tabulated from this watershed event, was that the Six-Day War, into which the USS *Liberty* had sailed, transformed Israel from a small state into a major, militarily powerful nation located in the center of the world's most ancient civilization.

LYNDON JOHNSON'S DEMONS

Robert Kennedy once said to JFK's aide and historian, Arthur Schlesinger, Jr.,: "How can we possibly survive five more years of Lyndon Johnson? Five more years of a crazy man?"[32] The many other references made in previous chapters to Lyndon Johnson's various untreated mental issues are merely random samples that were noted in various other books, including many memoirs from people who seemingly went out of their way to make that point in their recollections of their life's work. These were made by laymen, people who worked closely with Johnson and observed his behavior, but there were mental health professionals who affirmed those assessments as well:

Gerald Tolchin, PhD and psychology professor:[33]

> "Johnson may well have been the most psychologically unstable person ever to assume the presidency. He was a tragic figure pursued by demons, real and imagined …It appears likely that Lyndon Johnson suffered from bipolar (manic-depressive) disorder throughout his life, a condition that grew worse as he grew older, peaking just as he reached the zenith of his influence and power."

Dr. Bertram S. Brown, a psychiatrist, said:[34]

> "Johnson's humiliation of his employees was a way of exercising his power …Johnson was a megalomaniac …He was a man of such narcissism that he thought he could do anything."

Dr. Hyman L. Muslin, M.D. and Thomas H. Jobe, M.D. in their book, *Lyndon Johnson: The Tragic Self – A Psychohistorical Portrait*, said:[35]

> "Could or should a Lyndon Johnson with all the imbalances in his self lead our nation? We submit that the self-pathology of LBJ precluded this sensitive and unstable man from becoming an authentic leader of men …A tragedy such as the Vietnam war should not be recounted simply as a lesson of history; it should be blazoned in our books as a chilling example of the disasters overtaking the world when flawed leaders are given command of the engines of war."

Unfortunately, Drs. Muslin and Jobe, writing their book in 1991, neglected to even mention the attack on the USS *Liberty*, probably because of the secrecy surrounding it even then, twenty-four years after the fact. However, if they had known the full story, as we have recounted it here, it would have been an even more object lesson to their point. In due course Lyndon Johnson's real persona, and his brutal forcefulness on all of the men and women he commanded, should become his rightful legacy and replace the myth of presidential greatness that has been inserted in its stead.

Johnson's intent for such an elaborately planned operation would be to show the world how the United States had turned its entire foreign policy around and would now become not only the savior to "Little Israel," as he called it, but to be its chief supplier of armaments and financial subsidies from then on. That has been stated by many observers, but one of the first was Richard Parks, who in 1967 worked in the U.S. Embassy in Cairo as the Political Consul:

> It was a turning point. Up until that point we had avoided being a major arms supplier to Israel. Paradoxically, the security of Israel became one of our strategic objectives [as a result of the Six-Day War, and in the immediate aftermath of the Israeli attack on the USS *Liberty*], which it had never been in the past.[36]

Much has been written about the correlation of politicians – to a higher degree than most other professions – to having sociopathic or psychopathic personalities. In fact, there was one such article written in the British newspaper *Independent* several years ago, titled "Q: What's the Difference between a politician and a psychopath? A: 'None.'"[37] While that premise was a bit overstated, it could be argued that Lyndon Johnson was "Exhibit A" of such a predicate, for he exhibited every one of the attributes listed in that article, beginning with "pathological liar, remorseless, having a complete lack of empathy for others, and callous" and continuing through the rest of the list.

The overarching "moral" of this story might be stated thusly: Giving psychotics the keys to the White house, or even put into positions of power on the other end of Pennsylvania Avenue, will come back to bite the democracy that allowed them such easy access. That lesson is really the whole point of this book and it should be considered a warning to all: The lies and deceit are now fifty years old, and have become merely "ancient history" to younger people, but the rot induced into the foundations of the republic known as the United States of America has yet to be repaired. In fact, given the apparent trends toward greater levels of mendacity among aspirants to the Oval Office, it has only grown larger over those five decades.

How the USS *Liberty* Became "The Most Decorated US Warship in History," Including a Medal of Honor for Commander William McGonagle

Ex-CIA analyst Ray McGovern noted the circumstances of how Commander McGonagle received his distinguished Medal of Honor, in a less-than-memorable manner:[38]

> I remembered what a naval officer involved in McGonagle's award ceremony told one of the Liberty crew: "The government is pretty

jumpy about Israel ...the State Department even asked the Israeli ambassador if his government had any objections to McGonagle getting the medal." When McGonagle received his award, the White House (the normal venue for a Medal of Honor award) was all booked up, it seems, and President Lyndon Johnson (who would have been the usual presenter) was unavailable. So it fell to the Secretary of the Navy to sneak off to the Washington Navy Yard on the banks of the acrid Anacostia River, where he presented McGonagle with the Medal of Honor and a citation that described the attack but not the identity of the attackers.

Former Chairman of the Joint Chiefs of Staff, Admiral Thomas H. Moorer, commenting on the same point, said, "The way they did things, I'm surprised they didn't just hand it to him under the 14th Street Bridge."[39] Lyndon Johnson chose not to honor this man by personally awarding him the Medal of Honor because he knew that he could not look at him, eye to eye – knowing that this victim of his treachery was not supposed to have even survived, much less given such an award. This particular story should be taken for what it was: The President's subtle admission of his own cowardly actions, because he knew that the man who was given the medal stood in stark contrast to himself – and would be looking him in the eye.

But that ceremony was not the only tradition that would be broken by the president in this case: For over two hundred years, there had been no provision for awarding medals, especially the Purple Heart, in situations involving "friendly fire," which was purportedly the official excuse to be used for the attack. This prohibition was considered inviolate for all those years despite the fact that the *Liberty* crewmen were soon given a total of 840 medals, ranging from the Medal of Honor for the commander to Navy Crosses, Bronze Stars, Silver Stars, a Presidential Unit Citation, and over two hundred Purple Hearts, but not one of them indicated the whereabouts of the *Liberty* – and no mention was made of Israel's involvement. As noted earlier, a Silver Star awarded to Terry Halbardier forty-two (42) years later, in 2009, was the first one ever issued that did finally acknowledge that Israel was the attacker.

This must have been quite a conundrum for the officials handing out the original awards, while keeping that information off of the awards, monuments or gravesites in Arlington National Cemetery where many of the bodies of those killed were interred. It wasn't until 1993 that the standard changed, when Congress expanded eligibility after learning that some victims of friendly fire in the first Gulf War had been awarded Purple Hearts but others had not.[40]

The Medal of Honor for Commander McGonagle is arguably the most controversial of all, since it is also the highest possible award given within the military. Some believe it was because of his purportedly false testimony to the Court of Inquiry, which has been described in detail in other books, including James Ennes' seminal 1979 work. Yet Ennes himself stated that McGonagle was "...an authentic hero of rare courage," and describes his errors as being the result of his being "ill, weary, grief-stricken and apparently worried that he might be charged with some as-yet unidentified offense."[41] One of the survivors has stated "The crew's survival was part and parcel of him being there. He was old school Navy and I truly believe he would have been one officer who would have countered a "bad order" if it meant the taking of our lives. In my mind he did deserve the medal for accurately making the right decisions [relating to] his order to prepare to abandon ship and for staying at the helm despite his wounds ...his oath to protect classified data might have prevented his complete honesty. Nevertheless, as I said, he was a giant in my eyes." But other survivors disagree with such assessments, one of them asserting: "He sold the crew down the river because he was part of the cover up ...He took the rewards rather than stick by his crew that saved the ship, that is the way it was then and now." Still another one of the crew members stated, "I will only say this: to be around the Captain at a reunion or something like that, you could feel the stress dripping off him, like sap from a tree. I could feel it. I know this isn't fact, but it is what I felt. My thoughts were [that] the medals were an appeasement. We all knew it."

Regardless of how he is remembered by different crew members, it must be acknowledged that Commander McGonagle was put into a deadly, impossible situation by an unscrupulous politician obsessed with his own political agenda. McGonagle had simply sailed into waters that had seemed so tranquil and peaceful as he approached them, but then turned treacherous in an instant. Given the "stacked deck" that he was dealt, the unimaginable horrors to which he had to immediately respond, the unrelenting pressure from all of his superiors to "get along by going along"* and his overall responsibility for the safety of the remaining crew and his ship, one must put himself/herself into Captain McGonagle's shoes before considering how they might have handled the situation.

---

* A phrase famously made by LBJ's sycophant Bobby Baker, who used it often as advise to new senators, explaining what was expected by the "Master of the Senate:" Only "yes men" need our support; no mavericks needed here (which explains why the Wisconsin senators, Gaylord Nelson and William Proxmire, among a few others, were not among the "establishment"). It was a concept that Johnson expected of everyone under him, only rejected by a courageous few.

Endnotes

1. Cooper, pp. 3-5

2. Ibid.

3. http://www.renegadetribune.com/uss-liberty-survivor-says-us-submarine-filmed-israels-attack-torpedoed-ship/ and https://republicbroadcasting.org/news/ussliberty-the-unmentioned-parts-survivor-richard-larry-weaver/

4. Smith, Grant, "Most Americans Believe Palestinians Occupy Israeli Land" March 25, 2016. Anti-War.com. See: http://original.antiwar.com/smith-grant/2016/03/24/most-americans-believe-palestinians-occupy-israeli-land/

5. Ibid.

6. See: Anti-Media.org, Kit O'Connell, Oct. 27, 2015: "Before MSNBC's apology, pro-Palestinian activists praised the segment as a rare instance of mainstream media honesty about Israeli occupation" http://theantimedia.org/msnbc-apologizes-after-accidentally-telling-the-truth-about-israel/

7. Ibid.

8. Ibid.

9. Young, Cathy. "Ann Coulter's Anti-Semitism Runs Deep." *The Daily Beast* May 10, 2016. (See: http://www.thedailybeast.com/articles/2016/05/10/ann-coulter-s-anti-semitism-runs-deeper-than-you-know.html?source=TDB&via=FB_Page)

10. See: C-Span.org: 1967 Arab-Israeli War and USS *Liberty*

(http://www.c-span.org/video/?179892-1/1967-arabisraeli-war-uss-liberty)

11. Churchill, Randolph, and Winston Churchill, *The Six-Day War, 1967* p. 199 citing *The World at One*, BBC radio, 12 July 1967

12. See: http://www.zionism-israel.com/bio/biography_moshe_dayan.htm

13. Hounam, p. 185

14. Rusk, p. 388

15. Goldberg, J. J. p. 289

16. See: http://5tjt.com/our-first-jewish-president-lyndon-johnson-an-update/

17. See: http://www.haaretz.com/israel-news/.premium-1.701993?utm_campaign=Echobox-&utm_medium=Social&utm_source=Facebook#link_time=1454884938

18. Cohen, Michael A. *American Maelstrom: The 1968 Election and the Politics of Division*, London: Oxford University Press, 2016, p. 109. http://www.amazon.com/American-Maelstrom-Election-Politics-Division/dp/019977756X/ref=sr_1_1?s=books&ie=UTF8&qid=1459787303&sr=1-1&keywords=michael+cohen+american+maelstrom

19. *Newsweek*, September 4, 1967

20. See Peter Holley "Sirhan Sirhan denied parole despite a Kennedy confidant's call for the assassin's release" The Washington Post, February 11, 2015 (https://www.washingtonpost.com/news/post-nation/wp/2016/02/10/this-kennedy-confidant-has-spent-decades-calling-for-the-release-of-rfks-killer/?postshare=9771455345625972&tid=ss_fb)

21. Hershman, Power …, p. 212; Goodwin, Richard, pp. 402–403.

22. Califano, p. 205.

23. Ibid. (ref. personal papers of Jos. Califano: memo from Levinson and Wattenberg to LBJ, June 7, 1967)

24. Ibid.

25. Ibid., p. 206

26. Hounam, p. 136.

27. Ibid., p. 140.

28. Hounam, p. 233

29. Ibid., pp. 234–235

30. See: *A True Story Of The Sea* by Rear Admiral C. A. Hill, Jr., USN (Ret) 1 October 2005 http://www.newtotalitarians.com/index_files/TrueStoryOfTheSea.htm

31. See Herring, p. 8

32. Schlesinger, *RFK*, p. 836

33. Hershman, p. 6

34. Kessler, p. 32

35. Muslin and Jobe, p. 197

36. See: YouTube: "Documentary on the USS Liberty: Dead in the Water," (@ 3:20).

37. See: "Q: What's the Difference between a politician and a psychopath? A: "None." http://www.independent.co.uk/news/q-whats-the-difference-between-a-politician-and-a-psychopath-a-none-1361687.html

38. McGovern, Ray, A USS Liberty Hero's Passing, *Consortium News*, August 17, 2014

39. Gates, p. 65 (Ref. *Christian Science Monitor,* June 22, 1982)

40. See Military.com, "Marine Slain By Friendly Fire in Vietnam to Be Awarded Purple Heart," March 16, 2015 (http://www.military.com/daily-news/2015/03/16/marine-slain-by-friendly-fire-in-vietnam-to-be-awarded-purple.html)

41. Ennes, p. 150

Epilogue

On a Wing and a Prayer:
Sailing to Zion

"Everyone admits how praiseworthy it is in a prince to keep his word, and to behave with integrity rather than cunning. Nevertheless our experience has been that those princes who have done great things have considered keeping their word of little account, and have known how to beguile men's minds by shrewdness and cunning.

In the end these princes have overcome those who have relied on keeping their word."

– Machiavelli, in *The Prince*

A President of Machiavellian Dimensions

A common thread woven through the earlier chapters will now be tied together, and the tapestry we've already started should now become clearer: There were diabolical forces at work in the previous two years and the early months of 1967 that culminated, on June 2, in the voyage across the Mediterranean by the USS *Liberty*; it was then that the ship began the last part of the journey to its fateful assignment, according to plans ordered by the commander-in-chief. The depiction we have described, of how a very sophisticated plan had been executed – albeit one which failed to account for the unpredictable human foibles that caused it to unravel – illustrates with new clarity the underlying darkness that has been missing from the earlier accounts of the story of the USS *Liberty's* last journey. As we tie that last knot together, it will reveal the truly epic nature of the larger story about the reasons behind the *Liberty's* fate.

As the *Liberty* sailed off on its last voyage, into the same Mediterranean waters that were once the scene of Shakespearean drama, it too became caught up in the same kinds of power plays that William Shakespeare had only imagined. But some of the stories he described involved scenes near the same route which the *Liberty* sailed. As it passed to the south of Italy, scenes from *Othello, The Merchant of Venice, Julius Caesar,* or the star crossed young lovers in *Romeo and Juliet* might have been evoked in the imaginations of some of the crew; and again, as it sailed south of Greece, scenes from *A Midsummer Nights Dream,* or his descriptions of Troy in *Troilus and Cressida* might have been recalled by some of the nearly 300 men aboard. In the latter part of its voyage, the *Liberty* sailed through the very same waters described in the earliest "novels" such as *The Iliad, and The Odyssey,* written originally by Homer and followed later by other similar works by his many literary descendents.

These analogies will also be referenced in the Afterword, The Power of Myth, for the purpose of instilling a sense of the historical significance of the scene of the attack on the *Liberty,* a geographical area that was also the scene of many other events, and wars, in the three millennia since those earliest recorded histories of humanity. By looking at this story in the Shakespearean context, one can also see beyond the attack, or even the narrow slice of history called the "Six-Day War," because the similarities do not end with the Mediterranean metaphor. Even as the attack played out, another new play that evoked the Shakespearean genre had already opened on Broadway, titled *MacBird!,* by playwright Barbara Garson and writer/director Roy Levine. The obvious and explicit comparison of President Johnson to the murderous Shakespearean character Macbeth was merely the first instance of the creation of that metaphor; in this popular play that ran for nearly a year, the president was already being accurately cast as a shrewd, guilt-ridden, maniacal schemer. Lyndon "MacBird" Johnson was a president who uniquely evoked the darkness of *Richard III* and the cunning of *Macbeth.* Had Shakespeare gotten around to writing a play about Caligua, (born *Gaius Julius Caesar Augustus Germanicus* after his famous relative who preceded his reign), he would have come very close to describing the persona of Lyndon Johnson. Caligua was also known as a leader famed for his cruelty, sadism, extravagance, and sexual perversity.[1]

The context could not have been more explicitly drawn – even when he had done it himself – as noted in Chapter 1: While sitting in his throne chair on Air Force One, he declared to a group of reporters surrounding him, as he thumped his chest in Tarzan fashion: "I am the King!" And, as the "King," he would have literally considered all of the military assets under his command as being merely pawns at his beck and call. He would play them on a global chessboard which as the Machiavellian "King" he uniquely controlled, either indirectly through his highest level bishops and knights, or directly, as he felt necessary, as when he would personally deliver a telephonic message to one of those lesser chessmen. He did it routinely with military men in the Pentagon or those stationed in Vietnam. And on June 8, 1967, he did it with Admiral Lawrence Geis, when the "King" felt that his knight, Defense Secretary McNamara, wasn't getting through to his errant "castle," Admiral Geis, who had ordered two separate squadrons to go to the *Liberty's* defense. Johnson decided that only he could frame the order emphatically enough to get the message across to this wayward rook: "I want that Goddamn ship going to the bottom. No help. Recall the wings." LBJ had a remarkably unique way with words, and for Admiral Geis to recall that kind of profanity and treachery, and thereby ensure that they would eventually become part the future record of this despicable event, is proof enough that such a sentence could only have originated with him: no one else could have possibly uttered such a thing, a point that helps to prove everything else regarding his delusions and deceitfulness, which still comes as a stunning shock to most people who have never before been exposed to Lyndon Johnson's real legacy.

The Lost Battle-Cry: "Remember the Liberty!"

The sinking of the *USS Liberty* was the cataclysmic event that had been expected by President Johnson to produce a tidal wave of patriotic support once the anticipated public outcry had reached a crescendo, with a battle cry of *"Remember the Liberty!"* The plan called for deadly retaliation through an all-out attack aimed at the Egyptian (U.A.R.) President Nasser. "Operation Cyanide" (so named because, "If it ever became known, we would all be dead") was a subpart of the larger plan called Frontlet 615 and the weight of the evidence now available to us, even without the secret files that remain closed, indicates that it was instigated by Lyndon Johnson himself, in collaboration with his highest echelon of aides as well as several Israeli leaders. Who first thought up the diabolical plan can never be known, but the odds of it being President Johnson himself are certainly better than any other possible candidate.

It has been shown within these pages that Johnson was personally involved in all of the early planning, at least beginning in 1965 – if not before – indeed it is an axiom, because only he had the kind of power to have created such an audacious plan; anyone of lesser stature would have been risking his career, if not a lifetime in prison. His efforts to entice Canadian, and possibly other states, leaders just before the war was launched – clearly a task that he had assigned to himself – were also noted. The most critical element of the plan would depend upon his success at convincing Israeli officials to attack his own ship, and sink it, along with all the men aboard, for the purpose of blaming the attack on Egypt. Certainly they would not have advanced such an audacious, unspeakably brutish and cowardly action to their major benefactor, there would simply be no coherent motive for that and plenty of motive for not doing so. It was bad enough that they went along with it, but to put the blame on Israel, and only Israel, for doing it, is arguably the single greatest reason that the real cause of the attack has never been satisfactorily resolved. The limited evidence we do have suggests that Johnson had initially obtained the approval of Yitzhak Rabin, until he took it to David Ben-Gurion, whose furious reaction to it caused Rabin to back off further involvement, as Moshe Dayan then became Johnson's surrogate.

The reason that Israel, alone, got the blame, through the presumption by those who were unaware of Johnson's deceit – which Israeli leadership reflexively denied because they were only carrying out orders given them by President Johnson, their benefactor and protector – was because of the secretive but transparently deceitful cover-up that was immediately invoked: what else was anyone to think, who else could have possibly been responsible? The fact that the worst of the clues to Johnson's involvement were not exposed until years, even decades afterwards, ensured that his contrived legacy would protect him. When survivor Dave Lewis was finally able to reveal what Admiral Geis had told him, in 1987, and when survivor George Golden was able to reveal what Captain McGonagle had privately told him a decade after that – both of their statements being among the most incriminating evidence against Johnson – his presidency had already nearly recovered from his other exposed crime of Vietnam, when the public gave him "the benefit of the doubt" as to his tragic "error," still unaware of how he had set up the false flag operation that led to the Gulf of Tonkin Resolution.

By that time the still nearly complete secret of the attack on the *Liberty* became public, Johnson's "legacy" had become more centered on the "good things" that he had accomplished, designed by him specifically for that very purpose. He had never seriously come under suspicion for his other crimes, which became legend only within parts of the "assassination research community." Meanwhile, the story had become "off limits" according to the gospel of political correctness as practiced by the mainstream media (put there by the CIA's efforts simultaneously with the cover-up being implemented in 1967), to ensure that those secrets remained sealed: In April, 1967 the CIA sent a memorandum to their representatives in the journalism and publishing industries outlining how "conspiracy theories" and "theorists" should be handled. (The memo has been reproduced and printed as "Appendix D.") Among their instructions was this: "The aim of this dispatch is to provide material countering and discrediting the claims of the conspiracy theorists, so as to inhibit the circulation of such claims in other countries. Background information is supplied in a classified section and in a number of unclassified attachments." The fear, of course, was that these conspiracy theorists might become successful in their efforts to expose the truths that had been buried where the lies and myths had been planted in their stead.

This was one example, out of many, in which the CIA went well beyond its charter – which was to gather intelligence from other countries only – not to be involved in domestic operations. Harry Truman himself was so outraged by what he perceived as the CIA's brazenly illegal operations, which he implicitly believed had manifested into an involvement in JFK's assassination, that he wrote a strong, condemnatory statement in The *New York Times* a month later. It was an outgrowth of the program originated in the early 1950s by Allen Dulles and Frank Wisner, among the many other deluded officials of that agency who took themselves much too seriously in presuming that they were "above the law" ("Operation Mockingbird" as described in the Afterword). This was a direct assault on the U.S. Constitution, and its guarantees of freedom of speech, an independent press, and the right of the people to petition the government for a redress of grievances: The 1967 memorandum – which set the nation on a course still being followed, though even more secretly now – directed all its employees and resources to impede those rights to anyone daring to question the government's actions. This assault on American freedoms has continued its intrusive growth over the last fifty years as illustrated by the fact that President Barack Obama's choice to head the government's Office of Information and Regulatory Affairs, the "czar" Cass Sunstein, in 2010 developed a particularly onerous program targeted at anyone who advocated conspiracy theories which were deemed to be "false" by a government official[2] (It is interesting to note how so many of Obama's appointments would have made good candidates for Gestapo officials under Herr Hitler).

Such misguided thinking by government officials, whose unbridled thirst for greater power threatens the very foundations upon which America rests, has now become so engrained into the way of life that it will probably remain, and become just one of many such "grievances" that can only be dealt with by a newly energized citizenry that finally responds according to the remedy put forth over 200 years ago by one of the founding fathers, Samuel Adams:

> If ever a time should come, when vain and aspiring men shall possess the highest seats in Government, our country will stand in need of its experienced patriots to prevent its ruin.

The goals that Lyndon Johnson apparently sold Israeli leadership on were actually secondary to his own – within his deluded mind – to weaken the immediate neighboring countries and to eliminate Egyptian President Gamal Nasser, who Johnson hated because Nasser had begun distancing Egypt from the U.S. orbit while embracing that of the Soviet Union. Johnson undoubtedly took that as a personal affront – given how he perceived himself in the hierarchy of world leaders, yet jealous of how Nasser was hugely popular among Arab nations – and Nasser's popularity was undoubtedly a great embarrassment to him. The even-larger, longer-term objective of the Israeli leadership would have been to strengthen Israel by expanding its borders and providing it greater access to U.S.

weaponry, of both the conventional and nuclear kind. That objective was clearly met, and U.S. aid – of every kind, including financial, military, scientific, and nuclear – greatly increased after the successful Six-Day War. In the latest ten year period, the annual aid package was at an adjusted $3.1 billion per year, but according to a Reuters article dated November 4, 2015, "Israel has made an initial request for its annual U.S. defense aid to increase to as much as $5 billion [per year, for ten years] when its current aid package, worth an average $3 billion a year, expires in 2017."[3] (The aid package has since been set at $4 billion per year for the next ten years). While Israel's long-term objectives were met, the fact that their claims to the Palestinian territories they expropriated remain in contention makes their gains, in the eyes of many, a Pyrrhic victory that cannot be sustained. That unsatisfactory result should be added to the list of the numerous other "achievements" of the 36th President that comprise his true legacy.

The fact that practically everyone in the U.S. State Department in 1967 was convinced that the attack was intentional, yet by 2004 the staff there had come to the diametrically opposite position – as evidenced in the video of the official proceeding in which fabricated "evidence" was officially added to the files on the *Liberty* incident, reviewed in Chapter 7, that proved that assertion – could have only been for one reason: They knew that Israel held the "winning hand" because by then, both sides knew the real history and that it was much too embarrassing for U.S. officials to ever concede. It involved the official, sanctified legacy of the 36th President of the United States, and that was something that could not be sacrificed by admitting to the truth of the attack on the USS *Liberty*. That the ceremony was conducted with smiling, often smirking faces on camera – and probably "high-fives" off camera – is a particularly disgusting testament to the real motives for holding the hearing and making the findings the final official government word on the *Liberty* matter.

LAST LAMENTATIONS: THE LEGEND OF THE USS LIBERTY

The hope of the USS *Liberty* survivors has peaked many times, with the news of every new book on the *Liberty* story that is published, always with great expectations that this will be the one that will finally force the full truth out by possibly attracting the attention of congress or even the current president, to do "what is right." So far, that has proven to be a most elusive, maybe even impossible, dream. Yet that is probably the only way that a complete, honest and thorough investigation of the real causes of the attack might ever be accomplished. Only then might some scintilla of equitable justice be given to the survivors, their families and all caring citizens, to cleanse their consciences of the jaded myths, replaced by the real history of the event at last. And, even more importantly, that they know that everyone else – most of all, their fellow veterans, which has proven to be one of their biggest frustrations in the case of the American Legion – is conscious of the same epiphany, that the entire culture has finally been at least made aware of the tragedy they experienced, and still live with daily, and that all have at last been blessed with a sudden understanding of the true fate of their beloved ship.

Based on the lack of success to date, it is probably safe to assume that it won't happen in the lifetime of any of the survivors still alive today. Therefore, the simple and pragmatic goal of this book is to merely keep the hope alive that it may be done in a future generation, one that is more open to real truths than the Orwellian myths that have replaced them, and that their true legacy will have been enshrined into the official national records, and the lies and mythologies there now will have been expunged.

There were a number of still-unresolved treasons committed during Lyndon Johnson's reign, so to declare any one of them as being the "most brutal" is of course a very subjective question, but the reason the *Liberty* "incident" qualifies for that distinction is because the men who became the victims were not even his enemies; unlike most of the others, he did not know any of them personally. They were military officers, enlisted men and civilians who had volunteered to perform their patriotic duties and were following orders, as they were expected to do. But the commander-in-chief exploited their patriotism, and used these men like sacrificial pawns in a global chess match as he maneuvered the *Liberty* into the position that he had determined it would need to be, in preparation for the brutal attack that would allow him to enter the war that had been planned for several months. These assertions are not the idle conjecture of the authors, they are based upon statements made by the credible men whose first-hand testimony has been referenced within the previous pages and merely put into an overall framework that reflects the context of the epic story that should have been written a half-century ago.

One could argue that the 30,000 men killed in Vietnam under his command, a result of another of his treasonous lies related to the false flag operation that resulted in the "Gulf of Tonkin" resolution, far outnumbered the 34 men killed and 174 wounded on the *Liberty*; but the difference is in his specific order to sink the *Liberty*, with all 294 men on it. His intent was to sacrifice that specific ship and those specific men, all for the purpose of insinuating the U.S. military into the Arab-Israeli Six-Day War because he thought that it would gain him political favor from many thousands of people who would suddenly see the merits of his continued leadership. It was done merely to help Lyndon B. Johnson remain in the Oval Office for another term.

History is written by the victors, it has been said. Unfortunately, that has been proven over and again. Just as the history of the United States would have been profoundly different had John F. Kennedy lived, so too would it have been nearly as different had Robert F. Kennedy lived to fulfill his dream. Had Bobby lived to become president, he probably would have been able to solve his brother's murder, and Johnson feared that outcome more than anything. Even though it would have been too late to erase the disaster of Vietnam, and the attack on the *Liberty*, at least the history books would have been written differently and we, as a country, might have learned something from the mistakes of the past. As it was, Lyndon Johnson personally chose some of the men and women who would record American history circa 1963-69, and that history was recorded with the Johnsonian tilt that he had planted. Eventually, and inevitably, true history is revealed, and when it is, the mythological "history" is supplanted.

Unfortunately, in the case of the *Liberty*, the true account was put on hold by the president himself, through a cover-up that can scarcely be denied. The actual facts were replaced with lies that have now developed into a mythology that is nearly indestructible. In addition to the bogus official, mostly redacted or otherwise contaminated records, there have been overt attempts to place those myths into history books and the official records of the State Department and National Archives. Even the previous books that have courageously explored real facts, including the unfiltered testimony of the survivors and other eyewitnesses, the contemporaneous records that were, in some cases, inadvertently released, mostly stopped short of reaching the "critical mass" that put them all together into a complete and coherent document. And, it should also be noted, there were other, unfortunate attempts by some that were simply misdirected and merely added to the existential confusion: Such was the case with some of the, mostly laudable, work of Dr. Anthony R. Wells, whose career in the 1970s for the U.S. Navy caused him to attempt to add context to what was then still a state secret. During the course of that work, he interviewed former Secretary of State Dean Rusk and that resulted in a number of research papers, decades later, that mischaracterized much of the *Liberty* story. One such paper, "*Liberty* Victims Did Not Die in Vain" [4] for example, concluded: "The *Liberty's* crew did not die in vain. In extremely short order, her vital intelligence, and demise, helped convince two great Americans, Lyndon Johnson and Dean Rusk, that they must make swift and critical decisions. Those decisions saved the Middle East and U.S.-Soviet relations from a disaster course. They would want us to honor the USS *Liberty*." Not to put too fine a point on it, but that paper did not achieve its goal of putting the case into "better context." To call Lyndon B. Johnson a "great American" simply adds to the pile of deceit and confusion that has caused the case to still be unresolved fifty years after the event.

The key assertions made within these pages about Lyndon Johnson's actions regarding the *Liberty* attack cannot be denied: Among them is how he personally intervened to prevent help from being dispatched by fighter jets from the Sixth Fleet; how that action contributed to the torpedoing of the ship; how it took eighteen (18) hours to get them any help at all; how a super-secret cover-up was immediately ordered to prevent real truths from being revealed, replaced by vicious lies that told a completely opposite story of the attack than what actually occurred. No amount of rationalizations of all of that can possibly be accepted as unfortunate presidential "error." It is not a major leap from accepting these facts regarding Johnson's unmistakable complicity in all of those points, to putting them all into a larger envelop and stating that it was all pre-planned, by him. That is essentially what Captain McGonagle eventually told George Golden, as noted elsewhere. And with that, the remainder of this book is merely an attempt to explain that very point, in its complete and, unfortunately ugly, context.

After a half-century of mythological deceit and officious cover-ups, the nation must awaken and decide whether to allow Lyndon Johnson's brutal assault on his own ship, and the nearly three-hundred men on board, to stand. Do we leave that secret piece of his legacy in place as it is, to forever define the American-Israeli alliance, and continue to allow it to corrupt and compromise our nation's true interests? The betrayal of the American president to his own ship and all the officers, sailors, marines and civilians who were aboard the *Liberty* fifty years ago was a horrific injustice to them and all the others who served in the US Navy in the Sixth Fleet during that period who became entwined in that operation or its cover-up, and, by extension, to all other Americans, then and now. Moreover, the cover-up of that event still contaminates the relationship between the two countries as noted within this book, through such insidious manifestations as the Naval Academy's instruction to midshipmen to avoid even talking about it, especially in the presence of the Israeli ambassador. As long as our national understanding of that event remains incomplete, and the festering hurt continues to be unresolved, that betrayal will remain. Until we reclaim the heroes of that day – those who paid the ultimate price as well as those who survived the attack, but paid dearly in many other ways, as their stories within these pages reveal – their betrayal is for eternity.

THE HEROES OF THE STORY

The single most important unified message of this book comes, not from the authors directly, but from the heroic, yet militarily circumscribed men whose belated stories came too late for the secretively hidden, highly classified and "sham" investigation that was never intended to expose the truth of what happened to the *Liberty*. Yet their final acts of courage held the keys for unlocking the secrets locked away in government vaults. Those men, like all the survivors, were threatened in multiple ways to replace truth with lies, to create an official "mythology" to replace an honest and transparent, meaningful investigation. That is why Admiral Geis knew that he had to "go along" with the sham called a "Court of Inquiry" because he understood that it was what the higher-ups in the chain of command expected from him and demanded his compliance; to do otherwise would have been a form of suicide which would have destroyed his military career, and probably risked a prison term, according to the admonitions given to all the military men involved. But he redeemed himself ultimately, when he admitted the deceit to David Lewis. Geis must have taken a lesson from how Admiral McCain had shut out Captain Merlin Staring for not cooperating, or seeing how Ward Boston, Jr. had gotten the same message from his superior, Rear Admiral Isaac Kidd, Jr., when he, for a time, went along with the prescribed scenario; it was not until over three decades later that Boston finally, courageously, came forward with the truth which he wrote into the document that we reviewed in Chapter 5, dated January 8, 2004: The "Declaration of Ward Boston, Jr." Admiral Kidd himself never publicly atoned for what he had been forced to do, but Captain Boston confirmed how Kidd had been coerced by Admiral McCain to do it, and described Kidd's true feelings about the travesty of justice they had committed, as demanded by their superiors, all the way up to the commander in chief, from whom they had emanated.

Moreover, Captain McGonagle himself had purportedly gotten some information in advance about a possible "phantom" attack, but afterwards he admitted to George Golden much more about having been "set up," as noted previously, when he stated *"when they sent us up from over in Africa, we were there to have this happen."* Captain Joe Tully also knew from the start that "the fix was in" and, though he tried to speak up at the time, it was a futile effort. But the suppressed truth was tearing him apart from the inside and, by the time he was able to speak openly and honestly to the survivors, it was too late: he was already a "broken" man, according to the survivors who heard him tell his story. NSA Deputy Director Louis Tordella also reacted angrily when he was first informed of the attack and scrawled the "impolite" comment on the memo he read, which eventually also became public. The story was ultimately studied by no less an authority than former chairman of the Joint Chiefs of Staff, Admiral Thomas H. Moorer, whose 1997 statement cited in Chapter 5, and his 2004 document, written just before he died and included as Appendix A, came as close to the full truth of the matter as it was then possible to come: In both of these documents he labeled the *Liberty* attack "the most disgraceful act I witnessed in my entire military career," and in 2004 he stated that it "… can only be termed a national disgrace." Both of these statements were essentially ignored by the State Department in 2004 as they enshrined into the official archives the contaminated records that absolved the real culprits.

The honorable men noted above, reacting to events in the four decades after the attack, finally came forward to atone for their own actions, or to investigate the facts and attempt to redress the injustices done to the brave and heroic men who survived this grave assault and now seek an honorable resolution to it. The lengthier list of all the men who saw the jaws of the cover-up as they began to close is scattered throughout this book; their combined statements should be enough to cause all of the fabricated "official stories" held in the State Department, the Pentagon and all other government archives to be cleansed from the files and replaced with the real truths from these same sources. To accomplish that would require that all of the still-closed classified files finally be opened, and an honest and transparent investigation be conducted to expose the truth of the original despicable and disgraceful treasonous acts of the president in instigating the attack and again in orchestrating the immense cover-up that continues to this day.

Thankfully, because these high-level military men who were directly involved as eyewitnesses to the attack and/or its cover-up eventually came forward, the real truths were exposed for all to see. Unfortunately however, thus far, those truths were revealed "piece-meal," served up as small fragments of what should have been an epic story. As authors who have merely attempted to compile all of those pieces into a coherent record, this book serves as a proxy for the major news story that never was; it is about hidden treasons in high places, an incredibly outrageous story that should have appeared on the front pages of every U.S. newspaper fifty years ago. Had that been done in 1967, it would have potentially changed the course of history, but the decks were stacked against the journalists of that age by a man whose political power was of epic proportions. If the full truth of what has finally been sifted out – in tatters and crumbs five decades too late – would have been reported at the time, Lyndon Johnson would have certainly been impeached, and undoubtedly served time in prison. Vietnam would have inevitably been returned to its owners to resolve their own differences. Some form of rationality would have been restored in the 1968 elections instead of it becoming a year of chaos and assassinations. Had all of the secrets been exposed, the real legacy of Lyndon "Bull" Johnson – rather than the contrived, mythological legend that now exists thanks to the mythmakers identified herein – might have been revealed, despite its embarrassing details.

Since that did not happen, America is worse off because of the resulting unresolved damages, including its tenuous relationship with Israel. The billions of dollars of U.S. taxpayer subsidies diverted to Israel every year are inexorably linked to their continuing efforts to drive the indigenous Palestinians out of their homeland completely, despite the "disputed" claims to that territory as noted previously. In the absence of meaningful efforts by Israel to accommodate the international demands for resolving these differences, as previously examined, the United States thus remains linked as the centerpiece into an ageless clash of civilizations. All of this morass is part of the unheralded "legacy" of Lyndon Johnson's presidency, too embarrassing for contemporary politicians to acknowledge, or to ever attempt to reverse, with the lies now embedded by proxy. It is merely one set of lies now added to the multiple others which are part of the crumbling foundation of the former democratic republic called the United States of America. The myths have lived on and that makes it all the more difficult to envision a time when they will be replaced with the truths.

We can only be consoled by the fact that it is not too late to force what remains of the still-secret files to be opened, and to make them part of the real history that must eventually replace the myths planted fifty years ago. It would certainly be a good place to start the process of redemption, and that can only be done by cleansing the lies and deceit that have infested the official archives of the nation.

REMEMBER THE LIBERTY!

Short of a major change in national direction, a more realistic, achievable goal in the foreseeable future – for those who still care more about true history than perpetuating myths – might be to work toward spreading the story of the real heroes of the *Liberty* attack, and in so doing, to redress the many injustices done to so many great men, and thus begin treating them honestly, honorably, transparently and apologetically for what they have had to endure. That has been the worst part of this story, that they have been portrayed – by some people intent on replacing ugly truths with "feel good lies" – to look like the villains, rather than the heroes, of this tragic story. They need to be recognized for what they actually did in saving the USS *Liberty* from sinking: In doing that, they arguably also saved the world from a major nuclear conflagration, possibly one that might have led to "World War III." For that is precisely what the nuclear-equipped A-4 bombers were already preparing to do on June 8, 1967 as they sped towards Cairo, until they were grudgingly recalled by the president because the *Liberty* had not sunk according to his own plan.

Given the many "miracles" that have been referred to by the survivors, combined with their heroic work, there might have been another overarching reason that the *Liberty* did not sink. According to some of the survivors, it was not just the result of random, luck-of-the-draw, serendipitous events, but something more enigmatic and spiritual than that, which some have called "Divine Intervention." The multiple "miracles" – a few of which were recounted in the previous pages – were the manifestation of that cosmic guidance. Its immediate effect was to save America from the certain calamity that its primary leader had nearly wrought, and ultimately kept him from another term in office, which itself might have saved the world, yet again. If humanity was saved in that manner fifty years ago, there might have been even larger reasons for it that still have not been revealed, and probably will never be if justice for the *Liberty* survivors – being simply "the truth and nothing but the truth" – continues to be locked away and kept secret, for specious "national security" reasons.

If not for the heroism of the survivors, as well as possibly the "divine grace" that produced all of those miracles which kept it afloat, the world would be a far different place today, undoubtedly not a better one. That is why the *Liberty* story should not be swept away into the dustbin of history as prescribed by the one who created it, then buried it, while trying to shame those heroes in the process of salvaging his own political future and building his eventual, contrived, "legacy."

Endnotes

1. See: https://en.wikipedia.org/wiki/Caligula

2. See Greenwald, Glenn, http://www.salon.com/2010/01/15/sunstein_2/

3. http://uk.reuters.com/article/uk-iran-nuclear-israel-usa-idUKKCN0ST2SV20151104

4. http://www.usslibertydocumentcenter.org/doc/upload/Proceedings_US_Naval_Institute_2005.pdf

LBJ and Bill Moyers, 2/14/1967

Afterword

The Power of Myth

Wherever the poetry of myth is interpreted as biography, history, or science, it is killed. The living images become only remote facts of a distant time or sky. Furthermore, it is never difficult to demonstrate that as science and history, mythology is absurd. When a civilization begins to reinterpret its mythology in this way, the life goes out of it, temples become museums, and the link between the two perspectives becomes dissolved.

– *The Power of Myth*, Joseph Campbell and Bill Moyers (p. 2)

"So we tell stories to try to come to terms with the world, to harmonize our lives with reality?"

– Bill Moyers (Ibid. p. 249)

HOW LBJ AND BILL MOYERS HELPED REINVENT A LITERARY GENRE

MYTHOLOGY: FROM PRIMITIVE TRUTHS TO MODERN DECEIT

There is considerable irony in the fact that twentieth century mythmakers created the pseudo-story of an "accidental" attack on the USS *Liberty*, given the context of the history of where that attack occurred. The last tour of that now legendary ship, and its fate, occurred on the first day of the war – June 5, 1967 – when it sailed into the same ancient Mediterranean waters that had once been the scene of battles dating back at least three millennia, to the Argonauts as they sailed between Libya and Crete, as described in Homer's *Iliad* and *Odyssey*. Despite their being the foundation upon which Greek Mythology was based, there was immeasurably more truth contained in those ancient works than exists in the more modern version of that genre.

The term "mythology" today has a quite different meaning than it had in classic literature, when it was most often used to write essential truths about real events that had never been previously documented. It has now been reinvented, and its new purpose is to be an integral part of foundations built upon lies, the cornerstone of the cover-up. That people such as author Joseph Campbell, with help from a latter-day student of his, Bill Moyers, whose previous work for Lyndon Johnson prepared him well for his new avocation, have devoted their lives to perfecting this new art is testament to "The Power of Myth." The new kind of "mythology" created just for this purpose reached its zenith with the presidency of Lyndon B. Johnson. Moyers became the heir of the legendary mythmaker Campbell in the ensuing decades, and partly through his work, the term has now become synonymous with government-sanctioned deceit.

One example of an attempt by President Johnson and Bill Moyers to reframe real history, while vilifying an honest reporter occurred in 1965, when they called the president of CBS, Frank Stanton, to complain about a broadcast report by the late CBS reporter Morley Safer in an attempt to get Safer fired. The report was an accurate account of the torching of the village of Cam Ne, destroying one hundred fifty houses, and Safer's report noted that no Vietnamese soldiers had been captured or killed and the only fatality was that of a ten-year-old boy. He also reported that the four prisoners taken were all men in their late sixties or early seventies, and that the five wounded were all older women. Yet this honest reportage of an actual event set off a thunderous chain-reaction in the White House that was never reported until Morley Safer wrote about it in his memoirs twenty-five years afterwards, in 1990. President Johnson had become so furious with that report that, after calling Stanton the day following that report, he then summoned him to the White House so he could continue haranguing him about it. Safer wrote in his memoirs that Johnson, with Moyers present to support him with "facts," then threatened that, "unless CBS got rid of me [Safer] and 'cleaned up its act,' the White House would 'go public' with information about Safer's [alleged, but non-existent] 'Communist ties'. Johnson claimed that he and Moyers 'had the goods' on me as a result of an investigation launched by the FBI, the CIA, and the Royal Canadian Mounted Police."[1] This was an incredibly brazen and reckless assault on a television journalist whose only error was to assume that the public's right to know the truth of what had occurred in one of the early combat operations in Vietnam was an appropriate subject; he never considered that doing so might be such an embarrassment to the president and commander-in-chief that would put his broadcasting career in jeopardy.

According to Safer's account, Johnson – aided and abetted by Bill Moyers – spread the fallacious attack to all parts of the Executive branch, even to ambassadors such as Graham Martin, the last American ambassador to South Vietnam, that Safer "was a KGB agent." Decades later, as he wrote his 1990 memoirs, Safer stated that, as a result of Johnson's and Moyer's deceits, "To this day [Dean] Rusk believes the entire Cam Ne story was staged. He says that I convinced a Marine Corps unit to bring in some Vietnamese refugees to an abandoned village that the marines used for training exercises, that I then asked the marines to torch the village, and that, being susceptible, well-meaning young Americans, they obliged."[2] Moreover, he wrote that Rusk stated that it was "common knowledge at the White House" that Safer had ties directly to the Soviet Union's intelligence apparatus (i.e. the KGB) and that he had a particularly bad reputation as a "questionable character."[3] Finally, his characterization of Moyers' involvement with the bugging of Martin Luther King Jr.'s private life and numerous other instances of Johnson's and J. Edgar Hoover's illegal acts was summarized as being " ... not only a good soldier but a gleeful retainer feeding the appetites of Lyndon Johnson ... Moyers, the sometimes overly pious public defender of liberal virtue, the First Amendment, and the rights of minorities, playing the role of Iago."[4]

That the two of them would literally make up such heinous lies about Morley Safer, one of the most incorruptible, likeable and credible broadcast journalists in the history of television news broadcasting, for the purpose of attempting to destroy his career, is one more piece of evidence that must be factored into the story we are assembling. It was all done because Safer had accurately reported a story about the wanton destruction of an entire Vietnamese village – an act that Johnson, paradoxically, had been exhorting his highest level military officials to do, along with his constant refrain, to "Kill More Viet Cong!" – and that real truths could not stand, so lies had to be invented to replace the truth. It was a pattern that was used over and over again in the Johnson White House throughout his defiled presidency, though only a few instances of it were ever reported, due to exactly this kind of feared reaction by most other journalists. In this specific case, the truth according to Morley Safer took over twenty years to be revealed, and by then, it – like so many similar vignettes we have discovered and repeated here – became just another piece of ancient history, disconnected from all the rest and treated as just another anecdote of a bygone time.

Though a lot of the darker stories were kept secret throughout his reign, in fact, by 1965, press reporters who were assigned to cover the White House had become so accustomed to Johnson's propensity for speaking words that had no basis in fact, that they created a new term to describe it: "Credibility gap" was coined to describe the intrinsic worthlessness of President Johnson's words. He was distrusted by practically everyone who really knew him even before he had acquired the magical and near-universal imprimatur of public respect that is automatically conferred to whomever holds the office of the president of the United States. That trust only lasts until the new president destroys his own credibility through incompetence or having a tin ear to what the public really wants. Some people who knew him for decades had called him "Lying Lyndon" or "Bullshit Johnson;" to them, he was a former high school bully and college leader of his own secret society that eventually ruled the campus.

His followers in those early years were not much different than the syco-phantic aides he used and abused in later years; the only real difference was their age and the pay scales they were able to secure in exchange for continually "swallowing their scruples."

THE DEVOLUTION OF MODERN "MYTHOLOGY"

The modern form of the mythology genre, not about ancient truths, but of the newest, most politically salable lies, was born from the basest human characteristics: avarice, brutishness, cunning, deceit, evasiveness, fraud, guile – and twice through the rest of the alphabet to, finally – Zionistic Zealotry. After the attack, as the crew of the *Liberty* completed their last tasks aboard their listing, shot up, burned out hulk of a once-proud vessel, they again sailed back through the same ancient waters that had been the scene of original Greek and Roman, and eventually Shake-spearean mythology: those ancient stories that described pure, life vivify-ing and ageless truths. Little did the crew know that, on the other side of those ancient waters, their story was already being changed, not as clas-sic literature but to the hackneyed, secretive, illusive kind that modern mythmakers concoct to cover up the darkest secrets; this modern form of pettifoggery would pollute the real, truly historic, *Liberty* story for the ensuing fifty years.

It was those combined attributes that were employed to first keep the entire episode secret, and allowed more time to gather all the necessary re-sources to immediately "rewrite history," and then put into place all of the longer-term strategies to ensure that the same efforts would be sustained over many years to follow. That this strategy worked, for five decades now and counting, is the very evidence which proves the point: It was no "ac-cident" that other developments would occur to facilitate the process. It began with germinating the seeds of deceit into planted lies and then the growth of mythologies, from people who were trained well in all of those specialized skills, some of whom have been identified throughout the latter chapters. The harvested fruits of the planted lies have since been published, for example, in the later books authored by Michael Oren and Ahron J. Cristol and others, then memorialized into the "official record" at the State Department in a crowning act of political chicanery; it was the exact opposite position of their own predecessors within the Department of State, from the Secretary of State Rusk, on down through his direct As-sistant Secretaries and throughout the rest of the organization, including the ambassadors assigned to practically every country other than Israel.

Perfected and popularized for the exigencies of modern times, the twentieth century appellation of the terms "mythology," or "myth," de-scribes attempts to rewrite true history into more palatable versions, all as explained by such oracles as George Orwell and Aldous Huxley. Myths no longer serve the purpose of explaining ancient history in ways that were once used as proxy for testaments from eyewitnesses, or citations to previous veritable tomes – as Homer and his literary descendents were forced to do, by the circumstances of ancient civilizations, due to the absence of written words in historical documents (regardless of whether Homer himself was actually another part of the myths).

The modernized term "mythology" usually represents what is being, or has been, reported as fact, after being intentionally "spun" to portray covertly orchestrated events into "feel-good" stories for a public addicted to comforting, sanguine stories. They are prescribed for people who need quick fixes to assuage painful memories, just as most other modern inventions were created for purposes other than satisfying basic human needs. This metamorphosis in terminology was accomplished in the wake of Orwell's and Huxley's works, in the middle of the twentieth century; both described the new term thoroughly. That the phenomenon was perfected a decade or so later, during the presidency of Lyndon B. Johnson – just as the term "credibility gap" concurrently became part of the American lexicon – was no coincidence. Likewise, the term "political correctness" similarly became popularized during the same period, for essentially the same reasons. Another term for the new definition might be called "propagandized news," or what George Orwell described as the venal product of the "Ministry of Truth."

When considered in the context of the famous statement of Joseph Goebbels, the Nazi Minister of Propaganda, it is clear how this metamorphosis came about: "*If you tell a lie big enough and keep repeating it, people will eventually come to believe it… the truth is the greatest enemy of the State.*" Coming as it did in the immediate aftermath of World War II, Orwell undoubtedly learned a thing or two about irony from Goebbels. In a reverse twist of the same phenomenon, another illustration of that is how the legendary CIA "Black Sorcerer" and "Dirty Trickster" Sidney Gottlieb might have benefited from those works, especially of Huxley, which were intended to warn the masses of how methodologies such as psychological manipulation and Pavlovian conditioning could profoundly change society, and not for the better. Gottlieb turned the warning around, by exploiting them in his depraved plotting to develop lethal poisons and drug experiments in mind control; he became famous for his LSD research, a product that was then tested, unfortunately, by being forcefully administered to unwitting subjects, whose clinical experiences were most unfavorable, often even fatal. After becoming CIA director, Allen Dulles promoted Gottlieb to the head of Project MKULTRA, which conducted psychiatric research and development of "techniques that would crush the human psyche to the point that it would admit anything."[5] There were undoubtedly many others at Langley, some of which will be noted below, who were similarly involved in these nefarious schemes (another of the other notable madmen employed there, James Jesus Angleton, also comes to mind).

SHADES OF OPERATION MOCKINGBIRD

As soon as the CIA was formed, in 1947, Frank Wisner established Operation Mockingbird, which was the first attempt to influence the domestic and foreign media. As Allen Dulles began directing the nefarious research assigned to the "Black Sorcerer" noted above, in the early 1950s just after he became the Director of the CIA, he had also directed Wisner to aggressively expand the program and led it to become one of the several illegal acts of that agency which most undermined the Constitution of the United States. Its very purpose was to illegally compromise the responsibility of the press – print and broadcast media – to critically report to the American people on government's activities, as a means to control wayward politicians in order to ensure they did not misuse their power. Specifically, the First Amendment to the Constitution "frees" the press to ferret out cases of political malfeasance but that freedom carries with it the responsibility to remain the people's watchdog, which cannot be done if they are enticed to support the government's attempts to circumvent that duty. To say that this effort succeeded "beyond expectations" is a tremendous understatement, because even now, in the supposed absence of such a covert program, it is clearly still carrying out that original mission.

The phrase "estates of the realm" originated in the Middle Ages to denote the hierarchy of social orders for the clergy (first estate), the nobility (second estate), and commoners (third estate). The 18th Century politician Edmund Burke, who, in reference to the three "estates" of British government, likened them to the American government's three branches, or "estates" – legislative, judicial and executive – and thus the term "Fourth Estate" evolved to refer to the implicit role of the news media. The intrinsic reason for protecting journalism – especially newsprint, though the term was later naturally extended to broadcast news organizations – was their duty to expose governmental misconduct. It is difficult to argue that the term "journalism," therefore the "Fourth Estate" has any pertinence anymore to those original precepts, given the fact that the undermining of them by governmental actions has been among its "greatest" accomplishments.

Burke is also quoted for having said, "All that is necessary for the triumph of evil is that good men do nothing," which is a pertinent maxim that applies to the narrative that follows below. The First Amendment to the Constitution embodies the "freedom" of the press, but it has been eroded over time as a result of the insidious attempts of various agencies, and specific people, to compromise the press. Operation Mockingbird was arguably the biggest, boldest, most brazen effort ever done to destroy that role.

When Frank Wisner succeeded Allen W. Dulles as head of the Plans Division in the early 1950s, Wisner was intent on establishing direct contacts between the agency and the "Fourth Estate" – the American press – specifically to the journalists and book publishers who would willingly assist the CIA to communicate their view on any national or international political or military issue in a favorable light. The principal responsibility of both the Office of Policy Coordination (OPC) and the Plans Division was the conduct of secret political operations, in contrast to the other agency functions of gathering intelligence and the analysis of that intelligence. In 1951, Wisner revitalized Operation Mockingbird, to create new avenues to conduct more directly the sellout of American media and the resulting perfidy of the Constitution itself. "'Wisner recruited Philip Graham (*Washington Post*) to run the project within the industry," according to Deborah Davis, in *Katharine the Great*: "By the early 1950s, Wisner 'owned' respected members of *The New York Times*, *Newsweek*, CBS and other communications vehicles."[6] These journalists sometimes wrote articles that were unofficially commissioned by Cord Meyer, based on leaked classified information from the CIA.

By 1953 the CIA, through Wisner and Graham, had established direct linkages with at least 25 major newspapers and wire agencies.[7] Wisner also recruited several former members of the OSS to become CIA officials, such as Richard Bissell, Desmond FitzGerald, Tracy Barnes, and Cord Meyer.[8] To make Operation Mockingbird work effectively, Wisner realized that he could not rely only on journalists and publishers like Arthur Hays Sulzberger of the *New York Times*, who shared the Georgetown crowd's liberal view of the world. He therefore set out to recruit conservatives like William Paley (CBS), C. D. Jackson and Henry Luce (of *Time* and *Life* magazines). According to Alex Constantine (*Mockingbird: The Subversion of the Free Press by the CIA*), in the 1950s, "Some 3,000 salaried and contract CIA employees were eventually engaged in propaganda efforts."[9] One of the most important journalists under the control of Operation Mockingbird was Joseph Alsop, whose articles appeared in over three hundred different newspapers. Other journalists willing to promote the views of the Central Intelligence Agency included Joseph's brother, Stewart Alsop (*New York Herald Tribune*), Ben Bradlee (*Newsweek*), James Reston (*The New York Times*), Walter Pincus (*Washington Post*), Herb Gold (*Miami News*) and Charles Bartlett (*Chattanooga Times*).[10] In a remarkable irony, many of the same columnists targeted by Wisner and his men were already in the pocket of Lyndon B. Johnson – most notably

Joseph Alsop – and information in Hoover's "Official and Confidential" files, which was readily shared with Johnson on request and gave him an additional special entrée to these journalists.

NOAM CHOMSKY: "MYTHMAKER EXTRAORDINAIRE" OR, MERELY AN UNWITTING DENIER OF HISTORICAL TRUTHS?

CHOMSKY'S LINGUISTICS EXPERTISE FAILS TO TRANSLATE

Dr. Noam Chomsky's long and storied journey in life as a famed leftist iconoclast-philosopher has resulted in a legend that many thousands, perhaps even millions throughout the world, envy. His web page, "Chomsky.Info" confirms his bona-fides multiple times in numerous ways, one of which is this statement, apparently from about twenty-four year years ago, which would indicate the numbers behind the assertions have increased exponentially since then:

> According to the Arts and Humanities Citation Index in 1992, Chomsky was cited as a source more often than any other living scholar from 1980 to 1992, and was the eighth most cited source overall. He has been described as a prominent cultural figure, and he was voted the "world's top public intellectual" in a 2005 poll.

According to his lengthy Wikipedia page, "His public talks often generated considerable controversy, particularly when he criticized actions of the Israeli government and military. His political views came under attack from right-wing and centrist figures, the most prominent of whom was Alan Dershowitz; Dershowitz considered Chomsky to be a "false prophet of the left," while Chomsky accused Dershowitz of actively misrepresenting Chomsky's position on issues, calling Dershowitz "a complete liar."[11]

A lifetime of challenges to many precepts of accepted "conventional wisdom" has led some to wrongfully accuse Chomsky of being everything from a Neo-Con to an apologist for Cambodian leader Pol Pot.[12] Unfortunately, however, in some of the most elementally important matters, he – like many other famed members of his rarefied "erudite fellows" class – has failed to comprehend basic and profound truths. And the reason for that is because of an unfortunate misunderstanding and/or ignorance of basic facts, as we will examine shortly. Chomsky's acknowledged expertise in the field of linguistics has not always translated well into other fields, such as American history, circa mid-Twentieth Century, though he often expresses his views on that topic. Indeed, he has often repeated, as a matter of indisputable fact, statements which could be summarized as follows: "The assassination of JFK had no significant effect on the trajectory of the U.S. foreign or domestic policy."

That is arguably among the most inaccurate, misleading and un-prophetic assessments of history anyone in the public eye has ever made.

JFK's assassination marked the end of the republic that was once America and the complete reversal in foreign policy that quickly turned the country around and upside down and resulted in the most turbulent period in American domestic history – with the notable exceptions of the Revolutionary War and the Civil War – that Chomsky himself had participated in as an outspoken opponent of U.S. involvement in the Vietnam War. His 1967 anti-war essay "The Responsibility of Intellectuals" won him national acclaim, yet, his unfortunate, oft-repeated, completely erroneous statement about the JFK assassination being essentially inconsequential should cause most thoughtful people to re-evaluate his position of prominence. With JFK's murder, the ascension of LBJ into the presidency and along with it, the creation of the "National Security State," America experienced a coup d'état in 1963 which drastically changed the course of history while Chomsky, evidently, somehow lived through it all without realizing the full implications of what had happened.

Again, he is not alone: For example, Howard Zinn, the famed author of *A People's History of the United States,* similarly failed to note the sea-change in American foreign policy that occurred as a result of what has been referred to by more cognitively-aware people as the November 22, 1963 *coup d'etat'*. In fact, despite recounting dozens of other little-known or covered-up blemishes in U.S. history over the entire period of its existence, including some that were virtually unknown to most people, such as the great railroad strike of 1877, it is odd that the assassination of our 35th president did not merit even a footnote, never mind a short paragraph or even a sentence or even a word of acknowledgement; that singularly calamitous event was omitted by Mr. Zinn as if it had not even occurred. In his defense, he probably realized that it was a subject better left alone, as it would take an entire book to completely tell. However, a footnote about that point might have been useful.

There are many reasons why so many contemporary philosophers and historians have "missed the boat" on that seminal event, and that, too, might take an entire book to explain. A lot of it had to do with the immediate cover-up that was put into place by the National Security State, led by the CEO of that entity, the new president, Lyndon B. Johnson, beginning at about 1:00 p.m. CST in Dallas, Texas. As we will consider further, below, that was not the only official cover-up that Johnson put into place to protect his secrets, when we examine the 1967 Israeli attack on the USS *Liberty*. The complete and up-to-date book on how prominent authors "missed the boat" has yet to be written, but for anyone wishing to consider that point a little closer, I recommend a 2002 article titled "The Silence of the Historians" by David Mantik, MD, PhD., which can be found at the referenced website.[13]

The Three Reasons Given by Noam Chomsky for his Dismissal of Connections between JFK's Assassination and its Repercussions, including Vietnam

In the analysis to follow, we will examine the three reasons that Noam Chomsky has given for his position that there was no change in foreign policy, or any other policy, that substantively changed direction between the Kennedy and Johnson administrations.

1. That Kennedy had not made a commitment to withdraw troops from Vietnam;

2. That JFK had launched bombing raids and other aggressive, offensive military actions against Vietnam as early as 1961-62; and,

3. That there had never been sufficient evidence to doubt the official government findings that JFK was killed by a "lone nut" and therefore, absent evidence to the contrary, there was no reason to suspect a plot, or what might be considered a "coup d'etat," that created the perpetual war environment we live with today.

1. "JFK had not made a commitment to withdraw troops from Vietnam"

This point was already conclusively debunked by James K. Galbraith, fourteen years ago, in a September 1, 2003 article published in the *Boston Review* titled "Exit Strategy: In 1963, JFK ordered a complete withdrawal from Vietnam." In a lengthy, well-sourced and comprehensive article, Mr. Galbraith, the son of famed Harvard professor, economist and author John Kenneth Galbraith, who JFK had appointed ambassador to India, rebutted that argument in a detailed manner that needs no elucidation. The referenced article is incorporated by proxy into this thesis and a few short excerpts are noted to simplify and summarize the lengthy and scholarly article, and that should put item #1 of this list to rest. The following points summarize Galbraith's incisive article:

• Quoting Robert McNamara's 1995 book *In Retrospect*, "President Kennedy's decision on October 2 to begin the withdrawal of U.S. forces" he then traced eighteen months of detailed steps which JFK had taken to lead up to a planned withdrawal. He also referenced John Newman's seminal 1992 book *JFK and Vietnam*, which puts Kennedy's long-term strategy in historic context, and explains why the key parts of it were not contained in the Pentagon Papers released in 1971.

• Furthermore, he observed that Chomsky had incorrectly insisted that JFK's decision was conditional, that, "[t]he withdrawal-without-victory thesis rests on the assumption that Kennedy realized that the optimistic military reports were incorrect ... Not a trace of supporting evidence appears in the internal record, or is suggested [by Newman]. He puts to rest any notion that JFK's strategy was in any way equivocal.

•It examines Chomsky's repeated claim that the revised NSAM 273 was not substantively different than the original document: "There is no relevant difference between the two documents [draft and final], except that the LBJ version is weaker and more evasive." There are abundant reasons, he explains, why that is a serious misrepresentation of material fact.

• In his concluding statement, Galbraith wrote: "John F. Kennedy had formally decided to withdraw from Vietnam, whether we were winning or not. Robert McNamara, who did not believe we were winning, supported this decision. The first stage of withdrawal had been ordered. The final date, two years later, had been specified. These decisions were taken, and even placed, in an oblique and carefully limited way, before the public." [emphasis added].

2. THAT JFK HAD LAUNCHED BOMBING RAIDS AND AGGRESSIVE, OFFENSIVE MILITARY ACTIONS AS EARLY AS 1961-62;

Within Noam Chomsky's web page referenced above, the following erroneous assertion may be found (without citation), in the item called "On Democracy," a 1996 interview with Tom Morello, where he stated: "Kennedy is not even worth discussing. The invasion in South Vietnam – *Kennedy attacked South Vietnam, outright. In 1961-1962 he sent [the] Air Force to start bombing villages, authorized napalm.*"[14]

Short of digressing with an extended journey deep "into the weeds" of the story of how JFK, in his first two years as president, was at constant loggerheads with the heads of his own military and intelligence agencies, and his own vice president, let it suffice to say that, in fact, by 1963, he had gained the self-confidence and the resolve to finally resist their attempts to take the very actions attributed to him by Chomsky. A succinct description, however, would start with the fact that, throughout his vice presidency Johnson was getting more accurate accounts of the war effort, through his back channel connection from his long-time military aid Air Force Colonel Howard Burris, than was President Kennedy, who was briefed through the military's Pentagon regular channels, primarily emanating from General Paul D. Harkins, who seemed to be an unusually optimistic military officer. As author Newman described in great detail, while Kennedy had been given rosy, always hopeful, but misleading reports of how everything was going reasonably well and the enemy was suffering major setbacks, Johnson was being told the opposite: how the war was being lost to the stronger Viet Cong operations, which was becoming an even larger force.[15] The better intelligence Johnson had obtained, than Kennedy was receiving, gave him the advantage, and arguably allowed him to accumulate more power than the president himself with the military and intelligence organizations. That kind of power was what Johnson had always pursued, as illustrated by one of his favorite maxims: "Power is where power goes." It meant that one could define for themselves how much power, and clout, they held, regardless of their position; it may have even put him into a position to censor, or water down the intelligence reports that Kennedy received, however that is a speculative point that cannot be proven one way or the other.

Johnson's mission to Vietnam was followed in short order by another disastrous field trip led by Dr. Eugene Staley, an economist, whose intent was to produce a financial plan for the government of South Vietnam to develop a stronger economy, a plan which Lieutenant Colonel William R. Corson, in his 1968 book *Betrayal* said, resulted in "half-baked theories of economic development," written by supposed experts having "… no idea of the social fabric of Vietnam, or of the degree of political control and oppression there."[16] That was followed by still another ill-fated trip in October, 1961, by General Maxwell Taylor, along with "Walt Whitman Rostow, William Bundy, Sterling Cottrell, and a host of lesser lights … Taylor, the linguist [also out of his element], spoke in French to Diem and his henchmen about the "across the board problem." After a "quick two-day trip by air to see what was going on, a broad pronouncement of recommendation of strategy was made to the White House."[17] These trips resulted in an increase of the number of "advisors" from "… 685 in 1961 to 10,000 by the end of 1962. There was no change in the advice provided by the advisor; there were just more advisors."[18] But as noted above, President Kennedy had begun to have doubts about where this policy was leading and in the spring of 1962 asked McNamara to begin planning a reversal of that direction.

According to Arthur Schlesinger, Jr., in *The Imperial Presidency*, "In the Kennedy years [Vietnam] intervention was limited and provoked no constitutional questions. The dispatch of 'advisers' – 16,000 by the time of Kennedy's death – took place under familiar arrangements for military assistance based on congressional legislation and appropriations."[19] There are scores of other books including many commonly known to anyone with a modicum of knowledge about this seminal event, and some have been referenced below, for other related points.

To clarify and summarize the point, while the record shows that the troops in Vietnam under Kennedy were only "advisors," whether in the Marines, regular Army, Navy, or Special Forces (which had been deployed in remote regions to assist groups like the Montagnards)[20] it is true that, as their number increased so did their scope of responsibility, yet in those early years they were only fighting a defensive war south of the 17th parallel at the request of the recognized government there in an operation called "Farm Gate" (a fact that demonstrates that it was Kennedy who had inherited the outgrowth of decisions reached during the previous decade, and was put into the position of having to decide to perpetuate them or reverse them). The advisors accompanied South Vietnamese combat troops on their missions and were put into indirect combat situations with greater regularity by 1962. But the larger exception to that paradigm related to the defensive air operations and its Air Force code name "Jungle Jim" which, according to McNamara's decree, was used "for *training and operational missions* in South Vietnam with Vietnamese riding in the rear seats."[21] Though the air strikes during this period were flown almost exclusively by American pilots as they went about training Vietnamese pilots, the targets were selected by Vietnamese planners. And sometimes, as author John Newman noted, the Vietnamese man accompanying the American pilot was not even someone being trained, but merely an enlisted man sent along for the ride, to keep up appearances as cover for the fact that the actual preparations of the South Vietnam Air Force lagged behind the overly ambitious schedule. This arrangement was "grudgingly" implemented since it was inconvenient not only for the officers running it and the pilots flying the aircraft, but the Vietnamese men in the back seats didn't think too much of it either. According to author Newman, and to Air Force history, it "was more political than practical."[22] That point reinforces the fact, however, that the American pilots were there by invitation of the recognized government, whose representatives (whether actually being trained, or not) accompanied every *defensive* bombing run.

At the fourth SECDEF conference on March 22, 1962, the "glaring deficiencies" of the South Vietnamese Air Force were discussed and ultimately, the number of American aircraft and pilots were increased to address these deficiencies in the context of the only available alternative, which was to cede air superiority to the declared enemy's greater capabilities. There was also an effort, by Air Force Chief of Staff Curtis LeMay, to relax the restrictions that required a Vietnamese crewman on all combat flights, but McNamara would not budge on that because it would remove the "training cover" that allowed them to participate at all in these operations.[23] Although there was, admittedly, an element of deceit in these operations, this condition prevailed because of the rudimentary state of the South Vietnamese Air Force, and their military forces generally, until the hoped-for improvements could be achieved, coupled with the sudden need to expand the operations beyond their capabilities. Despite that concession, Dr. Chomsky nevertheless overstated this point on his website, where he maintains that Kennedy " ... *invaded Vietnam. He invaded South Vietnam in 1962. He sent the US Air Force to start bombing.*"[24] In the context of what is now "one Vietnam" he might have had a point; but given the political reality extant in 1962, saying that "he invaded South Vietnam to start bombing" was not an accurate or honest way to portray actual historic fact. Indeed, it could be charitably called "wishful thinking," or more accurately be called a gross misrepresentation, given that first, there was no *invasion* of South Vietnam since it was at their invitation, and second, the *defensive* bombing runs were being managed by South Vietnam against the Viet Cong, who were technically considered to be the aggressors in the territory involved (except by Chomsky, of course).

Dr. Chomsky's misstatements of historical truth are probably due to the fact that his expertise lies in the study of linguistics, not history, and that has led to his development of theories, according to author James McGilvray, "[w]ithin the field of linguistics, Chomsky is credited with inaugurating the 'cognitive revolution.'"[25] Based upon his erroneous descriptions of actual events, Dr. Chomsky evidently understands the theories of linguistics better than real-world communications, considering how most people would interpret the meaning of "cognitive ability" in comparing actual facts to his revisionist kind.

That series of misstatements, with more to follow, also illustrate how Chomsky intentionally uses words to completely reframe the meaning of a given set of facts: The first example is his repeated misstatements regarding Kennedy's purported responsibility for the original build-up of combat troops in Vietnam, which is simply not true; and based upon that inaccuracy, moreover, then to suggest that Johnson merely "inherited" that legacy and had no alternative but to pursue it vigorously, despite the advice both had received from, for example, Generals Douglas MacArthur, James Gavin and Matthew Ridgway, even the then-chairman of the Joint Chiefs, Maxwell Taylor, to stay as far away as possible from a ground war in Southeast Asia.[26]

Remarkably, that is precisely the case that Lyndon Johnson had always deceitfully made – that he had "inherited" the war and merely followed Kennedy's policies towards escalation – so Mr. Chomsky was at least paying attention then, to the prevaricating new president, apparently oblivious to the intrinsic worthlessness of his words; that, incidentally, was an issue so prominent among contemporary journalists that a new term was coined, and quickly added to dictionaries, to describe it: "Credibility Gap." The irony of Dr. Chomsky, publicly protesting a war – that most other cognitively aware people knew had not been ramped up and "Americanized" until 18 months after JFK's assassination, in the spring and summer of 1965[27] – apparently without realizing that it was President Johnson, not Kennedy, who did it, is astonishing. And revealing.

To the previous conclusion that JFK had definitely decided to end American involvement in Vietnam's civil war, we can now add the second conclusion: That JFK only reluctantly increased the number of "advisors" until the third quarter of 1963 when he revised official policy and planned to reduce them by the end of that year and withdraw them completely in 1965; he did not introduce "combat troops" nor "invade" South Vietnam and aggressively bomb them, since the Air Force was there by their invitation, and involved only defensive bombing runs managed by the Vietnamese military in operations within South Vietnam.

3. SINCE JFK WAS KILLED BY A "LONE NUT," THERE WAS NO REASON TO SUSPECT A PLOT, OR A "COUP D'ETAT."

Finally, the primary reason for why many people are baffled by the intransigence of a fabled, world-acclaimed man of supposed unmatched brilliance, the holder of numerous prestigious awards, honorary degrees and author of many scholarly works: The reason is that Dr. Noam Chomsky admits that he (unfortunately, like so many of his colleagues in the upper reaches of America's educational elite, regarding JFK's assassination), has never studied it, therefore, as he recently stated, "*I don't really have any opinion. I haven't looked into it in any detail, and I'm not that much concerned.*"[28]

For someone who is a self-professed expert on the world in general, and particularly the U.S. history and its foreign policy of the 1950s-1960s, that is a stunning admission, and it does not speak well for his "intellectual curiosity" to lack even a basic level of knowledge about the "Crime of the 20th Century," never mind having a basis for any opinion at all of the subject at hand. The issue that his position – "I haven't looked into it . . I'm not that much concerned" – allows him to avoid is whether the murder of the 35th president of the United States might have had something to do with what happened immediately afterwards: A major commitment of the U.S. military might on behalf of a despotic government fighting a civil war on the other side of the world (a government that Johnson once paradoxically, given the resources he had devoted to it, described as a "fourth-rate, raggedy-ass little country"). Johnson personally, nearly single-handedly, created the most turbulent domestic period of that particular century. It is unbefitting of a man of Chomsky's stature to not recognize the implications of JFK's assassination, and it suggests that his lack of interest in even wanting to know anything about that "incident" renders any opinion he might have on its impact to the nation, or lack thereof, meaningless.

There are only a limited number of potential reasons for his disinterest: Either,

> 1. He prefers not to invest his valuable time in analyzing it because of all the complications that would make it too difficult to sort out; or,

2. Despite his contrarian views on practically every other, less momentous, aspect of U.S. domestic and foreign policy of the 20th century, he accepts the government's official explanations as stated by the Warren Commission in 1964, without question, as specious and absurd as they are; or,

3. He has been conditioned by the very "political correctness" pressures of which he feigns his resistance, into a position of denial for the purpose of merely protecting his professional reputation, in order to avoid jeopardizing his stature as a professor emeritus of MIT by actively studying this clearly "off limits" national security state secret.

USS LIBERTY ATTACK SURVIVOR PHIL TOURNEY INTERVIEWS NOAM CHOMSKY

Regardless of his reason, Chomsky has previously repeatedly stated, essentially, that, "the answer doesn't matter anyway, so why bother." The referenced quote above (*I don't really have any opinion. I haven't looked into it in any detail, and I'm not that much concerned*) came from an appearance Professor Chomsky made on February 27, 2016, on an internet-radio program titled *Your Voice Counts* at "RepublicBroadcasting.org" hosted by Phil Tourney.

Unbeknownst to Noam Chomsky, until Phil Tourney pointed it out in his first interview with him, was the fact that Lyndon Johnson, with Robert McNamara at his side, personally cancelled two sorties of U.S. fighter jets sent to protect the *USS Liberty*; and that was only one of the several other treasonous acts committed by the president against his own ship that day, yet professor Chomsky had never been aware of it until Mr. Tourney explained it to him. There were several other troubling actions taken by Johnson and McNamara that day that have been covered at length in books and video presentations, but it is doubtful that Chomsky knows anything about all the rest of it since he was unaware of the one most stunning and incomprehensible of all. Yet several books have been written about the attack, including a very powerful one *What I Saw That Day*, by Mr. Tourney himself, and it was also featured in two chapters of my own book, *LBJ: From Mastermind to The Colossus*.

HOST PHIL TOURNEY ASKED PROFESSOR CHOMSKY TO RESPOND TO THIS QUESTION ON THE AIR:

The Question: "In recognition of the scholarship of Peter Dale Scott, John Newman and many others, is it not time to revisit your earlier assessment of the JFK assassination and accept the fact that it was indeed the sea change in U.S. foreign policy, that led to LBJ's escalation and even "Americanization" of the Vietnam War, as well as being behind the planning for the Six-Day War, including the "false flag" of sacrificing the USS *Liberty* as a pretext for inserting the U.S. military into that war along side of Israel, with a plan to attack Egypt – that failed only because the *Liberty* did not sink?"[29]

Chomsky's lengthy response to that question began:[30]

"We have plenty of evidence, I've reviewed it extensively myself, and I think that we can say with considerable confidence that it [JFK's assassination] was not a high level plot that led to a change in policy. Policies continued about as they were with regard to the Vietnam War. If Kennedy had had … [unintelligible] … the actual documentation shows, that Kennedy continued to be one of the more hawkish members of his administration until the very end, until the very day of the assassination practically, he was keeping to the same strong position, the U.S. could withdraw, as had been suggested by McNamara, but only after victory, that was a condition; and if indeed Kennedy had had any interest in withdrawal, there was a perfect opportunity just shortly before the assassination. As you know, in August, 1963, the U.S. government … determined that the South Vietnamese regime, the Diem regime, Diem and his his brother were negotiating with North Vietnam, and were seeking a peace agreement between the two, which would have ended the conflict. Uh, if Kennedy wanted to withdraw, that was a perfect opportunity …uh, let the Diem brothers pursue the negotiations and end the conflict and take credit for having implemented a peaceful end of the conflict. But they didn't do that, instead, what they did was instigate a plot to have the Diem brothers removed and it turned out they ended [up] being assassinated. But that was not Kennedy's proposal … rather, just remove them and put in place a more hawkish general who would then carry out Kennedy's policy of maintaining and escalating the the war … uh, I think that fact, along with the extensive documentation on Kennedy's actual position and the story that the evidence that has since been released about the [unintelligible] …the main documents [NSAM] 273 which called for an eventual withdrawal under the condition, as Kennedy insisted, that it be after victory. I think all of this shows pretty clearly that there was no … any plot had nothing to do with changing policy."

[…]

"Shortly after the Kennedy assassination, in Vietnam, it was learned that the optimistic forecasts coming from the military were not based …were based on highly distorted, misleading evidence and in fact the war was in much worse shape than they had thought and at that point the Kennedy advisors, including the most dovish of them, like George Ball, called for the policies which Johnson then implemented. But I don't think that one can tie this to the assassination, in any event. This still leaves open the question, "who carried out the assassination," and on that I have no particular thoughts ... uh, on the 1967 war, I don't think there is any credible evidence that the United States in any way instigated it, in fact they really didn't want it, they tried to keep Israel from attacking, but didn't block them. Uh, the war – the outcome of the war – was indeed very beneficial to U.S. policy, but not ... there was no indication that it was planned in any way." (Emphasis supplied).

Dr. Chomsky's response to the question ran on, for a total of over 1,500 words and twelve minutes altogether. The only pertinent additional comment regarding his response to the question above, was this: "... the real change in policy, the major change in policy, came in 1967, that's when U.S. aid to Israel started shooting up, when there was extraordinary enthusiasm about Israel in both political parties and among the general articulate community, the media and so on, changed radically after Israel's huge victory in 1967."*

The following observations will summarize what must be said regarding Professor Chomsky's statement:

- Regarding the outrageous, still-unresolved 1967 Israeli assault on a U.S. warship (which was quickly covered up by Johnson and no substantive punishment to Israel ever exacted) Chomsky's statement above, about "U.S. aid shooting up," was certainly true but there was a great amount of irony in that, even though this was not acknowledged; rather, his statement was more in the context of "win-win" atmosphere on the sides of both Israel and within the United States. But that should be no surprise, since the unfortunate attack by Israel on the USS *Liberty* was declared a state secret and thereby put to bed, and left for future generations to figure out.

- His first statement, that, "... *Kennedy continued to be one of the more hawkish members of his administration until the very end, until the very day of the assassination practically* ..." was the opposite of what the record clearly shows – that he was practically the only one in his administration who was striving to achieve

---

* For the sake of brevity in this essay, the remaining, approximately 1,000 additional words of Professor Chomsky's response to this succinct question have not been included, as they grew less and less responsive to the point at hand. However, the interview is available at the website referenced for anyone wishing to hear the remainder of it, up until the commercial break. After the break, the interview then resumed and his monologues continued on for another twenty minutes or so, in the same vein.

a lasting peace – as documented by practically every researcher who has ever studied this subject; and he seems wedded to
that position regardless of what anyone else might ever say. The
conclusions reached in the first two numbered paragraphs above
entirely disprove Chomsky's statement.

- Moreover, Chomsky is evidently unfamiliar with several additional specific, inarguable facts that contradict his mistaken por-
trayal of Kennedy being "hawkish:"

  - The first was demonstrated on June 10, 1963 when he
  gave his famous "Peace Speech" at American University,
  in which he, notably, did not bother to clear the content with any of his White House or military advisors,
  not to mention the high level intelligence officials. That
  speech only increased the acrimony towards JFK felt by
  his enemies across the Potomac River in the Pentagon
  and farther up the river in Langley, the CIA.

  - The second indication that he deeply wanted to achieve
  peace occurred three months later, in September, when
  Kennedy declared in an interview, "In the final analysis, it
  is their war. They are the ones who have to win it or lose it.
  We can help them, we can give them equipment, we can
  send our men out there as advisers, but they have to win
  it, the people of Vietnam, against the Communists …"

  - The third is the point already noted in Section No. 1
  above, where Chomsky does not yet understand the
  meaning of Kennedy's NSAM 263, and in fact, sees
  little difference in it and Johnson's NSAM 273, which
  effectively, though subtlety, turned Kennedy's policy
  around, by 180 degrees. (See pp. 7-9)

  - The fourth illustration of the point was Kennedy's final
  words on the subject, of which there were two instances
  that occurred on Thursday, November 21, 1963, before
  he left for his fatal trip to Texas:

    1. Just an hour before he departed, he told As-
    sistant Press Secretary Malcolm Kilduff, "I've
    just been given a list of the most recent casu-
    alties in Vietnam. We're losing too damn many
    people over there. It's time for us to get out.
    The Vietnamese aren't fighting for themselves.
    We're the ones who are doing the fighting …
    After I come back from Texas, that's going to
    change. There's no reason for us to lose anoth-
    er man over there. Vietnam is not worth anoth-
    er American life."[31]

2. Also, before he left the White House, he instructed Michael Forrestal, "I want you to
organize an in-depth study of every possible
option we've got in Vietnam, including how to
get out of there. We have to review this whole
thing from the bottom to the top."[32]

That Noam Chomsky denies all of these indisputable events is simply
incomprehensible.

Moreover, his statement " … the U.S. could withdraw, as had been
suggested by McNamara, but only after victory, that was a condition" is
yet another subtle distortion of fact, on the same point as also previously
addressed, above, and proved to be yet another misstatement.

Regarding his assertion that the "South Vietnamese regime, the Diem
regime, Diem and his his brother, were negotiating with North Vietnam,
and were seeking a peace agreement between the two, which would have
ended the conflict" is yet another smoke-screen. As explained in a recent
book, titled, *Hanoi's Road to the Vietnam War* by Pierre Asselin, that there
was no such peace initiative being pursued, even though in July, 1963, an
illusory effort [quoting from an Australian assessment of the proposal] by

"Hanoi and its allies in China and the Soviet Union 'have recently
stepped up efforts to gain international support for the convening
of a Geneva-type conference on south [sic] Vietnam,' the assessment began. Their aim was to 'exploit the precedent of the Laotian
settlement and the favorable atmosphere resulting from it to obtain
international support for a similar type settlement … [In pursuing
this proposal, Hanoi leaders] were playing down their parallel objective of achieving reunification of the south with the north on
their own terms. They might well expect that if they could obtain
the withdrawal of United States forces and the replacement of the
Diem Government [sic] by a regime amenable to communist pressure, a unified communist Vietnam would be the almost certain
outcome in the long run.' But since Diem was 'unlikely under any
circumstances to agree to internal negotiations for the withdrawal
of United States military aid and the neutralization of South Vietnam,' Hanoi had nothing to lose and much to gain domestically
and internationally by at least appearing to be open to negotiations
on those issues."[33]

Though this ephemeral idea had germinated within the Hanoi regime, it never blossomed south of the 17th parallel. Because they had
considered pursuing it – not through the Diem regime, but – through the
National Liberation Front (NLF), as a provisional revolutionary govern-

ment, since that entity was already "in place" with its own flag and anthem and "regularly addressed messages to sovereign states and the UN in the name of the South Vietnamese people," and, even though Hanoi portrayed it as a proxy for a shadow government, it was ultimately decided to drop the idea, because it had no territorial base; and if it claimed one, it wouldn't last long before Diem's forces would seek it out and destroy it.[34]

In other words, Professor Chomsky has taken this sliver of a suggestion that there was indeed a viable peace offering being actively negotiated by Diem and his cunning brother, Nhu, in July, 1963 and posited it as an actual fact. But in fact, the North Vietnamese government was merely exploiting international opinion by appearing to be open to negotiations, while never getting around to putting the offer on the table. So this is merely another Chomskyism, another deception used by Professor Chomsky to extend his oration as long as necessary to defray any attempt of the interviewer to interrupt him with a request for elucidation. The fact is that the first known peace offer to have come from North Vietnam was 18 months *after* JFK's assassination: In April 1965 Vietnamese Premier Pham Van Dong Pham proffered a four-point plan which called for a return to the provisions of the Geneva Accords of 1954, along with the withdrawal of US military personnel. And in 1966, in a casual gesture, Ho Chi Minh declared that North Vietnam was willing to "make war for 20 years" – but if the Americans "want to make peace, we shall make peace and invite them to afternoon tea." And of course President Johnson's public statements also regularly expressed a willingness to negotiate with Hanoi, but always through off-the-cuff comments he made for public consumption at press conferences or other empty gestures, not firm policy offerings, until 1967-68, and even then, they were half-hearted attempts aimed mostly at the voting public.[35]

What emerges from an intensive study of actual, documented facts – in contrast to the series of linguistically-challenged "Chomskyisms" – noted above is that the leading anti-war force, practically the only one, within the Kennedy administration, was President Kennedy himself. For Chomsky to continue his illusionary idea of the sincerity of the Diem brothers achieving a "peace agreement" with their sworn enemies in the North Vietnam government seriously undermines his credibility. To airily dismiss the well-established history of their plotting and prevarications toward the U.S., especially the cunning and deceitful brother Nhu, who had even been planning a false coup d'etat as a means to somehow regain popular respect, should be proof enough that this is a specious argument.

Combined, his weakly argued reasoning based upon non-factual assertions, demonstrates how his use of linguistic tricks ultimately produces nothing more than a more rarefied, higher-level version of mythology having the imprimatur of a legendary soothsayer. It vividly demonstrates how an exalted, clairvoyant oracle can "fall onto his own petard" all while it goes practically unnoticed by most of his followers. And it demonstrates, again, the effectiveness of the residual "Operation Mockingbird" program designed in the early 1950s to infiltrate publishers and journalists and feed them CIA propaganda ready for dissemination to the public. It inextricably evolved, over time, to its much more sophisticated, and subtle, manifestation: To install and sustain Chomsky (among others), in his influential position at MIT – notoriously famous for its history of being one of the CIA's most favored universities – for the very purpose of putting a politically correct imprimatur on official government dogma.

In this case, it was a "limited hangout" to acknowledge the diabolical Israeli attack on a U.S. Navy spy-ship, and to leave it at that. The real objective of his appearance on Mr. Tourney's radio show – not unlike his many other appearances – was to hide the fact that the attack was just another Johnsonian (governmental) "false flag" operation, which was the real (and only) catalyst behind that attack. His appearance there was merely another attempt to sandbag such attempts to reveal deeper truths, and to lead his students away from questioning the other larger, and unresolved crimes of the US government, starting with the 1963 coup d'etat and the endless wars now being waged around the world.

Commenting on this same point in a recent video "The Shame of Noam Chomsky," two notable authors of a number of books affirmed these assertions in their own observations:[36]

> James Corbett: "He uses his verbosity and loquacity to talk around various subjects and to mumble and mutter and stutter on for 8 minutes in ways that completely fail to address the original question and in ways that no one seems to notice. It's a key technique in his ability to deflect and avoid answering the question."

> Barrie Zwicker: "He engages in bizarre non-sequiturs all the time. This is a technique he uses."

Clearly, Joseph Campbell and Bill Moyers had/have no better exemplar for a mythmaking model: The key commonality Moyers and Chomsky share is their ability to perform uninterruptible monologues, extending their thoughts as though their space in time is infinite, their thought processes segued seamlessly together as though invisibly connected, even where one subject has nothing to do with the next. They, like their fellow practitioners of this art, were trained to use their voices in low, modulated, softly spoken monotones, caressing every syllable of each word as though, sufficiently squeezed, there could be hidden, implicit meanings revealed in each. When the subject turns though, and the audience needs a clarion call to act, the pace of the modulation increases in harmony with the temper, tone, and decibel level and the mesmerizing point is reached at the pinnacle of the oration. Only the occasional commercial break might interrupt them long enough to quickly have a drink of water and relax their vocal chords sufficiently to begin again, after all the soap, hemorrhoid elixirs and automobile ads have been completed and logged in.

Anyone attempting to interrupt them between those commercials will understand implicitly that to do so would be a very foolish mistake on their part, and could only cause them a special kind of embarrassment, or other discomfort. It is called a "Hobson's Choice" when there really is no free choice, other than the only one that will move both parties to the next level. Thus, under the understood paradigm of "facts be damned," their reputations as great oracles of worldly events is assured.

THE "HERO" WITH A THOUSAND FACES: PROOFS OF LBJ'S UNBRIDLED MALEFICENCE

We now turn to "connecting the dots" that have been placed on this historical matrix. As we simultaneously steer around the obfuscation of myths planted for that purpose, some of the narrative may appear to be speculative in nature, but the reasoning behind it should give the term clarity and justification. Indeed, as we examined in a previous chapter, what becomes clear is that it was J. Cristol's numerous unfounded, scurrilous attempts to reframe factual evidence outside of the original context that should be labeled as "unwarranted speculation."

The worst of the truths spilled out randomly, sporadically, and independently of each other over many decades. One piece of damning evidence presented earlier, discovered through the diligent research conducted by Mr. Ennes and others previously noted, came in the form of misfiled minutes from a meeting of the "303 Committee" – a reference to Room 303 of the Executive Office Building, only a few yards away from the Oval Office. That document revealed an important secret involving the plan for the *Liberty's* encounter with a "submarine in U.A.R. waters" as well as the key men on that committee who planned it, who could only make such audacious plans under the authority of the men they answered to: Secretary of Defense Robert Strange McNamara and his boss, President Lyndon Baines Johnson.

The worst, most incriminating assertions came from respected Navy officers, including what David Lewis was told by Admiral Lawrence Geis: "I want that Goddamn ship going to the bottom. No help. Recall the wings." And what Captain McGonagle told Lieutenant George Golden: *"It was the President and McNamara, when they sent us up from over in Africa, we were there to have this happen."* These assertions tell the real story of what happened and they cannot be ignored any longer. As they say, "You can't make this up."

Yet another piece of evidence was the letter, ironically from Moshe Dayan, which his daughter Yael Dayan furnished, admitting that it was preplanned Israeli provocations that led to the war. These and numerous other proofs previously cited show plainly that the overall plan was designed by the highest level councils of President Lyndon B. Johnson, in collaboration with key men in the Israeli leadership, and furthermore, that the plan was then referred to the Joint Chiefs of Staff – reporting through the Secretary of Defense, directly to the president – with orders to execute it. Through the most rigorous processes of deductive reasoning, it can therefore be reasonably posited that those orders could only have emanated from President Johnson himself. He was uniquely the only man who could order them executed through the military chain of command. The only thing missing – the proverbial "smoking gun" if it, or they, have not already been destroyed – might still exist within the files that have been designated "top secret" and barred from public inspection.

Only President Lyndon B. Johnson – whose obsession with acquiring and using power, and his other title, "Commander in Chief," put him into the position of control over both the "303 Committee" and the Joint Chiefs of Staff – could have possibly given such an order. This very kind of planning was his primary skill, practically a trademark, along with his obsessive accumulation of unbridled power. Despite the diverse opinions on Lyndon Johnson's many other traits, probably every book and news article ever written about him coincide on these two points. Ultimately, these skills and traits are the conclusive proof that he was uniquely responsible for both the plan's creation and its execution. Indeed, it would be grossly speculative to suggest that it could have been anyone else, for no one else had that kind of power, authority, and the audacity, to have promulgated such a plan, complete with a very sophisticated time-bomb set to give him the pretext for the insertion of the U.S. military into a Mid-East war that would guarantee him an election victory in the following year. Had the *Liberty* sunk, as he had planned, it would have guaranteed a repeat of his 1964 landslide election; it would have closely replicated the other false flag called the "Tonkin Gulf attack" which had been similarly planned and stunningly executed (except that it has long-since become clear that there was no such actual attack, only one of the "phantom" type) exactly three months before election day, ironically against a contender who he had successfully labeled as a "war monger" with considerable help from Bill Moyers and the "Daisy Ad." That the purported "attack that didn't happen" in the Tonkin Gulf succeeded in triggering the Vietnam War, but the "attack that failed because the ship didn't sink" caused the mission to insert the U.S. military into a Mid-East conflagration to be aborted, were, in juxtaposition, just another inexplicable irony. Or, in the latter case at least, it might have been yet another "Devine Intervention."

"Comparative Myths" Dissected

The men working within the White House and Executive Office Building, serving on the 303 Committee, had something else in common with their comrades located in Langley and Tel Aviv and Jerusalem: Regardless of their race, religion (if any), their skin hues and colors or even whether or not they were all circumcised, they were all Zionists, of the most zealous and treacherous sort. And they knew that the man then occupying the Oval Office next door was behind their planning, and would also be behind its execution and subsequent cover-up. It follows, axiomatically, that he was also the one man who could have instigated all of it and then would have the power to ensure that it would remain a secret. They further assumed that the secret would remain "forever." It was only because one facet of the plan failed that the secret would one day unravel: The USS *Liberty*, thanks to the brave and heroic men who survived the abominable plan to sink it, refused to sink. That a series of "miracles", as Ron Kukal has stated over and again, which prevented its sinking, proves his contention that those men were guided by Divine Intervention to do what they did, when they did, and how they did it. And everything they did after the torpedo created the massive hole, which was mostly below the waterline, saved the ship from sinking. They miraculously kept it afloat as they sailed their crippled ship across the choppy Mediterranean waters to get it into dry dock so that it could finally be repaired.

The handling of the *Liberty* investigation's adjudication of "facts" was contaminated from the start and has never been corrected. We have demonstrated that certain inconvenient facts were discarded and replaced by false testimony or fabricated "evidence." The real experts, the first-hand witnesses, have been replaced by men with their own agendas, operating from the comfort of their high offices within the Executive Office Building, the State Department, the CIA or the Pentagon, as illustrated by the January, 2004 State Department conference reviewed in Chapter 7. The discrete testimonies, or credible statements, of each of the men identified in the earlier chapters – ranging from numerous Naval officers on various ships of the Sixth Fleet to the Air Force B-52 pilot Jim Nanjo based in California, not to mention the men who survived the assault on the *Liberty* – combine to form a chorus of men whose voices have heretofore been systematically silenced. No amount of smug condescension, in abundance at Foggy Bottom in the State Department auditorium that day, January 12, 2004, when the testimony of the real "experts" – the survivors of that atrocity – was systematically ignored and replaced by that of the several men who were intent on securing the squalid, sleazy, cover-up story that never fit the facts in the first place. Only a few of the expert witnesses, led by James Bamford, were clearly interested in exposing the essential truths; they had the delicate task of remaining cordial to the others there whose mission seemed to be celebrating the final victory of sealing away into the final historical record of the "*Liberty* incident," files that would forever "prove" that it was all an unfortunate error and would now go away if those pesky and pedantic survivors would just stop talking about it. The video,[37] for those who might want to check these assertions, is recommended viewing; but since it is three hours long, it might be best to plan it for a rainy day when nothing else is on the calendar to mitigate its inevitable mind-numbing effects.

Other proofs of the real story were contained in the evidence presented in the earlier chapters, about how the IDF knew in advance what radio frequencies needed to be jammed, and when to jam them; how they knew precisely how many antennae were there, and exactly where each was; how to destroy them on the first pass to ensure they would no longer operate; how they knew the number and position of the gun tubs; and the need to slaughter the men in those tubs before they had a chance to fire those guns.

The military precision involved in orchestrating one wave after another of coordinated air and surface attacks was spectacular, as if it were all being done by a Maestro conductor performing with a philharmonic orchestra, so that each movement was in harmony with that which preceeded it, and the next one exquisitely timed to follow it, every instrument playing its part masterfully, though in this case, brutally and violently. The extensive training of those pilots, and the Israeli Navy men on the torpedo boats as well, tell the real tale – about the methodology used to destroy the remaining life rafts whose only function would have been to save a few of those lives, and that could not be allowed. When their "mission" was accomplished, the next movement, of large transporter helicopters filled with commandos armed with automatic rifles – clearly instructed to let no survivors live to tell of this horrendous experience – thus belie the reasons and rationale for why the men – not just the ship – had to be destroyed. They only left when it appeared that time had run out on them and they were about to be caught. Only then did they somehow begin their "acts" of contrition, explaining how they thought the U.S. warship was really an old, broken-down, rusty horse transport boat that had long since been scheduled for destruction; the IDF, the highly professional military command of Israel, undoubtedly knew that from the beginning. Now they begged the U.S.(everyone other than the few who had plotted the operation from the start) to believe that their once-glorious, and invincible IDF had just made a silly mistake.

When one juxtaposes all of the obvious evidence of a lengthy, meticulous planning operation that clearly took many months of preparation – with an alleged "accidental," yet sustained, brutal attack that was incredulously stated to be conducted against an aging, rusty old horse transport ship that was one-fifth the displacement of the *Liberty* in tonnage, half its length, with none of the forty-five antennae and other high-tech equipment festooned on its deck – the absurdity of the claim could not be more stark. The *El QusElr* was a ship that had one single thing in common with the *Liberty* – two masts – but in no other respect did it look anything like the well-marked ship, proudly flying the U.S. Old Glory high above its deck: The USS *Liberty*.

THE POWER OF TRUTHS: DESTROYING MYTHS

The hope of the survivors has peaked many times, with the news of every new book on the *Liberty* story that is published, always with great expectations that this will be the one that will finally force the full truth out by possibly attracting the attention of congress or even the president. So far, that has proven to be a most elusive, maybe even impossible, dream. Yet that is probably the only way that a complete, honest and thorough investigation of the real causes of the attack might ever be accomplished. Only then might some scintilla of equitable justice be given to the survivors, their families and all caring citizens, to cleanse their consciences of the jaded myths, replaced by the real history of the event at last. And more importantly, that they know that everyone else is conscious of the same epiphany, that the entire culture has been blessed with a sudden understanding of the true fate of their beloved ship.

Based on the lack of success to date, it is probably best to assume that it won't happen in the lifetime of any of the survivors still alive today. Therefore, the simple and pragmatic goal of this book is to merely keep the hope alive that it may be done in a future generation, one that is more open to real truths than the Orwellian myths that have replaced them.

Endnotes

1. Safer, pp. 92-95.
2. Ibid. pp. 95-96
3. Ibid. p. 96
4. Ibid. (Iago is one of the major characters in Shakespeare's play Othello, and, was "one of Shakespeare's most sinister villains, often considered such because of the unique trust that Othello places in him, which he betrays while maintaining his reputation of honesty and dedication." per Wikipedia).

5. Wikipedia - Entry for Sidney Gottlieb

6. Davis, Deborah, p. 146

7. Ibid., p 139

8. From The Arlington National Cemetery Web site: http://arlingtoncemetery.net/fgwisner.htm

9. Ibid.

10. Ibid.

11. Barsky, pp. 170-171

12. See Wikipedia: https://en.wikipedia.org/wiki/Noam_Chomsky#cite_note-FOOTNOTE-Barsky1997170-96

13. See Mantik essay: http://assassinationofjfk.net/wp-content/uploads/2014/04/The-Silence-of-the-Historians.pdf

14. See: https://chomsky.info/20131122/

15. Newman, Op. Cit., pp. 227-229

16. Corson, , pp. 44-45

17. Ibid.

18. Ibid. p. 46

19. Schlesinger, Jr., Arthur, The Imperial Presidency, Boston: Houghton Mifflin Company, 1973, p. 177

20. Ibid. 763

21. Newman, p. 159

22. Ibid. p. 161

23. Ibid., pp. 204-207, 210-211

24. See www.chomsky.info

25. McGilvray, p. 19

26. These generals were referenced in the author's previous work, *LBJ: From Mastermind to the Colossus* so the details of that testimony have been omitted here. But one example of it was that General Ridgway was quoted telling Senator George Aiken of Vermont that "even if two million men were sent to Vietnam they would be swallowed up."

27. Johnson, ever the politician, knew of course that he had to wait until after the 1964 elections to jump-start the war he had planned since (actually, before) he became president.

28. See Republicbroadcasting.org. For this interview go to: http://www.drtourneyarchive.com/show/february-27-2016/28 (@45:15)

29. Ibid. (@45:00)

30. Ibid (@ 54:20

31. Douglass, James W. *JFK and the Unspeakable. Why He Died and Why it Matters*, Maryknoll, NY: Orbis Books, 2008, p. 304

32. Reeves, Richard, *President Kennedy: Profile in Power*. New York: Simon & Shuster, 1993, p. 660

33. Asselin, Pierre, *Hanoi's Road to the Vietnam War, 1954-1965*, Berkeley: University of California Press, 2013, pp. 136-137 (Note: Including two references to secondary sources: [1] "South Vietnam: Communist Proposals for an International Conference" ([Australian Government Report]), 3 August, 1962, FO 371/166763, NAUK, 1., and [2] Canberra to All Posts: "South Vietnam's Communist Proposals for an International Conference," 1-3.

34. Ibid.

35. Alpha History, "U.S. Day of Reckoning?" Vietnam War Peace Talks. See: http://alphahistory.com/vietnam/vietnam-warpeace-talks/#sthash.Jev67TsE.dpuf

36. See: "The Shame of Noam Chomsky" (https://www.youtube.com/watch?v=BhrZ57XxYJU)

37. State Department Hearing 1/20/2004: "1967 Arab-Israeli War USS Liberty

http://www.c-span.org/video/?179892-1/1967-arabisraeli-war-uss-liberty

Admiral Thomas Moor

Appendix A

A Fair Probe Would Attack *Liberty* Misinformation

–By Admiral Thomas H. Moorer (From the January 16, 2004 edition of THE Stars And Stripes)

While State Department officials and historians converge on Washington this week to discuss the 1967 war in the Middle East, I am compelled to speak out about one of US history's most shocking cover-ups. on June 8, 1967, Israel attacked our proud naval ship – the USS *Liberty* – killing 34 American servicemen and wounding 172. Those men were then betrayed and left to die by our own government. US military rescue aircraft were recalled – not once, but twice – through direct intervention by the Johnson administration. Secretary of Defense Robert McNamara's cancellation of the Navy's attempt to rescue the Liberty, which I confirmed from the commanders of the aircraft carriers *America* and *Saratoga*, was *the most disgraceful act I witnessed in my entire military career*. [Emphasis added.] To add insult to injury, Congress, to this day, has failed to hold formal hearings on Israel's attack on this American ship. No official investigation of the attack has ever permitted the testimony of the surviving crew members. A 1967 investigation by the Navy, upon which all other reports are based, has now been fully discredited as a cover-up by its senior attorney.

Capt. Ward Boston, in a sworn affidavit, recently revealed that the court was ordered by the White house to cover up the incident and find that Israel's attack was "a case of mistaken identity." Some distinguished colleagues and I formed an independent commission to investigate the attack on the USS *Liberty*. After an exhaustive review of previous reports, naval and other military records, including eyewitness testimony from survivors, we recently presented our findings on Capitol Hill. They include:

- Israeli reconnaissance aircraft closely studied the Liberty during an eight-hour period prior to the attack, one flying within 200 feet of the ship. Weather reports confirm the day was clear with unlimited visibility. The Liberty was a clearly marked American ship in international waters, flying an American flag and carrying large US Navy hull letters and numbers on its bow.

- Despite claims by Israeli intelligence that they confused the Liberty with a small Egyptian transport, the Liberty was conspicuously different from any vessel in the Egyptian navy. It was the most sophisticated intelligence ship in the world in 1967. With its massive radio antennae, including a large satellite dish, it looked like a large lobster and was one of the most easily identifiable ships afloat.

- Israel attempted to prevent the Liberty's radio operators from sending a call for help by jamming American emergency radio channels.

- Israeli torpedo boats machine-gunned lifeboats at close range that had been lowered to rescue the most-seriously wounded.

As a result, our commission concluded that:

- There is compelling evidence that Israel's attack was a deliberate attempt to destroy an American ship and kill her entire crew.

- In attacking the USS *Liberty*, Israel committed acts of murder against US servicemen and an act of war against the United States.

- The White house knowingly covered up the facts of this attack from the American people.

- The truth continues to be concealed to the present day in what can only be termed a national disgrace.

What was Israel's motive in launching this attack? Congress must address this question with full cooperation from the National Security Agency, the CIA and the military intelligence services. The men of the USS *Liberty* represented the United States. They were attacked for two hours, causing 70 percent of American casualties, and the eventual loss of our best intelligence ship. These sailors and Marines were entitled to our best defense. We gave them no defense. Did our government put Israel's interests ahead of our own? If so, why? Does our government continue to subordinate American interests to Israeli interests?

These are important questions that should be investigated by an independent, fully empowered commission of the American government. The American people deserve to know the truth about this attack. We must finally shed some light on one of the blackest pages in American naval history. It is a duty we owe not only to the brave men of the USS Liberty, but to every man and woman who is asked to wear the uniform of the United States.

* * *

Admiral Thomas Moorer was chairman of the Joint Chiefs of Staff from 1970 to 1974 and once was 7th Fleet Commander. He was joined in the Independent Commission of Inquiry by Rear Admiral Merlin Staring, former judge advocate general of the Navy, and Ambassador James Akins, former U.S. ambassador to Saudi Arabia. General Ray Davis, former assistant commandant of the Marine Corps was also a member of the commission at the time of his death in September, 2003.

Three weeks after signing this document, and two weeks after it had been ignored by the State Department, on February 5, 2004, Admiral Moorer suddenly died.

Appendix B

The USS Liberty Alliance Letter, September 30, 2006 from Rear Admiral (Ret.) Merlin Staring to his fellow members (approx. 400) of the Navy – Marine Corps Retired Judge Advocates Association, laying out the reasons he believed that it was inconceivable to him that any of them, knowing the facts of the *Liberty* attack, would defend "the validity or the reliability of that farcical 1967 Court of Inquiry..."

U. S. S. Liberty Alliance, Inc.

1819 Horseback Trail
Vienna, VA 22182
(703) 938-4670

September 30, 2006

Dear Colleagues, and Their Families and Friends,

As a fellow member of the Navy - Marine Corps Retired Judge Advocates Association, I am directing this rather-imposing document package to each other member, plus a few of their friends – a total list of about 400 for the moment. As a preliminary, I address you on an interim letterhead of the U. S. S. Liberty Alliance, an organization which I presently serve as Treasurer. (That relationship will terminate shortly due to a relocation in store for me in the near future.) I was brought into the USS LIBERTY matter, in its present posture, chiefly by and through Admiral Thomas Moorer, our long-esteemed Chief of Naval Operations and later Chairman of the Joint Chiefs of Staff who most unfortunately passed away in early 2004. Admiral Moorer was succeeded in the letterhead organization by RADM Clarence A. (Mark) Hill, Jr., USN (Ret), with whom I now closely work.

So – what is this all about? It's about this: Back in June 1967 the USS LIBERTY, a U. S. Navy intelligence ship, was operating in the Mediterranean during the Israeli "Six Day War." A neutral ship in international waters, essentially unarmed, she was suddenly placed under concerted attack, over a period of several hours, by Israeli air and naval forces. Of a complement of 294 officers and men, she suffered 34 Americans killed and 173 wounded in action. The ship was badly damaged and never again sailed on an operational mission.

Admiral Moorer, who became CNO shortly after that attack, was personally convinced, based on information even then available, that the attack was a deliberate and knowing attack by Israel on our ship, despite the claim by Israel that it was a case of mistaken identity. He held that view through the rest of his active-duty career and through his retirement, to the time of his death. At his initiative, the U. S. S. Liberty Alliance was ultimately formed in support of the much-delayed public efforts of the survivors of the attack to determine, and to have accurately recorded in our nation's history, the true facts and nature of the event.

I, personally, had at the time only brief and glancing contact with the Navy's resulting investigation – a Court of Inquiry convened by Admiral John Sidney McCain, Jr., then Commander in Chief, U. S. Naval Forces Europe. My sole formal contact was to receive the record of that Inquiry when it was submitted to the Convening Authority for his action. As Admiral McCain's senior staff legal officer, I was asked to review that record of about 650 pages. I immediately undertook that review. I had the record for a total of about 18 hours, during 15 of which I concentrated solely upon it. At the end of that time Admiral McCain, learning that I was having problems finding evidence in the record to support some of the Court's findings (though only about a third of the way through it), withdrew the record from me. I had no input into his action upon it, and I had no further official contact with the matter during the rest of my active-duty career which concluded in 1975.

Not until many years later did I learn some of the facts related to the Navy's 1967 investigation and the experiences of the survivors both during and after the attack. I will mention here only these basic facts concerning that inquiry – though there are many others of significance: When the Court convened on 10 June 1967 in London, it was ordered to conduct <u>and to complete</u> its investigation <u>within one week</u>. It did so, meeting for portions of only five calendar days and having in the process requested of the Convening Authority additional time, which request was denied. In its report the Court cited, as an "unusual difficulty" it had experienced in conducting its proceedings, "the necessity of investigating such a major naval disaster of international significance in an extremely abbreviated time frame." During its three days with the ship in drydock in Malta, the Court heard from <u>only 14</u> of the 260 surviving members of LIBERTY's complement – many of her 172 <u>wounded</u> crewmen, including many who had been at the heart of the action, having been evacuated to other U. S. Navy vessels and shoreside facilities for medical attention. Never thereafter were those critically important eyewitnesses officially questioned concerning their observations of or experiences during the attack.

With that background of the matter – highly condensed for these present purposes – Admiral Hill and I wrote to the Secretary of the Navy on 27 July 2005, setting forth those and many other telltale facts. We respectfully asked the Secretary to examine and appraise the records of his Department to which we thus referred, and to consent to and support the efforts of the LIBERTY survivors to generate a full, fair, and objective U. S. Government investigation into the facts and records of the attack upon their ship. On 22 September 2005 a subordinate in the Office of the Judge Advocate General of the Navy, speaking on behalf of the Secretary, answered, stating that there was "no purpose to further investigation," thus refusing to examine the facts of record which clearly revealed that investigation to have been grossly and blatantly inadequate to its stated purposes.

On 8 June 2005 the survivors' Liberty Veterans Association had filed with the Secretary of the Army, as Executive Agent for the Department of Defense in War Crimes matters, an extensive, documented report of War Crimes alleged to have been committed against LIBERTY and her crew during the 1967 attack. The Secretary of the Army, under his charter, is responsible for ensuring that all such War Crimes allegations are "thoroughly investigated," so we in turn wrote to him on 20 April 2006, asking that he consider and appraise the Navy's 1967 Court of Inquiry, in all of its utter inadequacy, and that he institute a proper investigation <u>now</u> to supplant that inquiry and remedy its deficiencies. On 15 May 2006 a Special Assistant to the Judge Advocate General of the Army responded — again on behalf of his Departmental Secretary — taking no note of our demonstration of the superficiality and inadequacy of the Navy's hasty 1967 Inquiry and concluding that "further investigation by the U. S. military is unwarranted."

It's being then apparent that no cognizant Defense authority in the Executive Branch of the Government would consent or attempt to reopen the matter that had been so hastily swept under the rug back in 1967, and remained officially there, Admiral Hill and I have on 22 July 2006 written formally to Senator John Warner, Chairman of the Senate Committee on Armed Services, enclosing a complete file of the relevant documents I have described above. (I had earlier, myself, written informally to the Senator about the prior stages of the process, in light of his past service as our Navy Secretary and his known interest and fairness in related matters.) The package below this cover memo is the full file that we thus presented to Senator Warner and to each member of his Committee. We ask there that the Legislative Branch of our Government now step in to conduct or to order a full and proper official U. S. Government investigation of the 1967 assault on the LIBERTY while many participants and eyewitnesses remain still available to testify.

Our communication to the Congress was the subject of a personal meeting in late July between Liberty Alliance representatives, including Admiral Hill, and a designated member of Senator Warner's staff. At this writing we have an appointment for a further meeting with a cognizant member of his Committee staff. In our letter to the Senator we assured him of our keen awareness of the delicacy of the matter from a diplomatic standpoint – an earnest concern in which we yield to noone. In light of that very concern, when we next meet we will suggest – as we have long espoused – that Congress, rather than institute its own hearings, might direct instead that the Department of the Navy now conduct, for the record, the full, fair, and objective investigation that it should have conducted back in 1967.

I tell you all of this because, as "alumni" of the organization, I think you have a right to know, and should know, how the legal affairs of the Navy have been and are being conducted, both during our mutual service years and since. I submit that not a single Navy or Marine Corps Judge Advocate addressed by this letter would or could conscientiously spring to the defense of the validity or the reliability of that farcical 1967 Court of Inquiry and its sequelae. I cannot bring myself to think that any of our present or past Judge Advocate successors have allowed themselves to be coopted into ignoring the points we have thus repeatedly made, and I can only believe that they have either been denied the opportunity to apply their professional qualifications or directly ordered to ignore their clear professional duties.

I shall not report further, to this address list, on future developments in the matter. We have had recent changes in the management, organization, and administration of the Liberty Alliance, however -- explaining my use here of the temporary, interim letterhead rather than the one seen below in the document file. We shall in the very near future have a new letterhead reflecting those changes. I will then address a further, and far shorter, communication to each of you, explaining briefly who we are, where we may be reached, and what we are about.

Sincerely, and most cordially, to all,

Merlin Staring

Appendix C

The USS Liberty Alliance Letter, September 21, 2005 from Rear Admiral (Ret.) Merlin Staring to survivor Ron Kukal

September 21, 2005

☆☆☆☆
Admiral Thomas H. Moorer, USN
Chairman, Joint Chiefs of Staff
Retired
Founding Chairman

☆☆☆☆
General Ray Davis, USMC
Medal of Honor
General of Marines, Retired
Founding Vice Chairman

☆☆
RADM Clarence A. (Mark) Hill, Jr.
USN (Ret.)
Chairman pro tem

☆☆
RADM Merlin Staring
JAGC, USN (Ret.)
Former Judge Advocate General
Treasurer

Ambassador James Akins
Director

Captain Richard Kiepfer, MD
USN (Ret.), *Director*
U.S.S. Liberty Survivor

Richard Larry Weaver, SN.
USN (Ret.), *Director*
U.S.S. Liberty Survivor

M. I. Hakki
Director

Jack Tillar
Director

Tito Howard
Director
Executive Director

Mr. Ron Kukal
456 East Montana Street
Sheridan, WY 82801

Dear Ron,

I am writing, in advance of my planned visit to you some 10 days from now, to thank you for the help and information that you have so readily shared with me concerning the June 1967 Israeli attack on the USS LIBERTY.

As you know, I had only a surprisingly short, and at that time a profoundly puzzling, connection with the LIBERTY events as they unfolded. They were thereafter quickly screened from public view. Only many years later, long after I had retired in 1975 from my final active-duty position as the Judge Advocate General of the Navy, did I gradually start to learn some of the true - - and the unbelievably bizarre - - facts about:

1. the attack;

2. the manner in which the Navy's hasty Court of Inquiry had been conducted and handled;

3. the treatment and the oppressive threats to which you and the other LIBERTY survivors were subjected;

Liberty Alliance
P.O. Box 663, Front Royal, VA 22630 Tel: 540-631-9339 Fax: 540-636-6912 Email: lntaiyo@yahoo.com

4. and, ultimately, the manner in which the blatantly inadequate Navy Court of Inquiry became the peg from which successive administrations of our United States Government have attempted to hang a concealing screen over what was in fact a travesty of justice, of humanity, and of the fair and open government of men and women.

I now know that, only after two or more decades, did the suppressed and oppressed LIBERTY survivors, of all categories, venture to talk and to communicate with each other concerning the June 1967 experiences that they had until then been compelled to hold closely within themselves under duress - - a duress that was first applied to them at and by the farcical Court of Inquiry, and that continued later to be applied to some of them as they attempted to resume their lives in the isolation from their LIBERTY shipmates that had been immediately and deliberately imposed upon them.

Ultimately, and gradually, many of the LIBERTY survivors became sufficiently self-assured that they dared to speak out - - to reveal what had happened to them, and what they knew - - and to seek and to fight for the recognition and the benefits which they had deserved and to which they were entitled. For most of them, this period of openness, and of recuperation, came after years of inner conflict - - of private memories of horrible events - - of nightmares, and panic attacks, for some - - and of personal and/or domestic stresses that cast shadows over or radically changed their lives and their human relationships.

Against that general background, I now know that a few of the LIBERTY survivors - - including you - - found in their power and in their personal convictions a courage to speak out, and to strive for the justice denied to them, much earlier in their isolation than was true of many of their more cautious, or more browbeaten, shipmates. Many came to that point far later - - and some, only too late. Many were helped along the way by a loving and sympathetic family as they gradually mended and redirected their stricken lives. Some were not so fortunate, or not so blessed.

I now know, Ron, that you were one of the very first of the LIBERTY survivors - - or certainly among the first to fight the battle in which you are all without exception now united. I also know that, as an unquestionably direct result of your understandable preoccupation with that fight, your domestic life was radically affected, if not torn asunder. Finally, I am privileged and comforted to know that you were ultimately able to put those ruptures behind you - - yet to continue to support your shipmates in their still unresolved effort.

If I were one who pretentiously wore his religion on his sleeve, I would probably pronounce blessings upon you in some form. I am not one of those,

nor am I empowered to do that. I can however, do what a fellow member of the United States Navy is empowered to do:

Ron, I salute you!

Sincerely,

Merlin H. Staring
RADM, JAGC, USN (Ret.)

Appendix D

The CIA's Attempt to Denigrate "Critical Thinkers"

In April, 1967, the CIA, in a terrified reaction of the then-current attempt by New Orleans District Attorney Jim Garrison to conduct an honest and thorough investigation of the JFK assassination, introduced a new and dismissive term that was intended to ridicule and repudiate anyone having the temerity to doubt their consecrated imprimatur on the established mythologies they created: Call them a "Conspiracy Theorist." That term was created in this memo, which was written specifically not only their own employees, but, more importantly, for their many "stringers" in the journalism and publication worlds, who were paid to replicate whatever message the "powers that be" wanted to be written. Specifically, the memorandum coined the terms "conspiracy theories" and "conspiracy theorists," and included recommendations for discrediting and ridiculing such theories.

The text of that document is included below. To view the original document, see: http://www.maryferrell.org/showDoc.html?docId=53510#relPageId=2&tab=page

Concerning Criticism of the Warren Report

CIA Document 1035-960

RE: Concerning Criticism of the Warren Report

1. Our Concern. From the day of President Kennedy's assassination on, there has been speculation about the responsibility for his murder. Although this was stemmed for a time by the Warren Commission report, (which appeared at the end of September 1964), various writers have now had time to scan the Commission's published report and documents for new pretexts for questioning, and there has been a new wave of books and articles criticizing the Commission's findings. In most cases the critics have speculated as to the existence of some kind of conspiracy, and often they have implied that the Commission itself was involved. Presumably as a result of the increasing challenge to the Warren Commission's report, a public opinion poll recently indicated that 46% of the American public did not think that Oswald acted alone, while more than half of those polled thought that the Commission had left some questions unresolved. Doubtless polls abroad would show similar, or possibly more adverse results.

2. This trend of opinion is a matter of concern to the U.S. government, including our organization. The members of the Warren Commission were naturally chosen for their integrity, experience and prominence. They represented both major parties, and they and their staff were deliberately drawn from all sections of the country. Just because of the standing of the Commissioners, efforts to impugn their rectitude and wisdom tend to cast doubt on the whole leadership of American society. Moreover, there seems to be an increasing tendency to hint that President Johnson himself, as the one person who might be said to have benefited, was in some way responsible for the assassination.

Innuendo of such seriousness affects not only the individual concerned, but also the whole reputation of the American government. Our organization itself is directly involved: among other facts, we contributed information to the investigation. Conspiracy theories have frequently thrown suspicion on our organization, for example by falsely alleging that Lee Harvey Oswald worked for us. The aim of this dispatch is to provide material countering and discrediting the claims of the conspiracy theorists, so as to inhibit the circulation of such claims in other countries. Background information is supplied in a classified section and in a number of unclassified attachments.

3. Action. We do not recommend that discussion of the assassination question be initiated where it is not already taking place. Where discussion is active [business] addresses are requested:

a. To discuss the publicity problem with [?] and friendly elite contacts (especially politicians and editors), pointing out that the Warren Commission made as thorough an investigation as humanly possible, that the charges of the critics are without serious foundation, and that further speculative discussion only plays into the hands of the opposition. Point out also that parts of the conspiracy talk appear to be deliberately generated by Communist propagandists. Urge them to use their influence to discourage unfounded and irresponsible speculation.

b. To employ propaganda assets to [negate] and refute the attacks of the critics. Book reviews and feature articles are particularly appropriate for this purpose. The unclassified attachments to this guidance should provide useful background material for passing to assets. Our ploy should point out, as applicable, that the critics are (I) wedded to theories adopted before the evidence was in, (I) politically interested, (III) financially interested, (IV) hasty and inaccurate in their research, or (V) infatuated with their own theories. In the course of discussions of the whole phenomenon of criticism, a useful strategy may be to single out Epstein's theory for attack, using the attached Fletcher [?] article and Spectator piece for background. (Although Mark Lane's book is much less convincing that Epstein's and comes off badly where confronted by knowledgeable critics, it is also much more difficult to answer as a whole, as one becomes lost in a morass of unrelated details.)

4. In private to media discussions not directed at any particular writer, or in attacking publications which may be yet forthcoming, the following arguments should be useful:

a. No significant new evidence has emerged which the Commission did not consider. The assassination is sometimes compared (e.g., by Joachim Joesten and Bertrand Russell) with the Dreyfus case; however, unlike that case, the attack on the Warren Commission have produced no new evidence, no new culprits have been convincingly identified, and there is no agreement among the critics. (A better parallel, though an imperfect one, might be with the Reichstag fire of 1933, which some competent historians (Fritz Tobias, A.J.P. Taylor, D.C. Watt) now believe was set by Vander Lubbe on his own initiative, without acting for either Nazis or Communists; the Nazis tried to pin the blame on the Communists, but the latter have been more successful in convincing the world that the Nazis were to blame.)

b. Critics usually overvalue particular items and ignore others. They tend to place more emphasis on the recollections of individual witnesses (which are less reliable and more divergent--and hence offer more hand-holds for criticism) and less on ballistics, autopsy, and photographic evidence. A close examination of the Commission's records will usually show that the conflicting eyewitness accounts are quoted out of context, or were discarded by the Commission for good and sufficient reason.

c. Conspiracy on the large scale often suggested would be impossible to conceal in the United States, esp. since informants could expect to receive large royalties, etc. Note that Robert Kennedy, Attorney General at the time and John F. Kennedy's brother, would be the last man to overlook or conceal any conspiracy. And as one reviewer pointed out, Congressman Gerald R. Ford would hardly have held his tongue for the sake of the Democratic administration, and Senator Russell would have had every political interest in exposing any misdeeds on the part of Chief Justice Warren. A conspirator moreover would hardly choose a location for a shooting where so much depended on conditions beyond his control: the route, the speed of the cars, the moving target, the risk that the assassin would be discovered. A group of wealthy conspirators could have arranged much more secure conditions.

d. Critics have often been enticed by a form of intellectual pride: they light on some theory and fall in love with it; they also scoff at the Commission because it did not always answer every question with a flat decision one way or the other. Actually, the make-up of the Commission and its staff was an excellent safeguard against over-commitment to any one theory, or against the illicit transformation of probabilities into certainties.

e. Oswald would not have been any sensible person's choice for a co-conspirator. He was a "loner," mixed up, of questionable reliability and an unknown quantity to any professional intelligence service.

f. As to charges that the Commission's report was a rush job, it emerged three months after the deadline originally set. But to the degree that the Commission tried to speed up its reporting, this was largely due to the pressure of irresponsible speculation already appearing, in some cases coming from the same critics who, refusing to admit their errors, are now putting out new criticisms.

g. Such vague accusations as that "more than ten people have died mysteriously" can always be explained in some natural way e.g.: the individuals concerned have for the most part died of natural causes; the Commission staff questioned 418 witnesses (the FBI interviewed far more people, conduction 25,000 interviews and re interviews), and in such a large group, a certain number of deaths are to be expected. (When Penn Jones, one of the originators of the "ten mysterious deaths" line, appeared on television, it emerged that two of the deaths on his list were from heart attacks, one from cancer, one was from a head-on collision on a bridge, and one occurred when a driver drifted into a bridge abutment.)

5. Where possible, counter speculation by encouraging reference to the Commission's Report itself. Open-minded foreign readers should still be impressed by the care, thoroughness, objectivity and speed with which the Commission worked. Reviewers of other books might be encouraged to add to their account the idea that, checking back with the report itself, they found it far superior to the work of its critics.

Bibliography

"For there is nothing covered, that shall not be revealed; neither hid, that shall not be known"

~ Luke 12:2

Books

Albertazzie, Col. Ralph and J. F. terHorst. *The Flying White House: The Story of Air Force One*, New York: Coward, McCann & Geoghegan, Inc., 1979.

Asselin, Pierre, *Hanoi's Road to the Vietnam War, 1954-1965*, Berkeley: University of California Press, 2013

Ball, George W., with Douglas B. Ball. *The Passionate Attachment: America's Involvement with Israel, 1947 to the Present*. New York: W. W. Norton & Co, 1992.

Barsky, Robert F. *Noam Chomsky: A Life of Dissent*. MIT Press, (1998).

Burns, Stewart. *To The Mountaintop*. New York, NY: HarperCollins Publishers, Inc, 2004

Bamford, James, *Body of Secrets: Anatomy of the Ultra-Secret National Security Agency: From the Cold War Through the Dawn of a New Century*. New York: Doubleday, 2001.

Califano, Jr., Joseph A. *The Triumph & Tragedy of Lyndon Johnson*. New York: Simon & Shuster, 1991.

Campbell, Joseph. *The Hero with a Thousand Faces*. New York: Fontana, 1993.

Campbell, Joseph, with Bill Moyers. *The Power of Myth*. New York: First Anchor Books (owned by Random House), 1991

Caro, Robert A. *The Years of Lyndon Johnson: The Path to Power*. New York: Alfred A. Knopf, 1982.

Caro, Robert A. *The Years of Lyndon Johnson: Means of Ascent*. New York: Alfred A. Knopf, 1990.

Caro, Robert A. *The Years of Lyndon Johnson: The Master of the Senate*. New York: Alfred A. Knopf, 2002.

Caro, Robert A. *The Years of Lyndon Johnson: The Passage of Power*. New York: Alfred A. Knopf, 2012.

Churchill, Randolph, and Winston Churchill, *The Six-Day War*, CB Creative Books 2014

Cohen, Michael A. *American Maelstrom: The 1968 Election and the Politics of Division*, London: Oxford University Press, 2016.

Cooper, Charles G., with Richard E. Goodspeed, *A Marine's Story of Combat in Peace and War*. Victoria, Canada: Trafford Publishing, 2002.

Corson, William R. *The Betrayal*. New York: W. W. Norton & Co., 1968.

Cristol, A. Jay, *The Liberty Incident: The 1967 Attack on a U.S. Navy Spy Ship*. Potomac Books, 2002

Davis, Deborah, *Katherine the Great*. New York: Harcourt, Brace and Jovanovich, Inc. (1979).

Douglass, James W. *JFK and the Unspeakable: Why He Died and Why It Matters*. Maryknoll, NY: Orbis Books. 2008.

Dunn, Si. *Dark Signals: A Navy Radio Operator in the Tonkin Gulf and South China Sea, 1964–1965*. Austin, TX: Sagecreek Productions LLC, 2012.

Ennes, James M. *Assault on the Liberty*. New York: Random House, 1980.

Gallo, Ernest A. *Liberty Injustices: A Survivor's Account of American Bigotry*. Palm Coast, FL: ClearView Press, Inc. 2013

Gates, Jeff. *Guilt by Association: How Deception and Self-Deceit Took America to War*. State Street Publications, 2008

Goldberg, J. J. *Jewish Power: Inside the American Jewish Establishment*. New York: Basic Books, 1997.

Goodwin, Richard N. *Remembering America*. Boston: Little, Brown and Company, 1988

Goulden, Joseph C. *Truth Is the First Casualty: The Gulf of Tonkin Affair and Reality*. New York: Rand McNally, 1969.

Green, Stephen. *Taking Sides: America's Secret Relations with a Militant Israel*. New York: William Morrow and Company, Inc. 1984

Haley, James Evetts. *A Texan Looks at Lyndon: A Study in Illegitimate Power*. Canyon, Texas: Palo Duro Press, 1964.

Herring,Ggeorge C. *America's Longest War: The United States and Vietnam, 1950– 1975* (4th Ed.). New York: Mcgraw-Hill, 2001.

Hersh, Seymour M. *The Dark Side of Camelot*. Boston: Little, Brown and Company, 1997.

Hersh, Seymour M. *The Samson Option: Israel's Nuclear Arsenal and American Foreign Policy*. New York: Random House, 1991.

Hershman, D. Jablow. *Power Beyond Reason: The Mental Collapse of Lyndon Johnson*. Fort Lee, NJ: Barricade Books, 2002.

Hounam, Peter, and John Simpson. *Operation Cyanide: Why the Bombing of the USS Liberty Nearly Caused World War III*. Chatham, Kent, UK: Mackays of Chatham, Ltd., 2003.

Howe, Russel Warren. *Weapons: The shattering Truth about the International Game of Power, Money and Arms*. London, UK: Abacus, 1981

Isserman, Maurice and Kazin, Michael. *America Divided: The Civil War of the 1960s*, 4th Ed. New York: Oxford University Press , 2011

Isaacs, Stephen D., *Jews in American Politics*, New York: Doubleday, 1974

Joesten, Joachim, *The Dark Side of Lyndon Baines Johnson*, Ketchum, ID: Iconoclastic Books, 2013 (Orig. Pub. 1968)

Kalman, Laura. *Abe Fortas: A Biography*. Binghamton, NY: Vail-Ballou Press, 1990 (copyright Yale University).

Katzenbach, Nicholas deB., *Some of It Was Fun: Working with JFK and LBJ*. New York: W.

W. Norton & Company, 2008

Kessler, Ronald. *Inside the White House,* New York: Pocket Books, 1995McClellan, Barr. *Blood, Money & Power: How LBJ Killed JFK.* New York: Hannover House, 2003

McGilvray, James. *Chomsky: Language, Mind, Politics,* Cambridge: Polity (Second Ed. 2013)

Miller, Merle, *Lyndon: An Oral Biography* New York: Putnam's, 1980.

Muslin, Hyman L, MD, and Thomas H. Jobe, MD. *Lyndon Johnson: The Tragic Self: A Psychohistorical Portrait.* New York: Insight Books/Plenum Press, 1991.

Neff, Donald, *Fifty Years of Israel.* Washington, DC: American Educational Trust, 1998

Newman, John M. *JFK and Vietnam: Deception, Intrigue and the Struggle for Power.* New York: Warner Books, Inc., 1992.

Novak, Robert. *The Prince of Darkness.* New York: Three Rivers Press/Crown Publishing Group/Random House, 2007.

Oren, Michael B. *Six Days of War: June 1967.* New York: Presidio Press, 2003

Pearson, Anthony, *Conspiracy of Silence.* London, UK: Quartet Books Ltd., 1978

Reeves, Richard. *President Kennedy: Profile of Power.* New York: Touchstone, 1994.

Rusk, Dean. *As I Saw It.* New York: W. W. Norton & Co., 1990.

Safer, Morley. *Morley Safer, Flashbacks: On Returning to Vietnam.* New York: Random House, 1990

Schlesinger Jr., Arthur M. *Journals: 1952–2000.* New York: Penquin Press, 2007.

Schlesinger Jr., Arthur M. *Robert Kennedy and His Times.* New York: Ballentine Books, 1978.

Schlesinger Jr., Arthur M. *The Imperial Presidency.* Boston: Houghton Mifflin, 1973.

Schulman, Bruce J. *Lyndon B. Johnson and American Liberalism,* New York: Bedford Books of St. Martin's Press, 1995.

Scott, James. *The Attack on the Liberty: The Untold Story of Israel's Deadly 1967 Assault on a U.S. Spy Ship.* New York: Simon &Schuster, 2009

Shlaim, Avi. *The Iron Wall: Israel and the Arab World,* New York: W. W. Norton & Company, January 2001.

Shesol, Jeff. *Mutual Contempt: Lyndon Johnson, Robert Kennedy, and the Feud That Defined a Decade.* New York: W. W. Norton & Company, 1997.

Tourney, Phillip F. and Mark Glenn. *What I Saw That Day: Israel's June 8th, 1967 Holocaust of US Servicemen Aboard the USS Liberty and its Aftermath.* Careywood, ID: Liberty Productions,

Winter-Berger, Robert N. *The Washington Pay-off.* Secaucus, NJ: Lyle Stuart, Inc., 1972.

PERIODICALS

Crewdson, John, *Baltimore Sun* October 2, 2007

    (See http://www.baltimoresun.com/news/chi-liberty_tuesoct02-story.html#page=1)

Evans, Rowland and Novak, Robert. "The CIA's Secret Subsidy to Israel" *The Washington Post*, Feb. 24, 1977

Galbraith, James K. "Exit Strategy: In 1963, JFK ordered a complete withdrawal from Vietnam," *The Boston Review*, 9/01/2003 https://www.bostonreview.net/us/galbraith-exit-strategy-vietnam

Geller, Pamela. "Geller: Lamar Advertising Runs Libelous Anti-Israel Billboards" *Breitbart.com, April 25, 2016*. See: http://www.breitbart.com/middle-east/2016/04/25/lamar-advertising-runs-libelous-anti-israel-billboards-refuses-afdi-pro-freedom-billboards/

Greenwald, Glenn, "Obama Confidant's Spine-chilling Proposal," *Salon*, January 15, 2010 See: http://www.salon.com/2010/01/15/sunstein_2/

Halsell, Grace, "How LBJ's Vietnam War Paralyzed His Mideast Policymakers," *Washington Report on Middle East Affairs*, June 1993, Page 20 http://www.wrmea.org/1993-june/how-lbj-s-vietnam-war-paralyzed-his-mideast-policymakers.html

Holley, Peter. "Sirhan Sirhan denied parole despite a Kennedy confidant's call for the assassin's release" *The Washington Post*, February 11, 2015

Lambert, William, and Keith Wheeler. "How LBJ's Family Amassed Its Fortune," *Life*, August 14 and 21, 1964.

McGovern, Ray, *A USS Liberty Hero's Passing, Consortium News, August 17, 2014*

"LBJ in Trouble," *Newsweek*, September 4, 1967

Pearson, Anthony, "The Attack on the U.S.S. Liberty: Mayday! Mayday!" *Penthouse* magazine, May 1976

Reston, James, *New York Times*, May 7, 1969

Ricks, Thomas E. "Was there Academic Freedom at Annapolis During the Israeli Ambassador's Visit? *Foreign Policy, FP – National Security* January 23, 2012 FP National Security website:

   http://ricks.foreignpolicy.com/posts/2012/01/23/was_there_academic_freedom_at_annapolis_during_the_israeli_ambassador_s_visit

Witkin, Richard, "Johnson, in City, Vows to Maintain Peace in Mideast," *New York Times*, June 4, 1967.

Witkin, Richard, "Protests to Greet Visit of President," *New York Times*, June 3, 1967.

INTERNET RESOURCES

AlJazeera Website: "Remembering USS Liberty: When Israel Attacked America" http://www.aljazeera.com/blogs/americas/2015/06/israel-uss-liberty-attack-150608204015123.html

Alpha History website: : Vietnam War peace talks" http://alphahistory.com/vietnam/vietnam-warpeace-talks/

Arlington National Cemetery [The], website: http://arlingtoncemetery.net

BBC Documentary 'Dead in the Water' on various websites, including: http://www.bing.com/videos/search?q=bbc+documentary+dead+in+the+water&view=detail&mid=35163F5529ADE621098D35163F5529ADE621098D&FORM=VIRE1

Chomsky.com "Chomsky Weighs in on Kennedy Assassination Anniversary: 'It Would

Impress Kim Il-Sung." Noam Chomsky interviewed by Daniel Falcone, *Truthout*, November 22, 2013. See: https://chomsky.info/20131122/

Counterpunch.org: :"American Legion Honchos Betray Liberty Veterans" http://www.counterpunch.org/2014/05/16/american-legion-honchos-betray-liberty-veterans/

Darwish, Adel, "Analysis: Middle East Water Wars," *BBC News*, May 30, 2003: http://news.bbc.co.uk/2/hi/middle_east/2949768.stm

Findings of the Independent Commission of Inquiry into the Israeli Attack on USS *Liberty*, the Recall of Military Rescue Support Aircraft while the Ship was Under Attack, and the Subsequent Cover-up by the United States Government, Capitol Hill, Washington, D.C., October 22, 2003 (See for example: http://www.ussliberty.org/findings.htm)

Gilad Aztmon website: "What Phil Saw That Day." http://www.gilad.co.uk/writings/what-phil-saw-that-day.html

Giraldi, Philip, "Sinking Liberty" The American Conservative, March 17, 2011 http://www.theamericanconservative.com/articles/the-uss-libertys-final-chapter/

Greenwald, Glenn, "Obama Confidant's Spine-Chilling Proposal," *Salon.com* Jan. 15, 2010 http://www.salon.com/2010/01/15/sunstein_2/

Heretical Press (The). Richard K. Smith " The Violation of the *Liberty*" *http://www.heretical.com/miscella/liberty.html*

History News Network: http://historynewsnetwork.org/article/191#sthash.AQN-FqXhS.dpuf

If Americans Knew website: http://www.ifamericansknew.org/us_ints/ul-ameu.html

Independent [The] website: *"Q: What's the Difference between a politician and a psychopath? A: "None."* http://www.independent.co.uk/news/q-whats-the-difference-between-a-politician-and-a-psychopath-a-none-1361687.html"

Jewish Virtual Library - Attack on the Liberty: *http://www.jewishvirtuallibrary.org/jsource/History/liberty.html*

LBJ Library: Transcript, *George Ball Oral History Interview I*, 7/8/71, by Paige E. Mulhollan, Internet Copy,

LBJ Library: Transcript, *Harry McPherson Oral History Interview III*, 1/16/69, by T. H. Baker, Internet Copy.

Lopez, Ralph, "Declassified Israeli cables add evidence USS Liberty no accident." *Digital Journal*, Nov. 14, 2014. (http://www.digitaljournal.com/news/world/declassified-israeli-cables-add-evidence-usaliberty-no-accident/article/414951)

Mantik, David, "The Silence of the Historians." http://assassinationofjfk.net/wp-content/uploads/2014/04/The-Silence-of-the-Historians.pdf

Margolis, Eric, 'The USS *Liberty*': America's Most Shameful Secret. *LewRockwell.com*;

http://www.lewrockwell.com/ orig/margolis12.html;

also http://www.ifamericansknew.org/us_ints/ul-ameu.html;

Military.com,

Walsh, David C. "The Naval Institute: Proceedings -- Friendless Fire? http://www.military.com/NewContent/0,13190,NI_Friendless_0603,00.html

"Marine Slain By Friendly Fire in Vietnam to Be Awarded Purple Heart," (From *Stars and Stripes*, March 16, 2015)

Popp, Roland "Stumbling Decidedly into the Six-Day War" *The Middle East Journal* VOLUME 60, NO. 2, SPRING 2006 See: https://www.researchgate.net/publication/236885756_Stumbling_Decidedly_into_the_Six-Day_War

Rense, Jeff website: rense.com: *"LBJ's 'Passionate Attachment' to Israel"* http://rense.com/general44/lbj.htm

Reston, James, *New York Times*, May 7, 1969: http://jfk.hood.edu/Collection/White%20%20Files/Security-CIA/CIA%200228.pdf

Republicbroadcasting.org. Phil Tourney Interview with Noam Chomsky: http://www.drtourneyarchive.com/show/february-27-2016/28

Reuters: Patricia Zengerle: "U.S. Officials: Israel wants up to $5 Billion in Annual Military Aid" Nov. 4, 2015: http://uk.reuters.com/article/uk-iran-nuclear-israel-usa-idUK-KCN0ST2SV20151104

Safieh, Afif, *40 Years after the 1967 War: The Impact of a Prolonged Occupation*. Edited transcript of remarks titled *The 1967 Occupation: A Palestinian Perspective*, The Palestine Center Washington, D.C. 5 June 2007 (http://www.thejerusalemfund.org/ht/a/GetDocumentAction/i/2918)

Scott, Peter Dale, *The Pentagon Papers and NSAM 273* (Hood College, Weisberg Collection) See: http://jfk.hood.edu/Collection/Weisberg%20Subject%20Index%20Files/T%20Disk/Tiger%20to%20Ride%20Viet%20Nam%20Withdrawal/Item%2001.pdf

Smith, Grant, "Most Americans Believe Palestinians Occupy Israeli Land" *Anti-War.com*, March 25, 2016. http://original.antiwar.com/smith-grant/2016/03/24/most-americans-believe-palestinians-occupy-israeli-land/

Smith, Morris, *5 Towns Jewish Times* March 7, 2016, "Our First Jewish President Lyndon Johnson? – an update!!" http://5tjt.com/our-first-jewish-president-lyndon-johnson-an-update/

State Department Hearing 1/20/2004:

  http://www.c-span.org/video/?179892-1/1967-arabisraeli-war-uss-liberty

State Department website: https://history.state.gov/milestones/1953-1960/suez

Quandt, Dr. William The Palestine Center Washington, D.C. *40 Years after the 1967 War: The Impact of a Prolonged Occupation*. Edited transcript of remarks titled *The Johnson Administration and the 1967 War,* 5 June 2007 (http://www.thejerusalemfund.org/ht/a/GetDocumentAction/i/2918)

United States Cryptologic History: *Attack on a Sigint Collector, the USS Liberty*: http://www.nsa.gov/public_info/_files/uss_liberty/attack_sigint.pdf

USS *Liberty* - (General website with numerous links to others) http://gidusko.webs.com/

USS *Liberty* Document Center:

      http://www.usslibertydocumentcenter.org/doc/upload/CIA_from_Tel-Aviv_1967.pdf

      http://www.usslibertydocumentcenter.org/doc/upload/Proceedings_US_Naval_Institute_2005.pdf

USS *Liberty* Memorial: See http://www.gtr5.org

USS *Liberty Veterans Association: http://www.usslibertyveterans.org/*

War Crimes Report: A Report: War Crimes Committed Against U.S. Military Personnel, June 8, 1967 http://www.gtr5.com/evidence/warcrimes.pdf)

Weir, Alison. "American Legion Honchos Betray Liberty Veterans" Counterpunch May 26, 2014   http://www.counterpunch.org/2014/05/16/american-legion-honchos-betray-liberty-veterans/

Wikipedia.com:

> https://en.wikipedia.org/wiki/Caligula

> https://en.wikipedia.org/wiki/USS_Liberty_incident

http://en.wikipedia.org/wiki/Moshe_dayan#cite_note-66

https://en.wikipedia.org/wiki/Noam_Chomsky

https://en.wikipedia.org/wiki/Sidney_Gottlieb

WingTV: http://www.wingtv.net/documentaries.html

Youtube videos:

> Alex Jones, Video *Terrorstorm: USS Liberty White House-sanctioned attack, June 8, 1967*   (See: https://www.youtube.com/watch?v=ZnTdn1bSo-Q)

> "BBC Documentary on the *USS Liberty: Dead in the Water*," http://www.youtube.com/watch?feature=endscreen&Nr =1&v=va0shuZyJwU

> "Ernie Gallo: *The USS Liberty -- what really happened? What did not?*" (https://www.youtube.com/watch?v=rLr9fjg6cmM

> *Loss of LIberty* documentary video on USS *Liberty* cover-up: See: https://www.youtube.com/watch?v=ZluFfyQ7sAI

> "The Shame of Noam Chomsky & left gatekeepers: Zwicker (#3)" https://www.youtube.com/watch?v=BhrZ57XxYJU

Young, Cathy. "Ann Coulter's Anti-Semitism Runs Deep." *The Daily Beast* May 10, 2016. http://www.thedailybeast.com/articles/2016/05/10/ann-coulter-s-anti-semitism-runs-deeper-than-you-know.html?source=TDB&via=FB_Page

Young, Rick, PBS "Frontline" documentary *Give War a Chance* at the web site: http://www.pbs.org/wgbh/pages/frontline/shows/military/etc/lessons.html

Index